Cecily Duchess of York

Cecily Duchess of York

J. L. Laynesmith

BLOOMSBURY ACADEMIC
LONDON • NEW YORK • OXFORD • NEW DELHI • SYDNEY

BLOOMSBURY ACADEMIC
Bloomsbury Publishing Plc
50 Bedford Square, London, WC1B 3DP, UK
1385 Broadway, New York, NY 10018, USA

BLOOMSBURY, BLOOMSBURY ACADEMIC and the Diana logo
are trademarks of Bloomsbury Publishing Plc

First published 2017
Paperback edition first published 2017

For legal purposes the Acknowledgements on p. ix constitute an
extension of this copyright page.

Cover image: Cecily duchess of York, cloaked in the royal arms of England, at prayer behind
Elizabeth Woodville. Detail from the frontispiece of the Luton Guild Book, 1475. Image
courtesy of Luton Culture.

A catalogue record for this book is available from the British Library.

Library of Congress Cataloging-in-Publication Data
Names: Laynesmith, J. L., author.
Title: Cecily Duchess of York / J. L. Laynesmith.
Description: New York : Bloomsbury Academic, an imprint of Bloomsbury
Publishing Plc, [2017] | Includes bibliographical references and index.
Identifiers: LCCN 2017000055 | ISBN 9781474272254 (hb) |
ISBN 9781474272278 (epdf) | ISBN 9781474272261 (epub)
Subjects: LCSH: York, Cecily, Duchess of, 1415-1495. | York, Cecily, Duchess of,
1415–1495–Family. | Nobility–Great Britain–Biography. |
Great Britain–History–Lancaster and York, 1399–1485.
Classification: LCC DA247.Y67 L38 2017 | DDC 942.04092 [B] –dc23
LC record available at https://lccn.loc.gov/2017000055

ISBN: HB: 978-1-4742-7225-4
PB: 978-1-3500-9878-7
ePDF: 978-1-4742-7227-8
ePub: 978-1-4742-7226-1

Typeset by Newgen Knowledge Works (P) Ltd., Chennai, India.

To find out more about our authors and books visit
www.bloomsbury.com and sign up for our newsletters.

For my parents,
David and Judith Chamberlayne,
with love and thanks

Contents

Illustrations

Acknowledgements

In the twenty years since I first undertook research on Cecily duchess of York I have incurred debts of gratitude to a great many people. My first thanks must go to my tutors and fellow students at the University of York's Centre for Medieval Studies, especially Jeremy Goldberg, Felicity Riddy, Mark Ormrod and Richard Marks. I am indebted to the British Academy for funding my MA there and to the Richard III Society and Yorkist History Trust for a grant towards my initial research as well as for paying for the inclusion of pictures in this present book.

I am very grateful to Geoffrey Wheeler for sending me snippets about Cecily that came his way all through those twenty years, reminding me that my work on her was not yet complete, and for his advice on images for this book; to Michael K. Jones for his advice on my initial research and for first suggesting that I should write a biography of Cecily; and especially to Hannes Kleineke who brought me back to Cecily with an invitation to contribute to the *Yorkist Age* Harlaxton Conference and then generously read the entire manuscript of this book for me, not only saving me from various errors but also offering some fascinating extra references and insights.

I would like to thank the many other people who shared references to Cecily that they had encountered, sent me pieces of their published and unpublished research, or talked through aspects of this book with me: these include Marianne Ailes, Linda Clark, Michael Hicks, Steven Gunn, Livia Visser-Fuchs, Rowena Archer, Sean Cunningham, Jonathan Mackman, David Grummit, James Ross, Lynda Pidgeon, Brian Kempe, Anne Jeavons, Alex Brondarbit, Euan Roger, Lucia Diaz-Pascual, John Ashdown-Hill, John Goodall and Laurent Ungeheuer. I have very much appreciated the support and encouragement of the academic communities of the Fifteenth Century Conference, the Institute of Historical Research Late Medieval Seminar and the University of Reading's Graduate Centre for Medieval Studies. I am also grateful for the questions and suggestions from the various Richard III Society branches who have listened to me talk about Cecily over the years.

I am indebted to the staff at many libraries and archives, but would especially like to thank Marie Barnfield (papers librarian for the Richard III Society) and the archivists at St George's Chapel, Windsor and the Norfolk Record Office for going out of their way to find extra information for me. I would also like to thank Liz Lowth for so many enjoyable Latin lessons. I am similarly grateful to all those who provided hospitality for me on research trips, notably the Joneses, the Irvines and the Augustinian community at Clare Priory. My thanks too to Claire Lipscomb, Emily Drewe and Beatriz Lopez for so patiently guiding this book to publication at Bloomsbury.

Above all I would like to thank my family: Judith and David who first introduced me to the fascinating world of the fifteenth century, who proofread an earlier draft of this book and to whom this work is dedicated; James and Matthew who have put up with the chaos caused by a mother too often distracted by mysterious persons long dead; and above all Mark for his constant support, enthusiasm, faith, patience, advice, research help and for reading more drafts of these chapters than could possibly be considered reasonable. Of course, errors, omissions and confusions that remain in this work are very much my own.

J. L. L.
The Feast of St Hilda of Whitby, 2016
University of Reading

Author's Note

Quotations from foreign languages have been rendered in modern English except where translation seems superfluous or cannot convey an important subtlety of meaning. Where possible quotations from Middle English have been rendered in the original but contractions have been expanded and obsolete letters replaced. For ease of cross reference, names have been given in their commonest modern form. Inevitably this has led to some inconsistencies: for example, Katherine Swynford is best known by her first married name whereas Elizabeth Woodville is generally remembered by her maiden name.

Abbreviations

BIHR	*Bulletin of the Institute for Historical Research*
BJRL	*Bulletin of the John Rylands Library*
BL	British Library
Bodl.	Bodleian Library
CCA	Canterbury Cathedral Archives
CCCC	Corpus Christi College Cambridge
CCR	*Calendar of the Close Rolls*
CFR	*Calendar of the Fine Rolls*
Clare Roll	College of Arms MS Num/Sch 3/16. Published in K. W. Barnardiston, *Clare Priory: Seven Centuries of a Suffolk House* (Cambridge: Heffer, 1962), 65–6; C. Horstman, ed., *Osbern Bokenham's Legenden* (Heilbronn: Gbr. Henninger, 1883), 269–74.
CPL	*Calendar of Entries in the Papal Registers Relating to Great Britain and Ireland*
CPR	*Calendar of the Patent Rolls*
CSP Milan	*Calendar of State Papers and Manuscripts, relating to English affairs, existing in the archives and collections of Milan 1385–1618*, ed. A. B. Hinds (London: HMSO, 1912).
CSP Venice I	*Calendar of State Papers and Manuscripts, relating to English affairs, existing in the archives and collections of Venice*, volume 1, ed. Rawdon Brown (London: Longman, 1864).
CUP	Cambridge University Press
EETS	Early English Text Society
EHR	*English Historical Review*
ERO	Essex Record Office
GEC	G. E. Cockayne, *Complete Peerage*, rev. Vicary Gibbs, 25 vols (London: St. Catherine, 1910–59).
HMC	Royal Commission on Historical Manuscripts
JMH	*Journal of Medieval History*

NRO	Norfolk Record Office
OUP	Oxford University Press
Oxford DNB	*Oxford Dictionary of National Biography* Electronic resource, ed. H. C. G. Matthew and Brian Harrison (Oxford: OUP, 2004).
Paston Letters	Norman Davis et al., eds, *Paston Letters and Papers of the Fifteenth Century*, EETS, s.s. 20–22 (2004–5).
PPC	Nicholas Harris Nicolas, ed. *Proceedings of the Privy Council of England*, 7 vols (London: Commissioners of the Public Records of the Kingdom, 1834).
PROME	*The Parliament Rolls of Medieval England*, ed. C. Given-Wilson et al. (Leicester: Scholarly Digital Editions, 2005). Entries on this CD ROM are allocated the same pagination as the *Rotuli Parliamentorum*
RO	Record Office
SGC	St George's Chapel, Windsor
TNA	The National Archives
VCH	*Victoria County History*
WAM	Westminster Abbey Muniments
Will	TNA PROB 11/10/447, published in Alison Spedding, '"At the King's Pleasure": The Testament of Cecily Neville', *Midland History*, 35 (2010), 256–72.

Genealogies

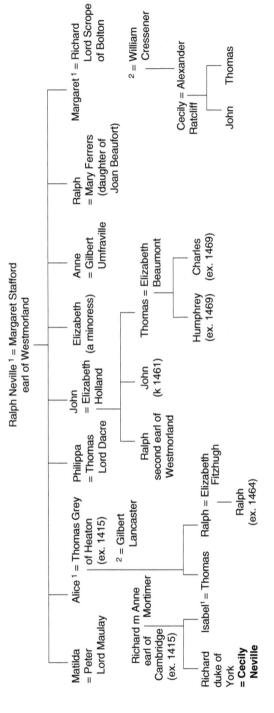

1 The first family of Ralph Neville, earl of Westmorland

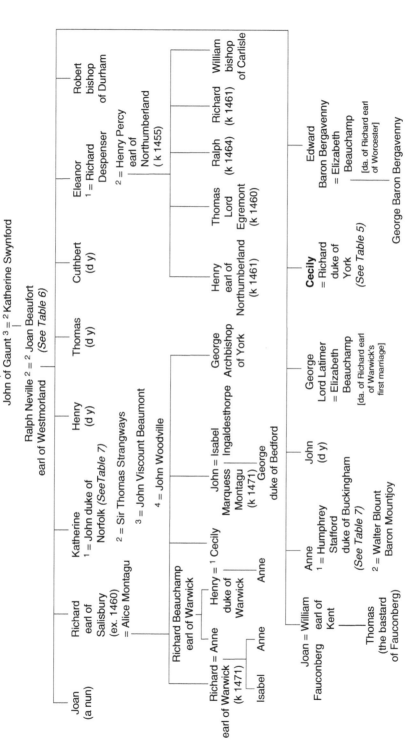

2 The family of Ralph Neville, earl of Westmorland and Joan Beaufort

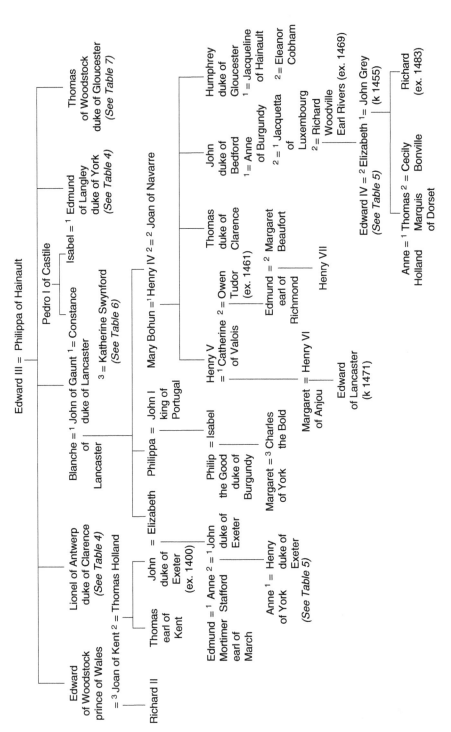

3 The Lancastrian royal family

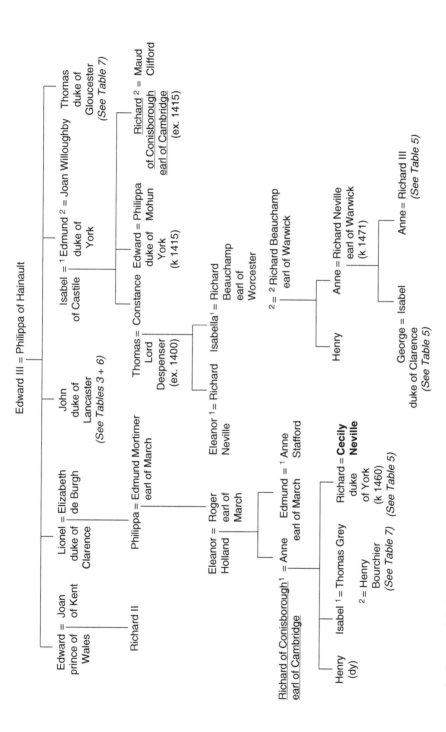

4 The descent of the house of York

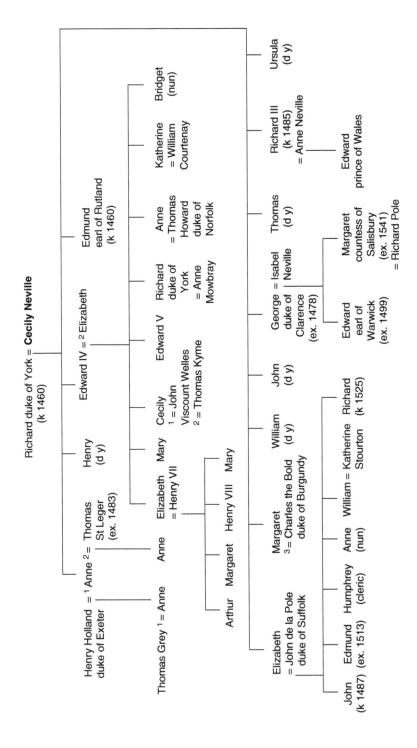

5 The Yorkist royal family

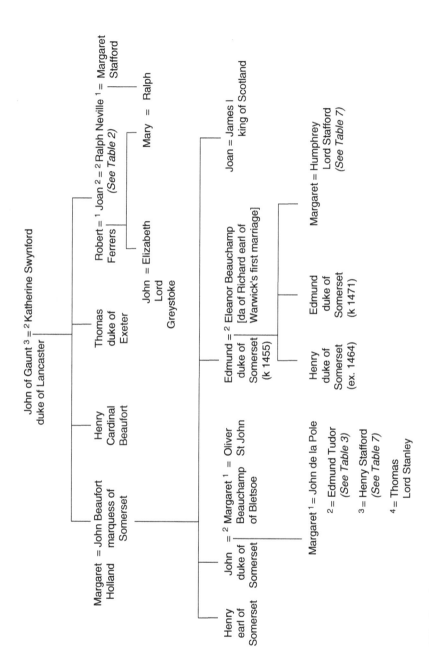

6 The Beauforts

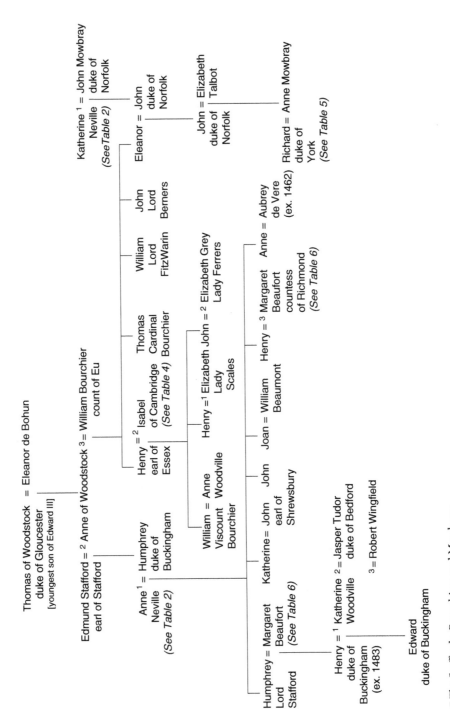

7 The Staffords, Bourchiers and Mowbrays

Introduction

1415: In this year, on the day after the feast of St Lawrence [10 August], king Henry set sail from Southampton with 1,787 vessels ... and on 25 October following, there was a battle at Agincourt, on which day the French were defeated, and many lords were captured and killed. In this year was born Cecilia, wife of Richard duke of York, daughter of the earl of Westmorland, on 3 May.

Annales of pseudo-Worcester[1]

Cecily Neville, mother of Edward IV and Richard III, was born in one of the most dramatic years of a tempestuous century. Later that summer Richard earl of Cambridge, younger brother of the duke of York, was executed at Southampton for plotting to overthrow the Lancastrian king Henry V. Weeks after that Edward duke of York himself was one of the few English dead at Agincourt, one of England's most spectacular victories in the Hundred Years War. The repercussions of these events provided the context for the Wars of the Roses that followed, wars that shaped Cecily Neville's life intimately and were sometimes shaped by her. From the first blood at Southampton until the last serious Yorkist pretender threatened Henry VII's throne in the mid-1490s was a span of eighty years. Cecily duchess of York was the only major protagonist of the Wars of the Roses to live right through those eighty years.

Yet the drama and bloodshed of civil war and conflict with France were only one part of her story. Her well-documented religious interests and book ownership have made her a popular exemplar in historians' assessments of lay piety. By contrast, her role as a major landholder and head of a powerful household have scarcely attracted any attention despite the wealth of sources that survive. Nor has there been any assessment of the way her own administration supported that of Edward IV. The story of Cecily Neville's life provides a rich insight into national and local politics, women's power and relationships, motherhood, household dynamics and the role of religion in fifteenth-century England.

It is common for biographies of such figures to begin with a narrative of events which is followed by thematic chapters. However, as Joel Rosenthal observed, Cecily's life is 'best seen, not so much in terms of a life cycle, but rather as a series of epic chapters that, by the end, were barely connected through living memory'.[2] Her dramatic changes in circumstance and the very random survival of sources for these different chapters in her life make a broadly chronological biography more effective. It is hoped that this approach will also provide a more useful foundation upon which further research on Cecily can be built. To avoid allowing the narrative to slide into a retelling of the Wars of the Roses from Cecily's perspective, the focus is on those political events in which her involvement can be traced and these are interwoven with discussion of other aspects of her life.

As with almost all medieval men and women, little is known about Cecily's childhood and so the first chapter of this book uses what little we do know to frame an introduction to the world in which she operated, the context of ideas and events that shaped her subsequent history. Chapters 2 to 4 cover most of the thirty-six years of her marriage to Richard, duke of York. Inevitably this part of her story has to be understood in the shadow of her husband's turbulent political career. The couple developed a close domestic and working partnership which produced twelve children in seventeen years and eventually led to Cecily representing her husband in both business and politics. In subsequent chapters Cecily comes to the fore, made visible by her husband's exile and death and by her wealth and power as the mother of two kings of England. That power came from her close relationship with Edward IV and from her acute skills in personal networking as well as a pragmatism bordering on ruthlessness.

Cecily is rare among medieval women in terms of the comparative profusion of sources for her life and the lives of those who served her that do survive.[3] Her long widowhood combined with her status as a mother of kings to contribute to this unusual abundance. In the National Archives there are dozens of account rolls for her estates, records of her courts, court cases involving her servants, and her fabulously detailed will. The British Library houses books that once belonged to her, details of her husband's expenditure on her behalf, various accounts of her religious patronage and a number of her letters. The largest single collection of her letters is to be found in Chelmsford at the Essex Record Office, but others are scattered from Nottingham and Leicester to Cambridge, Taunton and even the Huntingdon Library, California. In the library of the Inner Temple there is a copy of her fascinatingly detailed daily routine and household regulations. The Westminster Abbey Muniments Room and the Bodleian Library house manuscripts recording her administration, household members and family events while other administrative documents are housed in local record offices from Ipswich to Leicester and in Windsor Castle. Cecily's actions are documented in the patent rolls, the papal registers, ambassadors' letters, heralds' accounts, English and continental chronicles, poems and genealogies, various civic records (most of them unpublished), the letters of the Paston and Stonor families, and depicted in glorious colour on the frontispiece of the Luton Guild Book. In 2005 a unique version of *The Golden Legend* was discovered in Sir Walter Scott's library that seems to have been produced especially for her.

Most of these records are individually very brief and they are widely dispersed. Moreover, historians have generally been far more interested in exploring the stories of the men in her life than in Cecily herself. For centuries the absence of easily accessible information with only hints of power has allowed writers to shape representations of Cecily's character and actions to the needs of their wider narratives. Her story has generally been told as a means of illustrating their arguments about her closest kinsmen.

Rewriting Cecily's story

The earliest of these writers was Polydore Vergil, who arrived in England seven years after Cecily's death and began working on a history of England at Henry VII's suggestion. Vergil called Cecily a 'woman of most pure and honourable life'.[4] Her honour mattered to Vergil because he wanted to argue that she had wrongfully been accused of adultery by her wicked son Richard III as an excuse for seizing his nephew's throne. In contrast, Thomas More, writing in about 1513, depicted Cecily as an arrogant political meddler whose actions contributed to the tragedy of Richard's usurpation.[5] More was very likely influenced by the popular contemporary assumption that disaster ensued when women interfered in politics.

Nearly a century after Cecily's death, William Shakespeare drew on both More and Vergil in writing *The Tragedy of King Richard III* to construct his own enduring image of Cecily. She became a bitter and miserable crone in whose 'accursed womb, the bed of death. A cockatrice … [had] hatched'.[6] Yet only three decades later, Sir George Buck imagined a very different Cecily. In 1619 he published his *History of King Richard the Third* in an attempt to clear Richard III's reputation. Buck maintained that Thomas More had 'foully erred' in his depiction of Cecily.[7] Buck argued that she had 'so wisely and so earnestly' attempted to prevent Edward IV from making a genuinely illegal and invalid marriage.[8]

Seventeenth- and eighteenth-century accounts of Cecily's life frequently saw the tragedies she endured as something of a punishment for her pride in aspiring to be a queen. Typical of this is a letter of 20 August 1713 (published in 1787) in which the well-respected London bookseller Alexander Bosvile took it upon himself to educate the vicar of Fotheringhay, Rev. James Holicott, on Cecily as a former inhabitant of the latter's parish.[9] Bosvile wrote, 'I do not know, in all our English History, of any prince or princess that underwent such variety of fortune, or was a greater instance of the mutability of human affairs'. He averred that 'her natural temper was high and ambitious' and that she had married Richard, duke of York 'in hopes of being queen'. Despite the fact that Cecily clearly had no control over her marriage, subsequent writers have persistently accepted Bosvile's account of her character and in particular his assertion that after Edward IV became king 'her natural temper again appeared, even to a proverb at this day known in most counties, for she was *a proud Cis*'. This is the earliest reference I have been able to find for that epithet.

In 1768 Horace Walpole (probably unaware of Bosvile's work) reiterated the trope of 'a princess of spotless character' in using Cecily's actions to exonerate Richard III.[10] 'What man of common sense can believe', Walpole rationally asked, 'that Richard went so far as publicly to asperse the honour of his own mother?' Walpole argued that Richard could scarcely have used Cecily's lodgings for his first council meeting if he had so accused her.[11] Then in 1795 Cecily's reputation took a dramatic new turn when an anonymous four volume anti-Ricardian gothic novel titled *Cicely, or The Rose of Raby* was published. The adventures experienced by the romantic, heroic and beautiful protagonist of this novel bear scant resemblance to the life of the real Cecily Neville but the book became a bestseller. The author was eventually named as Agnes Musgrave who was at one time a resident of Staindrop, the village that borders the Raby Castle estate.[12] It would seem likely that it was her local connection with the Neville family's principal residence that had inspired Musgrave to weave what she knew of Cecily's story into a popular contemporary literary genre. It was almost certainly she who invented for Cecily the title by which she has been known ever since, 'the Rose of Raby'.

Perhaps in response to Musgrave's dramatic prose, the Rev. Mark Noble composed his 'Observations' on Cecily's life the following year.[13] This is Cecily's earliest biography and extended to eleven pages of *Archaeologia*, although much of this concerned her children and grandchildren rather than Cecily herself. Noble emphasized the turbulence and tragedies of her life but made no reference to her looks, place of birth or supposed arrogance, presumably because he knew there was no evidence for any of these. He traced the references to her in the *Paston Letters* and Tudor chronicles as well as arguing that the way in which she spent her time, according to her household regulations, 'does her great honour'.[14] He accepted Walpole's conclusions about Cecily's support for Richard's usurpation although he added that 'it must be supposed she was greatly shocked by his conduct ... when he had imprisoned, if not destroyed' Edward IV's sons.[15]

Despite Noble's attempt at a measured portrait, Bosvile and Musgrave's more imaginative and sensational depictions proved most influential. In 1848 the Strickland sisters published their widely read *Lives of the Queens of England* in which they included a detailed footnote on Cecily. They asserted that 'the duchess of York was remarkable for her beauty, and still more so for her indomitable pride ... She had a throne-room at Fotheringhay, where she gave receptions with the state of a queen'.[16] The Stricklands also implied that many on the Continent genuinely believed that Cecily had committed 'derelictions of her duty' and been unfaithful to her husband.[17] There is more than a hint of Victorian censoriousness in their sketch, again suggesting that Cecily had to some extent deserved the tragedies that befell her. Four years later Caroline Halsted similarly revealed Bosvile's influence in her adulatory biography of Richard III. Halsted argued that Cecily's husband, Richard duke of York, was 'remarkable for his peaceable and submissive disposition' yet was driven to challenge his king and to the tragedies that followed by his ambitious wife: 'the blood of the haughty Nevilles and the imperious Beauforts flowed in her veins'.[18] However, Halsted believed that Cecily redeemed herself, according to Victorian standards, by her behaviour in widowhood for 'with a high degree of moral courage and self command' she abandoned 'all thought of those regal dignities which she once so earnestly coveted, and had so nearly enjoyed' and abstained completely from 'interference in public or political affairs', thereby revealing 'the true greatness of [her] character'.[19] A broadly similar picture of Cecily's life emerged in Guy Paget's novel, *The Rose of Raby*, written in 1937.

It was not until 1942 that an academic chose to study Cecily for her own sake. In this year John Armstrong published a seminal study of her household ordinances and will. From these he concluded that she possessed a 'tranquillity of spirit, the existence of which has been insufficiently recognized in most appreciations of the fifteenth century', as well as displaying 'a disciplined gravity' and even 'a type of sanctity'.[20] Armstrong's conclusion fits closely with Polydore Vergil's record of a 'pure and honourable life'. This remained the predominant view of Cecily's character for almost sixty years, despite articles on Richard duke of York by T. B. Pugh which portrayed Cecily very differently. Pugh asserted that Cecily's 'reckless extravagance rivals the prodigality of that spectacular royal spendthrift Richard II'.[21] He also observed that she failed in her duty to limit her husband's years in purgatory when she did not try to pay off his massive debts after his death.[22]

In 1991 Joel Rosenthal summarized Cecily's widowhood, emphasizing her many personal tragedies, her 'vicarious identity' and the signs of 'half a life spent just this side of the church'.[23] Rosenthal's is the only published study so far to consider her exercise of 'good ladyship', although this is very brief and relies almost exclusively on the patent letters of chancery.[24] He also noted that her will 'is full of both the conventions of piety and the good things of this world'.[25] In 1994, I completed an MA dissertation on Cecily arguing that Armstrong's conclusions about Cecily's piety in the last years of her life should not be read backwards as a judgement on her entire career.[26] I argued that, contrary to Halsted's conclusions, she did involve herself in public and political affairs while her sons were king and that the queenly role she had almost achieved continued to shape her identity throughout her life.

Then in 2002 Michael K. Jones published a controversial reinterpretation of Richard III's career, *Bosworth 1485: Psychology of a Battle*. In it he argued that Cecily had had an adulterous affair with an English archer at Rouen in the summer of 1441 and that Edward IV was illegitimate. This dark secret ultimately tore the house of York apart when Cecily fell out with the cuckoo in the Yorkist nest. She first attempted to replace him on the throne with her son George and later 'directed' Richard III's coup against Edward IV's offspring.[27] Jones's idea of a complex and powerful Cecily is both plausible and attractive, but to some extent it is yet again the byproduct of a focus on her youngest son. This Cecily is implicitly the antithesis of Shakespeare's powerless and wretched duchess who had tried hopelessly 'in the breath of bitter words [to] smother [her] damned son', Richard.[28]

The following year Rowena Archer published an important riposte to the popular stereotype of devout widowhood that has characterized so many depictions of medieval women. Within this she argued that 'a woman more in and of the world [than Cecily] ... would be hard to equal'.[29] Nonetheless it has been Cecily's religious life that has continued to attract academic attention in illuminating articles such as Simon Horobin's assessments of her copy of *The Golden Legend*, Mary Dzon's interpretation of her ownership of the *Infantia Salvatoris*, Alison Spedding's edition of her will, and Sofija Matich and Jennifer Alexander's study of the Yorkist tombs at Fotheringhay.[30] Many recent fictional works, however, have been inspired by Michael Jones's theory of her catastrophic adultery.[31]

In 2004 Christopher Harper-Bill's short article for the *Oxford DNB* argued that Cecily's religion was 'essentially conservative', that the rumour of adultery was mere propaganda but probably not peddled by Richard III, and observed that despite contemporary comments about her great influence over Edward IV this can 'seldom be documented'.[32] Anne Crawford's 2007 history of the Yorkists and Sarah Gristwood's 2012 survey of the principal female protagonists of the Wars of the Roses included relatively brief references to Cecily which expanded upon Harper-Bill's summary somewhat but were broadly similar.[33] In 2014 Amy Licence produced a full length popular biography which added some further details from published sources and provided a vivid portrait of Cecily's fifteenth-century context. Licence offered the novel argument that Cecily had invented the story of her own adultery as a means of trying to control her wayward sons.[34] Adultery and piety are consistent themes that have dominated interpretations of Cecily's role while in most studies of fifteenth-century politics she has remained a very marginal and shadowy figure.

If Cecily had been only a pawn in, and witness to, her menfolk's tangled conflicts, as Shakespeare implied, hers would have been a fascinating story that deserved to be told in full, illuminating our understanding of women's lives in the fifteenth century. As it happens, Cecily was a far more significant player than that. Few noblewomen could avoid some political involvement in late medieval England. Kimberley LoPrete argued recently that the small number of very visible powerful women in the middle ages were long thought to be 'rule-proving exceptions' to a norm of domesticity, enclosure and submission, but now a 'swelling stream of document-based studies devoted to the particular lives of individual noblewomen is fast confirming the view that powerful women were not exceptional in the Middle Ages'.[35] Most elite men would at some point have interacted with a 'female lord' who not only commanded her household but also controlled extensive lands and revenues in her own right. It has become increasingly clear that 'to act authoritatively beyond the inner chambers of castles, the lordly women crossed no conceptual threshold separating domestic from public spheres'.[36] Cecily was very much one of those 'lordly women'. What makes her exceptional is her capacity to survive repeated regime changes so spectacularly, the sources for so many different aspects of her life, and her closeness to the fascinating and controversial men of the house of York. In the course of this biography her relationships with these men will be a major theme. Similarly important are the communities and networks that she inhabited as a result of literary and devotional interests, political and family connections, and her position as the head of a large household and as a major landholder. As Miri Rubin has argued,

> Identity can never be constituted through a single or overarching affinity – whether gender, class or age – but rather at the intersection and the changing dynamic negotiation of these and other positions in the world.[37]

In order to understand Cecily it is necessary to understand the affinities in which she operated. The earliest of these were her Neville family and the house of Lancaster which is where this biography begins.

1

Daughter of Lancaster: 1415–1425

Dame Cecile sir: Whos doughtir was she
Of the erle of Westmerlond I trowe the yengest
And yn grace hyr fortuned to be the hyest[1]

Dialogue betwix a Seculer . . . and a Frere

Cecily duchess of York was the youngest daughter of one of medieval England's greatest social climbers, Ralph Neville, earl of Westmorland, and his well-connected wife, Joan Beaufort, daughter of John of Gaunt, duke of Lancaster. Very little is known about Cecily's earliest years but records of her family and our wider knowledge of fifteenth-century childhood enable us to reconstruct not only plausible practicalities but also something of the ideas and ideals with which she would have been brought up, thereby providing a social context for understanding her adult life. An examination of the glittering marriages that her parents arranged for her siblings and herself similarly reveals the political context that shaped her later years.

Birth and baptism

Unusually for one of Ralph Neville's children, we do know Cecily's date of birth: 3 May 1415.[2] Very probably she herself had recorded it in the calendar of one of her devotional books along with the birthdates of her children (but not her husband). This list was then incorporated into a somewhat chaotic compilation of annals which were once thought to have been the work of William Worcester, secretary to Sir John Fastolf.[3]

There is no evidence for Agnes Musgrave's assumption that Cecily was born at Raby Castle in County Durham but this is a plausible location since Raby was Ralph Neville's principal residence. If so Cecily would probably have been baptized at Staindrop Church, a short walk from the castle. At Raby Castle there was a chapel above the gatehouse where her sisters Eleanor and Katherine had been married three years earlier.[4] However, parish churches jealously guarded the privilege of providing baptism and special licences had to be procured for baptism in a private chapel unless the child's life appeared to be in danger.[5] For the Nevilles of Raby their parish church, St Gregory at Staindrop, was as closely associated with their own family as was their castle chapel. Much of it had been built by their fitz Maldred and Neville forbears.[6] Consequently Cecily was most likely baptized in a space hallowed by centuries of prayer both by and for her ancestors.

Given the extensive evidence for Cecily's engagement with religion in later life, it makes sense to consider Cecily's baptism because the rite provides a vivid window into the thought-world that she was entering. Baptism was a much more public sacrament than marriage. This was the vital moment of a person's entry into the community of Christendom without which eternal damnation after death was assumed to be inevitable. It was a rite experienced by every child and one that people witnessed frequently in adulthood. Modern assessments of medieval women's relationship with religion habitually define the church as an essentially patriarchal and misogynistic institution. A recent encyclopedia on women and gender sums up church doctrine on women as 'an equation of women with carnality on the one hand and spiritual and intellectual weakness on the other' and concludes that in the later Middle Ages 'this suspicion of women turned into hostility ... and, eventually, to the witch craze'.[7] Yet studies of individual women like Cecily suggest a far more complex dynamic in which religion was frequently empowering to women operating, as they must, in the patriarchal and anti-feminist social framework of medieval Europe. In a study of late medieval women's relationships with their parish church, Katherine French has argued that 'religious practice was an important source of self-expression, creativity, and agency for women of every social status'.[8] The baptismal liturgy illustrates some of the potentially conflicting ideas about women that were held in tension by the medieval church.

Assuming Cecily's was a relatively uneventful, standard baptism, we may use the *Manuale et Processionale ad Usum Insignis Ecclesiae Eboracensis* to reconstruct her theatrical and symbol-laden entry into the Christian community.[9] By the late fifteenth century baptisms commonly began with a formal procession from the child's home. The midwife carried the child from her mother's chamber to the church door, within the porch, where the service began. Mothers were expected to remain at home recovering after the birth until the time of their churching, so the priest's first question was directed to the midwife. He asked whether the child was male or female. From this moment Cecily's identity as a member of the weaker sex began to be shaped. Boys were held on the priest's right, representing strength and dominance, but the godmother holding Cecily stood *a sinistris* (to his left).[10]

The priest blew three times into the child's face, telling her to receive the Holy Spirit and commanding the devil to flee. Even for those who did not speak or read Latin the liturgy was scattered with familiar words, phrases and especially names which they did understand and these were enhanced by the priest's gestures: the words 'Accipe Spiritum Sanctum ... effugare, diabole' (receive the Holy Spirit ... to drive away, the devil) were all they needed to hear to recognize an exorcism as the priest blew into Cecily's face.[11] Blessings and a prayer to resist temptation followed this and 'the salt of wisdom' was placed upon her tongue.[12] It was after this that the liturgy varied for boys and girls. Unsurprisingly the prayers for boys were longer. Strikingly the prayers for girls seem to have been shaped to reassure listeners about women's status before God and their fitness for baptism.[13] There was no hint of the common rhetoric that sin had come into the world through women. On the contrary, listeners were reminded that despite the limitations of her sex, this tiny girl still fully belonged to God's kingdom. Moreover, they specifically included reference to a female exemplar of faith, the Old Testament heroine Susannah whom God saved from wrongful punishment.[14]

After a brief Gospel reading, the priest placed the Gospel book against Cecily's lips so that she kissed it, something the priest himself usually did after reading the Gospel and thus a rather extraordinary privilege for a baby girl. Subsequently the priest spat into his left hand and touched the baby's ears and nose with his saliva, saying 'Ephphatha' (be opened), thereby placing the child into a re-enactment of Jesus's healing miracles. It was out of these sorts of experiences that a more personal, imaginative, 'affective piety' developed in the middle ages which influenced a number of the authors whom Cecily read in later life.[15] Once priest and godparents had together recited the essential doctrines of the faith contained in the Lord's Prayer, Hail Mary and the Creed, the priest would have drawn a cross with his thumb upon Cecily's right hand. He explained that he was giving her the power to make the sign of the cross in order to keep away danger and to have eternal life, essentially to call on God as her protecting lord just as a man might call for protection from the earthly lord whose livery he wore. Only now was she ready to enter the church, carried by one of her godmothers.

Cecily's godparents would have held her naked over the font to be anointed. The priest took her in his hands and immersed her three times in the water, vividly washing away sin, re-enacting Christ's own baptism and representing Cecily's rebirth in the three persons of the Holy Trinity. On the third occasion it was one of her godmothers who drew her out, the other godparents also quickly placing their hands on her. In the York rite even boys were to be received from the water by their godmother. This imitation of the midwife's role in lifting the child into the world visually implied the positive nature of that secular role too, despite the ideas of uncleanness that were also associated with that process. The priest then made a cross upon the baby's head with chrism. Her head and body were swiftly covered with a richly embroidered chrysom cloth.[16] Finally a burning candle was placed briefly into her right hand. For those watching and participating in the baptism, it was a remarkably generous and empowering rite promising God's presence within and beside them. Little wonder then that it was followed by jubilant festivities which sometimes prompted criticism for their excessive expense.[17] Godparents' gifts to high-status children were often pieces of plate, like the silver cup worth five marks and containing a further five marks that a prior of Durham purchased for one of Cecily's nieces.[18]

Most children were given their name at baptism, sometimes by one of their godparents.[19] Cecily's parents gave most of her older siblings names that belonged to close family members although her brothers Cuthbert and William may have been named for local saints and George for the saint whose cult Henry V was promoting at that time.[20] Quite possibly Cecily too was directly named after a popular saint. Her great uncle, Geoffrey Chaucer, had translated and adapted the *Legend* of St Cecilia into Middle English about forty years earlier and subsequently included it in his *Canterbury Tales*.[21] St Cecilia's legend was commonly used as an example of how married women could still be profoundly active Christians and so may well have been an inspiration to Cecily's mother, Joan Beaufort, whose remarkable piety is discussed below.[22] According to her legend, St Cecilia was a self-confident, determined, even sassy, but devoutly religious noblewoman who spent her wedding night converting her husband, Valerian, to Christianity and convincing him not to consummate their marriage. She subsequently preached regularly in the respectable confines of her home until the Roman prefect Almachius executed her husband and brought her to trial. Unbowed before the prefect, Cecilia mocked his religion and assured him that every mortal man's power is 'like a bladder full of wind' that collapses with a simple 'needle's point'.[23] (The reference to a tool more closely associated with women than men may have been deliberate.) Almachius attempted to have Cecilia boiled to death in a bath, appropriately in the home where she had preached. When the heat had no effect on her, Almachius sent a servant to smite off her head. Three strokes failed to achieve this and despite her pain as she slowly bled to death, she successfully prayed for three more days of life in which to arrange that her house might become a church. Such a brutal and improbable demise was typical of virgin martyr stories, as was the coarse hair shirt she wore next to her skin beneath her golden wedding dress. These were the tales that fifteenth-century girls like Cecily grew up listening to.

Family

Cecily's childhood was presumably divided between the various major Neville family homes: Raby, Brancepeth, Middleham and Sheriff Hutton. These splendid palace fortresses were the product of what has been called 'the most important residential building campaign in the north of England before the eighteenth century'.[24] Their 'princely' appearance was an ambitious strategy by Cecily's father and grandfather to belie the Nevilles' modest origins. The family had first arrived in England with William the Conqueror but were relatively minor Lincolnshire gentry until the 1170s when Geoffrey Neville married the heiress Emma Bulmer and so acquired her lands in Northumberland and Yorkshire.[25] In 1295 Ranulph Neville was called to Parliament as baron Neville of Raby thereby signalling the family's arrival in the ranks of the lower nobility just over a century before Cecily's birth.[26] The Neville lords spent much of the fourteenth century in service to successive kings and earls of Lancaster but it was only in 1397 that they became earls of Westmorland. The honour was granted by Richard II in part to try to ensure Ralph Neville's loyalty and in part to please the king's powerful uncle, John of Gaunt, whose daughter, Joan, Ralph had recently married.

Joan Beaufort was the only surviving daughter of John of Gaunt's infamous liaison with his daughters' governess, Katherine Swynford, who eventually became his third wife. Katherine's father, Paon Roelt, had arrived from Hainault with Edward III's queen and Katherine was considered by some to be a 'foreign lady' despite her English upbringing.[27] Her liaison with the king's third surviving son provoked chroniclers to label her 'an abominable temptress', 'a she-devil and enchantress'.[28] It was a commonplace of medieval culture to associate sexual immorality or the successful use of physical charms with witchcraft, but it must have been an uncomfortable legacy for her children and grandchildren. Katherine bore John of Gaunt four known children during the 1370s who took the surname Beaufort: John, Henry, Thomas and Joan.[29] In 1386 Gaunt arranged Joan's betrothal to one of his retainers, Sir Robert Ferrers of Oversley although they did not marry until 1392. She bore two daughters before Ferrers's death in the mid-1390s.[30] By then John of Gaunt's second wife, Constanza of Castile, had died and in 1396 Gaunt took the astonishing step of marrying his mistress twenty-four years after their liaison had begun.[31] That September their children were legitimated by papal bull and the following February Parliament approved the same.[32]

This dramatic change in status meant that Joan was now an appropriate bride for a nobleman and even before the parliamentary ceremony her marriage to baron Ralph had been solemnized.[33] For Gaunt this was a means of strengthening existing bonds between the house of Lancaster and an increasingly important northern family. It was also part of a strategy to rein in the power of the Percy earls of Northumberland who had long been dominant in this region.[34] The marriage proved far more valuable to Ralph than he could have anticipated when Henry Bolingbroke, the eldest son of Gaunt's first marriage, decided to seize Richard II's throne in 1399. Just days after Henry had landed at Ravenspur, Ralph Neville joined him at Doncaster. This was significantly before the most senior Beaufort brother declared his support.[35] Cecily Neville, matriarch of the house of York, was thus every inch a child of Lancaster. Thanks to her royal blood, Joan's lineage had a greater impact on contemporaries' perception of her daughter's identity than was usually the case for mothers. A fifteenth-century list of Richard duke of York's children identified his wife as 'Cecily, daughter of the illustrious lord, Ralph earl of Westmorland, by the most noble lady Joan, his second wife, daughter of the most powerful prince John duke of Lancaster, son of King Edward the third'.[36] Between them Cecily's parents had around twenty-five children. Joan's daughters by Ferrers, Elizabeth and Mary, have already been mentioned.[37] Earl Ralph had two sons and six or seven daughters by his first wife, Margaret Stafford. Together Joan Beaufort and Ralph Neville had a further nine sons and five daughters.[38] There are conflicting records of the dates and order of birth for Cecily's siblings but a pedigree of the lords of Middleham that was probably produced at Coverham Abbey before 1446 seems to fit best with what else is known about the family.[39] This states that only Cecily's brother Edward was younger than her.[40] By 1415 a great many of Cecily's siblings were already married. Indeed, two of the children from her parents' first marriages had been married to each other: Ralph Neville (the earl's second son) and Mary Ferrers.[41] Earl Ralph and his Beaufort wife were able to use their closeness to Henry IV to arrange what J. R. Lander called 'the most amazing series of child marriages in English history'.[42] Very commonly this involved purchasing the wardship of children who had been orphaned in aristocratic rebellions against Henry IV. Where their parents had been opposed to the king it was apparently hoped that marriage into Joan's family would provide an environment in which the next generation would grow up loyal to the Lancastrian dynasty.

Table 1.1 includes the earliest possible year of birth as well as marriages arranged and titles obtained before Ralph's death in 1425 (see also Genealogies section for subsequent marriages and titles).[43]

Table 1.1 The children of Ralph Neville earl of Westmorland and Joan Beaufort

Joan	1397	a minoress (i.e. a nun of the order of St Clare)
Richard	1398	m Alice Montagu (countess of Salisbury)
Katherine	1399	m John Mowbray (duke of Norfolk)
Henry	1400	died in infancy
Thomas	1401	died as a child
Cuthbert	1402	died in infancy
Eleanor	1403	m 1. Richard Despenser 2. Henry Percy (earl of Northumberland)
Robert	1404	a cleric (provost of Beverley from 1422)
William	1406	m Joan Fauconberg (baroness Fauconberg)
Anne	1408	m Humphrey Stafford (earl of Stafford)
John	1411	died in infancy
George	1414	
Cecily	1415	m Richard (duke of York)
Edward	1417	m Elizabeth Beauchamp (baroness Bergavenny)

Of Cecily's brothers, three or four had already died before she was even born. Robert, aged eleven, was destined for a career in the church and was very likely already living in the household of his uncle Henry Beaufort, bishop of Winchester.[44] Boys generally left the care of women and the family nursery when they were seven, so Cecily's eldest brother Richard (aged about sixteen) as well as William (not yet ten) would have seen little of Cecily in her childhood. They too may have been sent to other noble households in which to learn the skills and manners of young men. So, Cecily's earliest companions were her sister Anne and her brothers George and Edward.[45] It is perhaps unsurprising that Anne seems to have remained a genuine friend with whom Cecily shared religious interests and devotions decades later, despite their husbands' enmity, and that Edward's family also seems to have been more closely connected with her than most throughout her life.

Upbringing

Cecily's earliest days would have been spent close to her nurse rather than her mother. Breast feeding was regularly extolled as a maternal virtue but it was also associated with lowliness, notably in images of the Madonna of humility.[46] Cecily's nurse would have been, in Nicholas Orme's words, 'of good free status, not from the lowest orders of society'.[47] Until they were about six or seven girls and boys were dressed more or less alike but from an early age Cecily would have been aware that clothes were a marker of social position.[48]

Noble girls received confusingly mixed messages about the clothing they should choose. The clearest Biblical guidance came from the author of 1 Timothy who had advised that 'women should dress themselves modestly and decently in suitable clothing, not with their hair braided, or with gold, pearls or expensive clothes, but with good works'.[49] This provided justification for generations of Christian authors who associated fine clothing with sinfulness. Jean de Meun, whose *Roman de la Rose* was to be found in many fifteenth-century noble houses, asserted that 'a woman who wants to be beautiful ... wants to wage war on Chastity'.[50] Yet devotional books routinely indicated the high status of virgin martyrs and the Virgin Mary herself by depicting them in opulent and elegant garments, like the cloth of gold dress that St Cecilia wore over her hair shirt. The upper classes believed that 'in a well-ordered society, consumption patterns would reflect the hierarchy of status'.[51] In 1363 parliament had even introduced sumptuary laws outlining the types of clothing permissible to those of various stations. Gentlemen whose lands were worth less than £100 annually were forbidden to wear silk, embroidered clothing, gold jewellery 'or any manner of fur', and their wives and children likewise.[52] Knights whose land was valued at less than 200 marks annually were forbidden to wear the most expensive wools and furs or cloth of gold, and even those receiving £1,000 a year could only wear ermine or cloth embroidered with jewels in their headwear.[53] Although the legislation was repealed just over a year later, as Christopher Dyer has argued, it indicates the legislators' 'assumption that the higher aristocracy *ought* to wear' opulent apparel that distinguished them from their inferiors.[54]

One author who tried to steer a helpful middle course was Christine de Pisan, the daughter of an Italian physician and widow of one of the secretaries of Charles V of France.[55] Christine's international reputation as a writer was such that Henry IV of England had tried to persuade her to visit his court so Cecily's family was almost certainly familiar with her work.[56] In her manual, *Le Trésor de la Cité des Dames*, Christine advised 'the wise princess' to ensure that 'the clothing and the ornaments of her women, though they be appropriately beautiful and rich, be of a modest fashion, well-fitting and seemly, neat and properly cared for. There should be no deviation from this modesty nor any immodesty in the matter of plunging necklines or other excesses'.[57] What we know of Cecily's expenditure on clothing in later life suggests that she was not much persuaded by the approach of men like Jean de Meun and indeed that she used clothing and jewellery in shaping her own identity and promoting her husband's status.

Christian education

A nursery of several children, like that at Raby, would be presided over by a mistress of rather higher birth than the wet nurses. She was usually someone who also attended the lady of the house herself.[58] At some point after weaning a girl's primary carer became a governess or *magistrissa*, the role Katherine Swynford had occupied for John of Gaunt's older daughters.[59] The *magistrissa* for Cecily's cousins Blanche and Philippa, before their father became king, was Katherine Waterton, the wife of Henry Bolingbroke's chamberlain.[60] Even though royal and noble women were usually too busy to teach their children directly, these mothers were expected to take an important supervisory role in the early education of both their sons and daughters.[61] Christine de Pisan explained that 'the wise lady who loves her children' should ensure that 'they will learn first of all to serve God, and to read and write, and that their teacher will be careful to make them learn their prayers well'.[62]

For noble children, an awareness of God and the tenets of Christianity was woven closely into the fabric of each day. Daily routines drawn up for Cecily's nephew, John Mowbray, duke of Norfolk, and for her grandson, the future Edward V, reveal that they were expected to hear matins and then attend mass in their castle chapel before breakfast. They would also attend evensong later in the day.[63] Grace said before and after meals was another integral part of their routine. Religion also played a central role in the process of learning to read which generally began by learning to say aloud the sounds in Latin devotional works.[64] The skills of reading and writing were quite separate. Cecily could sign her own name, but the wide shapes of her letters suggest that she rarely if ever wrote anything else. When John Hardyng dedicated his *Chronicle* to Richard duke of York and his family in about 1460 he particularly directed it to Cecily's attention on the assumption that she could read English but 'in Latin hath little intellect'.[65] This should not be taken to mean that Cecily understood absolutely no Latin at all because she would have heard Latin words daily in the services she attended and like other girls would have begun to understand the sounds of letters from Latin books. Her cousins Blanche and Philippa were about seven and five when they were given such books for their own use.[66] Joan Beaufort could have allowed her children to read from a psalter that had once belonged to her own mother. This psalter was mentioned in Joan's will as the former property of 'the most illustrious lady and my mother Katherine Duchess of Lancaster' and was clearly one of Joan's most treasured possessions.[67] Once the skill of reading had been mastered, there were plenty of more secular books available for Cecily to read and indeed she would have heard others reading these out loud long before. Most of the books mentioned in her mother's will were religious, but from other sources we know that Joan's library was much richer and that contemporaries saw her as a woman with a particular interest in literature.

Joan owned a volume of stories of the crusades, the romance of Tristan and Iseult and a book by John Gower, very possibly his *Confessio Amantis*.[68] Thomas Hoccleve, a poet and former clerk in the Office of the Privy Seal, gave her a manuscript of his poems that he had written in his own hand and which is now held in Durham University Library.[69] It includes two parallel religious allegories that shed an interesting light on the morality Cecily was presumably learning. One told of a foolish young man who eventually slew the paramour who had stolen his magic jewels, but the other was about an innocent empress who forgave murderers, kidnappers and those who conspired to rape her. Implicit in these stories was the assumption that it was male nature to take revenge whereas women should suffer wrongs patiently. More positively, this attitude shaped the contemporary assumption that women were especially fitted for peacemaking. As Christine de Pisan explained, 'men are by nature more courageous and more hot-headed, and the great desire they have to avenge themselves prevents their considering either the perils or the evils that can result from war. But women are by nature more timid and also of a sweeter disposition, and for this reason ... they can be the best means of pacifying men'.[70] In adulthood Cecily frequently found herself in a position to use this expectation of feminine character in mediating between powerful men. She may also have been able to manipulate it to her advantage during political crises.

Cecily's education for womanhood must also have included horse riding, dancing, board games and needlework. Kim Phillips has argued that 'the training of medieval maidens was ultimately an education of the body ... it was educated in quietness of tongue, stillness of posture, and in keeping to a relatively limited space'.[71] Phillips contrasts conduct books aimed primarily at urban families with those whose concern was with women of the lesser nobility and finds important distinctions in ideas of respectability. Most women could prove their worth by hard work. However, while noblewomen had to work at managing their households and estates, for them respectability was 'tied firmly to the demands of piety' and a 'religious sensibility guiding all actions'.[72]

An even more striking class difference related to girls' responses to sexual temptations. Urban courtesy books advised girls to avoid any sort of situation in which they might be vulnerable to temptation and in this they reflected a common trope in literature in which servant girls 'have no defences against sexual advances' and are simply powerless to resist ruin.[73] By contrast, high-status women, like the many nobly born virgin martyrs, were assumed to have the capacity to protect their virtue inherent in their noble blood. Christine de Pisan explained that women at court

> should restrain themselves with seemly conduct among knights and squires and all men. They should speak demurely and sweetly and ... must not be frolicsome, forward, or boisterous in speech, expression, bearing or laughter ... This kind of behaviour would be very unseemly and greatly derisory in a woman of the court in whom there should be more modesty, good manners and courteous behaviour than in any others.[74]

Such advice was of course not always heeded. Consequently, Christine devoted a couple of chapters to guiding those in service with high-born ladies on the means of diverting their mistress from 'a foolish love affair'.[75] In the context of such upbringing it is easy to imagine why Cecily might have responded to rumours that she was an adulteress by developing an especially ostentatiously religious lifestyle later in her life.

Her mother's daughter

Another potential influence upon Cecily's later religious life was her experience of her mother's piety. Shortly before Cecily's birth, Joan had invited a controversial mystic, Margery Kempe, to her home to share her wisdom. Margery was a merchant's daughter from Lynn in Norfolk whose mystical experiences had begun after her first son's birth when a vision of Jesus cured her crippling postnatal depression.[76] Margery eventually bore fourteen children but finally in the summer of 1413 she persuaded her husband to adopt a chaste marriage. It was probably that same year that Margery made her visit to Joan Beaufort. Almost certainly Joan was one of those who helped to fund Margery's pilgrimage to Jerusalem by giving her money in exchange for her prayers.[77] Margery's way of life seems to have powerfully impressed at least one of Joan's daughters because in 1417 Margery was charged with trying to persuade Joan's eldest (Ferrers) daughter,

Elizabeth Lady Greystoke, to leave her own husband, presumably to live a similar chaste life.[78] Margery naturally denied the charge and Elizabeth did remain with her husband but the incident is suggestive of the religious ideas present in the household in which Cecily grew up.

In 1422 Joan acquired an indult permitting her to stay overnight with any order of nuns attended by 'eight honest women'.[79] This was effectively a licence to take religious retreats. Moreover, as a widow in 1428 she undertook a pilgrimage to 'many holy places' and joined the sisterhood of the abbey of St Albans where the abbey's chronicler judged her 'a woman devoted to God'.[80] As Rowena Archer pointed out, late medieval English noblewomen very rarely undertook pilgrimages.[81] At some point in her widowhood Joan Beaufort swore a vow of chastity dedicating herself to God in a public ritual not unlike that undertaken by nuns.[82] The ring she wore in token of this vow appears to have been particularly spectacular.[83] As a vowess her spiritual status was enhanced and her position as an independent woman of power made more respectable. During the 1430s, when she was in her fifties, Joan was regularly involved in the affairs of Durham priory.[84] Her only recorded religious foundation was a chantry at Lincoln cathedral over her mother's tomb.[85] Perhaps this model explains Cecily's own lack of interest in the grand foundations that would occupy her sons or women like Lady Margaret Beaufort. It is not unreasonable to speculate that Cecily's perception of appropriate behaviour for a widow was partly shaped by Joan Beaufort's ostentatious personal piety although there is no evidence that Cecily ever took a similar vow of chastity.

Matchmaking

Joan's most significant impact upon her children's lives was certainly in the marriages she arranged for them. The circumstances in which so many young noble heirs became available to marry the children of the new-made earl illustrate the political dynamics out of which some part of the Wars of the Roses grew. Both the first and the last of the exceptional husbands whom Joan and Ralph acquired for their daughters were grandsons of Edmund of Langley, duke of York, fourth surviving son of Edward III. The first of these was Richard Despenser, son of Edmund's only daughter, Constance. Her husband, Thomas Lord Despenser, had recklessly involved himself in the Epiphany Rising against Henry IV in 1400. After this plot to reinstate Richard II was foiled Lord Thomas had been betrayed by the captain of the ship he had hoped to flee in and then summarily executed by the townsmen of Bristol.[86] Thomas Despenser's fate was indicative of Richard II's unpopularity at the start of the fifteenth century. Constance's brother, Edward duke of York, then sought to take control of the Despenser inheritance during her son's minority. He eventually persuaded the king to grant him custody of the six-year-old Richard himself in 1403.[87] It was in this context that Constance Despenser became the first member of the house of York to conspire against the Lancastrian monarchy.[88]

At about the feast of St Valentine in 1405 Lady Constance abducted Edmund and Roger Mortimer, the great grandsons of Edward III's second son, Lionel duke of Clarence, from Windsor Castle. Her plan seems to have been to take them into

Wales where Owain Glyn Dŵr and Henry Percy, first earl of Northumberland, were plotting with the boys' uncle, Sir Edmund Mortimer, to rebel against Henry IV once more.[89] However, she was caught at Cheltenham and taken before the royal council. She then tried to blame the conspiracy on her brother Edward which has earned her the condemnation of modern historians.[90] Although York was briefly imprisoned at Pevensey for failing to reveal what he knew of the plot, Henry IV seems to have been unpersuaded by Constance's allegations.[91] Constance, like her brother, escaped the bloody fate of recent rebels, presumably as a consequence of the combination of her royal blood and her sex. In the medieval imagination there was a constant tension between the idea of women's changeable, corrupting, Eve-like influence in the world; the sense of their childlike inability to govern themselves or to be responsible for their behaviour; and the ideal of the vulnerable lady and mother who might intercede, Madonna-like, to create peace. While Constance certainly did not belong in the last category, her noble blood, widowhood and young children may all have made the king reluctant to be so unchivalrous as to impose harsh punishment. Nonetheless she had certainly forfeited any chance of arranging a marriage for her son Richard.

By August 1409 Edward duke of York had agreed that twelve-year-old Richard should marry Cecily's eldest full sister, Katherine.[92] As far as Ralph and Joan were concerned the potentially wealthy child heir of a disgraced peer was the perfect match for one of their children. The child was in no position to quibble as his parents might have done over the fact that Joan had been a bastard and Ralph had so recently arrived in his earldom (partly on his wife's coat-tails). Moreover, as the king's half-sister, Joan was well positioned to help negotiate her son-in-law's political rehabilitation. However, in 1411, before the marriage had been solemnized, Ralph acquired the custody and marriage of John Mowbray, at the substantial cost of 3,000 marks (£2,000).[93] Mowbray's father had died in exile in Venice in 1399 after a quarrel with Henry Bolingbroke that had provided Richard II with the excuse to banish them both.[94] John Mowbray's older brother Thomas had subsequently become embroiled in Archbishop Scrope's rebellion of 1405 during which Ralph Neville himself had tricked him and handed him over for execution.[95] One can only imagine how John Mowbray felt, aged nineteen, at being sold off to his brother's captor in this way. Since Katherine was the Nevilles' eldest marriageable daughter it made sense to rearrange their plans and wed her to their new ward. So in January 1412 a new dispensation was acquired permitting Richard Despenser (now fifteen) to marry Cecily's nine-year-old sister Eleanor instead. Despite the fact that Katherine can only just have reached the canonical age for marriage (twelve) and Eleanor was significantly younger, a licence was issued on the day before the dispensation allowing Richard, abbot of Jervaulx, and two other clerics to marry both couples in the chapel at Raby Castle.[96] Since both husbands were still minors, it it likely that they remained in residence at Raby until 1413, in which year Mowbray received full livery of his lands and Despenser died.

In northern Europe child marriage was very unusual for those below the ranks of nobility and even those of the highest ranks generally married in their late teens at least.[97] Both the high status of the families into which Cecily's siblings married and the young age of their unions may have been cause for some comment in their day as they have been among historians since. Some late medieval parents specifically elicited promises that a marriage would not be consummated until their daughter was sixteen.[98] Apparently no such limits were placed by Joan and Ralph since Katherine Neville's only child in her first marriage, another John, was born in September 1415 (she may just have been sixteen by then, but was certainly no older).[99] Eleanor's marriage to Richard Despenser was tragically brief and she was a widow at the age of ten. She was almost immediately betrothed again, this time to the twenty-year-old Henry Percy. Percy had grown up in Scotland after his father, the first earl of Northumberland's son 'Hotspur', was slain by the king's forces at Shrewsbury in 1403.[100] Henry V was trying to heal the wounds of his father's usurpation and he and Joan Beaufort seem to have worked in concert to bring Percy into the Lancastrian fold.[101] Eleanor married Henry Percy at Berwick as he returned to England to reclaim his grandfather's inheritance. By July of 1421 (when Eleanor was just eighteen) the couple had already had five children.[102] Cecily Neville consequently grew up with the knowledge that she should expect to leave her childhood behind as soon as she reached puberty.

On 13 December 1423 her parents acquired custody of yet another boy whose father had died opposing the house of Lancaster.[103] This was Constance Despenser's nephew, Richard duke of York. Constance's younger brother, Richard of Conisborough, earl of Cambridge, had been executed just a few months after Cecily's birth. It seems that Conisborough had long resented his lack of power or an income to match his status and perhaps imagined that he would share his sister's immunity when he became embroiled in rebellion. His motivation for an ill-conceived plot against Henry V on the eve of the Agincourt campaign remains something of a mystery. In 1408, without permission and in some secrecy, he had married Anne Mortimer, the sister of the boys Constance had abducted three years earlier.[104] Anne was to die in the autumn of 1411, very shortly after their son Richard was born.[105] After this Conisborough again married a woman of no great wealth, Maud Clifford. In 1414 he was approaching his thirtieth birthday when Henry V gave him the 'empty' title of earl of Cambridge.[106] The following summer Earl Richard schemed to take advantage of Henry V's long-planned absence abroad and initiate rebellion. It is unclear whether the initial plan was to replace Henry V with someone impersonating Richard II or with Cambridge's brother-in-law, Edmund Mortimer, earl of March.[107] Cambridge's co-conspirators were Sir Thomas Grey of Heaton (who was coincidentally married to one of the daughters of Ralph earl of Westmorland's first marriage) and Henry, Lord Scrope of Masham. Edmund Mortimer himself revealed the plot to Henry V as the king prepared to sail from Southampton. Cambridge, Scrope and Heaton were all executed in the first week of August 1415.[108] Less than three months later Cambridge's elder brother, Edward duke of York, died at Agincourt. Cambridge had not been attainted so his son Richard was permitted to inherit the title and lands of the duke of York.[109]

Richard duke of York was initially placed in the custody of Sir Robert Waterton, a former squire to Henry IV and the king's master of horse.[110] Earl Ralph took advantage of his position on the minority council of the new king Henry VI to acquire the wardship which, like Mowbray's, cost him 3,000 marks.[111] Earl Ralph had already negotiated a marriage for Cecily's older sister Anne with Humphrey Stafford (who had become a ward of Queen Joan after his father died fighting for the king at Shrewsbury in 1403).[112] So Ralph was clearly acquiring Richard of York's wardship specifically with the intention of arranging Cecily's marriage. When the earl drew up his will in 1424 he bequeathed a golden cup and a silver ewer to his daughter 'Ciciliæ Ducissæ Eborum'.[113] She was then just nine years old whereas Richard was thirteen.

In the context of her sisters' very youthful marriages it seems likely that this should not be read merely as a statement of intent but as evidence that Cecily had married Richard shortly after the earl acquired his wardship. Legally either party could still renounce the marriage at any time before they reached the age of consent – twelve for Cecily and fourteen for Richard – but in practice they were scarcely in a position to do so. Although most medieval weddings happened at the church door, those of the nobility commonly took place within private chapels and could be accompanied by several days of lavish celebrations.[114] Most likely Cecily and Richard were married, like her sisters Katherine and Eleanor, in the chapel at Raby Castle. Initially this can have made little practical difference to young Cecily's everyday life. However, Cecily must already have been conscious that as duchess of York her prospects were higher than those of any of her siblings.

In January of 1425 Richard of York's maternal uncle, Edmund Mortimer, died of plague at his castle of Trim. March had no children of his own, which meant that Richard now inherited his earldom and estates whose annual revenue sometimes approached £4,000.[115] Richard was consequently destined to be one of the richest magnates in England. He also inherited from Edmund Mortimer the potential claim to the English throne which would ultimately shape both his own and Cecily's lives so dramatically.

2

Becoming a Duchess: 1425–1438

Indults to the following to have a portable altar …
Richard, duke of York, and Cecily his wife, noblewoman.

Pope Martin V[1]

On 15 October 1429, in his elegant family palace beside the basilica of the Holy Apostles in Rome, Pope Martin V was issuing indults. These are special exemptions from normal church regulations. Among the indults Pope Martin granted that day were two which form the earliest evidence that Cecily Neville and Richard duke of York were married and operating as a couple, despite Cecily's youth. The first indult gave the couple permission to choose a portable altar on which mass might be celebrated for them when it was not convenient to attend a church. The second permitted them to choose their own confessor who could set penances, absolve them of their sins and provide spiritual direction.[2]

Cecily was by now fourteen years old and Richard eighteen. Until he turned twenty-one Richard should remain a royal ward. This meant that his lands were administered at the discretion of the king's council and much of his property was currently in the hands of favoured Lancastrian lords such as the king's uncle Humphrey duke of Gloucester. Only a year before the indults were issued York had been instructed to live within the young king's household, attending the king along with other royal wards.[3] Yet these documents suggest that Richard and Cecily were striving to define themselves as a married couple, with all that that implied about adulthood and independence. In stark contrast to her sisters' experience, Cecily's journey to full adulthood was to be long and slow.

Cecily's father had died on 21 October 1425, after which Cecily and Richard's lives gradually began to change. Her mother, Joan Beaufort, inherited York's wardship (and with it 200 marks annually for his 'sustenance' from the lands he would one day inherit).[4] Despite being the family of a second marriage, Joan and her youngest offspring were not cast out of the family home at Ralph's death. On the contrary, Raby, Staindrop, Middleham and Sheriff Hutton were all part of Joan's dower lands so that she could continue to reside there until her death in 1440. Throughout her marriage, she and Ralph had systematically reassigned the vast majority of Westmorland's possessions to Joan's children in what has been called 'an ambitious family fraud'.[5] This meant that most of the homes of Cecily's childhood would eventually pass to her eldest full brother, Richard earl of Salisbury and thence to his son, Richard earl of Warwick. The arrangement inevitably set generations of Nevilles at odds with one another and contributed to the baronial infighting of the Wars of the Roses. Ralph, second earl of Westmorland did eventually manage to wrest back Raby for his older line in 1443, after resorting to violence, whereas his brother, John Lord Neville, followed by their nephew, Sir Humphrey Neville, repeatedly opposed the house of York.[6]

Wife of a royal ward

Four months before the death of Cecily's father, the Privy Council at Westminster had agreed that all royal wards should be summoned to live in the household of their four-year-old king, Henry VI. Each could bring a master whose expenses would be defrayed from the king's own income. No provision was made for any wives.[7] It is likely that at this stage the council did not expect the fourteen-year-old duke of York to be a companion to his infant king immediately. Certainly there is no sign that any effort was made to send York south. However, on 4 May 1426 a summons was issued to Joan, Countess of Westmorland, to bring Duke Richard and her own sons William and George to Leicester to be knighted alongside the young king.[8]

Many historians state that it was the illustrious John duke of Bedford who knighted York.[9] That is what pseudo-Worcester's *Annales* record.[10] But this may rather have been how Richard and Cecily preferred to remember the day decades later. Some of the *London Chronicles* give a far more detailed account of the ceremony and explain that Bedford only knighted his nephew, the king. Thereafter it was four-year-old Henry who conferred that status on the assembled boys and men, most of them at least a decade older than him.[11] This knighting ceremony at Pentecost 1426 was essentially a morale boosting exercise to try to re-establish stability in the political community in the wake of a formal reconciliation between the king's antagonistic kinsmen. Earlier that year the supporters of his great uncle Henry Beaufort bishop of Winchester and of his uncle Humphrey duke of Gloucester had been on the brink of armed conflict in the heart of London.[12] The knighting ceremony in Leicester was an attempt to reassure and to reassert unified noble authority as well as an opportunity for a sense of brotherhood in arms to be established between the young king and those destined to be his principal councillors.

In May 1426 Joan Beaufort took advantage of her son-in-law's new status to petition for a rise in his allowance, explaining that now York was a knight his 'increase in honour, age and heritage demanded greater expenses and costs'.[13] A week after the knighting ceremony the king's council offered her an additional 100 marks from lands in Dorset and Suffolk formerly held by Edmund, earl of March.[14] This transaction indicates that for the moment York and Cecily were to remain in her mother's household and they probably returned to her northern residences. A year later Cecily turned twelve and her marriage became legally binding. Despite the youthful consummation of her sisters' marriages, it seems likely that Richard and Cecily waited. Their first child was actually not born until she was twenty-four. In the twelve intervening years the couple's lives would change radically.

Becoming a courtier

This change began in the spring of 1428 when it was decided that the king should be taken out of the care of women and given a household fitting to a prince who had left infancy. A schoolmaster, John Somerset of Bury St Edmund's, was employed as the young king's physician and master of grammar. Meanwhile the renowned commander Richard Beauchamp, earl of Warwick, began to take responsibility for the king's immediate welfare.[15] It was as part of this process that a letter was despatched in the king's name to Richard duke of York on 22 March summoning him to reside in Henry VI's household by the third Sunday after Easter at the very latest.[16] There were no women in the king's household so Cecily could not have joined her husband there. No evidence survives to indicate whose household she might have joined although a strong possibility is that of her sister Eleanor because York's biographer, P. A. Johnson, has suggested that Eleanor's husband, Henry Percy earl of Northumberland, now had some degree of guardianship over York. This guardianship seems to have been partly shared by William Alnwick, bishop of Norwich.[17]

Whichever household Cecily joined, she would have been furnished with servants of her own, chosen either by her mother or sister. Christine de Pisan advised that young married ladies should be served by gentlemen who were 'not too young, nor too talkative or gallant', and preferably married. Also 'she ought to have a lady or maiden of mature age – wise, prudent, good, virtuous and devout – who may be confidently entrusted with the chaperonage of the young lady'.[18] On those occasions when the household that Cecily had entered were in the king's company, Cecily experienced something of the life of a courtier, although it is moot whether the community around Henry VI in 1428 could properly be called a court. Certainly it was not the central political and cultural institution that the court had been in Richard II's day, or would be again under the Yorkist and Tudor monarchs. Nor was it even the centre of policy or 'exchange and mart of royal patronage' that it would become in Henry VI's adulthood.[19] Yet it was still a space for royal ritual and pageantry, for formality and opulence on a scale that Cecily had not previously experienced. Here she would have encountered the most powerful men in England and the most fashionable.

The indults

Richard and Cecily must have been living in separate households in the summer or autumn of 1429 when they applied to Pope Martin to have a portable altar and to choose their own confessor. Portable altars had initially been the preserve of clerics who needed to be able to perform mass in far-flung places or secretly, but by the fifteenth century laymen and women from merchants to nobles often petitioned for them, especially prior to travel.[20] Richard's uncle, Edmund, earl of March, and his (Edmund's) grandfather of the same name had made similar petitions in 1415 and 1368 respectively (in both cases prior to military expeditions to France).[21] Portable altars, like their larger counterparts, were always made of stone and contained a space for relics. They were often of marble or alabaster or even jasper or onyx and decorated with ivory or jewels set in precious metal. Portable altars were important tools for personal devotion but they also seem to have become markers of their owners' wealth or political importance in needing to travel regularly.[22]

It was quite common to apply for permission to choose a confessor at the same time as asking for a portable altar. In 1215 Pope Innocent IV had decreed that all Christians must make confession once a year at Easter, but many chose to make their confessions more often. One treatise translated by Walter Hilton recommended daily confessions if possible 'or else each third day, if a man may have leisure', but this was a council of perfection.[23] Usually confession would be made to the parish priest but many preferred to be able to confess to a friar.[24] Cecily and Richard, like many nobles, also sought someone highly qualified and it was probably at this time that they asked the Carmelite friar and doctor of theology John Keninghale to be their confessor.[25] Perhaps this decision was made under advice from bishop Alnwick since Keninghale was also based in Norwich. Confessors, unlike chaplains, tended not to be part of a nobleman's household but someone whose distance made them an appropriate person to listen to secrets and give spiritual advice. Keninghale's career was very much in the ascendant at this time. He was elected prior provincial of the Carmelite order in 1430 but resigned in 1440 to focus more fully on his role as a diplomat.[26] This combination of Carmelite spirituality and political experience presumably gave him an insight valued by nobles in Richard and Cecily's position.

These shared indults, the earliest recorded example of Cecily's religious life, set the tone for her subsequent piety. As will be seen, over the next few decades the evidence we have is almost always of religious interests shared with her husband. Many of these lasted throughout her life, particularly her devotion to religious houses associated with his dynasty. In his book of hours Richard duke of York was to add twenty-three pages of devotions that give a rare glimpse into his personal piety. These included memorials to six specific saints, three of whom were mentioned in various contexts in Cecily's will, thirty-five years after his death.[27]

The timing of the indults was almost certainly connected to the court's impending visit to France and suggests that in the autumn of 1429 Cecily expected to accompany her husband on the coronation expedition to France. This visit had been prompted by the sudden reversal in English fortunes in France marked by their humiliation at Orleans in the spring of 1429. Not only had the English failed to capture the town after a six-month siege, but one of their most able commanders, 'the worshipfull Prynce' Thomas Montagu, earl of Salisbury, had been killed by a cannonball (causing many of his men to desert), and their crucial ally Philip duke of Burgundy had been alienated by their choice of target (and so withdrawn his troops).[28] Above all, the army that drove them to abandon the siege had been led by a seventeen-year-old girl, Joan of Arc. Even before the siege was raised, the duke of Bedford had begun urging the council in England to plan a coronation in France. This would be an opportunity, he explained, for Henry's French subjects to declare their allegiance publicly in spiritually binding oaths of homage.[29] Bedford was probably also aware of plans afoot in Rheims to crown Henry's uncle Charles, the 'so-called dauphin', as king of France. The English council first had to arrange an English coronation. The duke of York was issued with clothing for that occasion, 6 November 1429, but seems to have had no formal role in the ceremony.[30]

There is no mention of Cecily in the narratives of Henry VI's French coronation but most accounts make no mention of any women at all. It is only thanks to the survival of the earl of Warwick's household book that we know that both his wife and his daughter Margaret Talbot were present and that they occasionally entertained women who were the wives of other English commanders.[31] What we do learn from the chronicler Enguerrand de Monstrelet, governor of Cambray, was that Richard duke of York already knew how to impress onlookers with his wealth and status for Monstrelet referred to him as 'le riche duc d'Yorch'.[32] He made no such descriptive comment about any of the other lords he was recording.

An early painting of Cecily

The royal expedition landed at Calais, appropriately on St George's day 1430, and spent several months there before moving to Rouen.[33] According to art historians, it was probably in Rouen that the earliest surviving image of Cecily duchess of York was painted, by an artist possibly associated with the creators of the Bedford Hours.[34] The image of Cecily is a gorgeously detailed scene of Neville women at prayer: Cecily and five of her sisters (two of them half-sisters) genuflecting behind Countess Joan.[35] A companion image was painted of nine male relatives and three more half-sisters behind Earl Ralph. (Neither Joan's Ferrers daughters nor the sisters who became nuns are included in either picture and it is not wholly clear which of Cecily's brothers are represented.)[36] In the bottom margin of both images there are shields displaying the arms of each member of the family (albeit inaccurately for some of Cecily's half-sisters). The images have been inserted into a Latin and French manuscript that included hours of Paris Use, Gospel extracts, prayers and psalms. The Neville illuminations are of a higher quality than the rest of the manuscript but all are of a similar date and in the style associated with the Master of the Munich Golden Legend who was a collaborator and perhaps a pupil of the Master of the Bedford Hours.[37]

We cannot be sure which of the women in the picture was meant to be Cecily. Indeed, the only clearly identifiable figures in either image are her brother Robert (wearing the mitre he had acquired as bishop of Salisbury in 1427) and her parents. If the artist did envisage any of the others as particular individuals, it is most likely that Cecily was positioned nearest to her mother, thereby mirroring the position of her coat of arms in the bottom margin which is next to Joan's. This was appropriate because her status as the wife of a royal duke was greater than that of her sisters despite her age. This figure's dress is of gold and blue with a rose-coloured girdle whereas her sisters wear dresses of only one colour. Cecily and her sisters each wear a gold Lancastrian livery collar of linked Ss (as Joan Beaufort, Margaret Stafford and Ralph all do on their funeral effigies at Staindrop). By contrast the men wear a more cumbersome collar of a stag jumping through a fence. This too may have been a Lancastrian livery collar, a variant of that famously worn by Sir Thomas Markenfield on his tomb effigy in Ripon

FIGURE 2.1 *Joan Beaufort, countess of Westmorland, with her daughters and stepdaughters at prayer c. 1435, from a Book of Hours of Paris Use. BnF Lat MS 1158 f. 34 v. Reproduced by permission of the Bibliothèque nationale de France*

FIGURE 2.2 *Ralph Neville, earl of Westmorland, with twelve of his children at prayer c. 1435, from a Book of Hours of Paris Use. BnF Lat MS 1158 f. 27 v. Reproduced by permission of the Bibliothèque nationale de France*

Cathedral.[38] These images of Neville family unity are strikingly at odds with the reality of conflict between the two branches of Earl Ralph's offspring.

Catherine Reynolds has speculated that one of Joan Beaufort's children acquired the book and had it altered in Rouen as a gift for their mother.[39] It may well have been that the purchaser chose a standard book of hours from a Rouen workshop and then asked both for additional prayers and the Neville portraits to be inserted. The prayers on the scrolls of the Neville images link them to prayers on the facing pages which are part of sections added in to the original manuscript.[40] The uneven arrangement of the members of the Neville family in these pictures is intriguing and it is perhaps worth noting that those of Joan's stepdaughters who were pictured with her and Cecily seem to be those who had some connection with Richard duke of York.[41] It is not impossible that Cecily and Richard had some role in commissioning these images.

If Cecily was indeed with the court for the French coronation expedition she would have been in Rouen for the duration of Joan of Arc's trial and her execution on 30 May 1431.[42] It was only in November 1431 that the English court moved on to Paris where they were entertained in the streets with tableaux of Biblical and legendary stories 'and a live representation of a stag hunt: very enjoyable to watch', according to one Parisian.[43] On December 16 Henry was crowned in splendour by Cardinal Beaufort at Notre Dame (much to the chagrin of the bishop of Paris who felt he should have performed the ceremony).[44] Having spent Christmas in Paris the king and his entourage made their way back home for a splendid welcome in London on St Valentine's day.[45] John Lydgate composed a somewhat over-optimistic record of the day, comparing Henry VI with the young king David and even with Julius Caesar arriving home from victory.[46]

Adulthood begins

Three months later Richard duke of York was granted livery of his estates. He was not quite twenty-one but in consequence of his 'good service both in France and England' he was allowed to inherit early.[47] It was a complicated inheritance. The estate of his uncle Edward duke of York was, in T. B. Pugh's words 'burdened with debt and dowagers', 'few English nobles in the later middle ages left their affairs and finances in a more ruinous state'.[48] Indeed it is likely that the old duke's debts amounted to more than the capital value of his estates. Richard's aunt Philippa (widow of Edward, duke of York) had died in July 1431 but York experienced problems claiming some of her income at least as late as 1439.[49] Richard's step-grandmother, Joan Holland, had been granted dower that included Hitchin in Hertfordshire, a substantial annuity from Grantham and the important northern castle at Sandal. She died just two years after Richard reached his majority and her York estates then passed to him.[50] By contrast Richard's stepmother, Maud Clifford, countess of Cambridge, lived on until 1446. Certainly in the 1430s York was paying her an annuity of £100 and this may well have lasted throughout her life.[51] Moreover, although the earl of Cambridge himself had inherited none of the York lands, Maud had taken possession of Conisbrough Castle and lived out her widowhood there.

Despite the limitations of his York inheritance, the wealth Richard inherited from his other uncle, Edmund Mortimer earl of March, made him the most powerful of Henry VI's subjects. This inheritance was also briefly limited by a dowager countess's claims: March's widow, Anne Stafford, who had gone on to marry John Holland, earl of Huntingdon. However, after Anne died in September 1432 her dower lands from her first marriage were handed over to Richard[52] In 1436 York declared that the taxable income on his English estates was £3,230.[53] His total income would have been significantly greater than this when his receipts from Wales were included. T. B. Pugh has estimated that by 1443 York's total landed income was over £6,000 besides which he was entitled to hereditary annuities of £761.[54] To understand the scale of York's wealth it helps to compare the 1436 estimate of the taxable income from his English lands with the sums declared by some other English landowners. The king's guardian, Richard Beauchamp earl of Warwick declared an income of £3,116 but Cecily's elder brother Richard earl of Salisbury declared only £1,238 and her brother-in-law Henry Percy earl of Northumberland valued his lands at £1,210.[55] The average taxable baronial income was about £865 and many men who described themselves as gentlemen received only £5 a year.[56] After so many powerless years controlled by Robert Waterton, Ralph and Joan Neville and then the king's household, it is scarcely surprising that the newly wealthy Richard duke of York seems to have been recklessly extravagant at times.

When Richard received livery of his lands Cecily was just turning seventeen. The couple could now begin to set up a household like those her sisters had enjoyed for so long. For a noble couple of their standing this was a complex structure. Just a few staff would be expected to reside at all times at each of their residences while the majority would be with the lord himself. If he was travelling abroad, or on a brief trip elsewhere in the country, the great household would remain in a major residence such as Fotheringhay or Ludlow, very often under the governance of his wife while only a small staff would travel with him. Married ladies usually had a small household of their own connected to the great household but capable of travelling with them as needed. The numbers involved could vary greatly. In the early years of her marriage to Henry Stafford, Margaret Beaufort, dowager countess of Richmond, had a household of thirty-two servants, including six gentlewomen. This was larger than average but Cecily's sister Anne, dowager duchess of Buckingham, enjoyed a household of about sixty during her second marriage.[57] Most of these servants were men. Just a handful of women were employed to provide appropriate company for the lady and the laundry was usually done by women who lived outside the great house.[58] The principal officials would usually come from gentry families and often held positions in the lord's administration too. The women were almost her social equals so Cecily may well have been expected to provide an education for some of her many nieces as well as the daughters of gentry families that York wished to favour. Women in a noblewoman's household were usually single but sometimes the wives of significant household members also served here.[59]

In most households many of the staff had a history of service to their lord's family and often kinship connections to one another as a result of previous generations' shared service.[60] The long period of Richard duke of York's minority would have made the process of building up a new household difficult since he could not look to those from his father's service. In the wider administration of his estates he clearly continued to employ many of those who had been performing these roles in his minority, some of whom had previously served his uncles. From here he also drew some of those who became his councillors and principal servants, such as Sir John Tyrell, steward of his Thaxted and Clare estates, who became his receiver general (and grandfather to the notorious Sir James Tyrell who was briefly Cecily's ward).[61]

Noble households were, as Barbara J. Harris has observed, 'stages for the display of their owners' status and wealth, headquarters for estate management, regional centers of consumption and social life, and the focal points for local and county government'.[62] Harris emphasizes that 'the public and political character of aristocratic households' shaped women's experience and provided them with the opportunity for a 'career' with 'as much political and economic as domestic importance'.[63] These careers 'were as crucial to the survival and prosperity of their families and class as the careers of their male kin'.[64]

As Cecily took up these responsibilities, she presumably drew inspiration from the practice she had witnessed in her mother's household and those of her elder sisters. Christine de Pisan advised 'the wise princess' to begin her day early with prayers and masses 'as many as accord with her devotion and as time and leisure will permit her' and to distribute alms as she left her chapel, mindful that her wealth was a gift from God which she must share.[65] The morning should be spent in administration with advice from well-chosen councillors, followed by the midday meal, 'and while the plates are still on the table (according to the fine custom of queens and princesses) she will have a gentleman at hand who will speak of the deeds of some good deceased person, or he will speak of some excellent moral subject or tell stories of exemplary lives'.[66] She should spend time in conversation with her household members and 'after the spices have been taken' might retire for a short rest and then spend the afternoon in more relaxed pursuits with her gentlewomen. Vespers should be said 'if no weighty business prevents her', after which she might 'go off to amuse herself in the garden … for her health' until supper-time and then pray before bed. This routine is broadly similar to that specifically attributed to Cecily in the 1490s and so it may well have been fairly close to her daily practice throughout her life.

The business to which Cecily would have to attend might be the administration of household matters or, in her husband's absence, those relating to his estates, or perhaps petitions from those hoping that she would influence her husband's judgement in their concerns, quarrels or career ambitions. Christine de Pisan emphasized the importance of developing good relations with her husband's counsellors and all those who were subject to him, particularly clergymen. She explained that this would strengthen their loyalty to her husband and these people would pray for the lady and defend her if her honour be impugned.[67] Christine also encouraged her readers to be 'thoroughly knowledgeable' about laws regarding landholdings, their expected revenues and the different types of farming on their estates, suggesting that they should find time to visit their fields and check up on workers.[68] This was of course easier for women with much smaller, concentrated landholdings than for women like Cecily.

Homes and castles

Cecily and Richard needed to set up homes for themselves across Richard's estates. Some of the residences York inherited had at times been occupied by those administering his lands during his minority. For instance, Henry V used Fotheringhay Castle to house his valuable French hostage Charles duke d'Orleans (captured at Agincourt) in 1421 and three years later Henry VI's council held seven Scottish hostages there.[69] Other sites had fallen into some disrepair. There was of course a very wide variety for the couple to choose from. Their manor at Cranborne in Dorset had been built as a hunting lodge by King John. Scant documentary evidence of time spent there survives but they presumably practised generous good lordship at the manor because Richard and Cecily's arms were displayed on either side of the west door of the neighbouring priory church of St Mary and St Bartholomew.[70] The decision to include Cecily's arms separately in this way suggests a desire to present the patronage as a joint enterprise by husband and wife.[71]

Another relatively small manor that the couple seem to have spent some time at was Fasterne near Wootton Bassett in Wiltshire.[72] This had been part of the dower lands of Philippa duchess of York (widow of Richard's uncle) so that she was responsible for it until her death in 1431.[73] Richard and Cecily's residence at Fasterne led to a tradition, recorded in the seventeenth century, that their youngest son Richard had been born at the manor.[74]

In stark contrast to such cosy residences, most of Richard and Cecily's time was spent in great castles. These included the imposing border fortresses that the Mortimers had maintained as earls of March. Montgomery, Usk and Wigmore Castles are today largely in ruins but the Yorks' most important and regularly used residence in this region, Ludlow, is one of the best-preserved castles in the marches, dramatically perched on a rocky plateau above the River Teme to protect it from Welsh attacks. As at Cranborne, Cecily and Richard involved themselves in the religious and civic life of the community at Ludlow. For instance, in 1438 they paid a princely £13 16s. 8d. to join the town's prestigious Palmers' Guild. Most members paid somewhere between 2s. and 20s.[75]

Not all the castles they inherited from the earl of March were located in the west of Britain. Clare Castle in Suffolk was the heart of the wealthy honour of Clare that Cecily would acquire in her own right as king's mother. The couple stayed here on occasion and arranged for various refurbishments there in the 1440s and 1450s.[76] They maintained connections with two important religious houses there. One was the college of Stoke by Clare which Richard's uncle, Edmund Mortimer, had re-founded for secular priests in 1415 and the other was the beautiful Clare Priory, the first house of Augustinian (Austin) friars in England.[77]

Cecily and Richard's most important York castle was Fotheringhay in Northamptonshire. This is located in 'the widest and richest part of the valley of the River Nene', just beside the medieval river crossing for the road linking Stamford to Oundle and only a few miles west of the Great North Road, making it a practical, accessible location from which to administer the majority of their English lands.[78] One of York's first priorities on entering into his inheritance was to complete the foundation of a college of secular priests at Fotheringhay in fulfilment of his ancestors' intentions. Edmund of Langley, first duke of York, had planned a college inside the castle, on similar lines to Edward III's foundations of St Stephen's at Westminster and St George's at Windsor. Like these the college would provide prayer for the well-being of the realm of England and in particular for the progress of the war with France. In founding such institutions noblemen discharged their moral obligation to use their wealth to benefit the wider kingdom.[79] Of course the college would also offer prayers specifically for York's own family and add to the family's prestige. Edmund's son Edward was more ambitious than his father and drew Henry IV into helping him attach the college to the parish church. Henry V helped him raise more cash to begin construction. The college statutes were published just months before duke Edward's death at Agincourt and building work does not seem to have begun before the 1430s.[80] Cecily and Richard consequently had moral as well as practical reasons for setting up their first home at Fotheringhay Castle.

York was also required to spend some time in London and Westminster for Parliament and meetings of the king's council. At this stage he did not yet own a London inn of his own. Edward duke of York's residence, 'le Olde Inn by St Paul's Wharfe', had passed into the hands of Humphrey duke of Gloucester who rebuilt it after a fire in 1428.[81] In the mid-fifteenth century it acquired the name Baynard's Castle, a name which had previously belonged to a property on the nearby site subsequently occupied by Blackfriars.[82] Richard duke of York was only able to acquire Baynard's Castle after Gloucester's death so would have rented accommodation belonging to another lord.[83]

Governor of English France

In the spring of 1434 York was at a Great Council in Westminster which tried to bring harmony between the dukes of Gloucester and Bedford as they disagreed over the conduct of the war in France.[84] In France events were unfolding that would soon draw Richard and Cecily into the miserable endgame of the Hundred Years War. In November 1432 Parisians had mourned the death of twenty-eight-year-old Anne duchess of Bedford, 'the most delightful of all the great ladies then in France, for she was good and beautiful'.[85] More importantly she was the link between her husband John, the English Regent, and her brother, the powerful Philip duke of Burgundy: 'with her died most of the hope that Paris had, but this had to be endured' one citizen stoically recorded.[86] The duke of Bedford and his wife were reputed to have travelled everywhere together and he seemed grief-stricken at her death, but just five months later he took a second wife. This was Jacquetta of Luxembourg, daughter of the Count of St Pol.[87] She was only seventeen to the duke's forty-four years but he was probably still hoping to father an heir. Jacquetta's uncle, Louis of Luxembourg, bishop of Thérouanne, was chancellor of France for the English so it should have been a constructive political alliance. However, the duke of Burgundy was offended and took Bedford's remarriage as the excuse he needed to begin to distance himself from the English. In the summer of 1435 attempts were made to negotiate peace between the

English and the French king at the Congress of Arras but on 4 September discussions ended in failure.[88] Ten days later John duke of Bedford was dead and within a week Philip duke of Burgundy had officially allied with Charles VII of France.[89] The English king now needed a new lieutenant in France but the appointment was surely a poisoned chalice.

The chosen candidate needed to be acceptable to all factions around the king. York's youth and lack of experience meant that he had not yet become associated with either party. His close kinship to the king made him acceptable to the duke of Gloucester, but Cardinal Beaufort considered him 'my very dear and most beloved nephew' on account of his marriage to Cecily.[90] Thus the post of king's lieutenant and governor general in France was given to Richard, duke of York.[91] This is a rare confirmation that York benefited from Cecily's powerful family who now considered him a close kinsman. The royal council then planned the largest military expedition of the 1430s. Naturally York was supported by many more seasoned commanders, most notably John Talbot, one of Bedford's most senior lieutenants. Cecily's brother William sailed with them and was to remain in Normandy until 1443.[92] Again there is no record of whether Cecily went too. One recent writer has asserted that Cecily must have travelled to France because her first child, Joan, was conceived while York was still in France.[93] Any internet search for Cecily's children will turn up dozens of references to this first child who died in infancy. However, Joan was conceived not in France in 1437 but through a twentieth-century scribal error. There is not a shred of fifteenth-century evidence for a child of this name among Cecily's offspring. If Cecily actually remained in England at this time that would go some way to explain the long delay before she really did conceive a child who survived to term. Since York was only meant to serve for a year and it was an explicitly military venture it is most likely that she did indeed remain in England.

York was apparently keen to return as soon as his one year term was complete, but the king's council were sufficiently content with his achievement to write persuading him to stay while an appropriate successor could be decided upon.[94] Richard Beauchamp earl of Warwick had resigned as the king's guardian in May 1436. His military experience, reputation and acceptability to both Cardinal Beaufort and Humphrey duke of Gloucester outweighed his lack of royal blood when it came to choosing a permanent replacement for young York in France. Unsurprisingly, Warwick does not seem to have been entirely willing but was persuaded of his duty to serve the king in this way.[95] York was at last free to return home. Chroniclers recalled that Warwick took his wife Isabella with him but notably made no mention of Cecily in their references to York's journeys.[96] Most likely Cecily was waiting for York at Fotheringhay, managing their relatively new household in his absence until his return in November 1437. Early the next year she probably accompanied him into Wales where he stayed at Usk Castle to oversee administration both locally and in his Irish lands.[97]

It was more than eight years since the couple had applied for a portable altar together, asserting their status as man and wife despite York's minority and their separation in different households. It was nearly six years since York had been declared legally of age and permitted to take control of his vast inheritance. He was now twenty-six and Cecily was twenty-two. They must have begun to wonder whether they would ever have a child to inherit all these riches, riches that had only come to them because Edward, duke of York and Edmund, earl of March had both themselves died without legitimate heirs. We do not know how many pregnancies Cecily may already have endured that failed to come to term, but in the spring of 1439 she knew she was pregnant. She was on the brink of fulfilling the role most esteemed in English noblewomen. She was on the cusp between Lancastrian daughter and Yorkist matriarch.

3

Motherhood Begins: 1439–1449

Here follows the family begotten of the most illustrious prince, Richard, Duke of
York, etc. by the most gentle princess, his wife, Cecilia ...

Anonymous, *Generacio*[1]

It was in the high summer of 1439 that Cecily duchess of York at last gave birth to a healthy baby in the family home at Fotheringhay. Richard and Cecily were now approaching the most successful period of their married life. On the morning of 11 August 1439 Cecily bore a baby daughter.[2] In the next ten years they would have seven more children. The couple spent much of the first half of that decade living in Normandy, ruling almost as king and queen of the English lands in France.

Anne of Fotheringhay

In 1439 Cecily was twenty-four, far older than her sisters had been when they became mothers. Although a contemporary writer remarked on Cecily's 'longe bareynesse', no reason for it was suggested.[3] It may well be that Richard and Cecily had not actually slept together until they moved into a household of their own in the summer of 1432 when she was seventeen. York was of course absent in France from June 1436 until November 1437 so only about four 'sterile years' would then have to be accounted for.[4] This period may of course have included miscarriages which naturally went unreported. If Cecily tended to remain on their estates while York had business in London this too would have reduced her chances of falling pregnant. Her situation bears comparison with that of Edward I's queen, Eleanor of Castile, who was married at thirteen but seems to have had no children until she was in her early twenties. She then bore twelve children over the next twenty years.[5]

Cecily's failure to conceive must nonetheless have been a cause of concern. The extreme pressure on women of her status to produce children was illustrated in the summer of 1441 in the catastrophe that overwhelmed her cousin's wife, Eleanor duchess of Gloucester, who had tried to procure fertility potions from one Margery Jourdemayne, 'the Witch of Eye'. Eleanor's association with Margery was to lead to disgrace and divorce.[6] Slightly lower down the social scale, an heiress of Cecily's acquaintance, Anne Harling, left substantial evidence of the grief and guilt that she suffered for her childlessness.[7] Anne chose to patronize a grammar school associated with Rushworth College (founded by her ancestors) so that 'the woman to whom God had denied the blessing of children will still leave children of her own who will call her blessed'.[8] She also arranged for shields of the arms of her husbands and of herself (including those of both her parents) to appear in the glazing of more than ten churches 'for a remembraunce to pray for us'.[9] As Anne Dutton has argued, this was very probably an attempt to compensate for her failure to perform her dynastic duty to her husbands as well as to her parents since she was their only heir.[10] For Eleanor and Cecily the dynastic responsibility was far greater. If it was assumed that the crown could not pass through the female line and as long as Henry IV's decision to exclude the Beauforts from the throne was not reversed, their husbands were second and third in line to the throne. The future of England might well depend upon their fertility.

Although medieval medical texts considered that either partner might be the cause of childlessness, the blame was usually placed upon women and it was more commonly women who took responsibility for seeking remedies.[11] Infertility and miscarriages were sometimes assumed to be a consequence of an enemy's sorcery and this might have motivated Eleanor duchess of Gloucester's recourse to counter-magic.[12] Suggested cures for infertility frequently mixed herbalism with prayer and incantations, a product of the porous boundary between medieval concepts of magic and miracles that had perhaps been Eleanor's undoing.[13] Kristen Geaman has argued that Richard II's childless queen, Anne of Bohemia, resorted to a variety of medicines, religious donations and a pilgrimage to the shrine of Our Lady at Walsingham in her efforts to conceive.[14] Many women focussed their prayers upon saints associated with fertility, particularly the Virgin Mary's legendary mother, St Anne, who was believed to have given up hope of pregnancy long before Mary was born. One of Cecily's acquaintances, Katherine Denston, owned a *Life of St Anne* which included a prayer to the saint to intercede with God to bring Katherine 'a sone/ Of her body'.[15] Richard and Cecily must have been conscious of this when they named their first daughter Anne, although it seems likely that the principal inspiration was Richard's mother's name.

Not long after Cecily was certain of her pregnancy, preparations for the birth would have begun. Letters despatched on behalf of Cecily's granddaughter-in-law, Honor, Lady Lisle, reveal that noblewomen lent one another rich hangings, screens, bedspreads and carpets that were reserved specifically for the delivery room. It has been suggested that the provenance of these furnishings could have been seen as markers of the mother's place in society because they illustrated her powerful connections.[16] There was perhaps also an emotional value in being surrounded by furnishings shared by close relatives who had survived childbirth. The precise details of appropriate ritual surrounding childbirth varied across medieval Europe and it clearly mattered a great deal to women that they performed this correctly. In 1430 Isabelle of Portugal, duchess of Burgundy, wrote to her sister-in-law, Margaret of Burgundy, countess of Brittany asking for advice on arranging the room for her lying-in. Isabelle also sought advice from an older lady at the Burgundian court, Madame de Namur, who apparently owned 'a great book in which were written all the honours of France'.[17] Having examined Burgundian evidence, Susan Broomhall has argued that 'women were key stakeholders in the maintenance and memory of honour conduct rituals'.[18]

It is likely that the arrangements Cecily made for her own delivery were similar to those described in *The Ryalle Book*, a fifteenth-century manual on royal protocol which has traditionally, but erroneously, been ascribed to Lady Margaret Beaufort.[19] The text was actually drawn up during the most powerful period of Cecily's own life, the early years of her son Edward IV's reign, apparently drawing on memories of Lancastrian practice, and later updated for the Tudor court.[20] In view of the Burgundian evidence, it is not unreasonable to imagine that Cecily or one of her ladies may have contributed to the sections of this text that would guide protocol for Cecily's daughter-in-law. The manual describes the preparation for a queen's lying-in so that even in the draughtiest castle a warm, dark and consciously womb-like space was created for the birth itself.[21] The ceiling, walls and all but a single window were to be thoroughly covered 'with rich arras' (a heavy cloth with interwoven patterns) and the floor 'must be laid with carpets over and over'.[22]

A few weeks before she expected to give birth Cecily would have made her confession and taken mass, conscious of the very real possibility that she might die as a result of childbirth as her mother-in-law had done. She then retired to her gilded bower accompanied only by her women. At all levels of society men were expected to stay away from the birthing chamber until after the child was born, unless the life of the mother or child were in such danger that it was necessary to call for a doctor or a priest.[23] Most births appear to have been attended by more than one midwife. These women had usually received training in matters like tying the umbilical cord and ensuring that the placenta had come out and were often also aware of how to respond to dangerous circumstances like incorrect foetal presentation.[24] Husbands generally carried on with their usual business while their wives were giving birth but would come into the chamber once the child was born.[25] After the delivery Cecily would have been expected to remain recovering in her secluded chamber for a month or more.

Although she must miss the festivities for her baby's baptism there was another opportunity for memorable celebrations at her churching. This commonly practised ritual had some links with Jewish purification rites but in later medieval England it was predominantly an occasion for thanksgiving.[26] It was not obligatory in canon law but most families wanted the opportunity to express their gratitude for the woman's survival, to mark her return to public life and to enjoy another feast. Indeed, at the Reformation the revelry associated with churching was a particular subject of criticism.[27] Like the preparations for the birthing chamber and the birth itself this was a predominantly female affair. Cecily would have walked down to Fotheringhay church, or perhaps to the castle chapel, with the women who had shared her confinement and with other female friends, relations and noble neighbours invited for the occasion. As with marriage and the initial stages of baptism, this rite was performed at the church door. Here the new mother knelt, holding a candle, as the priest blessed her and scattered holy water over her. The party then moved inside the church to celebrate mass before more secular festivities at the castle.[28]

Preparations for France

Beyond Cecily and Richard's personal celebrations in the Nene valley, discussions must already have been underway that would shape the next major chapter of their lives. Just over three months before Anne's birth, Richard Beauchamp, the 'gode Erle of Warwick' had died at Rouen.[29] The king was once more in need of a Lieutenant in France. As in 1436, York's high birth and his comparative political neutrality made him an obviously attractive choice. Now he was older and more experienced. Moreover, because his coming of age and first service in France had more or less coincided with the death of John duke of Bedford, many of Bedford's experienced men had moved into York's own new affinity. In the event Cecily's cousin, John Beaufort, earl of Somerset, briefly assumed command in Warwick's place because he was already in France, but on 2 July 1440 Richard duke of York was formally appointed Lieutenant-General of France once more.[30] This time he had been commissioned for a period of five years so Cecily was to travel with him to oversee the English headquarters in Rouen.

Before their departure, York made preparations to protect Cecily's financial future. As was commonly the case in marriages with royal wards, the arrangements at Cecily's wedding did not include a dowry from her father and probably did not make any provision for jointure. Jointure specified lands to be held by both husband and wife for life and was a means of guaranteeing some of the property a wife could expect to hold if she was widowed, in particular allowing her whole manors rather than just a third of the income of properties held by her husband's heirs, which was what she was entitled to through dower law. Few details of Cecily's jointure survive, but we do have a record that in March 1441 the king permitted York to enfeoff William Alnwick (now bishop of Lincoln) and others (including John Fastolf and William Oldhall) of various of his manors in the south of England to the use of the duke and Cecily together.[31] These included Marshwood in Dorset, the castle and town of Clare in Suffolk and the manor of Bardfield in Essex. However her jointure must have been far larger than this for, a few years later, the couple raised over £3,000 from the sale of their rights to a large number of jointly held manors.[32] In the months before their departure, Cecily and Richard were possibly travelling through their properties, setting matters in order before their departure. It was in about 1440 that the splendid stone and flint tower was constructed at Cranborne church in Dorset, near their manor house there, and very possibly at their expense.[33] In November 1440 Cecily's mother, Joan, died and was buried, as she had requested, with her own mother, Katherine Swynford, in Lincoln Cathedral.[34] Cecily may well have attended the funeral, but by now her mind was again focussed upon future generations because she was pregnant once more.

Henry of Hatfield

According to pseudo-Worcester's *Annales*, Cecily's son Henry was born at Hatfield on Friday 10 February 1441.[35] Unfortunately the author does not state which Hatfield. Some historians have reasonably assumed that this was Hatfield Manor House near Doncaster which Richard had inherited from his uncle Edward duke of York.[36] However, there is no evidence that the couple were in the north at the time. Another fifteenth-century list of York's children, henceforth called the *Generacio*, conflates Henry's birth with Anne's and claims that Anne was born at 'a certain manor of the Lord Bishop of Ely, called Hatfield'.[37] This would have been Hatfield in Hertfordshire. There are various mistakes in the *Generacio* and the compiler may have been confused by the fact that Anne did get married at the bishop's palace in 1446 but the Hertfordshire Hatfield does seem to be the more plausible location. On 14 February 1441 Henry VI at Westminster made mention of a son delivered to Cecily.[38] If the records of Henry's birth date are accurate, this would have required the news to travel improbably swiftly if it was coming all the way from Yorkshire. The bishop of Ely in 1441 was Cardinal Louis of Luxembourg, Jacquetta, duchess of Bedford's uncle. He was also archbishop of Rouen and still chancellor of France for the English. He had effectively governed Normandy for more than half the years since Bedford's death due to the frequent absence of a king's lieutenant.[39] Louis must have worked closely with York during the latter's first commission in France and would have been anticipating doing so again in the near future which is perhaps why Richard and Cecily came to be using his English home.

Henry VI ordered the keeper of his jewels, John Merston, to purchase £100 worth of jewels to be given as a baptismal gift to the child.[40] The jewels were entrusted to Cecily's nephew, Richard Neville earl of Warwick, presumably either because Warwick had been invited to be one of the boy's godparents, or because Warwick was actually standing proxy for the king himself in that role.[41] Henry VI's interest in the child was very natural since he might one day prove to be his heir. Tragically, however, the younger Henry was not destined to live long.[42] According to a sixteenth-century copy of a genealogy of the Yorkists that was probably originally drawn up before 1483 (now in Ashmole MS 831), Henry of Hatfield was buried at Fotheringhay.[43]

Rouen

We cannot be certain whether Henry of Hatfield died before Richard and Cecily's departure for Rouen, but it is not unreasonable to imagine that the brief life and death of their first son was one of the reasons that they delayed in England for so long. Richard duke of York finally left for Normandy in the early summer of 1441. A continuation of the *Brut* chronicle reported that 'with [the duke] went ouer the see the Duchesse of York, the Duchesse of Bedford, the Countesse of Oxenford, the Countesse of Ewe, and many other mo laydes with theire lordes, and other gentelwomen and damysels that bilonged to theym'.[44] This was to be Cecily's community for the next five years and most of their lives would be closely connected for decades to come. The women she travelled with presumably included friends, acquaintances and rivals.

The duchess of Bedford, Jacquetta de St Pol, had herself briefly been the first lady in English-occupied France so she was in a position to advise Cecily on her new role. It was almost a decade since Jacquetta's hasty marriage to John duke of Bedford had so enraged the duke of Burgundy. That marriage had lasted less than two and half years. Not much more than a year after Bedford's death, Jacquetta had taken a new husband, 'a young man, very handsome and well made' according to the chronicler Monstrelet, but 'in regard to birth inferior to her first husband, the regent, and to herself'.[45] Indeed he was only a knight. Jacquetta's family had been 'very angry' at news of this *mésalliance*.[46] The English seem to have been rather less appalled than their continental neighbours.[47] Perhaps they were beginning to become accustomed to such scandals after Gloucester's marriage to Eleanor Cobham (his first wife's gentlewoman) and the recent revelation that the king's mother, Catherine of Valois, had secretly married Owen Tudor, a mere squire from Wales. By contrast, Jacquetta's new husband, Richard Woodville, had been knighted alongside Richard duke of York and would acquire an international reputation for his jousting.[48] Under York's command in France Woodville was made captain of the garrison at Alençon. Like Cecily, Jacquetta had probably just begun bearing children.[49] One of her daughters, Elizabeth, would eventually marry Cecily's son Edward.

Another of Cecily and Richard's companions on the journey to Normandy, John de Vere, earl of Oxford, had also been knighted with York and indeed had lived in Henry VI's household as a teenager with York. Oxford's countess, Elizabeth de Vere (née Howard), was some five years older than Cecily but despite having married in 1425 may also have had only one surviving child at this point.[50] The third principal lady travelling to Normandy in 1441, the Countess of Eu, was someone else Cecily already knew well, for she was Richard duke of York's sister Isabel, wife of Henry Bourchier. Bourchier was to be governor-general of the marches of Picardy and captain of Le Crotoy.[51]

There were other English noble families already resident in Normandy, chief among them being John Lord Talbot, 'most dred of all other in France' and his wife Margaret.[52] Their family also already included a daughter whose name would eventually be linked romantically with Cecily's eldest surviving son: Eleanor, whom Richard III would one day allege had secretly married his brother Edward.

These nobles had their own residences in Rouen and in the towns to which they were despatched on military service. Most of them also spent time back in England on occasion. They must have socialized together, not only with dinners and games indoors but hunting in the Norman countryside, a pastime enjoyed by women as well as men. In 1444 the Yorks' household expenses included more than 40s. on equipment for hunting dogs, 20s. on arrows and 118s. on the purchase of twelve hunting horns.[53] Members of this community of English noblewomen would have been present for the births and christenings of many of each other's children and the subsequent churchings.

By the time Cecily and Richard arrived in Normandy, John Lord Talbot had been defending Pontoise against a French siege for almost a month. Consequently, the couple spent less than three weeks setting up their household at Rouen before Richard set out down the Seine to support Talbot.[54] Cecily was then left to represent her husband in the Norman capital. Political decisions would have fallen to Archbishop Louis of Luxembourg. Cecily's responsibility was to establish their new household there. Some of their senior household members had come over from England. These were men like Richard Leyland who had been the duke of Bedford's treasurer before he undertook the same role for Richard duke of York.[55] Like every noble household, a number of those in their service were recruited nearby. These included several clerks and their children's nurse, Anne of Caux.[56]

Richard duke of York's campaign in Pontoise was to prove the one great military triumph of his career. Enguerrand de Monstrelet recalled with admiration how he distracted the French and organized a daring river crossing on a rope bridge that prompted the French king and his men to flee to Poissy.[57] News of this must have reached Cecily on, or just before, 23 July which was when the Dominican prior, Jean le Sauvage, preached in the abbey church of St Ouen to celebrate the enemy's flight.[58] Four days after entering Pontoise, York 'advanced his whole army in battle-array before Poissy' and here 'a very great skirmish took place'.[59] Charles VII escaped and retreated to St Denis.[60] York's actions thereafter are by no means clear. Most chroniclers relate that he decided to return to Rouen at this point yet Michael K. Jones has recently argued that he was again at Pontoise on 6 August.[61] The war-ravaged lands in this region could not long support York's army and when he arrived back in Rouen his troops were 'haggard, starving and exhausted'.[62] Their achievements soon proved to have been for nothing. As one Parisian recalled, 'Pontoise was taken by storm on 19 September, some four hundred Englishmen being killed in the assault and about ten or eleven Frenchmen. A good many Englishmen were killed where they were hiding in basements and cellars'.[63] Many were taken prisoner and the writer continues with graphic details of those who were tied up and thrown into the river. It was perhaps this early military catastrophe that discouraged York from further direct engagements with the French. Instead he focussed on governing what lands the English still held and trying to build diplomatic alliances with Burgundy and Brittany against France. As early as September 1441 representatives of the duke of Brittany arrived in Rouen.[64]

Cecily too had a role in this diplomacy for noblewomen were expected to provide hospitality for diplomats visiting their husbands. Cecily needed to impress her husband's visitors with an opulence that would encourage them to trust his authority and influence. This meant that the furnishings of their home, the food they served and even the clothes Cecily wore should all contribute to this impression. Since married women were only rarely involved directly in political discussions this was Cecily's principal opportunity to support her husband's career. Sometimes their finery was borrowed, as at the feast of All Saints in 1442 when they were permitted to use ornaments and vestments from Rouen cathedral in the castle's chapel.[65] Much of it was bought. It is possible that it was in these wealthiest years of her marriage that Cecily acquired some of the jewels mentioned in her will. In 1444 purchases on her behalf included 325 pearls, most from the London goldsmith Matthew Philip, at a total cost of over £376. York too valued beautiful things. In the same year he spent £54 on a single gold cup for his own use.[66] More strikingly, when his finances were in trouble in the 1450s, he pawned some of his jewels to John Fastolf, including a gold brooch set with 'a greet poynted diamand settte up on a roose enameled white'.[67] This had reputedly cost a staggering 4,000 marks (£2,666) when first purchased.[68]

Expenditure made on Cecily's behalf while she was in Rouen has earned her a reputation for 'reckless extravagance'.[69] Undeniably the cost of the clothes and jewels she acquired in 1444 'amounted to more than an English baronial income'.[70] Yet they cannot be attributed simply to Cecily's 'craving for luxury'.[71] Indeed it is by no means certain that Cecily had any role in deciding on the purchases herself. They were made by her husband's men in London while Cecily was across the Channel and it is highly likely that they reveal York's own desire and even his duty to dress his wife in a manner that would impress others, particularly those familiar with the splendour of the French and Burgundian courts.[72] Almost a decade later we begin to get glimpses of Cecily as an independent, influential and self-confident woman but whether she had been so in her twenties can only be conjecture. If Cecily was the driving force behind this expenditure she was not being 'madly extravagant'.[73] At this point in time York could easily afford such outlay. T. B. Pugh estimates that York's annual income from lands and annuities was by then £10,000 even without his £20,000 salary as lieutenant general.[74] Moreover, there were very particular political circumstances at the time these clothes were bought, discussed below, which made it especially important for Cecily to remind those in her presence of just how wealthy, powerful and royal her husband was.

The Yorks' elegant lifestyle was enhanced further by the acquisition of beautiful books that were clearly meant to be seen by visitors as well as being enjoyed by the

FIGURE 3.1 *Detail from the first page of Cecily and Richard's copy of Christine de Pisan's* La Cité des Dames *c. 1442. © The British Library Board BL Royal MS 19 A XIX f. 4. Reproduced by permission of the British Library*

couple themselves. Marianne Ailes has argued recently that Cecily may have had a hand in acquiring a beautiful manuscript of a popular *chanson de geste* called *Les Quatre Fils Aymon* that was produced by a Rouen workshop that also provided some of John Talbot's books.[75] Another book with very similar decoration, and also in French, which certainly belonged in Cecily's household was a copy of Christine de Pisan's *Le Livre de la Cité des Dames*.[76] The book was probably not specifically commissioned by Cecily but was adapted for the couple's use with York's emblems of a white rose and a fetterlock painted into the illuminated lower margin of the first page. We cannot know whose decision it was to acquire the book, or if it was a gift, but it was most likely in Cecily's keeping since Christine de Pisan's works were very often owned by women, especially this volume and its companion *Le Trésor de la Cité des Dames*, quoted in previous chapters. *Le Livre de la Cité des Dames* was an eloquent defence of women, refuting the misogyny to be found in many popular literary works such as the *Roman de la Rose*.

Treatises condemning or celebrating women, like debates on the origins of nobility or the morality of courtly love, were something of a sophisticated medieval literary game. Christine seems to have been genuinely concerned that women's sense of their self-worth was affected by 'all manner of philosophers, poets and orators too numerous to mention, who all seem to speak with one voice and are unanimous in their view that female nature is wholly given up to vice'.[77] In *Le Livre de la Cité des Dames* she presented scores of positive images of women, their virtues, strengths and contributions to civilization. In its pages Cecily could find inspirational tales from classical mythology and history, from the Old Testament and more recent centuries of women who were warriors, scholars, saints and prophetesses.

The downfall of Eleanor duchess of Gloucester

Through the summer of 1441 chilling news of the consequences of one woman's ambition must have been filtering through to Rouen. Eleanor Cobham was the daughter of a knight and had become first mistress and then wife to Humphrey, duke of Gloucester who was Henry VI's only surviving uncle and the heir to the throne. In late June three men, including Eleanor's personal clerk and her chaplain, were arrested along with the 'witch' Margery Jourdemayne for trying to bring about the king's death through sorcery and other means.[78] On 24 July Eleanor too was brought to trial, and on 6 November 1441 the country's leading bishops officially 'deuorsed and departed the Duke of Gloucestre and Dame Alianore Cobham, as for matrymony made before betwene theym two'.[79] These bishops had ensured that even if Henry VI died childless and Humphrey became king, he could not make Eleanor his queen. She was forced to perform a humiliating penance whereas her fellow conspirators were executed.[80]

The downfall of the duchess of Gloucester was an incredible *cause célèbre* that was recalled in pages of lurid detail in contemporary chronicles. It subsequently provided generations of balladeers with a moving tale of the tragic consequences of pride and ambition. The duke of Gloucester's inability to protect the woman he loved was a shocking reminder of the fragility of power, even for the heir to the throne. We can only guess at the psychological impact of these events on his closest kinsmen and their wives, but the repercussions of Eleanor's trial and of the duke of Gloucester's mysterious demise a few years later may well have shaped Richard duke of York's own paranoia in later years.

Cecily's focus of attention in 1441, however, was surely on her own body. About six months after Henry of Hatfield's birth, she had fallen pregnant again. On 28 April 1442 her son Edward was born, the future Edward IV.[81]

Edward of Rouen

In 2002 Michael K. Jones controversially argued that King Edward IV could not have been conceived by Richard duke of York and must have been illegitimate. Citing a combination of unpublished manuscripts in French archives, he argued that York's Pontoise campaign had kept him away from Rouen far longer than previous historians had thought: from mid-July until after 20 August 1441.[82] Jones argued that Edward 'was likely to have been conceived in late July or early August 1441', precisely when he claimed that York was away from Cecily.[83] This was the starting point for his argument that later rumours of Cecily's adultery with an English archer at Rouen should not be dismissed automatically and that knowledge of this terrible family secret prompted Richard III to take the throne in 1483.

Highly respected medieval noblewomen certainly did indulge in adulterous affairs on occasion. Most famously Edward II's queen Isabel had done so a century earlier. However, redating the Pontoise campaign does not in itself prove Cecily's adultery. As many historians have pointed out, York was rarely more than a day's ride from Rouen and there is every chance that he travelled back at some point as Talbot certainly did.[84] Moreover, normal full term pregnancies can vary by 37 days in length and a thirty-six week gestation (possible if York returned on 21 August) would not be considered premature by modern doctors.[85] Jones rightly points out that a number of sources from the 1460s seem to have been especially keen to emphasize Edward's legitimacy, perhaps too keen he suggests. However, they were probably making a deliberate contrast between Edward of Rouen and the prince of Wales, Edward of Lancaster, Henry VI's son, whose legitimacy the Yorkists disputed. Importantly, there seem to have been no doubts about Edward's legitimacy in the months immediately after his birth. Richard duke of York was exchanging letters with King Charles VII of France throughout 1445 regarding plans to marry his infant son Edward to the French king's daughter Madeleine. Had there been the slightest uncertainty about Edward's legitimacy it is scarcely plausible that the king of France would have been 'pleased to take the said marriage into consideration'.[86] It is highly unlikely that Edward IV was illegitimate. It is possible that he was born a week or two early.

As with all medieval infants, Edward would have been baptized as soon as possible. One document drawn up in 1475 records that Edward was christened at Rouen cathedral, but no record of the event has survived in the cathedral chapter book.[87] Consequently, in 1910 Laurence Stratford speculated that Edward might really have been baptized in the chapel at Rouen Castle.[88] Thirteen years later Cora Scofield, in a much more influential and thoroughly researched biography, concluded that 'the evidence is of too negative a character to be of much value'.[89] Nonetheless, Stratford's guess has frequently been repeated as fact in subsequent publications.[90] If Edward was premature then the baptism may well have been a hasty affair, especially given the premature death of his brother Henry. Its exact location must remain uncertain. His godparents were chosen appropriately from the community of English nobility engaged in the war in France. One of them was Thomas, Lord Scales who spent most of his career in France and was lieutenant-general in western Normandy.[91] Another was Elizabeth Lady Say whose then husband, Sir John Montgomery, had been one of Bedford's councillors and who was now one of York's retainers.[92]

Edmund of Rouen

In the months after Edward's birth, the king's council were becoming increasingly disappointed by York's preference for governance and diplomacy rather than military engagements with the French. In September 1442 they began arranging a new military expedition under the command of Cecily's cousin, John Beaufort earl of Somerset. Rumours may have reached Rouen of the king's intention to raise earl John to the status of a duke which would make him almost York's equal. It was in the shadow of this significant threat to York's authority in Normandy that Cecily gave birth to her son Edmund on 17 May 1443, just thirteen months after Edward's birth. This time York had clearly had time to prepare a grand christening and motive to make it especially impressive. He arranged for Edmund to be baptized at Rouen cathedral in 'the long [?tall] font of Rollo, in which none other but him has been baptized from the time of the said Rollo'.[93] Rollo was a Viking chief who had established his rule around the mouth of the Seine during the early tenth century and had come to be seen as the first 'duke' of Normandy. York's decision to use this font was an unmistakeable signal of his own primacy in the duchy, quite possibly inspired by the challenge he felt that Somerset posed. This combination of opportunity and political need meant that Edmund received a far grander baptism than either of his elder brothers had.

In late July Somerset landed near Cherbourg. However, his campaign was poorly organized, ineptly financed and ended in disaster.[94] When Somerset returned to England in early 1444 it was in disgrace, barred from the court by a furious king. There were rumours that his death that May was suicide.[95] His only child was not quite a year old when he died but she would come to play a significant role in Cecily's life, for she was Margaret Beaufort, the future mother of Henry Tudor.

In the aftermath of John Beaufort's failure, the royal council decided the time had come to sue for peace and a marriage alliance with France. William de la Pole, earl of Suffolk, was charged with the politically hazardous task of leading the negotiations. He arrived at Harfleur on 15 March 1444. Naturally he visited Cecily and Richard in Rouen on his way to meet with Charles VII and René duke of Anjou.[96] René was the French queen's brother and it was his younger daughter, Margaret, that Charles VII had settled on as an appropriate bride for Henry VI of England.

On 27 March, shortly after Suffolk had left Rouen, Richard and Cecily too set out. They were in the company of Zano of Castiglione, bishop of Bayeux and other lords journeying 'to Caen, and elsewhere in Lower Normandy ... to provide for the necessities of the country, for the good and honour of the king ... for his justice and for the quiet of his subjects'.[97] It was something akin to a royal progress to check on administration and deal out justice. It had clearly been planned some time in advance because orders were sent to make the castle of Caen ready for Richard and Cecily's arrival. Serendipitously a receipt has survived for some of this work which affords us a rare glimpse of Cecily's domestic arrangements. The receipt detailed work produced over a combined total of 94 days by a pair of chest-makers, Guillaume le Tonnelier and Perrin Viart.[98] A *chaère servante en unes latrines* (cushioned toilet seat?) was provided in Cecily's own chamber which has been invoked as evidence of her luxury loving nature, although again the actual authorization for the expense inevitably came from Richard duke of York.[99]

What does not seem to have been commented upon by other historians are the rather more interesting implications in the receipt about Cecily's household arrangements. These point to the closeness of their domestic arrangements in sharing resources and personnel, but suggest that Cecily may have had some financial autonomy. It is apparent that the wardrobe was a room which Cecily shared with her husband, whereas Cecily had her own treasury. At Caen the bath house was to be converted into a treasury for her, furnished with a new trestle table and window.[100] It may have been not merely a store place for Cecily's jewels and plate but also a space for managing her personal financial accounts for her own household. However, while the accounts persistently refer to the duke's treasurer only a treasury for Cecily is mentioned. Administering Cecily's accounts was unlikely to have been a full-time job. It may well have been undertaken by a certain Geoffrey Spryng who spent some time in London that summer advising those making purchases on Cecily's behalf.[101]

The coming of the queen

While Cecily and Richard were travelling through Normandy, their country's future was being decided in Tours. It proved impossible to negotiate a genuine peace, but a twenty-two-month truce was sealed on 28 May 1444. It was hoped that this would be strengthened by Henry VI's marriage to the French queen's niece, Margaret of Anjou. Their betrothal had been performed by proxy, with William de la Pole, earl of Suffolk, taking the king's place at Margaret's side in St Martin's church on 24 May. The ceremony was followed by lavish celebrations which were repeated on a smaller scale as the news reached Rouen and London in June.[102] The new fifteen-year-old queen remained in France as Suffolk headed back to England. Cecily and Richard were still travelling when Suffolk passed back through Rouen.[103]

Richard and Cecily appear to have begun preparing a glorious reception for the new queen at Rouen within weeks of her marriage. It was in this summer that Cecily's famously 'extravagant' wardrobe purchases were made. They were not only intended to impress the new queen but also to assert York's pre-eminent position among the

English nobility, despite the rising status of Henry VI's closest kin, many of whom had recently received new titles.[104] Over £215 was spent on a single outfit which was very likely intended for the queen's reception. This was a surcote (outer gown), mantle and hood fashioned of 47¾ ells (nearly 50 metres) of crimson velvet, lined with ermine and embroidered with at least 200 pearls. The velvet was purchased for £53 13s. 4d. from Nicholas Michel of Lucca, Italy's premier silk-weaving city, where craftsmen specialized in weaving velvet in two different pile lengths to form exotic patterns.[105] The goldsmith who provided the pearls, Matthew Philip, was naturally one of the most prominent jewellers in the city. He became a sheriff of London in 1451 and mayor just over a decade later, in Cecily's son's reign, when he was also knighted.[106] Similarly Thomas Oulgreve, who was paid £93 13s. 4d. for ermine to line the outfit, became sheriff in 1455 and mayor in 1467.[107] The task of cutting and sewing these fabrics and attaching the pearls was given to the king's own tailor, John Legge. In a startling reminder of the different values of labour and commodities in fifteenth-century England, Legge received just 20s. for his work. Not all of the items purchased for Cecily in London that summer can have been connected to the impending arrival of the queen. More than £86 was spent on a variety of clothes from the dressmaker Margaret Chamberlayne, another £16 13s. 4d. on unspecified garments from a certain Greek merchant and £320 on pearls whose purpose was not mentioned.[108]

In early September Richard duke of York despatched a herald to Marie queen of France and to England's new queen Margaret with letters on his own behalf and on 'secret matters' from Henry VI.[109] Cecily must by then have been preparing herself for the imminent birth of yet another child. Elizabeth was born fifteen months after Edmund on 22 September 1444 at 2.00 am.[110] Elizabeth was baptized later that same day in Rouen cathedral. According to the cathedral registers her godmother was Jacquetta, duchess of Bedford and her godfather was John Talbot, earl of Shrewsbury.[111] Both these godparents had been members of Cecily's circle in Normandy for the past three years. Talbot's wife, Margaret, and Duchess Jacquetta were likely both present for Elizabeth's birth and for Cecily's own churching in October.

Shortly afterwards William de la Pole, now marquess of Suffolk, gathered a splendid entourage to return to France and collect Henry VI's new queen. He left London on 6 November but it was not until 18 March 1445 that he returned with Margaret to France's northern border.[112] York met Margaret here at Pontoise to escort her into Rouen for her ceremonial welcome to England's capital in France. The chronicler Matthew d'Escouchy especially noted that the English nobles were 'most highly and richly dressed', hence the need for Cecily's exceptionally luxurious outfit.[113] Unfortunately the teenage queen felt too ill to process through Rouen's streets. Alice Chaucer, marchioness of Suffolk, had to take her place in the chariot draped in gold cloth and pulled by six white horses that Henry VI had sent for the occasion.[114] Although the duke of York was riding on one side of this chariot Cecily had no part in the procession. This may have been because she was waiting at the castle to greet them, but it seems likely that as hostess it was she who was busy attending the sick girl who was her new queen. Her fabulous dress may never have reached the full audience it was intended for.

In subsequent days there was plenty of time for Cecily to build a degree of friendship with the queen for Margaret stayed at Rouen until 11 April.[115] At fifteen, Margaret was exactly half Cecily's age. There is every possibility that she admired Cecily's sumptuous wardrobe and that the duchess responded by recommending her dressmaker, Margaret Chamberlayne. Certainly one of the queen's first actions on English soil was to send her valet, John Pole, from Southampton to London with three horses to bring Margaret Chamberlayne into her presence 'for diverse business touching the said lady queen'.[116] Chamberlayne must have continued to work for the queen in subsequent years as she received New Year presents from Queen Margaret on at least two occasions in the 1450s.[117]

Marriage plans

Once the queen's fleet had set sail from Harfleur on 9 April, Cecily and Richard returned to business as usual in Rouen. A particular concern on their minds was to take full advantage of their current strong position to arrange prestigious marriages for their older children. As well as Richard's negotiations with Charles VII for young Edward's marriage, Richard and Cecily were also planning the marriage of their eldest daughter Anne to Henry Holland, heir to John Holland, duke of Exeter. Such a marriage would bind Richard and Cecily's family closer to the legitimate Lancastrian line which made political sense in the context of Henry VI's recent moves to promote his closest kin. Unfortunately, the Hollands were not especially wealthy and John duke of Exeter would have done better to have found a rich heiress who would enable his son to adopt a lifestyle appropriate to the family's status as royal dukes. York committed to pay the duke of Exeter a substantial, but not unprecedented dowry, of 4,500 marks in four instalments, beginning on the wedding day.[118]

By then York's term of office had expired. It looks as if contemporaries expected it to be renewed in due course but York and Cecily had a number of reasons to visit home. Parliament had been summoned and since this was meant to discuss a genuine peace with France it was in York's interests to attend. York was also aware of 'certain sclaindereux langaige' in England regarding his 'demenyng on the tother side of the see' which he was anxious to refute.[119] Moreover, the crown owed him an immense £38,667.[120] York presumably hoped to take advantage of time in England to try to settle some of this in person. He had no reason to fear the king's enmity at this point since Henry had only recently offered an 'exceptional mark of royal favour' in making York's sons the earls of March and Rutland at an unusually young age.[121]

The calm before the storm

For four years after Cecily's return from France, she disappears almost entirely from surviving sources. The locations in which her children were born are noted, but even here contemporaries occasionally disagreed. Her retreat into history's shadows is partly a consequence of the lack of household documents that survive. It almost certainly indicates that she was, like most women of her day, occupied discretely in her husband's service, focussing on bearing his children and running his household. Yet even for those years before the storm it is possible to piece together some sense of her life, in particular her continuing social networks and her literary patronage.

Historians for a long time envisaged the second half of the 1440s as a mere prelude to the strife that would follow, coloured by the duke of York's increasing political isolation and its consequent strain on Cecily's entire family.[122] However, since the 1980s, many scholars have argued that the court's hostility to York was largely a myth shaped by York's propaganda in the 1450s.[123] Admittedly charges of financial malpractice laid against York by Bishop Adam Moleyns appear to have been exaggerated in an attempt to provide an excuse not to repay debts to him.[124] Yet they were not entirely groundless.[125] Moreover, York was repaid a substantial amount of the moneys owed to him, despite the regime's perilous financial situation.[126] While there were undoubtedly periodic tensions between York and Suffolk or the Beauforts, there were also occasions when he worked together with each of them, and even in concert with Somerset against Suffolk.[127] Thus far Cecily and Richard's relationship with the young queen Margaret seems to have been entirely cordial.[128] In the late 1440s Cecily had no reason to guess at the bloody turmoil which would soon follow.

Two months after the family had returned to England, on 30 January 1446, her six-year-old daughter Anne married fifteen-year-old Henry Holland in the bishop of Ely's chapel at Hatfield, Hertfordshire.[129] A quarter of a century later, Cecily's former servant, Agatha Flegge, recalled it as the feast of St Bathildis.[130] Bathildis had been a Merovingian queen and a patron of Rouen's sainted bishop Ouen, so she had perhaps been mentioned in the service as an exemplar of noble womanhood for the new bride.[131] The presiding priest is likely to have been the bridegroom's choice, for this was Richard Caudray, master of King's Hall, Cambridge, where Henry Holland had resided as a commoner for about three years from 1439.[132] Anne then moved into the guardianship of John duke of Exeter but unfortunately Exeter fell ill the following summer. It is a further indication that York was not yet being ostracized from the centre of power that on 30 July 1447, six days before the duke of Exeter's death, the king granted York 'the keeping of Henry, son and heir of John, duke of Exeter, from the said John's death'.[133]

At the time of Anne's wedding Cecily had been six months pregnant and on Tuesday 3 May 1446 she bore another daughter.[134] This child was christened Margaret in a gesture of loyalty to the new queen, Margaret of Anjou. Margaret of York's birthplace has been disputed because pseudo-Worcester's *Annales* locate it at Fotheringhay whereas the *Generacio* gives the Abbey of the Holy Cross at Waltham, in Essex, twelve miles from Hatfield Palace.[135] However, a note in the lower margin of the calendar of her sister Anne's book of hours concurs with the *Generacio*, so it would seem that Fotheringhay was just a plausible guess and Margaret was indeed born at Waltham Abbey.[136] Two months later Richard duke of York was 9 miles away at the manor of Hunsdon, which he had acquired from the Tyrell family some months before.[137] Since the 'remarkable and significant' moated tower house that York was building at Hunsdon was very far from complete, Cecily may well have remained at the abbey somewhat longer with her baby daughter.[138]

The death of Humphrey duke of Gloucester

York was at Fotheringhay for Twelfth Night 1447, presumably with his family, and it was probably there that they had spent Christmas.[139] The following February a political scandal erupted that would cast a long shadow over the Lancastrian dynasty. Despite his marriage, Henry VI was now still frequently perceived as more of a child than a man, 'very young and inexperienced'.[140] The real ruler of England was William de la Pole, marquess of Suffolk, who led the king's anti-war policy. After decades of acrimony both Cardinal Beaufort and Humphrey duke of Gloucester were sidelined and largely spent forces. However, at the close of 1446 there was such popular resentment at the loss of French territories that Gloucester looked likely to rise politically as the voice of outraged war veterans and other enemies of the marquess. Against this background parliament had been summoned to meet in February 1447 at Bury St Edmunds, right in Suffolk's heartland.[141] On 18 February, shortly after his arrival at Bury, Gloucester was placed under house arrest, apparently accused of treason.[142] Two days later Gloucester, who was 57, collapsed, probably with a stroke, and on 23 February he 'passyde owte of thys wrecchyde and false trobely worlde'.[143] Inevitably his opportune death led to rumours that he had been murdered 'bitwene ij ffedirbeddes' or 'throst into the bowell with an hote brennyng spitte', but modern historians generally discount these.[144]

At the time Richard duke of York made no public criticism and seems to have joined the other principal lords in deciding that the kingdom's interests were best served by maintaining a display of unity among those who were trying to govern the country in spite of Henry VI's ineptitude and immaturity.[145] York continued to take an active role in council meetings and peace commissions. Moreover, he was one of many lords who benefited materially from Gloucester's death. His gains included the castle and lordship of Hadleigh, the manor of Great Wratting, the lordship of the Isle of Wight and, after some delay, Baynard's Castle.[146] There was as yet no reason to imagine that York wanted to offer an alternative form of government to that led by Suffolk.[147] It is even possible that when Cecily bore a son at Fotheringhay on 7 July 1447 the decision to call him William was meant to be a compliment to the powerful marquess.[148]

Sadly William did not live long and was buried in the family mausoleum at Fotheringhay.[149] He was the first of Cecily's children to die since Henry in 1441. After so many successful pregnancies she was moving into a traumatic time in which her babies would die more often than they lived. The following year another short-lived son, John, was born on 7 November at the abbot of Westminster's country home, the Neyte (in modern Pimlico).[150] There is now no record of when John too died, although he must have seemed healthy at birth since he was well enough to be taken from the house to be baptized in Chelsea.[151] It is possible that Cecily had undertaken the journey to the capital with her husband in expectation of spending some more time with the queen. Aside from her much debated letters to Charles VII of France regarding peace negotiations, Margaret had as yet taken little role in English politics.[152] Nonetheless, Helen Maurer has shown that some of the queen's letters from before 1450 reveal 'female networking' in which Margaret negotiated with the wives of some of the king's principal lords, asking them to influence their husbands.[153] Among Margaret's expenses for 1449 was a substantial gift of 66s 8d to Cecily's servants in reward for bringing the duchess's New Year gift to her. The same sum was given to the servants of the duchesses of Bedford, Buckingham and Exeter (presumably the widowed Anne Montagu rather than Cecily's daughter). In previous recorded years it was Duke Richard's servants, rather than Cecily's, who had received such rewards.[154] So this suggests that Cecily was spending more time with the queen, or at least communicating with her more frequently, than had previously been the case.

Literary patronage

Meanwhile Cecily had also become involved in a rather different network which was again predominantly female. This was a network of literary patrons centred near the Yorks' castle at Clare in Suffolk. There were a number of prominent East Anglian writers at the time, notably the Benedictine John Lydgate at Bury St Edmunds (who had produced a life of St Margaret for York's aunt, Anne countess of March) and John Capgrave who was the Augustinian prior at Bishop's Lynn.[155] The writer especially associated with the house of York was Osbern Bokenham, an Augustinian friar at Clare Priory.[156] It has long been known that in 1445 he composed a translation of the life of Mary Magdalene for the duke of York's sister, Isabel, countess of Eu, and probably also an intriguing edition of part of Claudian's *De Consulatu Stilichonis* (*On the Consulate of Stilicho*) for York himself, or for his supporters.[157] The latter consists of both Latin and English texts and seems to have been composed to give encouragement to York at a time of political troubles. Simon Horobin argued in 2007 that Bokenham also oversaw the production of a manuscript of his translation of the *Legenda Aurea* (*Golden Legend*) that was fashioned for Richard and, especially, for Cecily.[158] Bokenham mentioned in the prologue to his *Mappula Angliae* that he had compiled an 'englische boke ... of legenda aurea and of other famous legendes ... at the instaunce of my specialle frendis'.[159] All manuscripts were thought to have been lost until a vellum book, including saints' lives known to have been written by Bokenham, was discovered in Sir Walter Scott's library at Abbotsford early this century.[160]

The beginning and the end of this manuscript, where we might expect to find marks of ownership, are both missing, but at some time in the late sixteenth or early seventeenth century a John Jobson signed his name in the top margin of one page. Cecily had a great great grandson of that name. He was the grandson of Edward IV's illegitimate son Arthur, Viscount Lisle.[161] Cecily bequeathed her copy of the *Golden Legend* to her granddaughter Bridget, a nun, who might easily have chosen to pass this family heirloom to her half-brother's descendants since he was her father's only surviving son.[162] There is another possible link with Cecily in what appear to have been the most revered saints in the compilation. On some pages pieces have been cut out of the margins, most likely because these were covered in especially detailed decoration, marking the most valued stories. The stories in question are the Annunciation of Our Lady, and the lives of John the Baptist and Mary Magdalene. The life of Mary Magdalene had originally been composed for Cecily's sister-in-law but Cecily herself must also have revered this saint because she owned a tapestry of her and indeed another of John the Baptist, both of which she bequeathed to the future Henry VIII. Cecily's will reveals that John the Baptist was the saint that she was attached to above all others although she offered the keeping of her soul to the Virgin Mary too, as very many people did.

Several of the legends in the Abbotsford manuscript also appeared in the *Legends of Holy Women*, a much shorter compilation of female saints' lives that were composed by Bokenham but compiled by his fellow Augustinian Thomas Burgh in 1447. Burgh included prologues which reveal that many of these were originally composed for women of Cecily's acquaintance who look to have been sharing and reading each other's books.[163] At least three of these had been in Cecily's company in France: Isabel, countess of Eu; Elizabeth de Vere, countess of Oxford; and Agatha Flegge who had been in Cecily's service since the early 1430s and whose husband, John, had been one of the duke's captains in France.[164] A fourth recipient was Katherine Howard whose husband, John, was both a cousin of Elizabeth de Vere, and a nephew of Cecily's sister Katherine, duchess of Norfolk.[165] John Howard eventually became a steward of Cecily's East Anglian lands.[166] Finally there was Katherine Denston who received the life of St Anne. Katherine belonged to an important local family, the Cloptons of Long Melford. As a local justice of the peace Katherine's husband, John, must have had contact with the duke of York as the lord of Clare.[167] P. A. Johnson has speculated that John Denston may also have given explicit support to York in the 1450s.[168] Even without the evidence of the Abbotsford *Legenda Aurea*, it would have been reasonable to assume that Cecily was familiar with some of these women's books. Since some of the women in her circle were directly commissioning works from Bokenham it is not impossible that Cecily herself had some hand in recommending the author to her husband and the consequent translation of Claudian's *De Consulatu Stilichonis*. However, the motives and purpose of this last composition are matters of considerable debate, as indeed is its authorship.[169] It may be that the initiative for that manuscript came from the friars of Clare Priory themselves.[170]

Clare Priory had been the recipient of patronage by previous generations of York's family and the translator of Claudian's work may well have been attempting to encourage York to continue this tradition through the affirming comparisons that his text made between Stilicho and York. Just over a decade later another manuscript was produced at the priory which again affirmed York through parallel Latin and English poems. This was the Clare Roll which is dated 1 May 1456 and was most likely also composed by Bokenham.[171] It celebrated Cecily as much as it did her husband. Clare Hilles has argued that the Clare Roll 'constructs a lineage of holy women for Richard of York' in which readers were reminded that Cecily's 'fertility was one of York's major political assets'.[172] This emphasis on the women of York's line is reinforced by Latin captions above the shields of each of the lords and ladies of Clare which are painted down the centre of the roll, dividing the English and Latin poems. Richard and Cecily's arms are labelled 'Lord Richard duke of York son of the said Anne, and Lady Cecily daughter of the earl of Westmorland his wife'.[173] The women in this lineage, particularly Joan of Acre and Elizabeth de Burgh were valued not just for their royal bloodlines but also for their important patronage of Clare Priory. The author was perhaps attempting to remind Cecily of her forbears' achievements in the hope that she would emulate them as patron of his house, unless, that is, it was Cecily herself who had requested this work.

There are intriguing differences between the Latin and English poems in the Clare Roll. Surprisingly, it is the Latin version, which we might expect to be aimed more at York than his wife, which particularly dwells on those of their children who died young. It repeatedly describes a generous, nourishing God who seized the infants from this troubled world to live with him in paradise. Such an image was not just a comfort for their loss but a statement that children's deaths should not be seen as signs of God's disfavour. Cecily's prominence in these poems reflects her increasing visibility in other sources throughout the 1450s, as will be seen in the following chapter, coinciding with her husband's career becoming more turbulent and Cecily more often acting independently.

4

The Wheel of Fortune: 1449–1459

Also I geve to my lord Prince a bedde of arres of the Whele of Fortune
Will of Cecily, duchess of York: bequest to Arthur, prince of Wales, 1495[1]

On 30 July 1447 Richard duke of York was appointed king's lieutenant of Ireland for a term of ten years.[2] At the time it had seemed a very natural and logical step in his career. However, events across Henry VI's kingdoms while Richard and Cecily were in Ireland were to make this a turning point in their lives. Thereafter York's fortunes rose and fell dramatically and repeatedly, spinning like the wheel that was a hugely popular motif in fifteenth-century art. Cecily began to appear more often on the public stage as she negotiated on her husband's behalf for his political career and his business interests. It was in this decade that the last of her children were born and the Wars of the Roses truly began.

Departure

York's appointment as lieutenant of Ireland was later perceived as a form of exile, but there is little to suggest that Cecily and Richard initially understood it in this way. As a major Irish landholder, York was an obvious candidate for the post and the terms of his office permitted him to appoint a deputy so it was scarcely banishment. York at first appointed Richard Talbot, archbishop of Dublin, to govern Ireland for him while he remained in England and Wales for a further two years.[3] After his return to England in 1450 York was reappointed lieutenant of Ireland and, aside from a brief period in 1453, continued in that post throughout the decade without returning to Ireland until 1459. Nonetheless, his relationship with the king and court may already have been under some strain in 1449 for he later reported that 'certayn personnes [had] armed and lye in awayte for to herkin uponme' as he departed.[4]

These tensions may have related to policy in France and were probably aggravated by York's straitened financial situation. In the months before setting sail he sold off or mortgaged a large number of properties and these included some which appear to have been part of Cecily's jointure.[5] Most of these were mortgages which he presumably hoped to reclaim before she had need of them. Almost all were assigned to Cecily by their son in 1461.[6] One exception to this was the Northamptonshire manor of Wick Dive (now in Wicken) which Jacquetta duchess of Bedford and her husband Richard Woodville (recently created Lord Rivers) purchased outright for £100.[7]

Arrival

Cecily and Richard at last arrived in Ireland, at Howth, on 6 July 1449.[8] Here they were 'received with great honour' according to Irish chroniclers.[9] The names of the servants who had travelled with Cecily on this occasion are not recorded, although on 21 December 1449 York issued payment to a certain William Wynne for his expenses in conducting his wife from London to Ireland to enter Cecily's service.[10] At first York seemed to be very successful in winning support from both the English and Irish in his new domain. On one occasion Cecily found herself the recipient of a pair of expensive Irish warhorses, hobbies, among the many tributes paid to her husband.[11] At the time of their arrival, she had been five months pregnant and her sixth son, George, was born on 21 October 1449, not quite a year since her last confinement.[12] Despite the exceedingly brief period that Cecily's body had been allowed to recover between pregnancies, George was destined to survive into a tempestuous adulthood.

The name George was still relatively uncommon among the English nobility but Cecily had both a brother and a nephew called George. York inserted a short prayer to St George into his book of hours and Cecily eventually owned a tapestry of the saint.[13] It was perhaps also no coincidence that Dublin's only specifically religious guild (rather than a trade guild) was dedicated to St George and had come to be especially associated with the military culture and defence of the city of Dublin.[14] The choice of George's name was perhaps associated with this Anglo-Irish military identity in Dublin. His christening, at Dublin's Dominican priory, certainly operated in this way.[15] York invited James FitzGerald, earl of Desmond, and James Butler, earl of Ormond, to be godfathers in order to cement their new peace through their shared spiritual affinity to the duke of York's family.[16]

However, York was steadily realizing that many of the submissions he had received were hollow and he was becoming desperate for money. The exchequer owed him 4,700 marks and his personal income had substantially decreased due to a crisis in revenues in Wales.[17] On 15 June 1450, in an impassioned letter to Cecily's brother, Richard, earl of Salisbury, York wrote that he would rather be dead than fail in his responsibilities, 'for it shall never be chronicled nor remain in scripture, by the grace of God, that Ireland was lost by my negligence'.[18] York's fear of 'losing' Ireland and the shame it would bring was no doubt influenced by recent disastrous events in Normandy. On 29 October 1449 Edmund Beaufort, duke of Somerset, had surrendered Rouen to the French king's siege and negotiated his own escape with a humiliating ransom and hostages who included the highly respected earl of Shrewsbury, John Talbot.[19] In the words of one Irish annal, 'All the king of England's conquest in France was taken from him but only Calais, 3140 men being slain in Rouen'.[20] It is scarcely surprising that York and others were appalled. Henry VI's council tried to send further troops to Normandy, fitting out ships and mustering soldiers at Portsmouth, but they were desperately short of finance. The soldiers who were kept waiting at the port became angry and reckless. York's erstwhile opponent, Adam Moleyns, bishop of Chichester and keeper of the privy seal, finally arrived at Portsmouth with the soldiers' back pay in January 1450, only to be hacked to death.[21]

Those close to the king continued to come under attack. In early 1450 the commons in parliament were determined to make Suffolk a scapegoat for the loss of Anjou and Maine and the subsequent collapse of English power in France. Ultimately Suffolk was banished, but was murdered at sea. His severed head and body were cast onto the beach at Dover.[22] Fear of royal reprisal for this in Kent seems to have been significant in drawing together dissident groups who had been causing unrest since the previous autumn. The man who emerged as their leader, Jack Cade, was probably a Sussex yeoman. However, he took the name 'John Mortimer' and claimed to be a cousin to the duke of York.[23] Cade's rebellion was much the most serious of such risings since the Great Revolt of 1381. It shocked and deeply unnerved the political establishment and by drawing attention to York's Mortimer ancestry and calling upon him to right the wrongs of Suffolk's administration it placed York and his immediate family in a very dangerous political position.

One of the petitions produced in the course of the rebellion gave a list of four dukes of the 'trewe blode of the Reame' whom the king should take into his council. These were York, Henry Holland, duke of Exeter, Humphrey Stafford, duke of Buckingham and John Mowbray, duke of Norfolk (Cecily's son-in-law, brother-in-law and nephew respectively).[24] Yet it was actually only the duke of Norfolk who had certainly been an opponent of the duke of Suffolk for many years and who was excluded from power as a consequence. Even he, Norfolk, was in the company of the king and the duke of Exeter in early June as they followed Buckingham and Richard Woodville, Lord Rivers to London to try to suppress the revolt.[25] These four dukes seem to have been named by the rebels as a consequence of a long tradition of political rhetoric rather than because of their own actions or opinions. For generations political reformers had framed complaints against royal government by asserting that those who influenced the king were 'mene persones of lower nature' rather than the 'lordys of ryall blode' whom God had provided as councillors for the king.[26]

After days of violence, several high-profile murders and a nighttime battle on London bridge, Jack Cade's rebellion was finally quelled on 6 July 1450 when a delegation of churchmen received the rebels' petitions and offered a general pardon.[27] Cade himself was captured on 12 July and died of wounds sustained in the process. By then he had already been 'cryde and proclaymed traytoure' by the name of John Cade', and so disassociated from the name of Mortimer.[28] Nonetheless, Irish annals for that year referred to him without qualification as 'Sir Richard Mortimer'.[29] Whatever tangled tales may have reached Cecily in Trim that summer, it was clear that the political landscape in England had shifted dramatically and dangerously. Cecily was about to enter the most turbulent decade of her life.

Even before he knew of the rebellion, York had been contemplating return to England rather than risk presiding over the loss of territory in Ireland.[30] Now he also feared retribution from those who assumed that he had supported Cade. On 26 August he and Cecily left Trim and began to make their way to England.[31] York had appointed one of George's godfathers, James Butler, earl of Ormond, as his deputy to govern Ireland in his absence.[32] Cecily and Richard then took ship for Wales. When they tried to land at Beaumaris the king's officers forbade them to land, asserting that York was a 'traitor'.[33] As a child York had undergone the humiliation of being a traitor's son, but for Cecily it was a new experience to find herself set in opposition to her king.

Rise and fall

The couple eventually made their way via Denbigh to their fortress at Ludlow where Cecily was reunited with her elder sons, Edward and Edmund.[34] The boys, now aged eight and seven, had been living in their own household here while she was in Ireland. In the autumn of 1450 Cecily most likely remained in the Marches with her children while York headed towards London with a large force of men. Here the king apparently received him graciously (*gratissime*).[35] However, en route, York had followed up an earlier public bill asserting his loyalty with further bills offering his services in bringing reform and justice.[36] These were an implicit acceptance that Cade's rebels were justified in their complaints about governance and in their appeal to York as the king's senior magnate. Neither the king nor his fellow peers were persuaded. Nonetheless, York's support in the commons remained high. When parliament opened his chamberlain, Sir William Oldhall was chosen to be speaker of the Commons and a parliamentary petition called for Edmund duke of Somerset, Alice duchess of Suffolk and twenty-seven others to be banished.[37] Moreover a mob tried to lynch Somerset for 'so negligently and ignominiously losing all of Normandy'.[38] It was York and Thomas Courtenay, earl of Devon, who intervened to rescue Somerset although they subsequently lodged him in the Tower.[39]

Despite this, by Christmas Somerset was at liberty once more and the other twenty-eight accused were untouched. In the May session of the 1450–1 parliament York, or his supporters, pushed their luck too far with dramatic consequences. Thomas Young, one of York's legal advisors, presented a highly controversial petition. Its purpose was to recognize York as Henry VI's undisputed heir and the proposers refused to consider any other matters until this had been agreed upon.[40] Henry Holland and Edmund Beaufort were closer kin to the king, but the former was related to the monarch in a female line and the latter's family had been formally barred from the succession since Henry IV's reign. In the tangled history of succession since the Norman Conquest it was by no means clear whose right was genuinely superior. The king and other lords were not prepared to be held to ransom by the Commons in this way. Parliament was dissolved and Young was sent to the Tower with several others of York's servants.[41]

At some point amid this turmoil Cecily had conceived and given birth to a seventh son, Thomas. His name does not appear in either pseudo-Worcester's *Annales* or the *Generacio*, but he is mentioned in the Clare Roll and on a 1461 list of Cecily's children, as well as in the Ashmole 831 genealogy of the house of York.[42] Unfortunately these give no place or date of birth, but the Ashmole genealogy mentions that he died at 'Beuley' (most likely Bewdley) and was buried, like his brothers Henry and William, at Fotheringhay.[43]

Godmother to Warwick's daughter

Richard duke of York's whereabouts immediately after the 1451 parliament are hard to trace although extensive building work at Clare Castle that summer may indicate that either or both of the couple spent some time in East Anglia.[44] By late summer Cecily must have been at Warwick Castle where her nephew's wife, Anne Beauchamp, countess of Warwick, was awaiting the birth of her first child.[45] On 5 September Countess Anne gave birth to a girl, Isabel, and Cecily was one of the child's godparents.[46] Despite their closeness at the time of Henry of Hatfield's birth, Warwick had not yet aligned himself unequivocally with York in the aftermath of Cade's rebellion and York's more public opposition to Somerset. Cecily's role at the baptism was an important statement of affinity between the two families. As Warwick's aunt and as a woman she perhaps offered a safer point of connection than York himself.

By the time Cecily and her husband were together again for Christmas at Ludlow York had further alienated himself from the king by his handling of a dispute in Somerset between the earl of Devon and Lord Bonville. York refused repeated summons to explain himself before the king's council.[47] It appears to have been this confidence in his own authority that prompted those closest to the king to begin a more concerted attack on York's position, beginning with accusations against his most trusted councillor, Sir William Oldhall, who fled into sanctuary at St Martin le Grand in London.[48] The Christmas festivities at Ludlow must have been subdued, but it was during that time that Cecily conceived her youngest son, Richard, future king of England.

On 28 January 1452 Somerset persuaded King Henry to order that William Oldhall should be forcibly removed from sanctuary. For Henry this was an uncharacteristic violation of church rights and unsurprisingly the outraged dean managed to persuade the king to return Oldhall just two days later.[49] Nonetheless it may well have been news of this attack that provoked York to head for London with the expressed intention of removing the duke of Somerset from the king's side.[50] It proved a disastrous miscalculation. At Dartford armies led by York and the king came face to face. York was very possibly duped into backing down by the king's seeming willingness to arrest Somerset. York was then put under house arrest at his London home, Baynard's Castle. On 10 March he was compelled to swear a humiliating oath of allegiance to the king at St Paul's Cathedral.[51] This was probably the prerequisite for his release, although a late fifteenth-century London chronicler asserted that York was only 'libertid to goo at his wille' when news reached the capital that his son, Edward, earl of March was approaching the capital with 10,000 men.[52] If this is true, the nine-year-old earl can only have been a figurehead, much as Henry VI's own son would be in 1460 when Margaret of Anjou sent a letter to London in the seven-year-old prince's name and dressed men in his livery to march on the capital.[53] The only person with authority to despatch Edward in that manner in March 1452 would have been Cecily. However, T. B. Pugh was almost certainly right to dismiss it as an 'implausible tale' inspired by Edward's later military record.[54] Once at liberty, in the words of *Benet's Chronicle*, York 'rode up to his castle of Ludlow to his wife'.[55]

The birth of Richard III

In late August or early September, Cecily once again prepared herself for the dangerous experience of childbirth. In this instance pseudo-Worcester's *Annales* are corroborated in their record of the birth by an entry in a book of hours that belonged to Richard III himself. Against the calendar entry for 2 October someone, probably Richard, added in Latin the words 'on this day was born Richard III King of England at Fotheringhay AD 1452'.[56] Rowena Archer has recently uncovered evidence that York was not at Fotheringhay for Richard's birth because he was overseeing the king's justice at Thame in Oxfordshire.[57] Despite his disgrace after Dartford, York was still active in his role as Justice of the king's forests south of the Trent. No record of Richard's godparents has yet been uncovered but it seems likely that Joan Malpas, who had long been in his parents' service, was among the women who helped to care for him because thirty years later Richard mentioned her 'good service' to him 'in his youth'.[58]

Over half a century later Thomas More wrote his *History of King Richard III* in which he famously repeated stories that Richard's had been a troubled birth and that Cecily 'could not bee deliuered of hym vncutte'.[59] This is unlikely. A Caesarean would have killed Cecily and even an episiotomy would have been dangerous. Medieval manuals did not recommend this practice, although they gave advice on sewing up tears with silk thread.[60] Some recent works have suggested that the story was not purely propaganda and assert that Cecily herself referred to Richard's birth in a letter as a difficult 'encomerous labour, to me full paynfull and unesy'.[61] However, a close study of Cecily's letter and its context makes it clear that the 'disease and infirmite', which Cecily described as 'labour', was something she was suffering from early in 1453 and which became more severe in the following months and so is very unlikely to have been connected with Richard's birth in October 1452. Thomas More's own suspicions about the veracity of his report of Cecily's sufferings are perhaps the greatest reason to treat the story as anti-Ricardian myth-making.

It must have been another despondent Christmas that Cecily, Richard and their youngest children spent at Fotheringhay in 1452.[62] Katherine Lewis has outlined ways in which Henry, perhaps steered by his advisors, had been presenting a significantly more manly and authoritative persona since Cade's rebellion, including expressing an intention to lead an army into France.[63] York seemed further from influencing the king than ever. He still optimistically sent New Year's gifts to the royal family and Margaret as usual rewarded his servants in the same way as Somerset's, recognizing his equal status. Nonetheless she was by then paying Somerset an annuity of 100 marks 'for his good counsel and service' and she gave his duchess a jewelled salt cellar worth £28 at New Year.[64] In the spring of 1453 another bid was made to bring York back into the king's council, but this time it was to be done through their womenfolk.

Women's talk

Early in 1453 Queen Margaret had begun to suspect that after nearly eight years in England she was at last pregnant. She consequently planned a pilgrimage of thanksgiving to the shrine of Our Lady of Walsingham. Margaret had still not yet taken any visible role in political activities. Richard and Cecily must nonetheless have noted her potential to influence the king and planned to take advantage of it. Cecily set out to meet the queen as she left the shrine in April.[65] Later in the year Cecily mentioned the event in the course of a follow-up letter to the queen, reminding Margaret that she was 'replete with such immeasurable sorrow' because of York's own 'infinite sorow, unrest of hert and of worldy comfort, causid of that that he herith him to be estrangied from the grace and benevolent favour of … the kyng'.[66] Cecily did not indicate in her letter whether the queen had given her any assurances that she would plead her case with the king. However, Margaret's response was presumably not hostile either as Cecily meant to visit and press her suit further in the near future.

In the event Cecily became too ill to repeat her pleading in person as soon as she had planned. Her husband's fortunes dropped even further at a parliament held in Reading. On 12 May, in his absence, York was deprived of the lieutenancy of Ireland.[67] It was almost certainly in this context that Cecily dispatched her letter to the queen. In it Cecily assured Margaret that if she had been well enough she would have made the plea in person once again. Of course, had she done so no evidence would have survived of either of these attempts to influence national politics. The wording of Cecily's letter reveals her awareness that she was stepping close to ground that was not properly women's business. Doubtless she would have taken advice from her husband's counsellors in drafting her plea so it cannot be read purely as Cecily's voice. Nonetheless, it is the closest we can get to an understanding of Cecily's political acumen at this time. She emphasized her own fragility and humility as well as the queen's forthcoming motherhood in order to make their negotiation more politically acceptable and unthreatening to the male structures of government. She pleaded with the queen to be the 'gracious meane' by which the king's favour might be restored to the duke of York for the 'wele of this realme'. She also dwelt at great length on the queen's pregnancy and called the child Margaret carried 'the most precious, most ioyfull, and most confortable erthely tresor that myght come unto this land and to the people therof'.[68] Cecily was perhaps hoping to reassure Margaret that, far from being disappointed that the king would finally have an heir, she was relieved that this would end political tensions caused by uncertainty over the succession. Cecily's petitions seem to have been bearing fruit for in June 1453 the queen spent a night with her in York's house at Hitchin in Hertfordshire.[69] Whatever the women may have talked of together, their plans were swiftly overtaken by dramatic events on both sides of the Channel.

The madness of King Henry VI

In the autumn of 1452 John Talbot, earl of Shrewsbury had triumphantly reclaimed Bordeaux from the French who had temporarily succeeded in seizing it, but on 17 July 1453 his forces suffered a crushing defeat at Castillon. The renowned earl himself was slain among some 4,000 Englishmen. It was very probably this appalling news that caused even greater disaster for the Lancastrian kingship. In early August 1453 Henry

VI was staying at the royal hunting lodge at Clarendon when he was 'indispost sodenly … and smyten w[ith] a ffransy and his wit and reson w[ith]drawen'.[70] Henry VI's grasp on the real world had always been tenuous. Whether he was merely an incompetent ruler, or capricious and wilful, or actually lacked the mental capacity of an adult has been much debated, but there had at least been a façade of conventional kingship until this point.[71] In August 1453 he became incapable of communication or leadership.

Mental illness was a familiar trauma in Cecily's world. Henry VI's grandfather, Charles VI of France, had famously suffered frequent bouts of insanity. Nonetheless, it was accepted that no one had the right to depose the king and arrangements were made for Charles's queen, Isabeau, to govern with a chosen council during those periods in which he was incapacitated.[72] Closer to home, just two years before Henry VI's collapse, Cecily's own brother, George, Lord Latimer, had similarly suffered from an incapacitating mental breakdown and was placed in the guardianship of her eldest brother, Richard, earl of Salisbury.[73] Cecily's half-nephew, Ralph, second earl of Westmorland, was also described as 'simple minded'.[74] Moreover, in 1463 it was asserted that Cecily's sister-in-law, Joan Fauconberg, had been 'an idiot from birth'.[75] All three cases indicate a willingness in the fifteenth-century noble community to keep those whom they considered 'simple' within their normal sphere of life. George Neville was repeatedly summoned to parliament and Ralph Neville rode at the head of troops raised in his name in 1460 and possibly also in 1455.[76] Joan Fauconberg bore three children to Cecily's brother and in 1463 she and John Berwick esquire were pardoned 'for their trespass in intermarrying without licence'.[77]

When Henry VI fell ill, Cardinal Kemp, who was chancellor, and Edmund Beaufort, duke of Somerset initially tried to continue the government of England and Wales as if nothing had happened. They were presumably hoping that Henry would swiftly recover. On the feast of the translation of Edward the Confessor, 13 October 1453, a crucial new player appeared on the scene. In the palace of Westminster Queen Margaret was at last 'delyvered of a fair Prynce whos name was called Edward'.[78] The following day Bishop Waynflete of Winchester baptized the child in Westminster Abbey. His godparents were Cardinal Kemp, Edmund duke of Somerset and Cecily's sister, Anne duchess of Buckingham.[79]

Eleven days after the prince's birth, York was summoned to a Great Council at Westminster.[80] Now that Henry had a healthy son to succeed him, York's potential claim was less immediate and threatening. Some council members dared to hope that 'rest and union betwixt the lords of this land' could be achieved.[81] Moreover, since the king's council remained powerless to stop the continuing violence in the north of England that involved various of Cecily's Neville and Percy nephews, steps needed to be taken to build a stronger government around the helpless king. In the light of Cecily's negotiations, it may have been Queen Margaret who suggested this attempt at conciliation.

A week later, Cecily too was sent an invitation to Westminster.[82] This was to attend Queen Margaret's churching on 18 November. The *Liber Regie Capelle* (*Book of the Royal Chapel*) that had been written four years previously recommended that a queen wait sixty days between childbirth and churching.[83] However, in the unique circumstances in 1453 it was evidently deemed wisest for Margaret to re-enter public life as soon as possible. The letter to Cecily was written in the king's name although it was actually Cardinal Kemp and the dukes of Buckingham and Somerset who presided over the decision-making.[84] The invitation emphasized their sense of God's role in events as well as the vital responsibility that the queen bore: 'We holde for certaine that it is comen to youre knowlache howe that nowe late it hath pleased almighty god oure most entierly beloved wyf the Quene be delivered of the birth the whiche she by his mercy was charged with'.[85] A list of the thirty-five invitees (all women, of course) attached to the standard invitation letter ranked them in order of precedence. Jacquetta, duchess of Bedford headed the list as widow of the king's uncle, her rank unaffected by her marriage to Richard Woodville. Despite York's recent disgrace, Cecily's name came next, above those of the duchesses of Norfolk, Buckingham, Somerset, Exeter and Suffolk.[86]

Earlier in the year Henry had given Margaret 20 yards of russet cloth of gold and 540 brown sable backs to be fashioned into a gown for her churching. Along with the embroidered chrisom-cloth for Edward's baptism this had cost some £554 16s. 8d., which was more than twice the value of Cecily's famous crimson velvet outfit in Rouen.[87] If Margaret's churching followed the procedure laid out in the *Liber Regie Capelle* then she would have been dressed in these 'costly garments' and settled in a curtained bed in her great chamber to await the guests for the ceremony. As the première royal duchesses it was presumably Cecily, duchess of York, and Jacquetta, duchess of Bedford, who 'modestly and humbly' crossed the room to draw back the bed curtains. Two dukes then 'gently and humbly' lifted the queen from the bed and led her to the door of the chapel with all the women processing behind. After the service the queen was expected to return to her chamber with the ladies and damsels to feast 'solemnly', 'in great glory and honour'.[88] This is unlikely to have been an opportunity for Cecily and her kinswomen to gossip because these feasts were normally held in silence. She and Jacquetta were probably both required to stand or kneel on either side of the queen for a good part of the feast which may have lasted as long as three hours.[89]

Three days after these celebrations, the Great Council met in the star chamber at Westminster and all hope of reconciliation between lords was shattered. York's ally John Mowbray, duke of Norfolk, presented articles demanding Somerset's arrest for treason.[90] Those who had issued York's invitation to the council must have felt betrayed and disappointed as Somerset was incarcerated in the Tower of London once again.[91] It was this decision to exclude Somerset from government during Henry's madness that irrevocably established the conflict between York and Lancaster. In early January 1454 the queen, perhaps at Cardinal Kemp's prompting, sought to offer a solution to the vacuum in authority. According to a newsletter written on 19 January she desired 'to have the hole reule of this land'.[92] In earlier centuries English queens had been figureheads during their husbands' absence abroad but Margaret seems to have been looking for the much more powerful and formal authority commonly held by French queens. Her plan offered what could have been a much less partisan rule than a council dominated by York or Somerset. However, the most recent precedents for female 'regency' were scarcely auspicious: in France Isabeau of Bavaria had had to agree to a treaty disinheriting her own son and in England Edward II's queen Isabel, having deposed her own husband had in turn been deposed by her son.[93] Significantly

Henry VI's mother, Catherine of Valois, had been given no political role during his minority. The lords seem to have been undecided and spent several weeks entertaining the possibility of allowing a woman to hold this position. Nonetheless on 13 February York was given authority to open parliament the next day, implicitly recognizing his senior status among men.[94]

It was at this point that Margaret began to emerge as a political leader. Her motivation now seemed to be to check York's authority, but it is impossible to know whether she saw him as a genuine threat to her son's succession or simply as an overmighty subject to be reined in. On the morning of 22 March 1454 the power structure shifted dramatically when the chancellor, Cardinal Kemp, died suddenly at Lambeth Palace.[95] Margaret had lost her most vital ally. Moreover, it was essential that a ruler of some sort should be decided upon in order to appoint a new chancellor. Within a week the lords had chosen Richard duke of York to be protector and defender of the realm until the young prince came of age to replace him or the king recovered.[96] Shortly afterwards Cecily's brother, Richard Neville, earl of Salisbury, was appointed chancellor.[97] Once again Cecily was riding high upon the wheel of fortune.

Queen Margaret was by no means the only person disappointed by this outcome. The most bitter of all seems to have been Cecily's own son-in-law, Henry Holland, duke of Exeter, who had made common cause with Thomas Percy, Lord Egremont against Lord Cromwell and the Nevilles earlier in the year.[98] In May, Holland began orchestrating risings in the north of England, allegedly distributing Lancastrian liveries, as he claimed a greater right to rule on the king's behalf than York's.[99] Despite urgent business in the south, especially that of keeping control of Calais, Richard duke of York felt impelled to head northwards to try to achieve peace. In this he was successful and Exeter fled back to London.[100] Controversially York personally escorted Exeter out of Westminster Abbey sanctuary and swiftly organized for him to be taken back north for imprisonment at Pontefract castle.[101] As Christmas 1454 approached Cecily had every reason to feel secure and confident in her husband's power. He had reclaimed the lieutenancy of Ireland, made himself captain of Calais and initiated a reform of the royal household. The couple were most likely together in the capital that Christmas when the wheel began to turn briskly once more. By New Year's Eve King Henry had begun to show signs of recovery and a few days later York duly surrendered his office. Within the month Somerset was free and Exeter followed soon afterwards. In early March, York lost the captaincy of Calais, Salisbury was dismissed as Chancellor and Somerset was declared innocent, prior to resuming his place at the king's side.[102]

By now Cecily's brother, Richard, earl of Salisbury, and her nephew, Richard, earl of Warwick, were firmly bound to York. This was not only as a consequence of the outworking of the Neville–Percy conflict but also because of disputes with Somerset over property in Wales.[103] York and the Nevilles were excluded from a Westminster council and they justifiably feared that the forthcoming Great Council in Leicester would be debating their quarrel with Somerset, perhaps leading to their arrest.[104] Together the three of them withdrew to their northern lands where they raised an army to remove Somerset by force and forever.

Their forces met those of the king at St Albans on 22 May 1455. In hindsight this conflict has been identified as the first battle of the Wars of the Roses. Yet Cecily's menfolk still probably had no intention of toppling the House of Lancaster, only of cutting down its most troublesome (and illegitimate) scion in a single ambush. York's men surrounded the house in which Somerset tried to take refuge. When the duke emerged wielding an axe he apparently killed four of them before he was 'wounded in so many places that he died'.[105] Meanwhile two other lords were also slain, probably because of their rivalry with the Nevilles in the north of England rather than for their loyalty to the king. One was Lord Clifford and the other was Cecily's brother-in-law, Henry Percy, earl of Northumberland, husband to her sister Eleanor.[106] As Katherine Lewis has argued, at St Albans, 'Henry occupied a highly unusual position for a king, being in the midst of a battle by accident rather than design, and yet only observing it'.[107] The king's persistent failure to engage actively in the battles of the Wars of the Roses made it easier for the Yorkists to pose as enemies only of the king's men rather than the king himself. However, it also meant that 'the impression that Henry gave both to allies and enemies was that he simply lacked the strength and thus the manhood to exert himself in this crucial situation'.[108] Whatever their original intentions, York and the Nevilles increasingly appeared to be offering an alternative to this vacuum.

The second protectorate and its aftermath

Two months after the first battle of St Albans, Cecily gave birth to the last of her children, Ursula. The location is unrecorded but the date was 20 July 1455.[109] The child's name was unusual among the English nobility even though St Ursula was a popular virgin martyr and, like St Katherine, of royal blood.[110] In the pageantry that welcomed Katherine of Aragon to England in 1501 St Ursula was linked to King Arthur's lineage.[111] It may be that Richard and Cecily hoped to invoke the saint's support for York's political ambitions but inauspiciously their daughter died in infancy at Fotheringhay where she was then buried.[112] Very probably she had been born at that castle too.

After St Albans, York had swiftly positioned himself as the king's principal magnate and a parliament was called to negotiate some degree of reconciliation. York ensured that all those who had fought with him at St Albans were pardoned, that Thomas Young's reputation was restored and even that Humphrey duke of Gloucester was exonerated.[113] In August the earl of Warwick was appointed Captain of Calais. Another attempt was made to reform the royal household and in mid-November York was invited to take the role of protector once more. If the king had suffered another mental collapse this was not recorded. However, as Ralph Griffiths points out, it had been agreed on 11 November that Henry was unable to preside at the reopening of Parliament the next day which very much suggests some form of illness.[114] York's second protectorate began officially on 19 November but he did not possess a sufficient consensus of noble support. His alliance with the Commons over a bill of resumption (to reclaim lands distributed by the king back into royal hands) caused consternation among other lords.[115] Henry VI had presumably significantly recovered his health by now since the lords advised that the protectorship was no longer appropriate and York resigned again on 25 February.[116]

This dismissal was not like that in 1454. York was in no way disgraced and he was still entitled to sit in the king's council.[117] Nonetheless, York swiftly left the capital. He and Cecily may initially have withdrawn to Clare since the Clare Roll celebrating York's lineage was dated 1 May 1456 and was perhaps presented to him then. By 8 May the duke was at Sandal Castle in Yorkshire.[118] Cecily seems to have been engaged in trying to help her husband to build up popularity in the northern estates that he had so far largely neglected for in the summer of 1456 she visited the city of York, apparently without her husband, and joined their most powerful and fashionable religious guild, the Fraternity of Corpus Christi.[119] The cult of Corpus Christi was a relatively new one in medieval Europe and the fraternity in York had been founded in 1408.[120] In 1456 Cecily was much their highest status member so far.[121] When she joined she would have been expected to make a donation, either in coin or perhaps of jewellery to the Corpus Christi shrine which was carried at the heart of the feast day procession.[122] However, there is no evidence that she continued her patronage in later years and this appears to have been a primarily political short-term gesture.

Caister

In early autumn Richard and Cecily travelled back south. By mid-September York was in residence at the bishop of Salisbury's inn on Fleet Street.[123] Cecily, however, may have stopped in East Anglia. That November John Fastolf mentioned in one of his letters that Cecily had been visiting him at his sumptuous castle at Caister in Norfolk. Here she had 'soore mevid [him] for the purchas of Castre'.[124] This was presumably on York's behalf since, as a married woman, she could not own property in her own right. Fastolf had spent over £6,000 rebuilding his luxurious and well-fortified 'gret mansion', just a mile from the coast.[125] By 1456 he was in his late seventies and childless, so he knew he would soon have to pass this 'ryche juelle' to others.[126]

It seems that Fastolf was seriously considering Cecily's request to purchase Caister since her visit prompted him to try to speed up his plans to complete this splendid memorial of his life and achievements.[127] The finishing touch was to be a college within the castle to pray for his soul and that of his wife Milicent.[128] Cecily must have considered visiting Fastolf at Caister again either the following summer or in 1458 because in a letter dated simply 18 June, Fastolf expressed anxiety that he would be too ill to receive her.[129] It is plausible to assume that there were other, unrecorded, occasions upon which Cecily was transacting similar business with gentlemen on her husband's behalf, perhaps sometimes with greater success. Like her negotiations with Queen Margaret, the episode indicates York's respect for his wife and his faith in her abilities.

Elizabeth's marriage

Richard and Cecily were developing further interests in East Anglia through the marriage of their second daughter, Elizabeth, to the young duke of Suffolk, John de la

Pole, which seems to have been planned in February 1457.[130] After his father's murder, John de la Pole's mother, Alice Chaucer, had secured control of her son's lands and she had remained a close friend of the queen. However, the lands left to John after the many royal grants to his father had been resumed were valued at only £278 a year.[131] Like Henry Holland, John de la Pole should have married an heiress in order to maintain the status appropriate to a duke. Alice Chaucer's decision to allow the marriage suggests that she had faith in Richard duke of York's future political prosperity and believed there was a genuine commitment to reconciliation. At a council meeting later that year the king oversaw arrangements for a broader settlement which culminated in March 1458 with the extraordinary 'Loveday' procession through London's streets in which Richard duke of York walked hand in hand with Queen Margaret behind the king.[132]

By the autumn of 1458 plans were afoot to marry another of Cecily's children, Edward, in the cause of political unity. English ambassadors were sent both to France and Burgundy proposing an alliance in which brides should be found for Henry Beaufort, duke of Somerset and the sons of Henry VI and Richard duke of York.[133] This dual approach looks like a rather desperate search for allies. It backfired once the duchess of Burgundy discovered that the French were being made the same offer. Nonetheless, it reflects York's continuing peace with the king at this point.

Unfortunately, the earl of Warwick was not enjoying such harmony with the royal family. The impoverished exchequer had failed to pay the Calais garrison's wages and Warwick had consequently sought funds through piracy against foreign shipping in the English Channel. From that winter tensions escalated amid accusation and counter accusation, apparent assassination attempts and calls to arms.[134] York was persuaded to ally with Cecily's kinsmen once more.[135] By the summer of 1459 it was clear that the 'Loveday' peace had fragmented beyond repair.[136] Cecily was probably at Ludlow where her husband's forces were rallying. Her brother, Salisbury, was assembling his men in the north and on 20 September Warwick arrived in London from Calais. York and his allies may well have hoped to force the king into rearranging his government simply by showing the strength of their forces. However, the king and queen clearly felt that they could not afford to be pushed around by 'overmighty' subjects in this way any longer. On 23 September royal forces led by James Tuchet, Lord Audley, met the earl of Salisbury just south of Newcastle-under-Lyme, at Blore Heath. After four hours of bitter fighting in which two of Salisbury's sons had been captured, Lord Audley was dead and Salisbury's forces were triumphant.[137] A new phase of the war had begun.

5

A Paper Crown: 1459–1460

… my lady your wife dame Cecely;
… is electe,
Tyme commyng like to have the souerayntie,
Vnder your rule, as shulde feminitee,

Hardyng's *Chronicle*: dedication to Richard duke of York[1]

It was probably in the summer of 1460 that an elderly spy, forger and chronicler called John Hardyng composed these words speculating on Cecily's role as the future queen of England, inspired by York's very obvious ambitions.[2] For the last fifteen months of her married life Cecily would actually spend very little time 'under [York's] rule' because, unusually for them, the couple spent most of this time apart. Within weeks of Salisbury's victory at Blore Heath, York was an exile under threat of attainder yet Cecily remained in England to face humiliation and imprisonment. Throughout this she protected her younger children and tried to defend her husband's interests. She now became a far more public figure, carefully balancing her response to her family's needs within the boundaries of acceptable feminine behaviour.

On 12 October 1459 the forces of Richard duke of York, Richard earl of Salisbury and Richard earl of Warwick gathered at Ludford Bridge on the River Teme in Shropshire.[3] Henry VI had been pursuing the Neville forces across the Midlands in the aftermath of Salisbury's costly victory at Blore Heath. Now the king headed an army some 50,000 strong.[4] The Nevilles had met up with York outside his family stronghold, Ludlow Castle. Cecily's teenage sons Edward, earl of March and Edmund, earl of Rutland were with their father awaiting battle against their king. At the castle on the hill above the river Cecily waited too.[5] Her youngest children, Margaret, George and Richard, were with her.[6]

That evening Warwick's most senior commander became overwhelmed by qualms of conscience about facing his anointed king on the field of battle. This was Sir Andrew Trollope, captain of the Calais garrison. Under cover of darkness, Trollope and his men secretly made their way into the king's camp and 'there shewed the secretnesse of the Duke and his [h]oste'.[7] York and his allies knew that they could not win the battle with their forces so depleted and their plans betrayed to the enemy. In 'fere of dethe', York decided to send his heir, Edward, with Cecily's kinsmen to Calais, in the hope that Edward would survive even if he himself did not.[8] Meanwhile he took his second son, Edmund, via Wales to Ireland, breaking down the bridges behind him as he went.[9] Cecily's fate in the aftermath of the rout at Ludford is the one event in her life that attracted attention from more chroniclers than any other.

Humiliation at Ludlow

Cecily duchess of York, it seemed, had been abandoned at Ludlow by her husband, sons and brother. Perhaps the family had previously agreed that if the men were forced to flee Cecily should remain, trusting to the fact that fifteenth-century noblewomen were not usually held responsible for their husband's political actions. This meant that she could try to represent the family's interests in their absence. It would in any case have been very difficult to escape Ludlow with three young children in tow when the king's forces were already so close. On the morning of 13 October, 'King Harry rode into Ludlow, and spoiled the Town and Castle, where-at he found the Duchess of York with her two young sons'.[10] According to one Londoner, Henry's men looted the taverns, drunkenly striking open the 'pypys and hoggys hedys of wyne [so] that men wente wete schode in wyne and thenn they robbyd the towne, and bare a-waye beddynge, clothe and othyr stuffe, and defoulyd many women'.[11] The anonymous Yorkist who wrote *An English Chronicle 1377–1461* said simply that Ludlow was 'robbed to the bare walles' but he continued, 'the noble Duches of York vnmanly and cruelly was entreted and spoyled'.[12]

This sounds like some sort of physical assault. It has even been argued that she was raped.[13] Yet there is strong reason to be sceptical of this. In the first place, what interested all the other chroniclers was that Cecily was taken into custody and sent to the household of the duke and duchess of Buckingham. According to the London mayor who wrote a chronicle in *Egerton MS 1995* (commonly known as *Gregory's Chronicle*), Cecily 'was kept fulle strayte and many a grete rebuke' by the duke of Buckingham.[14] These writers seem to agree that Cecily was humiliated, but the culprits and means are very different. The word 'spoyled', used by the author of *An English Chronicle*, could mean 'raped' but was used most commonly to refer to robbery. His description calls to mind stories of the Great Revolt of 1381 when 'peasants' allegedly humiliated the king's mother, Joan of Kent. Two chroniclers related that rebels burst into Joan's rooms at the Tower, broke her bed and asked her for kisses.[15] Those stories were very likely apocryphal but they emphasized that the rebels were uncivilized, anarchic and ignorant of chivalric codes. The author of *An English Chronicle* was almost certainly using the same tactic to disparage the Lancastrians at Ludlow. The *English Chronicle* is one of the most partisan and sensationalist fifteenth-century sources we have and its most recent editor describes it as 'a carefully constructed piece of Yorkist propaganda or, more accurately, myth-making'.[16] The arrival of the king's forces in Ludlow must have been frightening for Cecily and her children, but there is no reason to believe that she was physically harmed.

What was shocking and humiliating for Cecily was the loss of her freedom. Even this was not as painful as it might have been. According to most chroniclers she was understood to be in the custody of her sister, Anne duchess of Buckingham.[17] Anne was the one sister with whom Cecily had grown up and indeed she was the only sister whom Cecily seems to have remained close to in later life. Anne's fate after Cecily's son became king suggests that Cecily felt no resentment towards her sister for her experiences that summer. Whatever criticisms Cecily may have received from the duke of Buckingham for the political turmoil in which her family had placed the country, this was a much less shameful confinement than Somerset or Wiltshire's custody would have been. Despite all that her husband and her kinsmen had done, Cecily was still being treated with respect by the king and his queen. This may well indicate that they did not consider Cecily to have been a significant political participant in her husband's schemes, or even that she had maintained some degree of friendship with the queen. Cecily was most likely kept at Maxstoke Castle, an exquisite red sandstone moated castle regularly used by the duke of Buckingham.[18] This lies just eleven miles from Coventry which was to be the location of a parliament which the duke would naturally attend.

The Coventry Parliament

From her gilded cage, Cecily presumably heard news from Coventry as men gathered for the meeting that was later known as the 'Parliament of Devils'.[19] It convened in the chapter house of St Mary's priory on 20 November 1459. Its principal business was the 'grete materes of atteyndre and forfeiture' against York, Salisbury and their followers.[20] Cecily's son-in-law, the duke of Exeter, and her nephew, the duke of Norfolk, were there with Buckingham. Sources for this parliament are not entirely clear in their chronology but at some point Cecily was permitted to leave Buckingham's household and to address the king. On 7 December John Bocking, a servant of the recently deceased John Fastolf, sent a letter from Coventry in which he mentioned that 'the Duchesse of York come yestereven late'.[21] This letter is usually read to mean that Cecily first arrived in Coventry on 6 December by which time the business of Parliament was almost over. There would seem to have been little point in Cecily addressing the king at such a late date. However, Cecily had probably been in Coventry for some days before, only personally calling on Bocking at his residence on the 6th.

John Bocking's letter mentioning Cecily was addressed to Justice William Yelverton, John Paston and Henry Filongley, all of whom were intimately concerned with the business of organizing John Fastolf's funeral, administering his will and determining the fate of his projected college and his castle at Caister.[22] Significantly, Bocking's letter concludes by explaining that the 'bringer' of his letter 'shall more pleinly declare yow', regarding Cecily's visit. He urged the recipients 'to gif credence' to the bearer's message about Cecily, which suggests that this was not simply a matter of news about her visit to the king. For more general news about the parliament he referred his readers to a 'grete bille of tidings' that he was sending to William Worcester. We can only guess what the 'bringer' had to report. It is unlikely that the matter was political since one of the recipients, Henry Filongley, was a committed Lancastrian.[23] Perhaps Cecily was concerned about the distribution of Fastolf's possessions.

If Cecily had first arrived in front of the king some days earlier, that would make much more sense of the account of her visit that was given in *Egerton MS 1995*:

The Duchyes of Yorke com unto Kyng Harry and submyttyd hyr unto hys grace, and she prayde for hyr husbonde that he myght come to hys answere and to be ressayvyd unto hys grace; and the kynge fulle humbely grauntyde hyr grace, and to alle hyrs that wolde come with hyr, and to alle othyr that wolde come yn with yn viij dayes.[24]

It seems unlikely that Cecily had any real hope of achieving a meaningful peace this late in the day. The eight-day time limit for submitting to the king may have been intentionally too short for York, March, Rutland, Salisbury or Warwick to make their way back to Coventry. Most likely Cecily's pleading on the duke's behalf was merely a formality that was necessary to achieve more realistic petitions for those York had abandoned at Ludlow. *Egerton MS 1995* continues: 'many men, bothe knyghtys and squyers, come whythe Syr Water Deverose, in hyr schyrtys and halters in hyr hondeys, fallynge by-fore the kynge, and alle hadde grace and marcy bothe of lyffe and lym'.[25] The parliamentary record explains that Devereux and others had made their submission at Ludlow, just after York's departure.[26] The theatrical affair indicated in the chronicle description was perhaps a later re-enactment for the benefit of parliament, unless the chronicler had conflated events at Ludlow and Coventry, in which case Cecily may already have pleaded for her husband and his men at Ludlow. Devereux and others were indeed granted 'lyffe and lym' but their goods were confiscated along with those of their absent lords and could only be reclaimed on payment of hefty fines. The following March Devereux acquired a pardon but he remained loyal to the house of York and entered Cecily's service shortly after her husband's death.[27]

Although it remains unclear whether Cecily was seeking pardons as late as the Coventry Parliament, what is certain is that she was looking to ensure financial provision for herself and her youngest children there. Through the last days of the parliament Cecily's former homes were being parcelled out to loyal Lancastrians: the earl of Shrewsbury's son, John Talbot, became constable of Sandal Castle; the young prince of Wales was given most of York's castles and lordships in Wales, although Jasper Tudor was given Denbigh where rebels loyal to York continued to hold out.[28] Cecily's son-in-law, Henry duke of Exeter, became constable and keeper of his wife's birthplace, Fotheringhay castle, 'for good service against the rebels'.[29]

It was standard practice for acts of attainder to stipulate that the widows of attainted rebels were still entitled to receive their jointure.[30] But for as long as their husbands lived, the wives of these men had no such rights. Consequently, Cecily needed to plead with the king to save her and her children from humiliating poverty. On the penultimate day of parliament letters were issued recording that

the king promised Cecily, duchess of York, for the relief of her and her infants, who have not offended against the king, 1000 marks yearly during her life from certain possessions late of Richard her husband, in the counties of Northampton, Essex, Hertford, Suffolk, Salop and Hereford.[31]

It was a highly respectable income, very similar to her mother's as a widow. The lands assigned to provide Cecily's income look to have been among those already chosen by

York for her jointure.[32] The manors were granted to a group of nine men for Cecily's use 'for her life'.[33] These men included John Stanbury, bishop of Hereford; John Chedworth, bishop of Lincoln; James Butler earl of Wiltshire (who had briefly replaced York as Lieutenant of Ireland in 1453) and her custodian, Humphrey duke of Buckingham.[34]

Cecily's comfortable income after the Coventry parliament seems to be testament to her powers of persuasion and political negotiation when compared with the fate of her sister-in-law, Alice Montagu countess of Salisbury, who was attainted along with her menfolk. Extraordinarily the act of attainder actually put more blame for the rebellion onto Alice than on her husband, son or brother-in-law. It was claimed that she had 'traiterously labored, abetted, procured, stered and provoked' her kinsmen into plotting the king's death.[35] York's chamberlain, Sir William Oldhall was similarly named as a malign influence along with Thomas Vaughan.[36] It seems unlikely that these three had really been the evil geniuses behind Salisbury, York and Warwick's actions. The lawyers who drew up the act, and their informants, seem to have been playing on anti-feminist and class assumptions to explain the ignoble behaviour of some of the kingdom's most senior lords. This approach meant that if it later seemed politically expedient to pardon the Yorkists there was still a framework within which this could be done.[37] In the context of Countess Alice's fate, Cecily's success at Coventry suggests that hitherto she genuinely had avoided political engagement other than acceptable ventures at creating reconciliation. Nonetheless, near the end of the fifteenth century one London chronicler recorded that Cecily, rather than the countess of Salisbury, had been attainted at Coventry.[38] Perhaps it was Cecily's powerful position in later years that led to the chronicler's assumption. Warwick's countess, unlike her mother-in-law, had remained in Calais and seems to have been ignored by those at the Coventry parliament.

A traitor's wife

Cecily and her younger children remained in her sister's household until the duke of Buckingham's death the following July.[39] A footnote in James Gairdner's edition of the *Paston Letters* has led a number of unwary writers to imagine that Cecily was in Kent by January 1460.[40] In fact the unnamed duchess who was in Kent must actually have been Jacquetta, duchess of Bedford.[41] The previous sentence in the relevant letter had referred to a humiliating incident for Jacquetta's menfolk: her husband, Richard Woodville, Lord Rivers, had been mustering men at Sandwich to attack Calais when John Dynham and a contingent of men loyal to Salisbury, Warwick and March raided the town and carried Rivers and his son back to Calais.[42]

Implausibly, the Burgundian chronicler Jean de Waurin claimed that Cecily joined York in Ireland.[43] Waurin's remark has understandably been ignored because so many other chroniclers were certain that she was with the duchess of Buckingham and we know from the Paston Letters that Cecily was in London before York returned from Ireland that autumn.[44] Yet his story may still tell us something about Cecily's comparative freedom within her sister's custody. Waurin's most important source of information was Cecily's nephew, Richard Neville earl of Warwick, and it is in the context of Warwick's visit to Ireland that Waurin mentions Cecily there. Richard duke of York had been 'worshipfully received' in Ireland, called a parliament at Drogheda, and then initiated a radical approach to governing which asserted his independence and security from the consequences of English law.[45] He also raised an army of archers, set about raising funds and began negotiations for an alliance with James II of Scotland.[46] His position was thus much more secure than that of the lords in Calais who had to rely on piracy for their income and who were under attack from Henry Beaufort, duke of Somerset. On 16 March Warwick arrived at Waterford for a conference with York. According to Waurin, he found 'the duke of York, the duchess his wife and all their children, except the earl of March'.[47] It is not at all plausible to imagine that their married daughters were present in Ireland or indeed that the Lancastrian authorities had allowed Cecily to take her younger sons out of the country. This statement looks like an ill-informed assumption to flesh out his story. However, when Warwick left, 'he set out with the lady his mother who had long been kept with my lady of York'.[48] Both pseudo-Worcester's *Annales* and *An English Chronicle* confirm that Warwick retrieved his mother from Ireland that spring and brought her to Calais.[49] How the attainted countess had made her way to Ireland does not seem to have been recorded. It may have been that Cecily had found some way to help her disgraced sister-in-law and that it was knowledge of this that led Waurin to assume that Cecily was actually in Ireland.

The road to Northampton

In June 1460 a manifesto was issued in the names of the duke of York and the earls of March, Warwick and Salisbury. It condemned the earls of Shrewsbury and Wiltshire and Lord Beaumont for leading the king astray and concluded with assurances of their own loyalty to the king.[50] The gossips in European courts were confident that their ambitions stretched further than they admitted.[51] As early as May it was rumoured at the papal court that the earl of Warwick had returned to England 'with a great following of other Englishmen … and it is hoped that he will deprive the king of that lordship'.[52] On 28 June James II of Scotland wrote to the duke of Milan, encouraging him to commit his aid to York. He claimed that he was himself supporting York's 'clear right to the crown and diadem of England'.[53]

On 26 June Warwick, Salisbury and March landed at Sandwich. They headed first to Canterbury and swiftly built up an army as they marched through Kent. Among them was Cecily's youngest brother, Edward Lord Bergavenny, in spite of the king's commission to him to resist the invaders.[54] In London a handful of Lancastrians took refuge in the Tower. These included Edward earl of March's godfather, Thomas Lord Scales.[55] Cecily's eldest daughter, Anne duchess of Exeter, was at the Tower too.[56] Anne was now twenty-one and had a young daughter, also called Anne. Her husband was among those who had most vigorously resisted her rebel family. However, it is likely that she was already resident at the Tower because her husband was its constable.[57] She was not fleeing from her brother but providing a refuge for those who shared her husband's loyalties. Her careful apolitical approach was like her mother's and similarly allowed her to weather the immediate storms. Richard earl of Salisbury took up governance in

London while 'that noble knyght and floure of manhode, Richard, Erle of Warrewyk', departed with his young cousin, Cecily's eldest son, to face the king at Northampton.[58] Warwick and March's entourage now included a papal legate, Francesco Coppini, who was meant to be trying to bring peace between the warring factions. However, Coppini had quickly been won over by the charismatic earl of Warwick so that he controversially excommunicated Shrewsbury, Wiltshire and Beaumont. Warwick and March encountered the king's army outside Northampton on 9 July.[59]

By midday on 10 July battle was inevitable. It was pouring with rain, flooding the ditches that the king's men had dug and rendering their guns useless. As at St Albans, what the Yorkists really wanted were the lives of certain key nobles. According to the author of *An English Chronicle*, March and Warwick 'leyte crye thoroughe the felde, that no man shuld laye hand vppone the kyng ne on the commune peple, but onely on the lordes, knyghtes and squyers'.[60] Shortly into the battle Lord Grey of Ruthin abandoned the king's forces, leading his men to join the earls of Warwick and March. After that, the fighting was brief, its casualties estimated at 300 or fewer. Among them were Cecily's brother-in-law, Humphrey Stafford, duke of Buckingham and her nephew, Thomas Percy, Lord Egremont, the second son of her sister Eleanor.[61] The victorious lords took possession of the king 'and entered with him into the house of monks, Delapré [Abbey], close to Northampton'.[62] Presumably they gave thanks to God for vindicating their cause. After three days in Northampton they returned in triumph to London bringing the king with them. Queen Margaret fled northwards and two chroniclers reported that en route 'she was robbed and dispoyled of all her goods' and 'in dowt of hyr lyffe and sonys lyffe also'.[63] As Margaret's position on the wheel of fortune plummeted, so Cecily's rose once more.

Cecily may still have been with her sister Anne duchess of Buckingham. We know too little about Anne to guess at her response to her husband's death or how that affected the sisters' relationship. However, Carole Rawcliffe has remarked on evidence of Buckingham's 'harsh and often vindictive disposition'.[64] Anne had borne him seven sons and five daughters but seems to have been content to allow his body to rest at Northampton where the Yorkist lords had laid him rather than moving him to a place with family connections. She was about 50 when he died and chose to remain a widow for the next seven years.

After the battle of Northampton, if not before, Cecily seems to have been free to go where she liked. Her properties were all still legally in the hands of Lancastrian loyalists but in practice she may have had access to some of their revenues since it was noted on 5 February that 'the lordships which came into the king's hands by the forfeiture of Richard duke of York, and Richard earl of Warwick, are detained from the king's possession by their adherents'.[65] Anne duchess of Buckingham had good reason to encourage Cecily to remain as her guest at this point now that the sisters' fortunes had been reversed and Anne needed the goodwill of Cecily's menfolk. Cecily is unlikely to have attempted to rejoin her eldest son immediately after Northampton since London was still in turmoil. The Lancastrians in the Tower had set their guns on London and the citizens of London had been attacking in return, setting a siege which meant the inhabitants of the Tower were running short on food.[66] Chronicles vary in their accounts of the consequences: either, on the night of 20 July many of the men attempted to escape by water, or they had negotiated a surrender but were then hunted down by angry Londoners nonetheless. Lord Scales was murdered by a gang of boatmen near Southwark. His body was thrown into the cemetery of St Mary Overy (now Southwark Cathedral) 'nakyd as a worme'.[67] Even Yorkists felt 'grete pyte it was that so noble and so worshypfull a knyght, and so well approued in the warrys of Normandy and Fraunce, shuld dy so myscheuously'.[68] Some of his erstwhile companions were slain as they reached Holborn, others were captured.[69] At least six of the duke of Exeter's household men were tried at the Guildhall and executed at Tyburn.[70] Duchess Anne herself may have been taken into custody just as her mother had been nine months earlier. The earls of Warwick and March took responsibility for providing the latter's godfather with an appropriate burial and issued a proclamation forbidding murder and theft on pain of death.[71]

In the last days of July a new regime was fashioned. The new chancellor was Warwick's younger brother, George Neville, bishop of Exeter. York's brother-in-law, Viscount Bourchier, became treasurer.[72] Writs were issued on 30 July for a parliament that October that would undo the work of the 'Parliament of Devils' at Coventry. By this point Warwick, Salisbury and March were confident enough of their authority in London to set out for Canterbury with the king to make a public pilgrimage to the shrine of that most famous victim of royal recklessness, Archbishop Thomas Becket.[73] It was sometime in the next few weeks that Cecily and her younger children rejoined her triumphant son, Edward earl of March.

Reunions

On 15 September 1460, a contingent of men arrived in Southwark on March's orders to establish lodgings for Cecily and her younger children.[74] These men included John Clay, who had been York's household treasurer in Normandy.[75] Their chosen location was one of the most sought after houses in London: Sir John Fastolf's place in Southwark. Within days of Fastolf's death (5 November 1459) the duke of Exeter had tried to take possession of this splendid manor. William Paston and William Worcester had resisted his attempts to enter, prompting the duke to threaten legal action.[76] Weeks later another loyal Lancastrian had taken up residence, James Butler, earl of Wiltshire, who celebrated Christmas there.[77] It was luxuriously secluded and easy to defend yet close to the Thames for boat trips to the Palace of Westminster or to Baynard's Castle where Edward earl of March had established his own headquarters.[78]

By the autumn of 1460 William Worcester was vigorously disputing John Paston's right to hold Fastolf's manor. A certain Christopher Hansson was supervising the property for John Paston when the earl of March's 'harbinger' and others arrived. Hansson took the opportunity to build support for his master by welcoming the duke of York's family in John Paston's name. Hansson agreed that 'my laydy of York myght lye her vn-tylle the comyng of my lord of York, and hir sonnys my lorde George and my lorde Richard and my lady Margarete hir dow3tyr, ... vn-tylle Mychelmas'.[79] Just two days after her arrival, Cecily received news that her husband had landed near Chester. On 23 September, a message came from the duke himself summoning her to Hereford.[80] She left Margaret, George and Richard in Southwark, presumably with instructions to Edward to ensure that they were well cared for since Hansson reported that he visited daily in spite of his other commitments at the time. Cecily left London in regal style, her carriage covered in blue velvet and pulled by eight coursers.[81]

Shortly after he landed, it became clear that York now intended to lay claim to the throne of England for himself. After his failure to muster sufficient authority to rule during his second protectorate this decision was hardly surprising. Only as king could he effectively marshal England's fractured polity and institute the government he wanted. Consequently, he was recruiting men and drawing up indentures that were unconventionally dated by the year of grace rather than with Henry VI's regnal year.[82] According to Waurin, when York reached Ludlow the local gentry gathered to call on him to assume the throne of England as the true and rightful heir of Richard II.[83] These border gentlemen were of course his most loyal supporters. At Shrewsbury he met briefly with the earl of Warwick and Countess Anne who then returned to London to make preparations. Warwick later maintained that he had been unaware of York's intention to claim the crown although this seems improbable.[84] If at Shrewsbury Warwick had tried to warn his uncle that the lords and bishops in London were still not ready to accept him as king it is unlikely that York would have been prepared to listen. After a decade of swinging between fear and fortune York was determined that the endgame had arrived.

Queen in waiting

While York may well have summoned Cecily so that he could share his triumph with her, he must also have been conscious that his fertile Neville wife was a political asset worth showing off. As Katherine Lewis has argued, the long delay before Henry produced his only child was associated by contemporaries with 'Henry's lack of manliness'.[85] One of the ballads composed in support of York's right to rule that summer significantly indicated that there were no questions over Cecily's chastity, unlike the queen's whose son's legitimacy had persistently been the target of Yorkist propaganda: the song told of a gentlewoman in Cheapside embroidering letters on a vestment including

> M for Marche trewe in euery tryalle …
> Conseived in wedlock, and comyn of blode ryalle.[86]

Another contemporary literary indication that Cecily was considered to be a very different wife from Margaret of Anjou is to be found in the lines with which this chapter begins. As Felicity Riddy has argued, it seems that John Hardyng had been commissioned to revise his chronicle in order to justify York's claim to the English throne and he had probably started some months before York was officially declared Henry's heir.[87] The assumption in his prologue is that Cecily would be under her husband's rule, as was proper for women. In the verse that follows Hardyng refers to

Cecily again as 'My lady that is vnder your proteccion'.[88] He surely meant his readers to recognize the contrast with Margaret of Anjou whose husband could neither rule nor protect her.

When Richard and Cecily reached Abingdon they adopted unmistakeable trappings of royalty. Whatever Cecily may have felt about the rightness of her husband's claim, she then had no option but to go along with it. Trumpeters and clarioners were summoned to march ahead of them and York gave these musicians 'baners with the hole armys of Inglonde with owte any dyversyte', that is, of the royal arms of England.[89] Moreover, York had 'his sword born vpright before him' as only a king should.[90] Parliament

FIGURE 5.1 *Richard duke of York c. 1444 with the coat of arms he used prior to 1460. Detail from the Talbot Shrewsbury Book of Romances. © The British Library Board BL Royal MS 15 E VI f. 3. Reproduced by permission of the British Library*

had already begun when they arrived on 10 October. A letter to John Tiptoft, earl of Worcester described the scene:

> ther cam my lorde of york with viij hundred horse and men harenysed atte x of the clok, and entred the paleis with his swerde born uppe right by for him thorowe the halle and parleament chambre. And ther under the cloth of estate stondyng he gave them knowlich[e] that he purposed nat to ley daune his swerde but to challenge his right.[91]

York did not receive the acclamation he was looking for but nonetheless took possession of the king's chambers in the palace. The second anonymous Crowland continuator [hereafter called Crowland Continuator] reported that the king moved out into the queen's chambers.[92]

In a council based at the Black Friars, the lords sought advice from judges and sergeants at law before finally establishing a compromise that everyone present was prepared to accept for the time being. Henry VI was to remain king but 'Richard duke of York rejoissh, bee entitled, called and reputed from hens forth, verrey and rightfull heire to the corones, roiall estate, dignite and lordship' of England.[93] He was granted the principality of Wales, the palatinate of Chester and the duchy of Cornwall which were expected to provide 10,000 marks yearly for his own upkeep and those of his eldest sons.[94] Henceforth it was considered treason if anyone 'spake any evil by the Duke of York or hys wyffe, or any of hys chyldryn'.[95] Cecily was at last officially a member of the immediate royal family. The accord was sealed in parliament on 31 October and was celebrated on the feast of All Saints with a procession to St Paul's in which the king wore his crown and was accompanied by all the lords who had signed the accord.[96] The king was then removed to the palace of the bishop of London so Cecily may have spent some time occupying the queen's rooms at Westminster.[97] York had not been formally invested with the titles taken from Henry VI's son, but this mattered little to Yorkist partisans. The author of *An English Chronicle* copied the accord into his work and immediately followed it with the assertion, 'Also it was ordeyned by the sayde parlement that the sayde Rychard, duk of York, shold be called Prince of Wales, Duke of Cornewayle, and Erle of Chestre'.[98] Perhaps York believed that his new status would prove sufficient to make this protectorate effective, although not all his supporters seem to have been content with the arrangement.[99] More seriously, there were important noblemen who had not been at Westminster to sign the accord. Among them were Cecily's nephews, Henry Percy, third earl of Northumberland and Ralph Neville, second earl of Westmorland, her son-in-law Henry Holland, duke of Exeter and her brother George Neville, baron Latimer.[100] Despite the fact that two of these men had previously been declared insane, their troops were now being mustered near Hull along with those of other northern lords and of Henry Beaufort, duke of Somerset while Thomas Courtenay, earl of Devon was marching to join them. At the same time, Margaret of Anjou had been negotiating support from the new Scottish regent, Mary of Guelders. (James II had been killed by one of his own cannons while besieging the English-held Roxburgh Castle on 3 August).[101] York had no option but to summon his men and fight once more.

Wakefield

On 9 December Cecily's husband left London to ride to York. With him travelled her eldest brother, Richard earl of Salisbury and his son Thomas. Beside them was Cecily's second son, Edmund earl of Rutland. Cecily would never see any of them again. Days after York's departure, Cecily's eldest son, Edward earl of March, also left the capital but he was bound for Wales. Cecily remained in London, probably now at Baynard's Castle, as did the earl of Warwick. On 2 January 'cam hevy word and tidings ... that the duke of york, the Erle Rutland his sone and the Erle Salesbury wer trayterously and ageinst lawe of armes be taking of Tretys graunted, mordred and slain in the north beside pountfreite [Pontefract] in a feld called wakefield'.[102] After that first stark news, rumours and whispers grew into stories told with certainty. The precise circumstances of Richard duke of York's death at Wakefield will never be known now. Cecily herself may have been equally uncertain. Some chroniclers told of Lancastrian treachery – a truce broken by Somerset; or a trap set by Cecily's nephew, John Lord Neville (Westmorland's brother), who had offered his service to the duke 'vnder a falce colour' and so lured York from Sandal into a battle he could not win.[103] Others believed that York had been over confident and 'incautiously engaged the northern army at Wakefield ... without waiting to bring up the whole of his own forces'.[104] It was reported that Cecily's seventeen-year-old son, Edmund, had escaped the battle but was chased onto Wakefield bridge and slain by John Lord Clifford in vengeance for his father's death at St Albans.[105] Salisbury was captured alive and there are various accounts of who was responsible for executing him. York himself died on the battlefield, 'without any mercy or respect, relentlessly slain'.[106] Then 'at Pontefract ... they beheaded the dead bodies of the duke of York, and the earls of Salisbury and Rutland, Thomas Neville [and five others] and set up their heads above various parts of York. Also they contemptuously crowned the head of the duke of York with paper'.[107] Richard duke of York had been the man through whom Cecily's identity was defined since she was nine years old, her bedmate and 'ruler' for three decades. It is impossible to be certain about the quality of their marriage but the overall impression of surviving evidence suggests that it had been a loving relationship. It appears from Cecily's very frequent pregnancies that they spent much of their time together and the occasions on which Cecily negotiated on her husband's behalf indicate that he respected her judgement and persuasive powers. Now he was gone and she would never be queen. She was denied the usual rituals and space for grieving because he and Edmund were interred at Pontefract by those who had slain them while she remained in London.[108] Christine de Pisan had recorded that the 'wise princess who is widowed' would stay in seclusion for a time 'with only a little daylight', dressed sombrely 'according to decent custom'.[109] For Cecily this was impossible because the fates of her other children were uncertain as indeed was the fate of the kingdom. Her new purpose was to support her eighteen-year-old eldest son as he took the throne his father had died for.

6

Her First Year of Widowhood: 1461

… write also to the duchess, who has a great regard for you, and can rule the king as she pleases.

Letter from the Bishop of Elphin to Francesco Coppino,
Papal Legate, Easter Week, 1461[1]

In the first few months after her husband's death, Cecily's family's fortunes would plunge deeper into the abyss before rising through the bloodiest battle ever fought on English soil into the triumph that had eluded York for so long. In the midst of this crisis Cecily's decisions revealed her mettle and her independent determination to fight for the cause that her husband had died for. At the age of forty-five she stepped at last into the forefront of the political arena and became the most powerful woman in England.

With the news of disaster at Wakefield came also the knowledge that the triumphant Lancastrians were marching back south, now accompanied by Queen Margaret of Anjou and reinforced with more troops from Scotland. Cecily's eldest son, Edward earl of March, had spent Christmas at Shrewsbury and it was here that he heard the crushing news of his father's death.[2] He had already begun preparations to intercept the queen's army before it reached the capital when he learnt of a second army. The king's half-brother, Jasper Tudor, earl of Pembroke, along with James Butler, earl of Wiltshire, was heading towards him from Wales, apparently with 'Frensshemen and Brettons, and Iresshe men … purposynge hem for to distroye hym'.[3] Edward swung back southwards. Ten miles beyond Ludlow he encountered Tudor's army at Mortimer's Cross at the feast of Candlemas. As Edward mustered his troops 'over hym men saw iij sonnys schynyng'.[4] Ice crystals in the February sky had created parhelia. Inevitably these were assumed to be some sort of omen. Edward was politically astute enough to declare it a sign of God's favour on his cause. He 'kneled doune on his kneis and made his prayers and thanked God. And anone fresshly and manly he toke the felde upon his enemyes and put hem at flyght, and slewe of them iij Ml [three thousand]',[5] or so chroniclers claimed. Pembroke and Wiltshire both fled the field but Pembroke's father, Owen Tudor, was captured and executed at Hereford in revenge for the earl of March's losses at Wakefield.[6]

The second battle of St Albans and its aftermath

In London, Cecily and Warwick were awaiting Edward's arrival with the troops needed to defend the capital – and Henry VI – from the army of northerners. Cecily tried to protect her youngest sons from capture, or worse, by putting them into the care of a certain Alice Martyn. All that we know about Alice is that by 1463 she was a widow and that in that year Edward IV gave her an annuity of 100s. in reward for her 'faithful service ... namely in receiuyng and keping of oure right entierli biloued Brethren The Dukes of Clarence and Gloucestre from daungier and perill in thair troubles vnto the tyme of thair departing out of this oure Reame into the parties of fflaundres'.[7] It looks as if the boys were being kept secretly in Alice's household while Cecily's residence, Baynard's Castle, remained a political hub.

By 12 February Richard earl of Warwick felt he could no longer wait for his cousin Edward. He marched out of the city with troops led by the dukes of Norfolk and Suffolk (who were Cecily's nephew and son-in-law respectively), as well as William Fitzalan, the earl of Arundel.[8] By the time he reached St Albans, Cecily's brother, Edward Lord Bergavenny was also with them.[9] The mayor and common council were now the principal authority in London once more and Cecily was presumably in close contact with them as each awaited further news. Warwick took the king with him, apparently hoping that Henry VI's presence would prevent some of the Lancastrians from attacking. He was mistaken. On 17 February, Shrove Tuesday, the second battle of St Albans proved a disaster for the earl of Warwick. Queen Margaret took back her king. Warwick's brother, Sir John Neville, was captured by the queen's forces. So too were Lord Bonville and Sir Thomas Kyriell who were executed in front of King Henry's seven-year-old son that evening.[10] Warwick himself and other lords fled towards Edward earl of March (he was now duke of York but contemporaries still most often referred to him by his earlier title). They eventually met up with him in the Cotswolds.[11]

Queen Margaret and the duke of Somerset could have marched on London and seized the capital. Cecily was in danger of a second humiliation like that at Ludlow, or worse. However, many of the capital's inhabitants were determined to keep the Lancastrian northerners out 'dredyng and weyyng the inconueniens and myscheues that myght folow'.[12] Rumours flew across the country that Margaret's army had been looting and pillaging all the way from York to London: a monk at Crowland explained that terrified local people came bringing their treasures which the monks stashed within the abbey walls.[13] A poem written months later imagined the northern men brutally boasting:

'We woll dwelle in the southe cuntrey [*sic*], and take all that we nede,
These wifes and hur doughters, oure purpose shal thei spede.'

Whether Margaret's army really deserved this barbaric reputation has been a matter of some debate among historians, but what is certain is the fear that gripped London's inhabitants.[14] It was scarcely dignified kingship or good publicity for a monarch to have to lay siege to his own capital, so the Lancastrians paused, uncertain how to respond to London's closed gates.

Mayor Richard Lee and the common council turned to women to help protect their city. In this they were putting their trust in the perception that noblewomen were by nature adept at peacemaking but they were also conscious that the king's principal negotiator would be a woman too, Queen Margaret. The council persuaded three ladies who had been close to the queen but were all familiar to Cecily to lead a delegation of 'wytty men', most of them clerics.[15] One of these noblewomen was Jacquetta duchess of Bedford. Richard earl of Warwick had brought her husband and son back to London along with his own wife and mother in the late summer of 1460 and some sort of conciliation had been made between the Woodvilles and the new regime.[16] Nonetheless Jacquetta was still essentially the most senior Lancastrian noblewoman by virtue of her first marriage. The second intercessor was the recently widowed Ismanie Lady Scales, who had been Margaret of Anjou's principal lady-in-waiting.[17] Both Jacquetta and the husband of Lady Scales had of course stood as godparents to Cecily's children in the 1440s. The third envoy was another recent widow and frequent companion of the queen, Cecily's sister, Anne duchess of Buckingham, godmother to Henry VI's son. With promises of food and money these ladies and their embassy bought some time for further negotiation. However, when the carts of food reached Cripplegate a mob of Londoners seized the food and would not let them pass through to the soldiers.[18] At news of Edward earl of March's impending arrival Queen Margaret decided to retreat northwards.

While the outcome of the negotiations with Margaret was still unclear, Cecily had acted to protect the youngest members of her family. York had repeatedly striven to safeguard the wider interests of his family by sending his eldest son by different routes from his own and with similar precaution Cecily now took George and Richard out of Alice Martyn's care and sent them overseas.[19] Strikingly Cecily did not choose to flee herself. Her chief priority was her eldest son, Edward, and his claim to the throne. She risked the incarceration and humiliation that would surely follow further Lancastrian victory in order to remain in London for Edward's sake.

The destination Cecily chose for her younger sons was important. Ireland and Calais were still in Yorkist hands and were places she knew, but both were also vulnerable to the arrival of a Lancastrian leader. Instead Cecily sent her sons to Philip duke of Burgundy in spite of the complex political loyalties in Philip's duchy.[20] Isabelle of Portugal, Philip's powerful duchess, was Cecily's cousin and a granddaughter of John of Gaunt. It is not clear whether the two women had ever actually met when York was negotiating with Isabelle but in 1454 Isabelle had been angling for a marriage between her eldest son, Charles, count of Charolais, and one of Cecily's daughters, whereas Duke Philip had disagreed.[21] It appears that Duke Philip personally disliked Henry VI but had avoided showing too much support for York in the late 1450s because he was unwilling to jeopardize his subjects' wider trade interests. Within Philip's realm was the court in exile of the French dauphin, Louis, who deliberately antagonized his father, Charles VII, with vocal support for York.[22] Unfortunately, Duke Philip also had his own rebellious son, Charles Count of Charolais, who resented the dauphin's influence and was inclined to support his Lancastrian kin.[23] In these complex circumstances it is unsurprising that Cecily's sons were lodged at Utrecht, an independent prince-bishopric, legally outside Philip's own jurisdiction, but ruled by his illegitimate son, Bishop David.[24]

On 26 February, just days after his brothers' departure for Flanders, Edward arrived in London, 'nobly accompanied' with the earl of Warwick at his side.[25] Apparently no one resisted his entry and many welcomed him. He took up residence at Baynard's Castle once more and gathered his closest advisers to plan his *coup d'etat*.[26] On the following Sunday, George Neville, bishop of Exeter and chancellor of England addressed some three thousand people at St John's Fields. He explained that after the second battle of St Albans Henry VI himself had 'wyckedly for sworne' his agreement with the Yorkists by abandoning 'his trewe lordis that stode in grete jopardy for his sake'.[27] This gave the Yorkists legal justification to ignore their oaths of loyalty to him. Having read out 'articles and poyntes that kyng Henry had offended in', Bishop Neville asked whether the crowds would accept Edward duke of York as their king and the crowds shouted 'Ye! Ye!'.[28] Certain 'Capitaynes' then went to Baynard's Castle to inform Edward that 'the people had chosyn hym kyng'. However, popular acclamation did not make a king in fifteenth-century England. Lords spiritual and temporal gathered at Baynard's Castle for a great council. Archbishop Bourchier, Bishop George Neville and the earl of Warwick were the most prominent among them although Cecily was presumably present too.[29] They arranged to issue proclamations summoning people to assemble at St Paul's at 9 am on Wednesday 4 March. Here, in an improvised inauguration ritual, Edward IV was recognized as king so that he had legal justification for summoning an army to fight the Lancastrians.[30]

King's representative

Before his departure, Edward summoned the mayor and 'all the notables of London' to gather and 'recommended them to the duchess his mother'.[31] In his absence she was to preside over his household at Baynard's Castle.[32] In practice it was not yet a king's household but in some ways this was the closest that Cecily came to being a queen and it demonstrates Edward's confidence in her political capacity. During his three month absence this household provided expenses, gifts and hospitality, including wine specifically for Cecily, that cost over £1,720.[33] Such hospitality was needed because those who wanted to learn news on the most crucial matters of the day were congregating at Cecily's home: the two most valuable letter collections that we have describing events at this time are the Paston Letters and the diplomatic correspondence now in the archives of Milan, both of which include mention of news gleaned at Cecily's house.[34]

On 13 March 'owre newe Kynge Edwarde' rode through London, his courser splendidly caparisoned with the royal arms of England, 'and soo owte at Bisshoppysgate, with a goodly ffelishyp with hym'.[35] As Cecily watched her handsome eldest son depart so triumphantly she knew that within a few days more of her closest kin must lie dead, whoever proved victorious. For three weeks she waited for news. Then, upon Easter Eve, 4 April, tidings were brought into London that Edward had won 'A gret batail in the north contre at A place called Towton, nat ferre fro Yorke'.[36] At 11 am Cecily received a letter under the king's sign manual. William Paston summarized its contents for his brother John: 'Fyrst, oure souerayn lord hath wonne the feld, and vppon the

Munday next after Palme Sunday he was resseyued in-to York with gret solempnyté and processyonz'.[37]

Among the dead he named John Lord Clifford who had reputedly slain Cecily's seventeen-year-old son Edmund just three months earlier, and Andrew Trollope who had betrayed her husband at Ludlow. The letter's list of the dead also included her nephews, John Lord Neville (the earl of Westmorland's brother) and Henry Percy, earl of Northumberland: he was the eldest son of Cecily's sister Eleanor who had already lost a son at Northampton and her husband at the first battle of St Albans. *The Great Chronicle of London* called it 'a sore & long & unkeyndly ffygth ffor there was the Sone agayn the ffadyr, The brothyr agayn brothyr, The Nevew agayn Nevew',[38] and the mayor who wrote *MS Egerton 1995* concluded: 'many a lady lost hyr beste be lovyd in that batayle'.[39] In fact, William Paston's letter included some names who later proved to have survived, among them Jacquetta of Bedford's eldest son, Anthony Lord Scales, whose recent rapprochement with the Yorkist earls had clearly been no more sincere than Devereux's submission to Henry VI had been.[40]

Further news arrived in the capital each day. The most common estimate of the dead was 28,000, a casualty figure 'hitherto unheard of in our country'.[41] This was probably greatly exaggerated but it indicates contemporaries' sense of the enormity of the carnage by which Cecily's family had taken the crown of England. Nonetheless, a Milanese merchant in Bruges received a letter from London the following week asserting that 'King Edward has become master and governor of the whole realm. Words fail me to relate how well the commons love and adore him, as if he were their God. The entire kingdom keeps holiday for the event, which seems a boon from above'.[42] On Easter Monday Nicholas O'Flanagan, the bishop of Elphin, had been in Cecily's house in time to receive more misinformation about events in the north. As he explained in a letter to Francesco Coppini,

> at the vesper hour, I was in the house of the Duchess of York. Immediately after vespers the Lord Treasurer came to her with an authentic letter, stating that the late King with his kindred … had been all captured and brought to King Edward. On hearing this news the Duchess [returned] to the chapel with two chaplains and myself and there we said "Te Deum"; after which I told her that the time was come for writing to your Lordship, of which she approved.[43]

In fact, neither Henry VI nor his closest kindred had been captured. This influx of constantly conflicting news must have added to the anxieties of those far from events so that the daily routine of chapel services provided valuable consolation. Bishop Nicholas was keen to impress Coppini with his own influence in Duchess Cecily's house. He concluded his letter 'write to the king, the chancellor, and other lords, as I see they wish it; also to the duchess, who has a great regard for you, and can rule the king as she pleases [*et habet regere Regem sicut vult*]. She will not fail you in anything you ask, as long as I have any power'.[44] O'Flanagan was not the only observer convinced of Cecily's new power. Coppini's physician, Master Antonio, was based in Bruges but he too was advising the Papal Legate on English magnates to whom he should send congratulatory letters, 'not forgetting, on any account, to write to the Duchess of York'.[45]

One of Cecily's earliest politically significant acts after York's death had been to send her youngest sons to the duke of Burgundy. O'Flanagan was probably reporting responses heard in Cecily's home, perhaps even Cecily's own opinion, when he informed Coppini thus:

> It is reported among the English lords that the Duke of Burgundy is treating the brothers of the king with respect. This pleases them wonderfully, and they believe that there will be great friendship between the duke and the English by an indissoluble treaty, and that one of these brothers will marry the daughter of Charles [i.e. the duke's granddaughter, Mary].[46]

Following news of Edward's victory, the duke of Burgundy invited George and Richard to join him in Bruges.[47] Thereafter they travelled by land 'with many great gifts' to Calais and by early June they had reached London.[48]

Establishing the new regime

Cecily apparently remained in the capital all this time. She perhaps bore some responsibility for the fact that as early as 9 April letters were issued at Westminster confirming the dower rights of her sister Anne, duchess of Buckingham.[49] By contrast their unequivocally Yorkist sister-in-law, Alice countess of Salisbury, was not granted rights to her inheritance and jointure until 5 July.[50] Cecily's daughter Anne, duchess of Exeter, was also acting swiftly to avoid poverty in the new regime despite her husband's loyalties: on 1 May, long before Edward had returned to London, Anne had persuaded him to grant a collection of her husband's lordships and manors to some of the most powerful men in the new regime which they would hold for her use.[51] Effectively Anne was acquiring the income from her jointure during her husband's life time, much as Cecily had done in 1459. Anne duchess of Exeter's new possessions included an attractive London home at Coldharbour, along the Thames from Baynard's Castle. The following year Anne duchess of Buckingham would also receive a London home, similarly close to Baynard's Castle, when the king granted her 'Lord Moleyns Inn' just outside Temple Bar.[52]

Cecily's own financial affairs, like her sister's, were arranged at Westminster while Edward was still travelling through his new kingdom. It is impossible to be sure how much of the decision making was Edward's and how much was Cecily's. In April, even before her estates had been officially assigned, Cecily's receivers were recording income delivered to her in London from York's manors.[53] On 1 June letters patent were issued granting Cecily lands and customs revenues that should ensure that she had an income of 5,000 marks (about £3,333) a year.[54] This set her among the very wealthiest landholders in England. There was inconveniently no clear precedent as to what income a king's mother should receive. The only recent example of one who had not previously been a queen was Joan of Kent but she had been able to supplement her dower lands as princess of Wales with her own inheritance as countess of Kent, making her wealthier than most dowager queens.[55] Lancastrian queens had repeatedly been promised 10,000 marks (£6,666) annually but in practice they rarely received all of this and in the thirteenth and fourteenth centuries queens had habitually been granted only £4,500.[56] The most optimistic estimate of Richard duke of York's annual landed income at this time is £5,000 to £7,000, so Cecily was clearly being provided with considerably more than the 'full recompense of her jointure'.[57] Despite the Yorkist manifesto promises of careful husbandry, Cecily's dower was a significant allocation of lands that the king himself might have benefited from. The next king's mother, Lady Margaret Beaufort, spent years trying to build up a similar fortune. Margaret's determination to pursue the most tenuous claims to land has been described as 'ruthless' and 'unprincipled greed' yet it was only in 1504 that her landed income reached £3,000.[58] That said, a few of Cecily's lands may not actually have brought her the income she anticipated at first. These included a number of those properties that she and her husband had granted to Thomas Browne and others in 1449 which she did not actually regain control of until 1472.[59]

As a widow Cecily was free to manage her own properties with full responsibility for her lands and actions. She could buy land for herself and go to law in her own name. She could continue to work with administrators whom she already knew from the occasions when she had had to assist her husband in the administration of his lands while he was caught up in affairs of national politics. Her estates from 1461 did not include her husband's former possessions in Wales or in the north of England. Pugh has speculated that Cecily deliberately avoided those in Wales because she knew that their value was diminishing.[60] It is also possible that she and Edward felt it was strategically sensible to keep these lands in the king's hands. Indeed, at the time of the grant Denbigh was still being held for the Lancastrian Jasper Tudor, earl of Pembroke, which could scarcely have made it a sensible proposition for Cecily.[61]

Cecily's possessions as king's mother were scattered across twenty-one counties.[62] They included the extensive lordship and honour of Clare, as well as Fotheringhay Castle and manor, Bridgwater Castle, Great and Little Walsingham, an inn called 'The George' at Grantham, the manors of Hitchin and Fasterne, and of course Baynard's Castle. The income from these properties was to be supplemented with over £789 from customs revenues from wool and sheep skins traded through the ports of Hull and London and from the issues of the county of York. On 29 June she appointed her husband's former counsellor, Sir Richard Quatremains, as supervisor of all her lands on a salary of £20.[63] On the same day she appointed Thomas Aleyn of Blakesley in Northamptonshire auditor of all her properties, for which he would receive 20 marks yearly as well as reimbursement for expenses incurred.[64] Aleyn had been the clerk of expenses for her household during her marriage.[65] He had also been Richard duke of York's auditor at Fotheringhay and various properties in the south west.[66] At about the same time she gave the post of great steward of her lands to John Clay who had been with her at Fastolf's place in Southwark.[67] Alongside their service to Cecily, these men would also perform important services for Edward IV: Quatremains became a member of the king's council, Aleyn was one of his auditors in the duchy of Cornwall and Clay became one of the knights of the king's body and victualler of Calais.[68]

Edward finally arrived back on the outskirts of London on 12 June and stayed at Sheen where Cecily may well have joined him.[69] On 26 June he made a formal state entry into the city, accompanied by the mayor and aldermen all dressed in scarlet and a procession of four hundred 'comoners well horsyd and cladde all in grene'.[70] The state entry marked the beginning of Edward's coronation celebrations during which he knighted both of his younger brothers as well as the duke of Norfolk's heir and Lord John Stafford who was a younger son of Cecily's sister, Anne duchess of Buckingham.[71] This last was one of many demonstrations of reconciliation with previously Lancastrian families that Edward made in the early months of his reign. For instance, only a fortnight after the coronation he pardoned Richard Woodville, Lord Rivers 'all offences committed by him' and eleven days later issued 'the like' to Anthony Lord Scales, Rivers's son.[72] Cora Scofield suggested that this very early pardon might have been a result of an encounter between the king and Rivers's daughter, Elizabeth, Edward's future wife.[73] However, the king was far more likely to have been influenced by the fact that Rivers was married to Jacquetta duchess of Bedford, who had previously been the second lady in the land and whose first husband was respected by Yorkists and Lancastrians alike. Given her earlier relationship with Jacquetta, Cecily is more likely to have proved influential than Elizabeth at this early date.

Edward IV's coronation is poorly recorded compared with those of Henry VI and Richard III or even of his own queen, so it is unsurprising that no mention of Cecily's role has survived. She was certainly at Westminster through July and so presumably also for the coronation on 28 June.[74] The only reference to her in the wardrobe accounts is in connection with a velvet dress that she was given as a gift at the time of the coronation.[75] It was a rather small gift compared with those lavished on George, Margaret and Richard but seemingly slightly superior to the dresses given to her married daughters. Edward IV was following the protocol set when Edward III similarly gave his mother a dress at the time of his coronation.[76] The coronation was a ritual lasting several days so the gift of a single dress very likely indicates that Cecily was only present for one day of the celebrations. The greater gifts given to Edward IV's unmarried siblings also reflected the fact that they did not yet have their own resources as his mother and married sisters did.

The coronation was swiftly followed by further family celebrations when Cecily's son George was created duke of Clarence.[77] Young Richard had to wait a few months longer before he too received a title, that of duke of Gloucester.[78] By then Richard was nine and George was twelve. Their new quasi-adult status was marked in November when their names headed a commission to array the king's subjects in Cumberland for defence against his enemies of Scotland and the former king, Henry VI.[79] They were now too old to remain in their mother's household. It is frequently reported that they were given a household with their sister Margaret at Greenwich, yet Anne Sutton long ago pointed out that the evidence simply does not add up to this.[80] The boys seem to have been attached, at least for some time, to the household of Thomas Bourchier, archbishop of Canterbury, albeit with a small household of their own servants.[81] Bourchier's sister-in-law was the king's paternal aunt, Isabel, whose husband, Henry Viscount Bourchier, count of Eu, was created earl of Essex just after Edward's coronation.[82] The archbishop himself was one of King Edward's councillors, very much at the heart of the new regime, so that in his company the boys could develop their political education.

Like her brothers, Margaret was provided with clothing from the Great Wardrobe but on a much smaller scale and she most likely remained within her mother's household for the next few years.[83] Christine de Pisan had advised that: 'As the wise princess watches over the upbringing and education of her daughters, the older they get the more careful she will be. She will have them around her most of the time and keep them respectful. Her prudent behaviour and virtue will be an example to her daughters to govern themselves similarly'.[84] Margaret had been the only child in her mother's household since shortly after her father's death. At fifteen she had every reason to expect to be married soon. Her new status as the king's sister meant that she could expect a far more glittering match than her elder sisters had enjoyed. She must now prepare for a life in which she would almost certainly be called to be an ambassador between her brother's kingdom and a foreign power.

The role of king's mother

Cecily's own change in status was every bit as dramatic and she now had to invent a new role for herself within the political community. At forty-six she was younger than many contemporary war widows who chose to remarry. Of the 160 widowed peeresses in the fifteenth century that Joel Rosenthal identified, nearly half remarried, although only twenty-eight united with another peer, whereas forty-five married commoners.[85] Some of these women may have taken the opportunity to choose a second husband for love. Others seem to have chosen men who could help them protect their financial interests. About six years into Edward IV's reign Cecily's sisters, Anne duchess of Buckingham and Katherine duchess of Norfolk, both remarried. Their husbands, Walter Blount and John Woodville, had both been born into the gentry but were new men in Edward IV's regime, seemingly well placed to guard their wives' interests.[86] The king probably encouraged his aunts to help him empower these men through their marriages and indeed Katherine's marriage to a man more than forty years her junior was probably arranged to smooth John Woodville's way into acquiring her Beaumont dower lands for himself 'and the heirs male of his body' after her death.[87]

For Cecily the situation was rather different. There was reason for concern that if she remarried she might jeopardize the balance of power at her son's court. When Henry VI's mother, Catherine of Valois, had tried to remarry in the mid-1420s the king's council had introduced a parliamentary statute forbidding anyone to marry a dowager queen without the king's permission (which could not be given until he had reached 'years of discretion') on pain of forfeiting all his lands and possessions.[88] Cecily's son was of course much older than Catherine's, but a king's stepfather might well have expected undue influence at court. In choosing not to remarry, Cecily ensured that her primary identity remained that of king's mother.

She was somewhat short on role models for constructing this identity. Richard II's mother, Joan of Kent, was her closest forerunner although Joan had enjoyed years preparing for queenship as princess of Wales and first became king's mother when her son was only a child. Joan's primary identity seems to have been as an intercessor, mediating not only between her son and his subjects but also between the citizens of

London and her unpopular brother-in-law, John of Gaunt, and even pleading mercy for the controversial cleric John Wycliffe.[89] Indeed Joan's reputation was such that she was even credited with bringing about a reconciliation between Richard II and his lords that actually happened after her death.[90]

Intercession, advocacy and persuasion were of course political tools for men as well as women but because noblewomen lacked access to many of the avenues of power enjoyed by noblemen their ability to influence the actions of others was more central to their identity. This was reinforced by the contemporary ideal of noblewomen who were expected to be gentle and to avoid confrontation. Inevitably, the more senior a woman's connections, the more valuable the potential influence of her persuasive voice became, as the bishop of Elphin's letter about Cecily indicated. The intercessor *par excellence* in medieval thinking was the Virgin Mary, mother of God, whose iconography was commonly shared with earthly queens but there seems to be no evidence that Cecily sought to appropriate this ideology into her own identity.[91] After 1461, Cecily's intercessory actions only attracted the attention of chroniclers in connection with conflicts between her sons.[92] Nonetheless, her influence was sought by a wide variety of contemporaries, from the countess of Warwick to an otherwise unknown prisoner in Ludgate, as well as her tenants and servants, religious institutions, and civic authorities in the lordships she owned and in the towns she visited.[93]

Other aspects of her role as king's mother were similarly shaped by contemporary expectations of noblewomen. For most widowed noblewomen, their chief responsibility was to administer the lands now in their trust efficiently as 'custodians of their families' futures'.[94] Depending on wardship arrangements, they were generally involved in ensuring suitable marriages for their children and often continued to take some responsibility for their adult children's well-being.[95] As will be seen in succeeding chapters, this sense of responsibility is evident in Cecily's actions throughout her widowhood in which she worked to promote Edward IV's policies and interests as well as his reputation.

Religious activity

Despite her subsequent reputation for piety, Cecily's religious interests do not initially appear to have impacted significantly upon her public identity. T. B. Pugh has argued that she also failed in a very significant moral responsibility for a widow by ignoring many of the debts her husband had left at his death, thereby condemning York to a longer time in purgatory.[96] In fairness a good many of those debts were to Lancastrians so that her dereliction is understandable.[97] It may partly have been with this in mind that she and King Edward arranged a huge number of prayers for York's soul.[98] Early in Edward's reign these arrangements also reveal Cecily's continued concern for the souls of her dead children.

About a month after news of Edward IV's victory at Towton reached London, all of his immediate family were admitted as members of the Fraternity of St Nicholas in London, including his dead siblings and 'Prince Richard duke of York of illustrious and noble memory'.[99] The combination of the date (when Edward was still in the north) and mention of all her dead infants suggests that this was on Cecily's initiative. Hitherto the fraternity's only noble members had been her brothers, Richard earl of Salisbury and Robert bishop of Durham, and her nephew John duke of Norfolk, who had all joined the fraternity along with the king himself in 1449 when Henry VI issued a charter incorporating the fraternity.[100] Cecily rarely seems to have been interested in religious institutions patronized by her natal family but in the aftermath of Salisbury's death and Norfolk's crucial military support at Towton their connection may have played some part in her motivation. It is also likely that the fraternity's masters had personally sought out her patronage, eager to make a statement of their loyalty to the new regime. In doing so they perhaps encouraged Cecily's patronage by drawing her attention to her existing family connections with the fraternity.

Other religious institutions were committing themselves to pray for Cecily at this time. This was because Edward was issuing various confirmations of grants previously made by Henry VI to religious houses and colleges and grateful recipients were expected to pray for the king in return. It is possible that the reason that Cecily's name sometimes appeared with that of the king in these grants was that she had played a part in persuading the king to make the confirmation. More probably, the communities were simply acknowledging Cecily's quasi-queenly role at this time. In similar circumstances Cecily's name would appear beside the king's for the next four years, but after his marriage such institutions usually prayed only for the king and his queen.[101] The institutions praying for Cecily in 1461 were primarily those with strong royal connections, including Syon Abbey and the Carthusian monastery at Sheen which were both Lancastrian foundations, as well as St Stephen's Chapel, Westminster.[102]

Early days as king's mother

Edward had initially intended to hold his first parliament days after his coronation. However, news that an alliance of Scots and Lancastrians was besieging Carlisle prompted him to postpone the parliament until 4 November, only for John Neville, Lord Montagu (Warwick's brother), to raise the siege shortly afterwards. Spared the necessity to return northwards to defend his kingdom again for the moment, Edward instead took the opportunity to make a royal progress through some of the south and west parts of his kingdom.[103] Cecily remained in London at Baynard's Castle where she was busy establishing the arrangements for the administration of her estates and finding ways to reward those who had served her in the past.[104] She also took time to issue letters confirming many of her husband's grants.[105]

Even while she remained in London, Cecily's influence and importance was recognized by those whom the king met on his journey. While he was at Canterbury the prior and chapter of the cathedral granted her a useful tool of patronage in the right to present whoever she chose as minister next time there was a vacancy at the church of St Denys, Bakchurch, off Fenchurch Street.[106] The grant identified her as 'the very powerful and illustrious Lady Cecily, mother to the supreme Lord our king Edward, duchess of York'.[107] The king journeyed through the West Country and the Midlands, after which Cecily and her younger children joined him at Greenwich where they stayed for much of October.[108] Despite being away from Baynard's Castle, Cecily, like the king, was still involved in business administration at Greenwich.[109] At the end of the month they travelled to Westminster for more family celebrations on All Saints Day.[110] Cecily's brother William, Lord Fauconberg, was rewarded for his loyalty with the title of earl of Kent, and her son Richard became duke of Gloucester.[111]

Three days after this ceremony, Edward's first parliament met in the painted chamber at Westminster.[112] Cecily was still conducting business from Westminster, so may have remained there for the duration of the parliament.[113] The parliament's principal task was to establish the legality of Edward's regime. This included the attainder of Henry VI and his supporters as well as a bill annulling certain Lancastrian judgements. This parliament also discussed Cecily's income. A bill read on 28 November ensured that her right to £789 6s. 8d. from the customs of Hull and London and from the county of York was given precedence 'afore every other persone and persones havyng any interesse' in money from these sources.[114] Cecily may well have been aware that Margaret of Anjou had received very little of the customs revenues to which she had been entitled and was determined to ensure that her own income was more secure.[115] On 9 December a specific 'bill of confirmacion for my lady of York' guaranteed that nothing in the act of resumption for that parliament should impact on any grants the king had made to 'the full noble, high and myghty princesse Cecille duches of York'.[116] Once Edward had given the royal assent to the attainder against Henry VI on 21 December, parliament was prorogued and its participants prepared for Christmas.

Christmas 1461

This was Cecily's first Christmas without her husband. She chose not to spend it at Greenwich with Edward. Instead she held Christmas at Eltham. The fact that a London chronicler took sufficient notice to mention Cecily's celebrations may well indicate that they were significantly sumptuous.[117] *The Ryalle Book* included guidance on the seating and serving appropriate in the king's mother's household on such special occasions. She was not to share a mess with anyone except for her younger sons. At the table any bishop present would be seated at the upper end of Cecily's table whereas earls, countesses, barons or baronesses would sit 'at the neder end of her board'. Her daughter Margaret took precedence 'above all the Duchesses in England' (presumably excepting Cecily's elder daughters), despite her lack of title.[118] That Cecily's independent household was included in the regulations of the *Ryalle Book* suggests that at this point it was understood as an extension of the king's own estate and display.[119] The particular distinction given to Cecily and the king's siblings inevitably emphasized the contrast between Henry VI's tiny family and the seemingly more dynastically secure house of York.

Midway through the Christmas celebrations 'theire was the yeres mynde kepte of the duke off yorke rially on New Yeres even the masse'.[120] This was a Requiem Mass on the anniversary of Richard duke of York's death. Usually such services would be held in the church where the subject was buried. The parish hearse was covered with a pall and set up before the high altar, tapers burning at each end, while the funeral rites were repeated as they had been in the corpse's presence. In Clive Burgess's words, 'the dead were not so much remembered as "re-evoked", being brought before the living for prayer'.[121] Richard duke of York's year's mind took place in St Paul's Cathedral. Over £150 was spent on candles for this hearse, but further details about the preparation or who was present do not seem to have survived.[122]

It must have been a bittersweet day for Cecily as she looked back over her first year of widowhood and her dramatic change in fortune since York's death. The extravagance of this 'year's mind' and even of Cecily's Christmas festivities were no doubt intended to impress the king's subjects with the financial resources of the house of York and the authority that this implied. It was a fragile authority which Henry VI and his queen might yet reclaim. The first four years of Edward IV's reign would be dogged by Lancastrian challenges but they would also be the most powerful years of Cecily's life.

7

The King's Mother: 1461–1464

Cecill the Kyngis moder Duchesse of York To alle thoos that thees oure lettres shall see or here Greting.
                                    Letter written at Westminster 20 November 1461[1]

For the first four years of Edward IV's reign Cecily styled herself, as in the quotation above, 'king's mother, duchess of York'. There was no need for the more grandiose titles that she would adopt later. Not only was she fabulously wealthy, with all the power that naturally accrued to a significant landholder and head of a large household, but she was also the woman who could most easily influence the new young king of England. During this time most of Cecily's days were spent like those of other wealthy dowagers, managing her estates and household, pursuing her financial interests, promoting her family and members of her affinity, or engaging in the generous acts of charity and piety that were expected of nobility. The influence she exerted through conversations with her son naturally left scant trace in the historical record so we cannot know for how long Cecily maintained the political status that Francesco Coppini's correspondents had noted in the weeks after Towton. Nonetheless, her own letters and financial accounts combine with state and civic records and chance references to her household members to reveal a good deal of this highest point in Cecily's career. It emerges that she was actively involved in the administration carried out by the men in her service, and that she worked with the king both in helping to promote men whose power he wished to increase and in bringing former Lancastrians into his new regime. Conversely, she herself was courted by civic authorities who were conscious of her influence with the king.

Securing the throne 1462–1464

In the early part of Edward IV's reign much of his time was consumed in suppressing challenges to his recently acquired throne. Inevitably most of the plots against him impacted upon Cecily, too. In February 1462 Edward ordered the arrest of John de Vere, twelfth earl of Oxford.[2] Oxford had accompanied Cecily and Richard duke of York to France in 1441 along with his wife Elizabeth (one of Osbern Bokenham's patrons). With five other men, Oxford was now accused of 'high and mighty treason that they imagined against the king'.[3] All but one were executed on Tower Hill within days of their arrest. Among them was William Tyrell whose father had been Richard duke of York's receiver general. Custody of his lands and his son, James, passed into Cecily's hands.[4] Cautiously Edward had chosen not to attaint the traitors, presumably hoping thereby to achieve reconciliation with the men's families eventually. In the event, Oxford's heir, another John de Vere, reverted to his family's Lancastrian loyalties within a decade. However, James Tyrell grew up to be a loyal servant to Cecily's youngest son, Richard. It was quite common for lords who controlled lands during a child's minority to extract as much as they could from the property but Cecily opted, like Edward, for a conciliatory approach. On 6 March 1462, she sold James Tyrell's wardship for 'a token' £50 to his mother, Margaret, and to Margaret's feoffees.[5]

That October another serious threat arose when Margaret of Anjou landed a small army near Bamburgh Castle in Northumberland. Bamburgh, Alnwick and Dunstanburgh castles all welcomed the Lancastrian invaders. The constable at Dunstanburgh was Sir Ralph Percy, a son of Cecily's sister Eleanor. His family's traditional hatred of the Nevilles clearly continued to outweigh any sense of kinship with the new king. At news of Margaret's landing King Edward swiftly left his capital and marched northwards, gathering forces at such a pace that Margaret herself rapidly withdrew to Scotland. Percy's garrisons were reduced to eating their horses by the time he surrendered just before Christmas.[6] Edward took the risk of pardoning both Sir Ralph Percy and Henry Beaufort, duke of Somerset, who had fled from England after Towton but had returned with Queen Margaret the previous October.[7] On the journey back southwards, in company with Somerset, Edward stopped at Fotheringhay to commemorate his father in the collegiate church there.[8] Edward may have chosen to arrange this expensive month's mind then because his cousin, the earl of Warwick, was at the same time organizing a sumptuous reburial service at Bisham Priory for his own father Richard Neville, earl of Salisbury. Salisbury's widow, Alice Montagu, had died late the previous year and her coffin lay waiting in the sanctuary of the priory while the bodies of her husband and her son Thomas were solemnly removed from Pontefract and conveyed to Berkshire so that all three could be interred together on 15 February 1463.[9] Cecily's thirteen-year-old son George represented the royal family at Bisham in company with his sister and brother-in-law, the duchess and duke of Suffolk.[10]

Neither Cecily nor any of her sisters attended their brother's reinterment and it seems most likely that she remained in London throughout the winter.[11] At some point there must have been discussion about when Richard duke of York and their son Edmund would be similarly reburied. Cecily was only forty-seven so it would scarcely have been appropriate to follow the Salisburys' model and plan to rebury York when his widow died. Instead it seems to have been decided that York's work in building the church and cloisters of his ancestral college should be completed before he was laid to rest there. Richard Marks has suggested that Cecily herself played a central role in designing and overseeing the elaborate glazing scheme that was installed there during Edward IV's reign.[12] The basis for this argument is the fact that she owned the manor of Fotheringhay until 1469 and that the images in the glazing reflected her known religious interests. However, there seems to be no evidence that Cecily ever visited

Fotheringhay after her husband's death or that she bore any financial responsibility for the work at either the college or the castle.[13] Although Cecily received income from the manor, official records called it 'the king's castle of Fodrygnhey', Edward appointed one of his men as keeper of the castle in January 1464 and expenses for building work at the castle occur in accounts of the king's expenditure.[14] That said, it is not unreasonable to imagine that Edward discussed duke Richard's plans with his mother and that Cecily contributed her ideas to the final appearance of the college.

Edward continued his journey south from Northamptonshire in leisurely fashion but before he had even reached London, Cecily's nephew, Sir Ralph Percy, 'by fals colysyon and treson' had once again turned coat and handed the castles in his charge to Margaret of Anjou.[15] Edward did not turn back because he had summoned parliament to meet at Westminster that April and he needed the Commons to grant an aid for the defence of the realm. In May, while parliament was still meeting, Sir Ralph Grey also turned traitor and handed Alnwick Castle to the Lancastrians.[16] This Ralph was another of Cecily's kinsmen: his grandmother was her half-sister Alice who had married the Southampton conspirator Sir Thomas Grey of Heaton half a century before. King Edward's next few months were dominated by attempts to negotiate with both the French and the Scots in order to cut off external support for the Lancastrians.[17] Despite leading his forces as far as Yorkshire, Edward avoided battle, even after Henry duke of Somerset betrayed his trust and returned to support the Lancastrians. By the end of February 1464 Edward was back in London, negotiating a possible alliance with Castile.[18]

Ultimately it was again John Neville, Lord Montagu who defeated the Lancastrian threat. Percy was slain at Hedgeley Moor on 25 April.[19] Somerset and others were caught and executed following a second battle at Hexham on 15 May.[20] King Edward arrived in York and rewarded Lord Montagu with the Percys' hereditary title, earl of Northumberland. Within two months Montagu had received their confiscated lands too.[21] After generations of Neville–Percy feuding it appeared that the younger branch of the Nevilles had now emerged victorious in the north of England. Despite her Neville parentage it was a further blow to Cecily's sister Eleanor, countess of Northumberland, who had lost a husband and four sons in battle since 1454. Montagu swiftly recovered the castles of Alnwick, Bamburgh and Dunstanburgh. Cecily's great nephew, 'that fals traytur' Sir Ralph Grey, was taken to Doncaster and 'there hys hedde was smete of and sent to London, and hyt was sette a-pon Londyn Bryge'.[22]

Edward remained in the North and the Midlands throughout the summer of 1464 and as plague raged through London he arranged for his Great Council to meet in Reading that September. The news he brought to that meeting astonished his lords, scandalized the royal houses of Europe and realigned Cecily's identity once more.

Travelling as king's mother

While Edward was so often absent from London, Cecily too took the opportunity to travel outside the capital occasionally. Late in 1462 she visited Kent in company with her daughter Margaret and may have taken the opportunity to look over some of her properties there. When she reached Dover she was entertained in style by the mayor. Cecily and her household were also given gifts of wine and capons.[23] By December Cecily and Margaret were both in Canterbury where they joined the cathedral priory's confraternity.[24] The cathedral at Canterbury was considered, in Barrie Dobson's words, 'the most efficacious prayer-house in the kingdom' and it was regularly visited by royalty.[25] Among those buried in the cathedral were the founder of the royal house of Lancaster, Henry IV, and Richard II's father, Edward, the Black Prince. Richard duke of York had joined the confraternity long before, on his return from France in 1436.[26] Cecily's membership of their confraternity was inevitably a statement of her dynasty's investment in this politically complex institution, even if it was also an expression of her personal religious interests. Membership was a privilege sought by many nobles in the fifteenth century and the priory expected generous gifts or political support in return.[27] Cecily was well placed to offer both and indeed the prior and chapter may have encouraged her to join by giving her the right to present to St Denys, Bakchurch the previous year.[28] Canterbury's civic authorities were also keen to cultivate a positive relationship with Cecily. They gave her two horses (at a cost of just over 50s. for the pair) as well as various breads and a variety of wines, including Tyre, a particularly expensive and prestigious sweet wine from the Eastern Mediterranean.[29]

In October of 1462 Cecily was travelling through East Anglia. On 6 October she was at Stamford and a few days later received a royal welcome at Norwich where the mayor, sheriffs and aldermen all rode out to meet her accompanied by many men on foot.[30] She may well have travelled back via Clare Castle and seems to have been at Clare again the following autumn.[31] Her 1463 visit may have coincided with the funeral of her half-sister Margaret, Lady Scrope, who chose to be buried at Clare Priory.[32] Margaret's son, Alexander Cressener, would eventually enter Cecily's service on her estates in Essex.[33] Despite their age difference and the rivalry between the men in each branch of their family, it may be that Cecily still valued Margaret's kinship.

Like the civic authorities at Canterbury and Dover, the gentry families in East Anglia perceived Cecily's visit as an opportunity to further their own position in the locality. In November 1463 Margaret Paston wrote a letter to her husband suggesting that their daughter should be offered as a bride for the son of Cecily's chamberlain, Sir John Clay.[34] Clay of course had important roles in the king's service but Margaret referred only to his role in Cecily's household, presumably because it was his involvement in Cecily's East Anglian estates that most interested her. Unfortunately, despite being the same age as Cecily, Clay died in September 1464, and the wedding never took place.[35] Young Margery Paston later scandalized her parents by marrying the family's bailiff instead.[36]

Residence at Clare Castle would have given Cecily the opportunity to spend time at the college of Stoke by Clare where the new dean was a man who had long had connections with the house of York. He was William Wolflete, former master of Clare Hall, who had been confessor to the duke and duchess of York during the 1450s and was one of Richard duke of York's administrators in southern England.[37] Wolflete may still have been Cecily's confessor in her widowhood. Cecily was to remain an active patron of the college of Stoke by Clare throughout her life and a number of her surviving letters from the early 1460s relate to her interests there.[38] Strikingly one of these letters also sheds a rare light on her relationship with her son George at this time. She had written to the dean and canons recommending her servant, William Lessy, for the vacant office of verger at the college, but then rescinded the suggestion because George duke of Clarence wanted the post to go to his 'welbeloved John Davy'.[39] Cecily chose to endorse George's recommendation. Clearly George had persuaded his mother to abandon her own protégé for his. It is an early hint of the charm and persuasiveness by which George was to retain his mother's affections despite his reckless behaviour in the future.

Cecily must have made other visits to her properties during these years. A copy of a grant that was probably signed at Cheltenham in late April 1464 seems to be the only surviving indication that she ever visited her possessions in the Cotswolds.[40] She also stayed at the king's palaces such as Sheen where she was resident in the summer of 1464 while Edward himself was still in the Midlands.[41] She looks to have spent much of the 1460s in central London and Westminster. Her principal London residence was Baynard's Castle, the elegant 'inn' on St Paul's Wharf that had been built for Humphrey duke of Gloucester in 1428 and was very close to the king's Great Wardrobe on St Andrew's Hill. Baynard's Castle was not only Cecily's home but also the centre of her business affairs. It was here that the receivers of her lands brought their accounts and presumably here also that her treasury was kept.[42] Men paying homage for lands they held from her would be summoned to Baynard's Castle. For instance, on 22 March 1462 the London alderman, stockfishmonger and former sheriff, John Felde, came there to pay homage for the manor of Bromley Hall in her lordship of Standon, Hertfordshire.[43] Officials from towns associated with her properties would also meet here with her council, as various Bridgwater officials did to discuss 'the mater of the Castell Diche'.[44] The majority of her surviving letters for this period, be they on private business or letters patent, were produced either here or at the king's palace of Westminster. Her means of authenticating these letters are a valuable key to her sense of her identity at this time.

FIGURE 7.1 *Cecily duchess of York's seals.* (Left) *Engraving of her great seal from F. Sandford and S. Stebbing,* A Genealogical History of the Kings and Queens of England *(London, 1707), p. 374. Reproduced by permission of the University of Reading, Special Collections.* (Right) *Privy seal.* © *The British Library Board BL Add MS 16564. Reproduced by permission of the British Library*

Seals and signatures

By the later middle ages seals were in common use for authenticating letters among all landowning classes.[45] The earliest women to use them had been queen consorts and many married noblewomen used seals, despite their ineligibility to hold land independently. When women's seals first emerged in the twelfth century they tended to be oval in shape to accommodate the usual image which was that of a woman standing. However, when heraldic seals emerged for women in the thirteenth century they were the same circular shape as men's.[46] None of Cecily's seals have survived from before 1461. However, in the early 1460s she used a small seal which was almost certainly that which she had used during her marriage. It is less than 2 cm in diameter, with small sprays of foliage on either side of a shield that has a little foliage sprouting above it, too. On the shield are the arms of York impaled with the Neville saltire.[47] Since her husband had abandoned the York label on his arms in favour of the royal arms of England some months before his death it is surprising to find Cecily still using such a seal. It is hard to find an explanation other than sentiment and affection for her husband. This was the seal which had represented her marriage for over thirty years. Cecily mentioned a signet ring in her will which could have been her matrix for this seal. Such rings had become commonplace only in the fifteenth century and the design was usually engraved onto a semi-precious jewel.[48]

Like other major noblemen and (occasionally) women, Cecily employed more than one seal.[49] The small seal was her privy seal or signet. By contrast, the surviving version of her great seal measures a much more impressive 8 cm across.[50] Her mother's principal seal seems to have been a modest 4 cm and fifteenth-century noblewomen's seals were usually about 5 cm in diameter.[51] Joan of Kent's only surviving seal from her son's reign similarly measures 5 cm.[52] It gives her title as 'Joan, Princess of [Aquitaine?], Wales, Duchess of Cornwall and Countess of Cheshire and Kent'.[53] Cecily's great seal was actually wider than those of some previous queens, so it may have been in response to Cecily's seal that Edward IV's queen, Elizabeth Woodville, adopted a 9 cm great seal.[54] A seventeenth-century engraving of Cecily's great seal from 1463 does bear the royal arms of England undifferenced, again impaled with her father's Neville saltire.[55] Above the shield is a bird of prey, probably a falcon in reference to her husband's device of a falcon and fetterlock. Unfortunately, the title on this is largely missing. By 1477 her great seal, described in more detail in the following chapter, included her full title, concluding *matris reg[is] Edwardi quarti ducisse ebor'* (mother of king Edward IV, duchess of York).[56]

Like her seal, Cecily's signature may also have been a statement of her quasi-queenly status. Throughout her years as king's mother Cecily unusually signed herself simply with her Christian name. Most aristocratic women and men habitually included the place name from which their title derived in their signature.[57] Given her continued use of her earlier signet, Cecily's failure to use the York title in her signature is surprising. She may have been consciously emulating English queens such as Joan of Navarre and Margaret of Anjou for whom letters survive signed similarly with just a Christian name.[58] Elizabeth Woodville was to follow the same practice whereas the next king's mother, Lady Margaret Beaufort, took Cecily's innovation a step further.[59] Sometime after 1497,

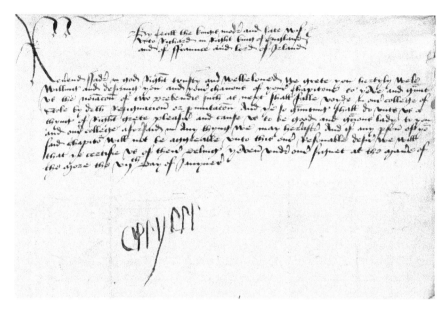

FIGURE 7.2 *Signed letter from Cecily duchess of York to the dean of Stoke by Clare. CCCC MS 108 p. 95. Reproduced by permission of the Master and Fellows of Corpus Christi College, Cambridge*

Margaret changed her sign manual from 'M. Richmond' to 'Margaret R', apparently playing on the possible double interpretation of the 'R' for Richmond or Regina.[60]

Margaret Beaufort also imitated Cecily in styling herself 'the king's mother'. Narrative accounts, particularly chronicles, had naturally used the phrase 'the king's mother' to describe women in the past, especially Joan of Kent. However, it was Cecily who turned this into a specific title in her letters and on her seals. Susan Johns noted in her study of twelfth- and early-thirteenth-century noblewomen's seals that these women never defined themselves as mothers, echoing Brigitte Bedos-Rezak's findings for France between the mid-twelfth and mid-fourteenth centuries.[61] No similarly detailed study has yet been undertaken for fifteenth-century England. Bedos-Rezak concluded that on seals maternity had been 'appropriated for, and thereafter exclusively reserved to, the Virgin Mary'.[62] Cecily appears to have had little interest in the possible theological implications of her decision to reclaim maternity for her own identity. As mentioned in the previous chapter, she never seems to have borrowed the iconography of the Virgin Mary which appears so commonly in images of late medieval queens. So it was the secular, rather than the spiritual, aspects of queenship that Cecily aspired to weave into her own identity through her title and splendid seal. At this time it was her son's position as king more than her husband's as rightful heir that created her sense of royal status. Her decision to innovate perhaps drew some inspiration from Humphrey duke of Gloucester who had styled himself 'son, brother and uncle of kings'.[63] Ralph Griffiths has suggested that Gloucester had been responding to the relatively new perception that the king's closest kinsmen comprised a distinct elite within noble society.[64]

It is a commonplace of medieval studies that identity was shaped by kinship and community. For Cecily, finding herself the widowed mother of children who were being treated as adults before their time, that kinship connection was potentially vulnerable. It needed to be restated with vigour. The community of her household and wider affinity enabled her to reaffirm that identity through widespread use of her heraldry, often in conjunction with emblems adopted by Edward IV. For instance Sir Henry Heydon, steward of her household, later included her coat of arms along with those of the king and queen in glazing either at his splendid new home at Wickham Court in Kent or in the church beside it.[65] Other churches associated with Cecily similarly bore her arms, including St James's Church in Oddingley, Worcestershire, which was one of the manors she had been granted in 1461. The church's fifteenth-century glass once included suns, roses and ducal coronets in the east window.[66] The little that remains now includes a shield of Cecily's arms that has been moved to the east window from the south aisle where it was originally paired with a slightly incorrect version of the Mortimer arms, flanking the royal arms of England surmounted by a sun.[67] That window seems to have been celebrating the fact that the church's dynastic patrons had produced a king of England. The emblems of Cecily and her son were not just a celebration of their authority but also a wordless request to viewers in this holy space to pray for them in life and in death.

Before the Great Fire of London, Cecily's arms were also depicted on the tower of St Benet's Church on St Paul's Wharf, behind Baynard's Castle.[68] Here the shield was supported by angels standing on roses-en-soleil. Edward IV himself often combined his white rose and sun in splendour badges in this manner. Consequently, at St Benet's Cecily's arms were again a celebration of her son as well as herself. They would have been seen by the many visitors and traders using St Paul's Wharf each day. They were also a reminder that Cecily's own centre of business was just a stone's throw away.

The household of the king's mother

As king's mother Cecily is likely to have headed a household of over a hundred men and women.[69] In the Inner Temple Library there is a seventeenth-century copy of a *Compendious Recytation* of regulations for this household.[70] The *Recytation* consists of four separate documents which give vivid details of the everyday running of Cecily's home. The first document, 'the order', is a summary of her daily routine, structured around religious services both in her chamber and her chapel. It is largely on this that her recent reputation for piety has been based even though, as mentioned in Chapter 2, it is actually very similar to the ideal noblewoman's day outlined by Christine de Pisan.[71] The second section is titled 'the rules of the house' and is largely concerned with the management of mealtimes, wages and the provision of food. For instance, most residents at her home were entitled to 'lyvery of bread ale and fyer and candle' but the fuel and candles were only available in full measure through the winter season (All Hallows until Candlemas) and were reduced to half measure in the weeks up to Good Friday 'for then expyreth tyme of fyre and candle also'.[72]

FIGURE 7.3 *Cecily duchess of York's arms as they appeared in a niche on St Benet's steeple, near Baynard's Castle, before the Great Fire of London. Reproduced from F. Sandford and S. Stebbing,* A Genealogical History of the Kings and Queens of England *(London, 1707), p. 388. Reproduced by permission of the University of Reading, Special Collections*

The 'rules' are followed by a record of officers' 'fees' which outlines privileges, such as the master cook's right to keep the skins of rabbits cooked for the household. It provides particular details of the important responsibilities of the purveyor of beef and mutton.[73] The final section was the 'Constitutions of the House' which listed punishment to be meted out for misdemeanours including late attendance at mass on a holy day or drawing a weapon in anger. Despite the presence of a small number of ladies and gentlewomen in her household, each of the rules referred only to men. The only reference to women was an injunction that 'no man misintreate any man his wife his daughter or his servant on payment of leesyng his servyse'.[74] The effect of this is to represent a world in which no woman, other than Cecily herself, was envisaged as an autonomous individual.

These ordinances were published in 1790, although the latter two sections were printed under the heading of Edward of Westminster's regulations rather than Cecily's.[75] The original documents on which the seventeenth-century copy was based appear to have been drawn up late in her widowhood and gathered in the form we now see during Henry VII's reign.[76] The 'order' possibly includes rather more time for prayer than would have been practical earlier in her widowhood, before her sons had died. Nonetheless, most of the document would have been broadly applicable throughout the last thirty-five years of her life. Those who composed it may have been drawing on the fashion for owning books of advice on household organization which had become increasingly popular towards the end of the Middle Ages. The earliest surviving treatise for a layperson was produced in the mid thirteenth-century by Robert Grosseteste, bishop of Lincoln, who adapted his own regulations on estate administration and household management for Margaret de Lacy, the widowed Countess of Lincoln.[77] Grosseteste's *Rules* clearly influenced generations of households since fourteen manuscripts survive, two of them from the fifteenth century.[78] Despite their dedication to the countess, these copies of the *Rules* were presented as being equally applicable to a 'lord or lady', indicating that a noble widow was expected to be able to run her estates and home with exactly the same authority as a man.[79] Cecily's *Compendious Recytation* is likely to have been particularly inspired by Edward IV's version of the *Ryalle Book* and perhaps his later *Liber Niger Domus Regis Anglie* as well as George duke of Clarence's *Ordinances*.[80] It appears that Cecily shared her sons' perception that formal written regulations were both a valuable tool in ordering a large household and an outward sign of an institution that was conducted with proper honour and wisdom.[81]

The persons in Cecily's household inevitably formed a fluid community. Like John Clay, most of the senior members had roles and responsibilities beyond Cecily's home. For instance, Lady Margaret Harcourt who accompanied her on her visit to Canterbury had her own household and husband to attend to.[82] Richard Gilmyn, who was also with Cecily at Canterbury, was the king's servitor and had been appointed one of Edward's sergeants-at-arms in August 1461.[83] Nonetheless, he continued to serve Cecily into the 1470s.[84] Such overlapping service must have helped Cecily to stay closely in touch with her son's affairs.

Cecily's choice of female companions in particular seems to have been designed to help in Edward's policy of conciliation. Among the women who accompanied her to

Canterbury there were several with previously Lancastrian connections. Lady Margaret Harcourt may well have met Cecily first when her husband, Sir Robert Harcourt, escorted Margaret of Anjou to England. Sir Robert had gained his pardon from Edward IV in February 1462 and swiftly became a loyal Yorkist.[85] Another companion was Isabella Browe who was almost certainly the wife of John Browe, a former member of the duke of Suffolk's affinity.[86] Browe had probably first come to Cecily's notice during the negotiations for her daughter Elizabeth's marriage and he had been pardoned by Edward IV in December 1461. However, unlike Robert Harcourt, John Browe's loyalty seems to have wavered again in 1469 and 1471. Edward IV nonetheless pardoned him on each occasion.[87] The value of such appointments was probably very similar to those illustrated in studies of waiting women at the Tudor court. These women's kinship networks enabled queens to spread their influence beyond their palace into the women's families while the noblewomen in turn were empowered by opportunities for patronage and the acquisition of 'gossip'.[88]

Not all Cecily's attempts at peace-weaving proved fruitful. Her principal lady at Canterbury was an Elizabeth Grey. There were many Elizabeth Greys among the nobility at this time, including a future queen and a granddaughter of John Talbot, earl of Shrewsbury. However, the woman most likely to have been Cecily's senior gentlewoman then was the widowed daughter-in-law of her half-sister Alice Grey.[89] Elizabeth had been one of Margaret of Anjou's daily attendants through the 1440s and probably the following decade, too, but her family did not flee England with the old queen.[90] Elizabeth's son Ralph appears to have fought for Henry VI at Towton but then swiftly committed himself to the Yorkists, probably encouraged by Cecily's brother, William Neville, Lord Fauconberg whose affinity he had joined a decade earlier.[91] By inviting Elizabeth Grey to serve in her household as her kinswoman, Cecily presumably hoped to encourage continued loyalty from the Greys. Edward instructed his followers in the north not to rob or trouble Grey's tenants on pain of death.[92] However, Sir Ralph's allegiance was easily swayed and, as noted earlier in this chapter, he ultimately lost his head at Doncaster. Wedgwood, in his *History of Parliament*, observed, 'it is difficult to explain Edward IV's tenderness to Sir Ralph Grey' or the speed with which his lands in Northumberland were restored to his widow.[93] If the Elizabeth Grey in Cecily's service was Ralph's mother, it may be that this 'tenderness' had been at Cecily's request.

There is a suggestion of a further, and even more surprising, rapprochement with a former Lancastrian lady in an addition to the Rous Roll. This states that Eleanor Beauchamp died at Baynard's Castle in March 1467.[94] Eleanor was the widow of Edmund duke of Somerset, who had been slain at St Albans, and mother of duke Henry who was executed at Hexham. Edward IV granted her annuities in 1463 and 1465 which indicates that she was not held responsible for her menfolk's loyalties.[95] Eleanor's apparent residence with Cecily is another indication of medieval women's capacity to set aside their menfolk's conflicts in their relationships with one another.

Naturally Cecily's household also included women whose families had long been in Yorkist service too. Joan Malpas seems to have remained in Cecily's service for most of her life. She was widowed early in Edward IV's reign and swiftly married John Peasemarsh whose family had also served the house of York for many years.[96] Katherine FitzWilliam, who retired from Cecily's service early in 1464, looks to have been connected to the FitzWilliams who had served Richard duke of York in Yorkshire.[97] Meanwhile, Agnes Walgrave, who was among those at Canterbury with Cecily, was possibly connected to the Yorkist Sir Thomas Walgrave whom Edward IV had knighted at Towton.[98] Other women in Cecily's service included the wives of some of her household men, like Katherine Holt whose husband Alexander was the sergeant of the duchess's pantry.[99]

Service in Cecily's household was clearly seen as a position that guaranteed influence in other avenues of life. One of her new yeomen of the chamber, William Cokys, took advantage of his confidence in his post to pursue an old grievance in the court of chancery. As he explained in his deposition, he had not previously dared to do so because his opponent 'stode grete in favour with the duke of Suff[olk]', Cecily's son-in-law.[100] Only now that Cokys was in Cecily's employ did Cokys dare to seek redress for a confidence trick played on him some years earlier. Cecily's household 'constitutions' stipulated that no member should go to court without the knowledge and advice of her council, 'on paine of loosyng his service'.[101] Cokys must therefore have acquired their permission, and presumably that of Cecily too, before using her name to guarantee a sympathetic ear from the chancellor. Some years later one of her tenants tried to use Cecily's name to similar effect when he explained to the chancellor that without redress he would be unable to pay the rent he owed to the duchess.[102]

Cecily's home would have housed regular visitors. There her family and friends would encounter gentlemen who served on her estates and acquaintances who needed to stay in London. Cecily evidently kept a lavish table. When the king decided to ban the import of wines from Gascony and Guienne in 1463, she swiftly petitioned for an exemption 'for hir owne drinking'. She acquired a license for her butler, factor or attorney to purchase sixty tuns of white or red wine from these regions 'at hir fredome and liberte'.[103] (The definition of a tun varied but these were presumably Bordeaux measurements according to which a tun was 210 gallons/954.7 litres.)[104] Cecily also acquired wine directly from the king. For Christmas 1464 he gave her six tuns of 'red wine of Gascony such as [to] her servant shall seem good and according to her mouth'.[105]

As Kate Mertes has argued, all medieval noble households functioned to some extent as religious communities, observing regular religious services in their private chapels, celebrating major festivals together and marking rites of passage in community. She suggests that these practices enabled families and their servants to bring God more closely into their personal lives, but that they also helped to create a cohesive and harmonious household and provided an attractive opportunity for showing off wealth and status.[106] Cecily's 'constitutions' indicate the importance she placed on this community activity: any man who arrived so late for matins on a holy day that he missed the third lesson would be condemned to the humiliation of eating nothing but bread and water for the next meal he attended in her household.[107] Because not all members would necessarily be present at major feasts, every man was required to bring a witness or a signed document to prove that he had been to confession and taken communion at Easter 'on paine of loosing of his servyce'.[108] This last regulation particularly suggests Cecily's sense of responsibility for the spiritual welfare of those in her service as well as concern to run a reputable household, much as Robert Grosseteste had advised Margaret de Lacy.[109]

Cecily's will gives some indication of the way her chapel similarly contributed to her honourable image in the way Mertes suggests. Some of the rich altar cloths and vestments that Cecily bequeathed had probably been acquired during her marriage and she presumably added to the collection throughout her widowhood. Those she deemed worth mentioning in her will included twenty-eight altar cloths, twenty-three copes and fourteen chasubles. Many of these were fashioned from materials such as crimson cloth of gold, embroidered white damask and embroidered blue velvet.[110] As Nicholas O'Flanagan's letter to Francesco Coppini from Cecily's household revealed, visitors as well as servants were expected to attend services in this splendid setting.[111]

Some of the clerics who served Cecily on occasion must, like her senior officers, have been men who were only occasionally present in her household. One such man was Thomas Candour (or Condover), a graduate of the university of Padua, whom the early humanist scholar Poggio Bracciolini described as 'a most cultured man and bound to me by close acquaintance'.[112] Candour had been a chamberlain to popes Eugene IV and Nicholas V and was an important scribe of humanist writings.[113] He had also been Richard duke of York's proctor in Rome so he may perhaps have been the man who first drew Richard and Cecily's attention to the work by Claudian that Bokenham translated.[114] For many years Candour drew an income as rector of the churches on York's manors at Pimperne and Tarrant Gunville on Cranborne Chase, lands which passed into Cecily's hands in 1461.[115] A papal letter of 1476 specifically referred to Candour as one of Cecily's chaplains as well as a chaplain to the king.[116] It is likely that he had remained in her affinity since York's death.

Estate management

Beyond Cecily's immediate household there was of course also the wider network of men who helped in the administration of Cecily's lands. The supervisor of her lands, Richard Quatremains of Rycote in Oxfordshire, was among those gentlemen who combined years of service for the king's mother with service to the king and with his responsibilities as a substantial landholder himself. He was one of four of her servants whose involvement in her early relationship with the borough of Bridgwater provides a helpful illustration of how her administration worked in practice. Her earliest receipts from her lands in Somerset and Dorset were delivered to Cecily on 10 July 1461 with a further instalment on 4 September. Several of her manors were somewhat in arrears but only Exmoor and Bridgwater had paid nothing at all.[117] Exmoor's fate is unrecorded, but on 20 November Cecily appointed her 'right trusty and wel-beloved servants' Richard Quatremains, William Brownyng, Thomas Aleyn and Stephen Preston to enquire into delays in payments from her property at Bridgwater. The men were to establish the names of the tenants who had not paid and who was responsible for reparations so that she might 'by the advise of oure Counsell purveye for Remedy'.[118]

William Brownyng of Melbury Sampford in Dorset was her receiver in Somerset and Dorset and, like Quatremains, a member of Cecily's council.[119] Brownyng had been York's receiver in the same counties from at least 1437 and in November 1453 Duke Richard had charged Brownyng to investigate the 'decay of his revenue from Bridgwater'.[120] The burgesses of Bridgwater were quick to refer Cecily back to Brownyng's report shortly after she became their lord. They reminded her that Brownyng had found that the rents due from Bridgwater had decreased by 25s. Optimistically they asserted that these had actually dropped a further 10s. since Brownyng's investigation and asked her to accept this and persuade the king to ratify the lower rent.[121] However, their failure to make any payment at all when Brownyng held his audit at Shaftesbury was behaviour that could not be tolerated. Cecily authorized Brownyng to send a stern letter to them demanding a fee that was only 20s. less than the traditional payment.[122] Clearly Cecily and her council were prepared to make some allowance for financial difficulties in Bridgwater but were also determined to show that she would be a strict lord. Brownyng concluded his letter to the town with a demand that the payment be given directly to the servant bearing the letter or else the reeve would be summoned for a reckoning 'that shall turn you to little ease'.[123]

Another of those appointed to investigate Cecily's Bridgwater income was her auditor Thomas Aleyn. The Bridgwater Borough accounts record that in 1462 they granted Aleyn a gallon of red wine, worth 10d., in his capacity as her auditor, which suggests that they had by then decided that conciliation was a wiser approach to their new lady than their earlier attempt to ignore her summons to pay on time.[124] The fourth investigator, Stephen Preston, was a Dorset man and a lawyer who would eventually stand as MP for Lyme Regis.[125] In November 1460 Richard duke of York had appointed him constable of Bridgwater Castle and keeper of the nearby deer forest, Petherton Park, an appointment confirmed by Edward IV on 24 July 1461.[126] He does not seem to have held other posts in Cecily's service, or indeed the king's, so was probably not on her council but his position as constable at Bridgwater naturally meant that he should be involved in pursuing Cecily's financial interests there.

Later receipts indicate that the officials in Bridgwater did manage their payments to Cecily eventually.[127] She subsequently had cause to complain that another lord with interests in the town, Lord Zouche, had received 40s. a year in 'casualtes' (payments due as a result of casual events) whereas she had received none, 'wheryn she fyndith her grevid'.[128] Nonetheless a sergeant-at-law negotiating with Cecily regarding the council's concerns about work that needed to be done on the castle ditch seems to have been relatively confident that they would 'haue good spede' in the matter.[129] The surviving evidence of Cecily's relationship with Bridgwater echoes Alan Rogers's conclusions about her lordship of Stamford.[130] In Stamford occasional disputes arose over financial matters but the borough council 'suffered little interference' in its day-to-day business.[131] In this Cecily was emulating previous medieval lords, although the situation in Stamford changed significantly when the lordship reverted to the Crown on her death.[132]

Bridgwater was perhaps not the only town that proved reluctant to start paying moneys owed to Cecily in the early part of Edward's reign. Letters were despatched from Westminster on 30 January 1462 to a variety of bailiffs, collectors and receivers reminding them of the letters patent issued the previous June and instructing them to backdate their payments to the time of Richard duke of York's death on 30 December

1460. These debts included more than £70 owed from Droitwich, over £289 from the port of London and £400 from the port of Kingston upon Hull as well as much smaller sums, like the £4 7s. 17d. owed from Chichester.[133] The port of London received another similar reminder three years later, as did Chichester and York in 1486.[134] As early as October 1461 the king had decided to supplement Cecily's immediate income by asking two men to collect all arrears and rents from farmers and tenants in a Buckinghamshire lordship that was currently in the king's hands and to deliver these to Cecily 'for her own use'.[135] One of the men appointed to this task was Richard Quatremains's nephew and heir, Richard Fowler, who often worked with his uncle.[136] Fowler was the king's solicitor and in the following year he became Chancellor of the Duchy of Lancaster.[137] He nonetheless continued to work for Cecily too until his death in 1477.[138]

The king was not the only lord who shared the services of Cecily's administrators. Richard Dalby of Brookhampton in Warwickshire regularly served the dukes of Buckingham and Norfolk, who were the families of Cecily's sisters Anne and Katherine.[139] In May 1463 Cecily appointed him to collect her knights fees in Buckinghamshire, Bedfordshire, Northamptonshire and Oxfordshire.[140] The steward of her honour of Clare in East Anglia was John Howard, a nephew by marriage to her sister Katherine duchess of Norfolk. (He was also the husband of one of Osbern Bokenham's patrons.)[141] Howard had been in the service of the Norfolk family for many years and acted as steward for a variety of lay and religious landholders. In July 1461 he had been appointed to several important positions in the king's service too.[142]

As Cecily's steward, Howard would have had to work with the dean of Stoke by Clare, William Wolflete, whom she appointed as surveyor of her estates in Suffolk, Essex, Cambridgeshire, Huntingdonshire and Hertfordshire.[143] Cecily's surviving letters to Wolflete all addressed him as the 'Dean of our College of Stoke', emphasizing her role as the college's patron and perhaps also her power over his position.[144] Cecily's letters to Wolflete, like her correspondence regarding Bridgwater, reveals her personal involvement in matters of land administration which she could have chosen simply to leave to her council. One of her letters to Wolflete complained severely that her 'lyvelode' in the counties under his jurisdiction had not been surveyed or approved as it should have been. Under threat of the 'perill that may ensue with our great displeasure and hevy ladyship' she demanded that he amend matters forthwith.[145] The language reflects Cecily's confidence that it was entirely appropriate for a noblewoman to demand this service, just as a lord would do, even from a highly respected churchman like Wolflete. It is perhaps worth noting that at the time that Wolflete resigned as Master of Clare Hall that college's finances were in a parlous state.[146] It is possible that despite his brilliance as a scholar Wolflete may not actually have been well suited to administrative roles and that Cecily had chosen him because of their other connections rather than because he was the best man for the job.

Like other senior politicians and landholders, Cecily was sometimes asked to hold land with other lords on behalf of their owners. In October 1462 Sir John Savile of Thornhill arranged for his manors of Eland and Tankersley to be delivered to Duchess Cecily, William Lord Hastings, Lord John Wenlock and others.[147] Savile had been chief steward of the manor of Wakefield and constable of Sandal Castle until December 1459, so he had probably encountered Cecily during her residence there as well as on business visits to her husband.[148] He would eventually become an important member of her son Richard's affinity in the north.[149]

Patronage

Many of the records of Cecily exercising ladyship at this period relate to her patronage of religious institutions. They reveal both her concern to continue the obligations of her husband's family and a particular interest in influencing the choice of clergymen on her own estates. However, on occasion her determination to provide well for men in her service was at odds with the interests of the church itself.

In 1462 Cecily nominated her chaplain John London as rector of Brinkworth in Wiltshire, presumably having been granted the privilege to do so by the abbot of Malmesbury.[150] Brinkworth bordered several of her own Wiltshire manors which explains her interest there. However, it was not the needs of the parishioners that attracted Cecily's attention. Rather, the church's revenues provided a good income for her chaplain who continued to attend Cecily in London and on her travels.[151] Presumably London had appointed a vicar to perform his duties in his absence. Naturally Cecily's involvement in church appointments was most often focused on her own estates. It was very likely during Edward IV's first parliament that Cecily despatched a letter on 4 December from the palace of Westminster appointing two of her clerks to be rectors at prebends in the patronage of the college of Stoke by Clare.[152] Because many of the manors in her possession were those from which the college's founder, Edmund earl of March, had endowed the college, she had a particular interest in choosing the men who would be rectors on those manors. Consequently, she provided rectors for Bisley in Gloucestershire and Great Dunmow in Essex throughout her life.[153]

Similarly, she ensured for herself the right to choose a clergyman for her Gloucestershire manor of Brimpsfield even though it should originally have been in Eton College's gift and later in that of St George's Chapel, Windsor.[154] Before the right was granted to Eton it had been kings of England who were patrons of the living, rather than the Mortimer lords of the manor. Cecily was apparently determined to use every opportunity for patronage that she could. She also seems to have been responsible for changing what had been a vicarage at Brimpsfield into a rectory so that the great tithes of the parish now went directly to the incumbent rather than to herself. In this context, a historian of Brimpsfield church has speculated that Cecily might have helped provide some of the important developments in the fabric of the church that occurred while it was under her patronage, including a new tower, two windows in the nave and a font 'decorated with carved quatre-foils, each with a rose centre'.[155]

She did not always consider clerical vacancies an opportunity to promote her own men. When the prior of Anglesey Priory in Cambridgeshire resigned in January 1462 she acceded to the subprior and canons' petition to choose their own leader. On 10 January, just two days after Prior Daniell's resignation, she sent a letter granting a licence for this election. Four days later John Wellys was elected as the new prior.[156] Cecily had been in London but the state of the winter roads between there and Cambridge did not delay this important business. Anglesey Priory, an Augustinian house like Clare Priory, may have been founded by Henry I but it had long been in the patronage of the de Burghs and the Mortimers.[157] Cecily had inherited her husband's family responsibility to protect the interests of this house which were clearly best served by allowing an existing member of the community to take the role of prior while she could be their advocate if required.

In light of her active involvement at Stoke by Clare, we might expect to find a similar engagement with Fotheringhay, the college where she would eventually be buried. In her will both colleges would be generously endowed. However, Edward IV had swiftly taken Fotheringhay under his own protection. Within a year of becoming king he had issued the college with a new foundation charter in which he, his parents, his brother Edmund and his paternal grandparents were added to those the canons were to pray for.[158] When he granted more properties to the college in August 1462 it was described as 'the king's college of Fodrynghey ... lately founded for the good estate of the king and Cecily his mother, and for their souls after death, and the soul of the king's father Richard, late duke of York'.[159] Cecily had the reassurance that the master, twelve chaplains, eight clerks and thirteen choristers there were praying for her without any need to become actively involved in its business.

The situation was very different for Folkestone Priory where Cecily became embroiled in a vitriolic dispute over the choice of prior even though her family had no history of patronage there.[160] Shortly before Edward IV became king, one of Cecily's chaplains, Thomas Banns, had been appointed prior at Folkestone.[161] However, Banns continued his service to Cecily in London. The local patron, John Lord Clinton, took advantage of Banns's absence to establish his brother-in-law, Henry Ferrers, in Banns's place. Banns enlisted Cecily's support in his attempt to regain his position. On 25 May 1463 Lord Clinton dispatched a letter to the mayor and leading citizens of Folkestone demanding that they should arrest the 'late pretended Priour' Thomas Banns if he should attempt to return to his position. Two days later Cecily wrote to these same authorities from Baynard's Castle, mentioning that 'my lord and son the Kyng, and also our cousin tharchebisshope of Caunterbury' were both writing on this matter too. Despite the distractions of parliament and alarming news of developments in the north of England, Cecily had found time to draw the king and primate into supporting the rights of 'oure welbeloved Chapellaine' and now she urged the mayor of Folkestone to carry out these men's instructions 'withe the more dilegence, at our especiall contemplacion'.[162] Lord Clinton, who was also in the capital at the time, must have been communicating with the king, Duchess Cecily and others of the king's council. His next letter assured the authorities at Folkestone that Edward and Cecily were on the point of changing their minds, although this was wholly untrue.

In the meantime, the would-be prior Henry Ferrers had appealed to the Archbishop of Canterbury's Court of Arches alleging that Banns was 'pretending himself to be a monk, wandering to and fro in the world as an apostate, notoriously excommunicated' and having confessed to sodomy.[163] Banns was duly summoned to appear before that court at the end of June. Nonetheless, it is apparent from Clinton's letters and from Archbishop Bourchier's that the mayor had been 'helping and assisting' Banns in accordance with the instructions from Cecily and the king. Throughout June Lord Clinton's letters became increasingly libellous, accusing Banns of 'certain felonies, treasons, insurrections, trespasses, robberies and riots' and then, like his brother-in-law, resorting to the allegation that 'Banns is a fals sodomyte, and for opene and proved sodomyte stante acursed, and may not be assoyled of no Bisshop in England … And alle that eet and drynk with hym are cursed'. He was still adamant that Cecily and the king were being misinformed and that by supporting Ferrers the mayor would ultimately find that he would 'plese the King and my Lady'.[164]

The archbishop's court eventually found in Thomas Banns's favour and he was re-established as prior. Banns remained in post until 1493 and the pope even permitted him to draw further incomes from the church of Hawkinge and the vicarage of Appledore in conjunction with his role as prior.[165] However, Banns also continued his role at court. This may initially have provided benefits for his churches, but increasingly his absenteeism led to a decline in discipline, the decay of buildings and rising debts at the priory. In 1480 he was called to the Court of Common Pleas to answer for a series of debts racked up through the 1460s. Coincidentally the attorney pursuing the case against him was also working for Cecily at the same time, so it may well be that Banns was no longer in her service by then.[166] Complaints were made about his ability to perform the office of prior in October 1491 although it was not until March 1493 that he was formally accused of using the receipts of the priory and parish church for his own use over the past thirty years, incurring personal debts under the conventual seal and allowing the priory buildings to fall into ruin.[167] Moreover, he was accused of having lived at Westminster, not setting foot in Folkestone Priory for over twenty years. On 2 June Banns was deprived of his office.[168]

Christopher Harper-Bill pointed out that Banns 'was not necessarily an evil man'.[169] It was not uncommon for the heads of religious houses to spend much of their time in royal service as administrators and often this was an advantage to the religious community there. But Folkestone was too small an institution to bear the expense of an absentee prior of this nature. Indeed, as early as April 1460 Banns had persuaded Pope Pius II that the profits from the priory were 'too slight for his support'.[170] In pressing Banns's case Cecily must have known that he would not be providing effective leadership for this house of God. She must also have known that he had a tendency to attract trouble since he had brought a case against the abbot of Westminster and others in May 1462 for beating and wounding him and imprisoning him in the abbey gatehouse for five days. Their defence had been that they were trying to bring him to justice for the theft of £24 from a certain John Gybon and threatening Gybon's life within the abbey sanctuary.[171]

Naturally Cecily's religious patronage continued to include provision of prayers for the well-being of her family. In April 1464, she allocated 40s. from her revenues in Hereford and Worcester for a chaplain to celebrate mass at St Andrew's Church, Droitwich, for the good estate of herself, her sons and daughters and for Richard duke of York's soul.[172] Like Oddingley, Droitwich had been associated with Edmund earl of March whose right to a large share of its fee farm had passed to Cecily.[173]

As yet there is no sign in the surviving sources that Cecily was interested in the role of pious widow that has been so commonly ascribed to her. She was still far more concerned with the kingdom of England than with the kingdom of Heaven and her very active patronage of churches and religious institutions was more about good ladyship and dynastic responsibility than devotion. Her potential for influence meant that service to her increased men's status, as Cokys and Clay both proved. Cecily was able to remain close to the king's affairs both by locating herself in or close to his palaces and through sharing his servants, many of whom had previously served her husband and were helping her to act as a confident and engaged administrator of the hereditary York and Mortimer lands.

Among the ladies of Cecily's household, previous political affiliations were more mixed. As a woman Cecily had a unique role to play in supporting her son's policy of conciliation by drawing previously Lancastrian women into her sphere of influence. In other circumstances this peace-weaving role might have been taken up by a queen. Between the spring of 1461 and the autumn of 1464 various ladies had been considered as possible queens: the dowager queen of Scotland, the child heiress of Castile and a sister of the French queen. Cecily was well aware that her position as the première lady in England could only be brief but the woman who eventually took her place in September 1464 took all England by surprise.

8

Wife of the Rightful Inheritor: 1464–1471

ye kinges mother obiected openly against his mariage, as it were in discharge of her conscience.

Thomas More, *Richard III*[1]

In September 1464, three and a half years into Edward's reign, Cecily ceased to be the most powerful woman in England. Her son Edward announced that he had made a secret marriage to the beautiful widow of a Lancastrian knight, Elizabeth Grey (née Woodville). Edward had chosen his wife not for her political value but for love. For a young king who had so recently seized the throne it was an astonishingly reckless act. Stories of Cecily's wrath at his marriage have been oft repeated and have become central to her posthumous reputation. Yet the details of those stories are highly contentious. After the king's marriage, Cecily remained a central figure in the royal family, constructing a new role and an identity for herself that emphasized her late husband's status as much as her son's. She also developed her interests beyond the court and was supported in this by the king. However, the security of her position was threatened once more when her son George allied with the earl of Warwick in a series of rebellions which eventually deposed Edward IV.

News of Edward's marriage

Edward made his dramatic announcement at Reading Abbey where he was meeting his Great Council in order to discuss changes to the coinage. When his councillors pressed him to decide on a proposed marriage alliance with France he revealed that he already had a wife, the widowed daughter of Jacquetta duchess of Bedford and Richard Woodville, Lord Rivers. Inevitably the news was greeted with astonishment. Venetian merchants who were in London when they heard the news subsequently reported that 'the greater part of the lords and the people in general seem very much dissatisfied at this, and for the sake of finding means to annul it, all the peers are holding great consultations in the town of Reading, where the king is'.[2] Cecily is unlikely to have been in London at that time since the merchants also reported that 'the plague is at work there, at the rate of 200 per day'. Possibly she was in Reading herself because the only other source that mentions attempts to annul the marriage, Thomas More, cites Cecily as the principal instigator. Whether such attempts were really being made in September 1464 remains unclear, but by the end of the month Edward's marriage had been formally accepted. In a ritual designed to compensate for the absence of a public marriage, George duke of Clarence and Richard earl of Warwick formally escorted Elizabeth into the abbey church where she was 'openly honoured as queen by the lords and all the people'.³

Elizabeth Woodville was the first English-born queen of England since the Norman conquest, an achievement that Cecily herself once had reason to hope for. Elizabeth's father's comparatively low social status and her previous marriage to a Lancastrian knight meant that many considered her a highly unsuitable queen. Some even believed that 'royal custom in England demand[ed] that a king should marry a virgin'.⁴ Unfortunately the controversial nature of the match swiftly led to romantic stories that further obscure the poorly recorded circumstances of the event and consequently of Cecily's response. Sometime around 1470 a story emerged that the secret marriage had taken place on a day especially associated with romantic love, 1 May.⁵ This is still the date most commonly recorded in histories, implying that Edward had concealed his marriage from his family and his lords for over four months. Such deception would surely have added to their anger. However, Michael Hicks's research indicates that the wedding is highly unlikely to have occurred before mid-August and very possibly only days before the announcement.⁶

Cecily as mother-in-law

There are two records of Cecily's immediate response to Edward's marriage, both of them unusually detailed for narratives of moments in her life. However, both stories emanate from very problematic sources which probably reveal more about contemporary ideas on nobility and marriage than they do of Cecily herself. The earliest was written by Dominic Mancini after his visit to England in the fevered summer of 1483 as the citizens of London struggled to understand how Cecily's son Richard came to be taking his nephew's throne. Mancini's story was that when she heard of the marriage Cecily 'fell into such a frenzy, that she offered to submit to a public inquiry, and asserted that Edward was not the offspring of her husband the duke of York, but was conceived in adultery, and therefore in no wise worthy of the honour of kingship'.⁷ For a king's mother to impugn her own reputation in this way would have been staggering. Not only would it have cast Cecily herself as a woman without virtue but it would also have made a mockery of Richard duke of York, a man who could not control his own wife. It seems most likely that Mancini's informants were conflating more recent gossip about Edward's legitimacy with older memories of the sense of scandal surrounding Edward's marriage. In doing so they were responding to contemporary ideas about the source of noble character: a man of royal blood should be inherently incapable of demeaning himself by marrying a woman of low birth (despite the many recent *mésalliances* in the English royal family or indeed the contradictory role the narrative demanded of Cecily in which, outraged by her son's ignoble behaviour, she reveals her own). Had Cecily really made such statements in public it is scarcely likely that they would have been unrecorded by the ambassadors gossiping in 1464 or indeed by the earl of Warwick as he challenged Edward IV's kingship five years later. Cecily could not have imagined that it would be to anyone's benefit for Edward to be replaced on the throne by his fourteen-year-old brother George at this point.

It was commonplace in medieval narratives for women to be twisted into implausible roles by authors who were actually only interested in the men in their story. Much the same had happened to Isabeau of Bavaria in the 1420s in the wake of the Treaty of Troyes. This treaty had disinherited Isabeau's son, the future Charles VII, in favour of Henry V of England and it was rumoured in Burgundy that in the process Isabeau had acknowledged that her son Charles was illegitimate. However, Charles VII's historiographer, Jean Chartier, was adamant that Isabeau had fallen ill as a consequence of these wicked 'English' smears on her virtue.[8] It may well be that rumours of Isabeau's imagined confession had helped to shape gossip about Cecily among London's continental communities in 1483.

The second account of Cecily's reaction occurs in Thomas More's *History of King Richard III*. More was writing in the early years of Henry VIII's reign, almost half a century after Edward IV's marriage. The unfinished *History* was a study of tyranny and the corrosive effects of fear and disharmony. Like Mancini, More drew upon contemporary gossip as well as reports from men and women who had known Richard III and his family.[9] More's lack of interest in historical precision combined with the impact of the passage of time on his informers' memories to provide a bewildering mixture of glaring errors and occasional surprisingly accurate minor details. It is consequently a minefield for historians. Since More's description of Cecily has been so influential, it cannot be ignored. His account of Cecily's outrage was very different from Mancini's. More imagined Edward consulting his mother before the marriage, upon which Cecily soberly advised that Elizabeth was wholly unsuited because she was the king's subject, a widow, and her social status was too low, whereas it was a king's duty to marry a foreign noblewoman who would bring allies and wealth to his realm. Edward answered 'as he that wiste himself out of her rule' that he intended to marry Elizabeth anyway. Edward argued that God had surely inspired the couple to love for a reason, one of his kin could just as easily seal a foreign alliance with their marriage on his behalf, and as king he should be at liberty to choose his own wife. He added that because Elizabeth was a widow with children he knew her to be fertile. Cecily was unpersuaded and 'shee deuised to disturbe this mariage, and rathr to help that he shold mary one dame Elizabeth Lucy, whom ye king had also not long before gotten with child'.[10] According to More, despite Cecily's attempts to persuade Elizabeth Lucy to claim that she had secretly married the king, the girl confessed under oath that she had slept with Edward in hopes of marriage but that this had never occurred.

Michael K. Jones has speculated that the eloquent argument was inspired by a genuine quarrel which the king had later mentioned to his mistress, Elizabeth (Jane) Shore. Shore, he suggests, then shared the story with Thomas More.[11] More's account of the argument reiterates the contemporary perception that Cecily was a valued adviser to her son who had once been able to 'rule' him, or expected to. His story also echoes Mancini's belief that the most adamant opponent of Edward's marriage was his mother. However, it makes no sense to imagine that Cecily would have tried to undermine her son's marriage to the widowed daughter of a foreign duchess in favour of a gentlewoman who had been foolish enough to bear the king's child out of wedlock. Understandably Jones ignores this part of the tale which had surely been concocted as a means of ridiculing Richard III's later assertion that Edward IV had secretly married Lord Talbot's daughter, Eleanor Butler. Ultimately More's story, like Mancini's, includes too much fabrication for us to be wholly confident that any of it is true.

There is frustratingly little contemporary evidence by which to judge Cecily's relationship with Elizabeth Woodville. The dating clauses of Cecily's letters suggest that she was no longer to be found at Westminster as often as she had been, but this does not indicate any falling out with the king and queen. Widows rarely lived with married children in any noble household at this period.[12] Joan of Kent's biographer, Penny Lawne, points out that when Richard II married Anne of Bohemia, his mother withdrew from court into retirement, and she argues that this was 'entirely voluntary'.[13] The exceptionally politically active Isabelle of Portugal, duchess of Burgundy, withdrew from court shortly after her son Charles the Bold married Isabella de Bourbon even though her own husband, duke Philip the Good, was still alive. Isabelle was by then in her late fifties and had apparently chosen to emulate her saintly ancestor Queen Isabelle of Aragon by devoting herself to 'meditation and charitable works' now that her adult son was married.[14] Isabelle nonetheless still visited court for major occasions, such as her son Charles's subsequent marriage to Cecily's daughter Margaret in 1468.[15] By contrast, Margaret Beaufort's failure to make way for her daughter-in-law, Elizabeth of York, attracted adverse comments from both Englishmen and foreign visitors.[16] Cecily's lower profile role after 1464 probably indicates nothing more than her respect for aristocratic and royal tradition.

Cecily did not formally attend Elizabeth Woodville's coronation ceremony or banquet on 26 May 1465 or indeed her churching after the birth of her daughter Elizabeth less than a year later.[17] There is no obvious precedent that might be used to judge whether this was a matter of etiquette. Neither of Cecily's married daughters attended the churching and Anne, like Richard duke of Gloucester, missed the coronation too.[18] Nonetheless, Cecily was certainly present at court in February 1466 since she was the princess Elizabeth's principal godmother alongside Jacquetta duchess of Bedford and Richard earl of Warwick.[19]

Even if Mancini and More were right to assume that Cecily was initially angry at Edward's misspent opportunity, this need not mean that the women loathed each other for the rest of their lives. Indeed, Cecily appears to have provided one of her longest serving ladies, Joan Peasemarsh, to help establish the queen's new household and to guide the queen in her new role.[20] Cecily may have offered further support by giving the new queen her copy of Christine de Pisan's *Cité des Dames*. There is no record of when this book passed into the royal library. It seems unlikely that Cecily would have given it to Edward. Records of events in 1471 also imply that the relationship between the queen and the king's mother was at least cordial, which is scarcely surprising given their families' history.[21] In 1444 Cecily (or her husband) had chosen Elizabeth Woodville's mother, Jacquetta, as godmother for their own daughter Elizabeth. Once king, Edward had swiftly brought the Woodvilles into the Yorkist polity and given

Elizabeth's father a place on his council. Early reports of Edward's marriage assumed that Edward had come to know Elizabeth through socializing in London.[22] Despite Richard Woodville's significantly lower status, the new queen and her family still belonged to the same social circles as Cecily, read the same books and must have patronized the same merchants and craftsmen.[23] In many ways there was a greater chance for a positive relationship between Cecily and Elizabeth than there would have been with proposed foreign brides such as Mary of Guelders or Isabella of Castile.

After the initial shock, most of the royal family seem to have been happy to integrate the new queen and her family into their own. The situation in 1464 echoed that of a century earlier when Joan of Kent had married Edward of Woodstock, the prince of Wales. Joan's children from her previous marriage were very like Jacquetta's in that their father had been a mere knight. Nonetheless Joan's Holland offspring made glittering marriages, including two into European ruling houses and her son John married Elizabeth of Lancaster, daughter of John of Gaunt, thereby founding the dynasty to which Cecily's prodigal son-in-law Henry Holland belonged.[24] Many of those who married into Elizabeth Woodville's family in the 1460s were clearly taking advantage of the opportunity to bind themselves closer to royalty after the recent political upheavals.

Cecily's nephew, Richard earl of Warwick, was later widely believed to have taken a different attitude and eventually been driven to rebellion by the marriage. But, as Michael Hicks has argued, this is an oversimplification. He was 'disappointed, even dismayed ... but he was not humiliated by public promises about Edward's marriage that he could not keep ... He recognized at once that he must make the best of the king's choice'.[25] He did object to those Woodville marriages that limited the options for his own family's dynastic alliances but this did not irreparably damage his relationship with the king. Despite the fact that Edward now needed lands with which to endow his dowerless queen and was expected to help provide for some of her family, Cecily's property holding was unaffected. Indeed, when an act of resumption went through parliament early in 1465 the king instructed the queen's father to deliver a proviso clause for Cecily's possessions to be completely exempt once again.[26]

'Wife of the rightful inheritor'

Whatever her feelings had been about Edward's choice of wife, it was inevitable that Cecily would need to construct a new identity for herself. Hitherto she had often omitted her title as duchess of York, styling herself simply 'the king's mother'.[27] However, in the 1465–6 entry of his *Abbreviata Cronica* John Herryson of Cambridge noted that the duchess of York had begun to style herself 'By the ryghtful enheritors Wyffe late of the Regne off Englande & of Fraunce & off ye lordschyppe off yrlonde, the kynges mowder ye Duchesse of Yorke'.[28] It was perhaps not such a directly self-aggrandizing title as that bestowed on her by the prior and chapter at Canterbury a few years earlier, but it made it clear that Cecily should have been queen. In practice, she used a number of variations on this style, all serving both to emphasize her own significance and to reiterate her son's inherited right to be king. In light of Edward's

FIGURE 8.1 *Great seal of Cecily duchess of York. Reproduced by permission of the Society of Antiquaries of London*

recent rash and arguably ignoble marriage it may be understood as an attempt to strengthen his position as well as her own.

This title eventually appeared on her great seal. By the mid-1470s and probably earlier the falcon above her shield wore a ducal coronet. Two more heraldic beasts supported the shield itself. One was clearly the lion of Mortimer that Richard duke of York had used as a supporter on his great seal.[29] The other has previously been identified as an antelope ducally gorged.[30] However, it has branched antlers like the stag on the collar worn by her father and brothers in the painting of the Neville family at prayer, or the Markenfield Collar. Moreover, below the crown around its neck hangs a chain, very like that worn by the white hart used by Richard II on the Wilton Diptych and elsewhere. In a Yorkist genealogical chronicle produced in Coventry early in Edward IV's reign the white hart seems to represent Edward's family as a whole, apparently symbolic of the family's position as the rightful heirs of Richard II.[31] A sumptuously decorated genealogy that was probably produced at Edward IV's accession likewise bears Richard II's white harts along with the black bull of Clarence and the white lion of March.[32] Richard II's mother's very similar emblem, a white hind, had been used for Richard duke of York in the manuscript of *De Consulatu Stilichonis* where it appears among falcons, fetterlocks, white roses and a dragon.[33] It is consequently most likely that Cecily's seal was deliberately evoking Richard II's distinctive badge. The seal was designed to remind every witness that the sender belonged to the true royal line of England. A scroll issuing from the falcon's beak read in Latin 'the seal of the lady Cecily, wife of the true heir of England and France and lord of Ireland, mother of King Edward IV, duchess of York'.[34]

Business as usual

Now that Cecily was spending less time at Westminster she was more often to be found at Baynard's Castle, a short boat ride away. In March 1467 Edward arranged for repairs to be carried out 'for the pleasure of oure moost derest lady and moder' at his manor of Kennington, not far from Westminster. He had just granted her the manor to use as her own residence.[35] The palace at Kennington had originally been built by Edward of Woodstock, Richard II's father, and archaeological excavations indicate that the complex included elegant chamber suites in a private garden that separated them from the public space of the great hall and more functional rooms.[36] In 1472 Edward IV paid for further building work at Kennington, including a new chapel to be built at the manor.[37]

Cecily was conducting business from Kennington in May 1468 and again that November, so she may well have spent much of that year in residence there.[38] At other times she used houses near London that were not her own, such as Merton Priory from where she wrote a letter to the mayor of Windsor one autumn.[39] It is possible that she travelled widely around her estates but the surviving evidence for her travels relates principally to East Anglia and the South East. For instance, she probably spent one Christmas near St Albans since she sent a letter to William Wolflete from the Manor of the More dated 7 January.[40] The More belonged to St Albans Abbey but had been leased to Cecily's nephew George Neville, archbishop of York and the king often visited him there.[41]

She spent time at Clare Castle in the summer of 1465 and presumably on other occasions, too.[42] In the summer of 1467 she apparently became involved in helping one of her widowed tenants in Sudbury, near Clare, who had received unwelcome marital advances and subsequently threats on her property from a man called Benet.[43] The following July Cecily's son Richard was in Colchester and Anne Crawford has suggested that he was then most likely on his way to or from visiting Cecily at Clare.[44] That same summer she had significantly extended her landholdings in the region when the king granted her some 600 acres of pasture, woodland and meadows including the manors of Newhall and Greys and a watermill in Cavendish all of which Richard duke of York had previously held. At the same time Edward granted her a court of honour, every three weeks, just over the Essex border in Stambourne, and 'a cottage called "le Courtehouse"' in the same town.[45] The Stambourne court of honour had operated for neighbouring tenants of the honour of Clare since the early fourteenth century, hence Cecily's interest in holding jurisdiction here.[46]

Her impact on local politics on her estates has left little trace for the first half of Edward IV's reign. Unlike the dukes and duchesses of Suffolk, Norfolk and Oxford, her name rarely appears in the Paston letters. This is perhaps in part because the majority of her East Anglian manors were further south and west than the Pastons' own interests. It may also have been that Cecily's possessions were too widespread for her to operate in the way that Alice Chaucer or Elizabeth Talbot did. Since women could not exercise the judicial or military authority used by men it is unsurprising that the king did not try to look to his mother to exercise royal authority in the localities as he did with Richard earl of Warwick, William Lord Hastings, Sir Walter Devereux, William Lord Herbert or other trusted men.

Edward nonetheless continued to reinforce his mother's financial rights through the 1460s, sending out letters reminding those who owed her money.[47] When the ports of London and Kingston upon Hull persistently failed to provide income due to her from customs he instead granted her the right to ship large quantities of wool without paying customs and subsidies, which proved a much more effective means of increasing her income.[48] Cecily in turn worked with Edward. In March 1465 she appointed his councillor, Sir Humphrey Stafford, Lord Stafford of Southwick as constable of Bridgwater Castle and keeper of her park at Petherton.[49] Edward had been steadily building up Stafford's power in the west country, apparently intending Stafford to function as the crown's principal representative there. This arrangement meant that the man who owed his place at Bridgwater to Cecily was especially high in the king's favour and so should have been able to serve her interests well, too, although Stafford was to prove unpopular with the people of Somerset.

A more significant example of the king's involvement in Cecily's properties was his continued use of Fotheringhay Castle as if it were his own. Edward regularly stayed at the castle and in March of 1464 it had been the king, not Cecily, who appointed Guy Wolston to the posts of constable and receiver of Fotheringhay Castle and lordship. This grant also made reference to a garden and spinney 'which the king has made to enclose the little park of Fodringhay'.[50] In February 1469 they finally regularized this situation when Cecily formally restored all her rights and title in the manor of Fotheringhay to the king.[51] Edward nonetheless reaffirmed her appointee as porter there a few months later.[52] Days after she had surrendered Fotheringhay, Cecily was recompensed with a much more practical grant of the castle, manor, lordship and honour of Berkhamsted and the manor of Kings Langley, both in Hertfordshire.[53] There is no surviving evidence that Cecily in any way resented this arrangement in the way that Margaret Beaufort very clearly baulked at her son's decision to make her exchange her house at Woking for Cecily's former home at Hunsdon in 1503.[54] Cecily does not seem to have used Kings Langley, a former residence of Joan of Navarre, but after 1471 Berkhamsted Castle became Cecily's favourite residence.[55]

Berkhamsted was one of the foremost towns in Hertfordshire, having developed as an important centre of trade because of its position on Akeman Street and like Clare it enjoyed a flourishing wool trade.[56] The castle there had once been the home of an earlier queen mother, Henry III's mother, queen Isabella. Thereafter the manor had belonged to various queens who were probably not resident before it came into the possession, like Kennington, of Edward of Woodstock. A survey of Berkhamsted Castle in 1336 indicated that at that time it was in a very poor state of repair, the great tower was split in two places with its roof leaking, many of the gates were much decayed and even some of the elegant interior rooms were in serious want of attention. In 1361 Edward of Woodstock decided to house his royal prisoner, King John of France (captured at Poitiers) in Berkhamsted Castle. Accordingly he arranged for repairs and refurbishing to make it a suitable prison for a king.[57] Richard Barber judged Berkhamsted 'one of the prince's favourite residences'.[58] During Richard II's reign Cecily's great uncle, Geoffrey Chaucer, was clerk of the works there.[59] The house does not seem to have been used much by the Lancastrian kings or their queens but it was evidently kept in sufficiently good repair to be used as a royal residence on occasion since Henry VI stayed there in September 1437 and again in May 1444.[60] It is likely that Cecily herself paid for any repairs and refurbishments when she took possession in 1469 but records for this do not survive. Certainly, Cecily had wealth enough from her other estates to restore this royal residence appropriately.

Cecily and the wool trade

One of Cecily's most valuable sources of income was the sale of wool. On 7 July 1468 Edward granted her, or her factors or attorneys, the right to ship 854 sacks and bales of wool over the next two years through the ports of London, Sandwich or Southampton without paying customs or subsidies, and to take them not to the Calais staple but 'by the straits of Marrok'.[61] Thereafter she was permitted to ship 258½ sacks and bales annually 'in like manner'.[62] The grant included a provision that the king would eventually provide the equivalent income from elsewhere, but in practice this arrangement continued beyond his death and was reiterated by his successors. The arrangement must have related to wool bound for Italy as the fine wool trade with Italian city states was one of only two exceptions to the rule that all English wool should be traded through Calais.[63] Most of this Mediterranean wool went via Southampton or Sandwich although Cecily certainly used London too to send some of her wool on this route in 1468.[64] The 259 sacks that she shipped through Southampton in 1479 were perhaps pushing her quota of tax free exports a little over its limit. But in 1481 she shipped 333 sacks from the same port, so must have been paying customs on some of these.[65] Her wool for Calais of course also continued to incur customs and subsidies and indeed in 1468 her attorneys paid just over £200 to ship 52½ sacks to Calais, an indication of just how much Cecily was saving on her exports through the straits of Gibraltar as a result of Edward's grant.[66] No other noblewoman seems to have been exporting wool on anything approaching this scale.

Like the king and many other landowners, Cecily granted the business of shipping her wool to foreign merchants. These included one Pietro de Furno, who probably came from Genoa. He transported 180 sacks of her wool from London in August 1468.[67] Most of her attorneys, however, appear to have been Venetian, including Marco de Pesero, Stefano Contarini and Ludovici Malumbere.[68] Another Venetian attorney who served not only Cecily but also her daughter, Margaret duchess of Burgundy, was Hieronimo Contarini.[69] These arrangements meant that most of Cecily's wool was normally taxed at alien rates, which were higher than those for English merchants.[70] The value of wool varied across the country with Shropshire and Cotswold wool bringing in the highest rates (up to 14 marks per sack) whereas the wool from Cecily's Suffolk manors was worth only about £2 12s. a sack.[71] Cecily's forerunner as Lady of Clare, Elizabeth de Burgh, had established flocks in Suffolk and Essex in the 1330s and sold this wool for the cloth industry in England.[72] Cecily may well have done the same although the local cloth trade had declined somewhat since Elizabeth de Burgh's day. Cecily's particular interest in the churches of her Cotswold manors was very likely to some degree influenced by her appreciation of their community's wool. Her special affection for St John the Baptist may have been enhanced by the fact that he was a popular dedicatee of Cotswold churches because their wool fairs began on his feast day.[73]

Warwick's first rebellion

In the autumn of 1468 Cecily was fifty-three years old and at last had reason to hope that she had attained a position that could be maintained for the rest of her life. Despite local disputes and the occasional arrest of Lancastrian plotters, Edward had now successfully held onto his throne for more than seven years. That summer Cecily's youngest daughter, Margaret, was finally married with exceptional pomp and splendour to Charles duke of Burgundy, a far more prestigious match than either of her sisters had made. Surprisingly, among the many detailed reports of that event on both sides of the channel, there is no mention of Cecily herself. Perhaps she was unwell. It is hard to imagine that there was any political reason for her absence from the match which she had helped lay the ground for when she despatched her youngest sons to Burgundy seven years earlier.

Yet behind the mask of brilliant display, Edward's kingship was under strain. Richard earl of Warwick escorted Margaret on her wedding journey through Kent, but he had refused to be a guarantor of her dowry because he preferred an alliance with France.[74] This difference over foreign policy led to increasing tensions between Warwick and the Woodvilles who were enthusiastically promoting the Burgundian alliance and opposed any treaty with France. King Edward consistently tried to reconcile Warwick to his policies and even promised a marriage between Warwick's nephew, George Neville (John Lord Montagu's son), and his eldest daughter Princess Elizabeth.[75] However, the king forbade marriage between Warwick's daughter, Isabel, and his own brother, George duke of Clarence. Edward may well have been hoping to use Clarence's marriage in his foreign diplomacy but both Clarence and Warwick deeply resented this high-handedness. In these disputes lay the beginnings of the next turn of fortune's wheel for the house of York.

Cecily's role in the upheavals of the summer of 1469 is tantalizingly obscure. That March she had enjoyed the role of godmother to her new royal granddaughter and namesake, the Princess Cecily.[76] The next record of Duchess Cecily's activities is at Canterbury on 14 June.[77] She stayed the night there at the prior of Christ Church's lodgings with a small household. She then travelled to Sandwich where she joined men who were deeply discontented with the balance of power in England: her son George, duke of Clarence and her nephews, the earl of Warwick and his brother George, archbishop of York. As I have argued above, the surviving evidence does not suggest that Cecily had any reason for sympathizing with them. Conversely, it is unlikely that she was actually trying to dissuade Clarence and Warwick from rebellion since there is no indication that she knew they meant to rebel. The king seems to have been blithely unaware of their plotting and was at the time making a pilgrimage to Walsingham and Bury St Edmunds.[78]

If there was any political significance to Cecily's journey to Sandwich then it most likely concerned George's marriage alone. In light of the king's reckless love match it would be understandable if Cecily sympathized with George's desire to marry England's wealthiest heiress, her own god-daughter, Isabel Neville. Cecily remained at Sandwich for five days and then left her kinsmen in order to spend a further week in Canterbury.[79] On 6 July Clarence and Warwick sailed to Calais, where Warwick was Captain, and here George Neville, Archbishop of York solemnized the marriage between George duke of Clarence and Isabel Neville. It looks as if Cecily may have signalled her own support for the match by permitting her minstrels to contribute to their celebrations.[80] Shortly afterwards the lords in Calais issued a manifesto condemning 'the disceyvabille covetous rule and gydynge of certeyne ceducious persons' about the king, including the queen's parents and Cecily's constable at Bridgwater, Humphrey Stafford, who was now earl of Devon. The rebels summoned their supporters to meet them at Canterbury on 16 July 'defensabyly arrayede' to face the king and make him change his councillors.[81]

It was at Edgecote, near Banbury, that the rebels' forces met the king's troops, led by William Herbert, newly created earl of Pembroke, on 26 July. The royal forces were defeated and Pembroke was captured. Shortly afterwards the queen's father and her brother John (Katherine Neville's latest husband) were also seized and all three were executed at Northampton. Humphrey Stafford should have been with Herbert but the two earls had fallen out, apparently over their lodgings.[82] At news of the disaster at Edgecote Stafford tried to flee to the security of Cecily's castle at Bridgwater but was prevented by the townspeople who seized and, eventually, beheaded him.[83] Popular rumour claimed that Stafford had engineered the arrest and execution of Henry Courtenay, nominal heir to the forfeited earldom of Devon, earlier that year in order to acquire the earldom for himself and he seems to have been widely resented for his greed and his influence over Edward IV.[84] Nonetheless he was Cecily's appointee in Bridgwater so that the townspeople's action reflected poorly upon her authority. But this was surely the least of her worries for shortly afterwards the king himself was made a prisoner first at Warwick Castle and then at Middleham. Jacquetta duchess of Bedford was also summoned to Warwick Castle, accused of sorcery, apparently as a preliminary to dissolving the king's marriage just as Humphrey duke of Gloucester's marriage to Eleanor Cobham had been.

Initially Warwick tried to rule the country with Edward as his puppet king, but there were rumours on the Continent that Warwick planned to depose Edward IV by claiming that the king was a bastard and not the son of the duke of York.[85] This is the earliest record of that slur on Cecily's chastity. It occurs in a letter from the Milanese ambassador in France, Sforza de Bettini, written to the duke of Milan on 8

August 1469. It may have been no more than the gossip of the French court. Yet it is also quite possible that Warwick had indeed considered making his son-in-law king in this manner. Less than a decade earlier the earl had been credited with spreading similar rumours about Edward of Lancaster's illegitimacy in order to further the Yorkist cause.[86] At that time he was very much the enemy of Margaret of Anjou whose reputation he was trying to destroy. Cecily's reputation, on the other hand, seems to have been collateral damage.

Warwick seriously misjudged his own authority in England. Ironically it was the actions of Lancastrian sympathizers that ended the coup. Sir Humphrey Neville (grandson of Cecily's half-brother John) attempted to destabilize his hated kinsman by initiating a Lancastrian rebellion. Warwick was unable to muster sufficient forces to counter this without the king at his side and was forced to liberate Edward. Together they marched on the Lancastrians. Humphrey and his brother Charles were captured and executed at York. Edward's initial reaction to Warwick and Clarence's rebellion appears to have been to plan revenge, but he eventually decided (or was persuaded) that conciliation was still possible and preferable.[87] Cecily may have played a part in this reconciliation. It was the sort of role a royal mother would have been expected to take and the author of the *Great Chronicle of London*, writing early in the sixteenth century, believed that she was still engaged in trying to rebuild her sons' relationship after Warwick had left London early the following year. He recorded that Edward and George both stayed at Baynard's Castle with Cecily in early March and harmony seemed to have been restored but 'everych to othir made ffayre dyssymylid countenaunces'.[88] George had no intention of keeping the promises his mother was asking him to make.

The rebellion in Lincolnshire

On 6 March 1470, the royal brothers 'took theyr leve of theyr modyr' and left London together.[89] On that very day rebels who had been summoned on behalf of the duke of Clarence were gathering at Ranby in Lincolnshire. Clarence had taken advantage of local unrest in that county to whip up a rebellion that gave him and Warwick an excuse to ride at the head of armed men once again. They claimed to be trying to put down the rebellion, but they were actually planning to trap the king himself between armies.[90] Fortunately for Edward their plotting failed when Sir Robert Welles led a premature attack against the king at Empingham near Stamford on 12 March. Welles's forces were utterly inadequate and the battle became a rout. As the ringleaders were captured the king swiftly learned that this was far more than a local dispute, but 'theire porpos was to distroie the king, and to have made the saide duc [of Clarence] king'.[91]

Strikingly none of the surviving records from 1470 cited the king's legitimacy as an issue. It is quite possible that Edward ensured that there was no mention in official reports at the time but more likely that George preferred not to slander his mother's virtue unnecessarily, despite later allegations against him. Sir Robert Welles's confession suggests that the justification for rebellion was more akin to Henry IV's excuse for taking Richard II's throne: Clarence's yeoman of the chamber, a certain Walter, had allegedly persuaded the rebels that the king 'was aboute to distroie [the men of Lincolnshire] and all this realm'.[92] So Clarence was taking the throne for the common good. The means of disposing of the king was clearly to be death in battle.[93]

After this second failure, Warwick and Clarence decided not to attempt any further pretence of reconciliation with the king. They ignored his summons and began to prepare for a renewed assault from Calais. Edward was more cautious now, taking steps to thwart their flight. Eventually they managed to leave from Dartmouth with Warwick's wife and daughters but were denied harbour at Calais and had to seek sanctuary from the French at Honfleur.[94] Faced with the possibility of living their lives in exile, Warwick and Clarence instead made an extraordinary alliance with Margaret of Anjou, committing themselves to reinstate Henry VI as king. Never had the interests of Cecily's children been so divided.

The readeption

While Edward was in York, Warwick and Clarence landed in Devon on 13 September 1470 and swiftly gathered support.[95] Edward was wrong-footed when the previously loyal Marquess Montagu turned coat to join his brother the earl of Warwick.[96] Recognizing his limitations, Edward and some of his closest associates fled from King's Lynn to the Netherlands.[97] The queen, still in London, took sanctuary at Westminster Abbey. Cecily's youngest son, Richard duke of Gloucester, had been entrusted to the earl of Warwick for his education and lived in his household until shortly before the latter's first rebellion. However, as Charles Ross noted, seventeen-year-old Richard had shown an 'early independence of character' in not joining Warwick and Clarence in 1469.[98] According to a Cistercian monk at Les Dunes Abbey, after Warwick landed in 1470 Richard 'put up as much resistance as he could' but eventually he too escaped to join Edward at the Hague.[99] Henry VI had been incarcerated at the Tower of London since the summer of 1465, but in early October 1470 he was brought out to be king once more.[100]

As in 1459, Cecily chose not to flee. Presumably she felt sufficiently confident in her relationship with the duke of Clarence to expect to be unmolested by the returning Lancastrians. George took up residence, as his father had sometimes done, at the bishop of Salisbury's house, near Dowgate, and was 'the faction's representative at London' while Cecily remained at Baynard's Castle.[101] Strikingly, whereas George was forced to give up most of the lands previously granted to him by Edward IV because their earlier Lancastrian owners were back in power, Cecily's estates were untouched. George attempted to construct a new role for himself as duke of York yet he made no attempt to confiscate any of his father's hereditary lands from his mother.[102] Cecily seems once more to have been playing on the relative political neutrality that her gender allowed. Her officials tactfully dated their accounts for her at this time according to the year of grace, rather than entering that of either king.[103]

There were those who assumed that Cecily's influence had significantly decreased. Her tenant at the manor of Compton Bassett, Walter Breche, suddenly found his family's liberty under threat from his neighbour Robert Baynard in Hilmarton when the latter thought Cecily could no longer protect Breche from Baynard's claims that the Breche family were his bondsmen.[104] By contrast, those closer to the centre of power seem to have continued to see Cecily as an important influence. Lady Margaret Beaufort and her husband Henry Stafford (Cecily's nephew) saw the readeption as an opportunity to restore the fortunes of Margaret's fourteen-year-old son, Henry Tudor, who had previously been a ward of the recently deceased William Herbert, earl of Pembroke. It looks to have been for this reason that they were in London for several days in October, in November and again in December of 1470.[105] On each occasion their household accounts record frequent boat hire from and back to Baynard's Castle, suggesting that for some of their time in London they were staying at Cecily's home.[106] If so Cecily may well also have been party to Margaret's discussions with George duke of Clarence about Henry Tudor's potential claim to Clarence's honour of Richmond.

Cecily's relationship with Margaret Beaufort is an intriguing one. Michael K. Jones and Malcolm G. Underwood have argued that in later life Margaret consciously emulated Cecily's model of royal motherhood and that the women 'held each other in great respect'.[107] It is unclear how well they knew each other in 1470. They may have spent some time in each other's company when Cecily was in the custody of the duke and duchess of Buckingham in 1459 since Margaret had married Buckingham's second son, Henry, the previous year, very possibly at Maxstoke.[108] At that time Margaret was only a teenager, albeit one matured beyond her years by bitter experience. It is quite possible that Cecily and Margaret encountered each other on subsequent occasions when Stafford was attending Edward IV.[109] It seems likely that Margaret was close to her mother-in-law, Anne, duchess of Buckingham, who in turn was the sister with whom Cecily shared most. In Anne's will every named book was bequeathed to Margaret.[110] Indeed, it has become a commonplace of studies of women's book ownership to discuss Anne and Margaret's book sharing.[111] However, this perception relies on a suggestion that Anne lent books to Margaret during her lifetime.[112] The evidence for this is an entry in the Stafford household accounts for payment to two men to 'bring to my lady of Bukyngham Books & vestmentes fro Wokyng to London'.[113] Since they were being transported with vestments, these are most likely to have been liturgical books for the couple's chapel, perhaps some of the 'stuffe to be hadd of my lady of Bukyngham for Cristemasse' that had been mentioned a few pages earlier.[114] There is thus insufficient evidence to suggest a special relationship between Margaret and Cecily's sister, Anne, at this period, but there are plenty of indications that Anne was close to her married son, Henry, who seems to have been as concerned to protect the interests of his stepson as Margaret was.[115]

In June of 1470 the Staffords' household accounts record rewards to a messenger carrying various letters to Baynard's Castle but whether these were from Margaret or Henry is unstated.[116] The Staffords attempted to negotiate with Clarence in both 1469 and 1470–71, which indicates their sense that Edward IV had treated Henry Tudor unfairly, but this is not necessarily evidence that Margaret nurtured a deep underlying loyalty to the Lancastrian dynasty. Indeed, after 1471 and her marriage to Lord Stanley, Margaret became much more closely connected to the Yorkist royal family and played a prominent role in major family events.[117] The negotiations in 1470–1 must have proved a disappointment to Margaret Beaufort. The settlement that was eventually reached allowed Clarence to keep the honour of Richmond for his lifetime, although he agreed that on his death it would pass to Tudor. Neither party seems to have been happy with this.[118]

Cecily may not have been entirely disappointed to see George's marginalization. According to the author of *The Historie of the Arrival of King Edward IV* (who was one of Edward IV's servants), Cecily was using 'right covert wayes and meanes' to lure George back into alliance with his brothers.[119] In this she was aided by her daughters, particularly Anne who was appalled to find her estranged husband back in power, and Margaret duchess of Burgundy who was 'moste specially' busy in trying to undermine the Lancastrians for the sake of her Burgundian family.[120] Louis XI of France had declared all Charles of Burgundy's possessions forfeit to the French crown and was prepared to make good that threat by force of arms, so Burgundy desperately did not want England to be in alliance with France.[121] The king's Bourchier kinsmen, the archbishop of Canterbury and the earl of Essex, were also named as mediators (despite their brief imprisonment by Warwick). So too was the former chancellor, Robert Stillington, bishop of Bath and Wells, who had taken sanctuary at St Martin le Grand. These ladies and lords used 'certayne priests, and othar well disposyd parsouns' as their go-betweens.[122]

On 14 March Edward IV landed at Ravenspur and began to make his way southwards. At Banbury he was once again reconciled with his brother George.[123] Before Edward reached London his supporters had retaken possession of the Tower so Edward entered his capital without resistance on Maundy Thursday, 11 April 1471.[124] From here he went on to Westminster where his queen was able to show him, 'to the Kyngys greatyste joy, a fayre sonn, a prince' born the previous November.[125] The king took Elizabeth and his children back through the city walls to Baynard's Castle and lodged for the night with Cecily. This would have been a very curious move if Elizabeth and Cecily really loathed each other or if Cecily had helped to engineer Clarence and Warwick's rebellion. That night the family all gathered together to hear divine service for the Good Friday vigil in Cecily's chapel.[126] The next morning Edward met with 'the great lords of his blood, and othar of his counsell' at Baynard's Castle, just as he had done a decade earlier before Towton, and there he took advice 'for the adventures that were lykely for to come'.[127]

It was decided that the king's family should return to the relative security of the Tower. Clarence's defection had made Cecily's position vulnerable to any of his erstwhile allies resisting Edward IV, so this time she joined the queen and her grandchildren within the royal fortress.[128] Edward left London on Easter Eve and shortly before five the next morning his forces opened fire on those of the earl of Warwick at Barnet in heavy fog. At one point rumours reached London that Edward had lost the field but after three hours fighting 'the perfite victory remayned unto hym'.[129] Warwick was slain 'somewhat fleinge' and Marquess Montagu 'in playne battayle'. Cecily's estranged son-in-law, Henry duke of Exeter 'was smytten downe, and sore woundyd, and lafte for dead'.[130] One of his followers carried him from the field and helped him to take sanctuary at Westminster.[131] On the Yorkist side, Henry Stafford was also severely wounded and his injuries eventually contributed to his death six months later, leaving Margaret Beaufort a widow once more.[132] Only two days later news reached London that Margaret of Anjou and her son had arrived at Weymouth on the very day of the battle.[133]

Henry VI was brought back to reside in the Tower of London, while Cecily and the queen remained in the fortress's royal apartments. The queen's brother, Anthony earl Rivers, was left to defend them while Edward and his brothers once more set out to face a Lancastrian army together. The battle of Tewkesbury, on 4 May 1471, was perhaps the ugliest of all the engagements of the Wars of the Roses. John Lord Wenlock, who had kept Warwick out of Calais in 1470 but then joined the Lancastrians by 1471, may have been slain by his fellow Lancastrian Edmund Beaufort duke of Somerset for failing to follow orders.[134] As the Lancastrians realized their cause was hopeless, Henry VI's seventeen-year-old son Edward 'was taken, fleinge to the towne wards, and slayne, in the fielde'.[135] Somerset and others made it to the sanctuary of Tewkesbury Abbey, only to be hauled out and executed two days later.[136]

While King Edward marched northwards to deal with further opposition in Richmondshire, London came under siege from Thomas Neville, the Bastard of Fauconberg (the son of Cecily's brother William). The mayor and aldermen wrote anxiously to the king that his family and the city 'was likely to stand in the grettest ioperdy that evar they stode'.[137] Earl Rivers and Lord Dudley led the city's defence and when news arrived that 1,500 of the king's men were approaching, Thomas Neville at last withdrew.[138]

Edward arrived back in London on Tuesday 21 May and joined his family at the Tower. By 24 May, Henry VI was dead. The official explanation was that the news of his son's death, his wife's imprisonment and the loss of his throne had caused him to die 'of pure displeasure and melencoly'.[139] Was it merely ironic coincidence that this was the very cause of death predicted by Eleanor Cobham's associates thirty years earlier? Most contemporaries thought Henry's death was far too convenient. The gossip in France was that 'King Edward has had him put to death secretly, and is said to have done the like by the Queen, the consort of King Henry'.[140] Yet a far less serious disappointment had provoked Henry's collapse into a catatonic stupor in 1453 and mere arrest had brought on Humphrey duke of Gloucester's fatal stroke. Henry VI may well have collapsed with a stroke or a heart attack as the Yorkists claimed. Edward IV was well aware that the death of the ageing, discredited and childless Henry VI opened up the possibility of a challenge from younger Lancastrians. Just days after Edward's return to London, Henry Holland was once again dragged out of sanctuary and moved into the Tower where he was granted a relatively comfortable imprisonment, probably much like Henry VI's before the readeption.[141] However, Henry Tudor and his uncle Jasper held out at Pembroke Castle until early September when they fled to the continent, free to fight another day.[142]

9

Queen of Right: 1471–1478

there was an imperiall of clothe of gould in manor of a canopie; and under the saide
canopie was the King, the Queene and my Lord the Prince, and the right high and
excellent Princesse and Queene of right, Cicelie, Mother to the Kinge …
Wedding of Richard duke of York and Anne Mowbray, 1478[1]

It had been military victories rather than loyalty to the house of York that enabled Edward IV to reclaim his throne after Henry's VI readeption. From 1471 Edward IV again needed to persuade his subjects of his legitimate right to the throne. One response to this need is apparent in the quotation above which was written in 1478. It comes from a herald's account of the wedding of Edward's youngest son, the new Richard duke of York. This record is the clearest surviving indication that by then Cecily's acknowledged role was not merely that of a previous heir to the throne's widow, like Joan of Kent, but actually that of a rightful queen, essentially an uncrowned queen mother. Yet by then Cecily had stepped back from the political maelstroms in London.

In public Cecily largely remained aloof from the quarrels between her sons which dominated much of Edward IV's second reign. It seems to have been Edward and Richard whom she saw most often and whom she continued to influence while her attitude to the rebellious George has left scant trace. The sources for this period of her life relate primarily to her estate administration and her practice of good ladyship. Her grandson's wedding was a rare instance of her taking a central role in courtly pageantry. One other such occasion, the foundation of the Luton Guild of the Holy Trinity provides the earliest suggestion that she was beginning to cultivate a consciously pious self-image. This was perhaps in response to the fractures in her sons' relationships and the slur on her virtue circulating in 1469.

The aftermath of the readeption

One of the most significant developments in the aftermath of the readeption was the change in fortunes for Cecily's youngest son, Richard duke of Gloucester. Richard was still only nineteen when Edward IV reclaimed his kingdom but he had emerged as the king's new right-hand man. Richard received the northern lordships that Warwick had inherited from his father, including some of Cecily's childhood homes, as well as all the properties confiscated from the earl of Oxford.[2] By the late spring of 1472 Richard duke of Gloucester had also acquired a wife. Typically mothers expected to have some involvement in choosing spouses for their younger children but Richard's bride was very much his own selection. She was Anne Neville, the younger daughter and coheiress to his cousin, the earl of Warwick, sister-in-law to his brother George. Like George, Richard presumably asked his mother's blessing on his decision, but surprisingly no record remains of the date, location or witnesses to the wedding itself. Nor is it entirely clear when their only son, Edward of Middleham, was born.

The quarrel between Richard and George over their wives' hereditary lands was to prove the 'most difficult domestic problem in the second decade of [Edward IV's] reign'.[3] As Charles Ross argued, 'both brothers showed a greed and ruthlessness and a disregard for the rights of those who could not protect themselves which shed an unpleasant light on their characters'.[4] The principal victim of their ruthlessness was Warwick's widow, Anne Beauchamp, whom they eventually chose to consider as legally dead in order to carve up her Beauchamp and Despenser lands between them. Anne Beauchamp was essentially a prisoner at Beaulieu Abbey where she had taken sanctuary on learning of her husband's death as soon as she arrived back in England. She wrote begging letters to the king and his brothers, asking for her rights to be upheld. She also wrote to a number of powerful women including 'my right redoubted lady the king's mother', but her letters proved fruitless in a dispute so bitter that some feared civil war would erupt once more.[5]

Cecily was perhaps more active in aspects of the formal reconciliation between the king and his subjects. In May 1471, all three of her sons made a splendid entrance into Canterbury where the council ransomed the city's charter at considerable cost. The king and his brothers were lodged, as most royal visitors since 1446 had been, at the Hall-in-the-Blean, an elaborate but temporary pavilion constructed for each occasion in the Forest of Blean at Harbledown.[6] Cecily seems to have been with them although the only reference to her presence is a record of bread supplied to her at the city's cost.[7]

The household at Berkhamsted

Cecily continued to reside at Baynard's Castle on a regular basis in the 1470s, but after the readeption Berkhamsted gradually became her principal home.[8] This was not only the centre of her administration but also the location for courts convened to arbitrate on disputes involving her tenants.[9] Her home was still regularly visited by friends and family as well as by petitioners and of course her various officers. In 1476 Elizabeth Stonor, wife of an Oxfordshire gentleman, wrote to her husband describing a visit to Cecily's household in the company of Cecily's daughter, Elizabeth duchess of Suffolk. Elizabeth Stonor reported that she had been able to discuss business there with Richard Fowler, Chancellor of the duchy of Lancaster, and with her kinsman Thomas Rokes. She had not, however, found the opportunity she had been hoping for to speak with Duchess Elizabeth on a financial matter.[10] Clearly this was more like the busy household of any major lord than the reclusive retreat sometimes implied in representations of Cecily's widowhood.

The arrival of this large permanent household in Berkhamsted was inevitably important to the local economy. The acquisition and distribution of food was a core function of any noble household, and the majority of Cecily's 'Rules of the house' were concerned with this. They stipulated that four times a year enquiries should be made in Berkhamsted and neighbouring market towns to ensure that her servants had been paying 'true paymente' on her behalf and that they had not been running up personal debts either.[11] This was not simply a matter of avoiding ill feeling in the locality. As Christine de Pisan had observed, if people were 'cheated or incommoded unreasonably' on a lord or lady's behalf it would be a burden on the latter's soul 'until they made amends for it'.[12]

Cecily's relocation inevitably affected the personnel in her household and she came to employ a number of local Berkhamsted men. These included Robert Incent whose memorial brasses in Berkhamsted church recorded his service to Cecily in both Latin and English.[13] Incent belonged to one of the most prestigious families in Berkhamsted and his son John went on to become Dean of St Paul's in 1540, perhaps having acquired his early education from the clerics in Cecily's household.[14] The 1470s also saw a very significant returnee to Cecily's household, Richard Lessy, who was to become Cecily's most trusted servant, despite his controversial career. Lessy had probably first been employed in Cecily's household as a child because in 1464 his parents were promised an annuity of 20s. for as long as he served in her chapel.[15] In 1471 he received a music degree from Cambridge, one of the first men to do so.[16] Unfortunately, during his studies Lessy had also made a reckless marriage that he swiftly came to regret. After a certain Agnes Cokkesson complained that he had abandoned her Lessy was briefly excommunicated. The excommunication was soon suspended but the status of his marriage was under debate for more than three years, being brought before various church courts.[17] Lessy argued that his marriage was invalid because Agnes already had an earlier husband. In a society that forbade divorce this was one of the few excuses by which marriages could be annulled. Ultimately Lessy's version of events was accepted.

By 1481 Lessy was practising as a priest but seems still to have been somewhat cavalier in his attitude to the law because he had not acquired the papal dispensation he needed for this calling following his bigamous marriage. He was by this point one of Cecily's counsellors and Edward IV himself successfully petitioned Pope Sixtus IV for a dispensation on Lessy's behalf.[18] Cecily's favour ensured an increasingly successful career for Lessy in spite of his youthful errors. Like her chaplain Thomas Candour he became a papal chamberlain, but he was also the dean of her chapel and would be the principal executor of her will.[19] Cecily may have envisaged a similar career for the son of her servant, William Stephen, when she endeavoured to secure him a place at the newly built Magdalen College, Oxford. In a letter to the college's founder, William Waynflete, bishop of Winchester, Cecily explained the boy's desire to be a priest 'yf that God will give him abyylite and conyng' and vouched for his 'godly disposicion'.[20] Typically she assumed that expectation of her gratitude would be the strongest incentive for Bishop Waynflete to admit the boy: 'ye so doing shalle in oure oppynyone do a righte meritorious dede, and also cause vs to be your loving lady in anything we may do for you hereafter, as knoweth God'.[21]

Administration

From her new base at Berkhamsted, Cecily continued to protect her financial rights and to ensure that men she trusted held responsibility on her estates. On some occasions her performance of good ladyship and responsible administration involved working with her sons Edward and Richard. Despite the great wealth that she already enjoyed, she was still pursuing her claims to property that she had had to part with when Richard duke of York's finances were under strain in the late 1440s. The original grant of lands that had been arranged for her in June 1461 included a number of manors in Kent and Surrey which she and York had remised and quitclaimed to Thomas Browne in 1449.[22] In November 1472 she was finally able to reclaim them from Browne's son, George.[23] These Surrey properties included Pirbright which she then granted to her servant Henry Lessy eighteen months later.[24] However, Edward IV wished to anticipate his eventual ownership of this manor and start enclosing a hunting park there. Mother and son may have been operating together in resolving this since Henry Lessy, like so many of her servants, was in the king's service too as a sewer of his chamber. Lessy was soon recompensed by the king with income from nearby Worplesdon.[25]

The king may sometimes have proposed suitable candidates for the offices on his mother's lands, as he seems to have done at Bridgwater in the previous decade, but where her motivation can plausibly be traced it indicates an independent exercise of Cecily's own good ladyship. For instance, in December 1473 she appointed her servants Richard and John Gilmyn jointly to the office of keeping her park and hunting chase at South Frith in Kent.[26] The following year she gave the same role at Marshwood in Dorset to one of the sewers of her chamber, Ralph Kyrisshawe.[27] On other occasions she appointed men who themselves owned property in the relevant neighbourhood, such as John Felde who became keeper of her park at Standon in 1476.[28] She also continued to find opportunities to promote clerics of her choice to churches that were not within her own jurisdiction: in August 1477 she acquired the right to appoint the next rector of St Peter's Westcheap, a London church in the patronage of St Alban's Abbey.[29]

The clearest evidence of Cecily's effective good ladyship comes from a dispute over lands in Essex that belonged to her servant John Prince. Prince had formerly been a servant of the earl of Oxford, but he had since entered Cecily's service and his wife, Lucy, had a nephew who was apparently one of Cecily's councillors.[30] Lucy also had a slightly more distant kinsman called Richard Brocas who was very likely the gentleman of that name employed by Cecily as her clerk of the kitchen, a senior household officer.[31] Consequently, the Princes were confident of Cecily's help when their ownership of the manor of Gregories in Theydon Bois was challenged in the early 1470s. This was despite the fact that their principal opponent, a former London goldsmith called Thomas Wethiale, was in the service of Richard duke of Gloucester and indeed that the duke himself was among those who had been enfeoffed in the manor by Wethiale's fellow goldsmith, William Floure.[32]

According to John Prince, on 19 September 1474 Wethiale with one Thomas Dalalaund and some twenty others in Gloucester's livery entered Gregories, some on horseback, all 'defensibly arrayed in maner of werre – that is to sey, with doubletts of defense, standards of mayle, bowes bent, arowes, speres, gleyves, bills, swerdes, bokelers and other defensible wepyns'.[33] Having seen this array, John understandably fled home. But Lucy Prince dared to trust that a member of the weaker sex would not be physically attacked. With one man servant and three other women she returned to Gregories with a writ from the sheriff and found Dalalaund and his men rounding up cattle where she challenged them: 'Sirs, what doo ye here in this wyse upon my husbands grounde? I doo you to wit that he is servaunt with my lady the Kyngs moder and my lady will not be wele pleased with you thus to entrete the catall of any servaunt that bilongeth to her good grace.'[34] Dalalaund of course retorted, 'We be servaunts to my lord of Gloucester, and he woll mayntene his servaunts as well as my lady hirs' and departed with twenty-four bullocks and calves. A few days later Wethiale returned to Gregories in an attempt to seize John Prince himself but Prince was absent. Wethiale told Prince's farmer 'Now shalt thou see whether of my lords man, or of my ladies, shall have the better'.[35]

Fortunately for John and Lucy Prince, Cecily and Richard did not see the conflict as an opportunity to test each other's authority. Cecily sent her steward, John Howard, to meet with Gloucester's council at his London residence.[36] However, agreement had not been reached before Howard needed to return to Calais on the king's business and Cecily then arranged to meet to discuss the matter with Richard herself at Syon Abbey. Here Richard promised his mother that he would sort out the matter and that he would not allow anyone other than her lawyers and his to shape negotiations.[37] The language of both Richard's letters and Cecily's throughout this dispute indicates her conviction that Prince was right as well as Richard's willingness to acknowledge that his 'welbeloved servant' Thomas Wethiale might be in the wrong.

After Richard had summoned Prince to come before his council and show his claim, the duke's steward in East Anglia, Sir Robert Chamberlayne, tried to put pressure on Prince 'to ende his matier' with Wethiale.[38] Cecily was now back at Berkhamsted but wrote swiftly to her son, thanking him for his 'good lordshippe' to Prince but asking him to command Chamberlayne to stop interfering. She also wrote to Chamberlayne himself, asking him to keep out of the negotiations.[39] Nevertheless her letter was carefully diplomatic and conciliatory in its tone. She assured Chamberlayne that she assumed he had her interests at heart 'as ye have done evyr in al other things' and she promised to continue 'to be youre very good lady in everything we may do for you hereafter'.[40] Presumably Chamberlayne, a Suffolk man, cousin to James Tyrell and knight of the king's body, had performed services for Cecily herself in the past and it was worth her while to retain his favour.[41] It is striking that her tone in writing to Chamberlayne is much less strident than in her letter to William Wolflete, dean of Stoke by Clare, when she felt the latter was failing in his duties as her surveyor.[42]

Soon afterwards it was established that two of Cecily's lawyers and two of Gloucester's would be chosen to arbitrate by Prince and Wethiale respectively. Prince elected John Catesby and Roger Townshend so Cecily wrote to them promising that she would see them 'so rewarded for youre labour as ye shal holde you right wele content and pleased'.[43] Catesby and Townshend must have proved John and Lucy Prince's right to continue their possession of Gregories in peace for the eventual settlement was entirely in their favour while Wethiale and Dalalaund were summoned before the king's council at Westminster to answer for their 'right grete riotes and misgovernances'.[44] John Prince seems to have responded to Cecily's support by serving her with a dedication that his kinsmen and others of her household deemed far beyond expectation for his pay.[45] Cecily in turn continued her good ladyship towards the family. By 1482 Lucy was a widow, and perhaps again facing a challenge to her rights in Gregories for Cecily then issued letters patent confirming Lucy's right to hold the land for the term of her life.[46]

This last document highlights an interesting link in Cecily's administration. It was confirmed not only by her steward, John Howard, but also by her nephew George Neville, lord Bergavenny. John Howard's personal connections with the Bergavenny family perhaps reinforced Cecily's own: Howard's sister Catherine had been first mistress and then wife to Cecily's brother (George's father) Edward Neville.[47] The lords of Bergavenny, like Cecily, owned property in Essex and may have worked with Cecily in administration here on other occasions. Certainly they did so in Kent where she appointed George as her bailiff on her manor of South Frith on the edge of Tonbridge.[48] It was perhaps because of these additional connections between Cecily and the lords of Bergavenny that a certain Joanna Conwaye, who was involved in a legal dispute with one of them, was moved to write to Cecily. Conwaye's undated letter explained that she had 'long bene in the myserous prisone of ludgate at the sute of the right noble lorde the lorde of Bergeveny to her confucion and mortal distruction for ever'.[49] She pleaded with Cecily to persuade lord Bergavenny to withdraw his various suits against her, although she gave no explanation of what these were. All the prisoner could offer in return were 'incessant' prayers for Cecily's welfare and for 'many prosperous dayes' in her 'most Rial estate'.[50]

Religious patronage

From the 1470s there is greater evidence than previously of the way in which Cecily's good ladyship operated through religious patronage. There was still nothing obviously exceptional in her piety. Nonetheless, the increasingly public nature of her religion may have been a strategic attempt to construct a more devout identity as a riposte to the rumours of her adultery that had circulated in 1469. It should be noted that no English evidence of these allegations survive from before 1478, although it seems likely that courtly circles were aware of Continental gossip. Philippe de Commynes, a Burgundian in the service of Louis XI of France, claimed to have overheard a conversation in 1475 in which an emissary to the duke of Burgundy recalled that duke's fury on learning of Edward IV's recent alliance with the French king: 'stamping his foot against the floor, and swearing by Saint George, he called the king of England Blaybourgne, son of an archer who bore that name, and all the insults in the world that it is possible to call a man'.[51] Abusing a man's wife or mother is common practice in such tirades of insults but, like Mancini's use of the story, it was especially pertinent in suggesting that Edward IV had behaved ignobly. It is no more likely that Duke

Charles actually believed this story than that noble contemporaries accepted tales that Edward of Lancaster was the child of a wandering player or Owen Tudor was the son of an innkeeper.[52] Nonetheless, it may suggest that the scandalous rumours of 1469 had not been forgotten. Cecily's increasingly public piety was perhaps also a response to her awareness of Henry VI's growing saintly reputation in contrast to her own children's in-fighting and a popular perception that Edward IV was a man 'who loved his comforts and his pleasures'.[53]

At Berkhamsted, as at Baynard's Castle, Cecily's local church expected her patronage. A much-restored glass escutcheon of her arms which is now in the west window of the south aisle celebrates her connection with St Peter's Great Berkhamsted. As well as providing material and financial gifts, it was also her responsibility to present rectors to the living. One of these, John More, she subsequently moved from Berkhamsted to the neighbouring Northchurch in 1484 and he clearly remained close to Cecily since she bequeathed him a purple altar frontal, a 'Legend boke' and a collect book. The other men she presented to Berkhamsted were Henry Matthew and Thomas Lee. Despite the significance of Cecily's own household chapel, these rectors of Berkhamsted had an important relationship with the inhabitants of the nearby castle, hence Cecily's servant Nicholas Talbot arranged for a year's prayers for More, Matthew and Lee when he drew up his own will in 1501.[54]

Cecily probably also developed a constructive relationship with the nearest major religious house to Berkhamsted, St Alban's Abbey. As mentioned earlier, the abbot there granted her the right to present to one of their London churches in 1477. Churches on her estates further afield certainly looked to Cecily for financial support and a voice in the king's ear. The white roses and suns in the glazing at Winterbourne Steepleton in Dorset were probably either a compliment to or a gift from Cecily who was patron of the church as well as lord of the manor there.[55] The most significant such patronage for which records survive occurred in 1472 when a wealthy Cirencester lawyer, John Twyneho, and the vicar of St Lawrence's Lechlade, Conrad Nye, involved Cecily in supporting the rebuilding work of the latter's church.[56] Despite its distance from her usual residences her involvement in Lechlade made sense on several counts. This rich wool producing region was naturally a property where it was appropriate for her to extend her generous good ladyship in order to maintain good relations with its inhabitants. It was also a town with a long history of enjoying the patronage of her husband's family where she had a responsibility to nurture dynastic memory. Now that the king already had one son, he had very likely discussed with his mother his hopes for a second son who would eventually be the new duke of York and inherit many of those lands now in Cecily's possession.[57] Consequently her responsibility was to future generations as well as to the memory of those who had died.

On a more immediate level, Cecily was also motivated by her relationship with the men most closely responsible for the church's rebuilding. When Conrad Nye was appointed vicar in 1468 Cecily had very unusually committed to paying him an annuity of 6s. 6d. from properties in Lechlade so she seems to have had a personal interest in his career.[58] John Twyneho was recorder for Bristol, a member of Henry Stafford duke of Buckingham's council and was possibly, like other members of his family, part of George duke of Clarence's affinity.[59] He was also steward of duchess Cecily's lands in

Gloucester and in 1472 her accounts record his income of £4 for 'good and laudable service' in this role.[60]

It may have been Twyneho who first suggested that Cecily should found a chantry at Lechlade in the process of Nye's rebuilding there, as he himself planned to do also. In order to fund her foundation Cecily persuaded the king to grant her the patronage of an Augustinian house in Lechlade that had 'fallen into decay' along with a licence to suppress the house and divert its wealth to the church. Within the church she then founded a chantry dedicated to St Mary.[61] Cecily would make mention of her particular devotion to the 'Mother of God' in a licence she granted in 1482 so this dedication presumably reflected her devotional interest rather than the vicar's.[62] As mentioned earlier, Cecily does not seem to have been concerned with the Virgin's ideological association with queenship and, like most of her contemporaries, looks to have been moved more by Mary's maternal role. Three chaplains were to celebrate divine service daily in her chantry, praying for the welfare of Edward IV, his queen and the duchess herself as well as their souls after death and that of Richard duke of York 'late lord of the said town'.[63] The inclusion of these last words in the instructions for the foundation emphasized her dynasty's investment in the neighbourhood. This dynastic connection was manifested to worshippers and visitors through the church's clerestory windows which were decorated with crowns, repeated images of the sun in splendour and gold and white roses.[64] Very possibly Cecily had helped to pay for some of this, too. She also arranged for £10 a year from the priory's revenues to fund John Twyneho's chantry which was appropriately dedicated to the patron saint of wool merchants, St Blaise.[65]

Another Gloucestershire beneficiary of Cecily's patronage was the Augustinian priory known as Llanthony Secunda. On this occasion it seems to have been the king himself who persuaded his mother to extend her generosity. The prior at Llanthony Secunda was one of Edward IV's chaplains, Henry Deane, and the priory was suffering from a 'great want of fuel'. Cecily arranged to supply as many trees as four horses could transport daily from her woodland in Brimpsfield to their priory or one of their manors.[66]

More significantly, Edward also involved Cecily in the foundation of a new guild at St Mary's Church, Luton, north-east of Berkhamsted. The guild was dedicated to the Holy Trinity and it was probably Thomas Rotherham, bishop of Lincoln and chancellor of England who initiated the foundation. The original foundation licence, in May 1474, made no specific reference to Cecily, other than a promise that the guild's two chantry chaplains would pray for the king's progenitors.[67] However, Cecily appears to have been present for the official inauguration and her role as a founding member was used by Rotherham in shaping the fraternity's sumptuously illuminated guild book into an eloquent statement of loyalty to the king. As befitted her status, Cecily's name appears on the first page of the guild book above Rotherham's and directly below those of the king and queen. However, her title takes up a great deal more space than theirs since she was entered as 'the most excellent princess Lady Cecily mother of the supreme and illustrious lord our King Edward and recently wife of the renowned and famous and very powerful prince Richard true and undoubted heir to the crown of England father to the most noble lord our king abovesaid'.[68]

FIGURE 9.1 *The Yorkist court at prayer. Frontispiece to the Luton Guild Book. Image courtesy of Luton Culture*

The frontispiece of the book similarly depicts Cecily almost as a queen. This frontispiece is a gloriously colourful image, probably by a Flemish artist, of members of the royal family and court kneeling before the Holy Trinity enthroned.[69] Although Cecily is depicted kneeling behind Elizabeth Woodville, she is visually united with the royal couple and the archbishop. Her style of headwear and clothing is identical to the queen's (unlike those of the other ladies present), but whereas the queen's dress is of gold embroidered or woven with blue designs, Cecily's mirrors the king's gown (and the bishop's cope) on which the designs are a deeper shade of gold than the main cloth. The king and queen both wear ermine-edged purple cloaks but Cecily's cloak marks her out as the vessel through whom Edward claimed his throne and as wife of a true king: her cloak is decorated with the royal arms of England. There are other intriguing details suggesting Cecily's importance. It may be mere artistic chance that Cecily is the only woman not looking at the bishop. She instead has her eyes raised towards God the father who is himself looking down towards the women. What cannot be chance is that Cecily is the only figure depicted with prayer beads hanging from her waist.

This blending of the pious and the political is typical of surviving evidence for Cecily's religious expression. It suggests utter confidence that those in authority had been placed there by God so that there was nothing incongruous in fashioning religious devotion that celebrated their own political status. The house of York had been bitterly tested by the readeption but their faith in God's favour had been proved in trial by battle at Barnet and Tewkesbury as it had at Mortimer's Cross and Towton. Cecily's central role in the public image of the foundation of the Luton guild was certainly intended to celebrate the king's political legitimacy. However, the prayer beads at her waist suggest that she was also seen as her dynasty's most devout member, or was being constructed as such, despite her comparative lack of religious patronage.

Heavenly treasures

The artist who depicted Cecily's prayer beads in the guild book had perhaps actually seen some of her sumptuous religious jewellery. Many such items are listed in her will and they must have been a collection that she had been building up over decades. She owned at least a dozen decorated pendants for holding wax *Agnus Dei* discs blessed by the pope. These discs were talismans fashioned from Paschal candles and were traditionally distributed by the Pope at Easter. She may have acquired them through those of her servants who also worked as papal chamberlains, Thomas Candour and Richard Lessy. The pendants in which she kept them, however, were likely to have been fashioned in England. These were usually round and their decoration frequently included the same image of the Lamb of God holding the banner of the Resurrection that was stamped onto the discs themselves. Commonly the cases also bore a Latin inscription of the words spoken by John the Baptist as Jesus first approached him 'Behold the Lamb of God who takes away the sin of the world'. Since *Agnus Dei* discs were especially associated with relieving the pain of childbirth, some may have been in Cecily's possession during her marriage.[70] Her 'Agnus of gold with our Lady and saint Barbara' was perhaps especially suited for this given the Virgin's role as supreme mother and Barbara's promise to protect her devotees from dying without receiving the last rites.

John Cherry has speculated that the Middleham Jewel, which also bears the traditional words and image of *Agnus Dei* pendants, was designed for this purpose, although no other lozenge-shaped *Agnus Dei* containers are known.[71] Like the Middleham Jewel, most of Cecily's *Agnus Dei* pendants were decorated with the Trinity so her particular devotion to 'the Holy and Undivided Trinity' may well have predated her involvement with the guild of that name at Luton. Certainly it was something she mentioned in 1482 in the same licence that referred to her affection for the Mother of God.[72] Her mother had also owned a spectacular gold 'jewel' (*jocale*) called 'le Trinitee'.[73] In 1440 Joan Beaufort listed this in her will ahead of her own mother's precious psalter (which was to be held by each of her sons for the term of their life) and before the gold ring set with a jewel 'of great virtue and precious' with which she had dedicated herself as a vowess. So this Trinity jewel was presumably an ornament of exceptional value. It is perhaps worth noting that she bequeathed it (like the ring) to her eldest son, Richard earl of Salisbury, lord of Middleham. Although the Middleham Jewel is most often ascribed to the third quarter of the fifteenth century, estimates of its age vary enough to allow for the possibility that this was Joan's pendant: John Cherry observes that the iconography on it 'could occur as early as the 1430s' whereas R. W. Lightbown states that the jewel was fashioned in the second quarter of the fifteenth century.[74]

Cecily's prayer beads were also spectacular pieces of jewellery. They included one set of white amber 'with vj grete stones of gold'; one of ten gold beads and five coral; a 'litell' set of white amber with seven stones of gold; and another of sixty-one round gold stones that were divided by six square stones 'enameled', and from these hung a gold cross and a jet scallop shell. It was in the fifteenth century that rosary beads became standardized in the form familiar today with groups of ten beads for reciting the *Ave Maria* divided by larger beads for the *Paternoster*.[75] The gold beads attached to the scallop shell sound very similar to the Langdale Rosary, the only Medieval English gold rosary known to have survived the Reformation. Every one of the fifty-seven Langdale beads is enamelled in black with images of saints, scenes from Christ's passion and nativity or emblems of the Evangelists.[76] Cecily's set of fifteen gold and coral beads does not fit the standard rosary form but they might perhaps have been used as 'pardon beads' for a special devotion promoted by Syon Abbey. These were usually a string of five beads used in praying a five line, thirty-three-word verse prayer celebrating the Name of Jesus in a cycle with *Paternosters* and *Aves*. Those who prayed this cycle fifteen times daily were promised a staggering 5,745 years of pardon from purgatory.[77]

Cecily was to bequeath all her beads, like her *Agnus Dei* pendants, either to women or to married couples in her household. The only jewellery that she passed to a family member was her 'crosse croselette of diamantes' which she gave to her granddaughter, Elizabeth of York, probably because it was much the most valuable of her pendants. John Ashdown Hill has also identified Cecily as 'perhaps the most likely' owner of a tiny gold reliquary cross that was found during excavations at Clare Castle.[78] It seems safe to suggest that she must at least have known its owner and worn jewellery similar to it.[79] It is 3.1 cm long with pearls set into each angle of the cross. There is a crucifixion engraved on the front which was originally enamelled and on the back

FIGURE 9.2 *Engraving of a fifteenth-century gold reliquary cross, set with pearls, which was found at Clare Castle in 1866. Reproduced from* The Archaeological Journal *vol. XXV (1868) facing p. 60*

are scrolling leaves (perhaps meant to be olive leaves). When the front was lifted off tiny fragments of wood and stone were found. These were almost certainly supposed to have been taken from the true cross and the rock of calvary. It was typical of the Christian amulets that had been popular among wealthy Europeans for more than a thousand years, functioning as 'objects of personal adornment and symbols of social status as well as powerful protective devices'.[80] However, Cecily's efforts to project a respectable image of herself and her dynasty and to protect them with her prayers were undermined by the ambitions and appetites of her children.

Family matters

The first breakdown among Cecily's offspring's relationships in the 1470s was entirely understandable and had been inevitable for more than a decade: her daughter Anne's decision to divorce her determinedly Lancastrian husband, Henry Holland, duke of Exeter. Anne had presumably already elicited a promise from the king that this would not affect her control of the Exeter lands or her daughter's inheritance, despite the lack of legal justification for such an arrangement.[81] Anne intended to profit from her position just as her youngest brothers would do at the Countess of Warwick's expense a few years later. Almost certainly she had already chosen her new husband, a loyal Yorkist knight, Thomas St Leger, who could not bring her the wealth of her first husband but who was perhaps already her lover.[82]

On 18 January 1470 Anne's brother George hosted the initial legal meetings at the bishop of Salisbury's inn on Fleet Street. The archbishop's court eventually convened at Lambeth Palace to assess the evidence and interview witnesses from 15 June 1471. The witnesses called included some of Cecily's former servants: Agatha Flegge, by now a widow living in retirement at Marlow, and Geoffrey Spryng whose attention to Cecily's fabric and jewel purchases in the 1440s had prepared him for his role as clerk of the king's jewel house.[83] Anne's argument hinged on the absence of adequate papal dispensations, as was usually the case in noble divorce suits. Unsurprisingly it was eventually accepted that the dispensation provided at the time only covered her kinship to Henry Holland through her father. The couple were of course even more closely related through Cecily since both were descended from John of Gaunt and on these grounds Anne's marriage was deemed never to have been valid.[84]

Cecily herself was not called to witness the announcement that she and Duke Richard had contracted an illegal union for their eldest daughter. Indeed, the nature of her relationship with her daughter Anne seems to have left no trace in surviving records. By contrast, as we have already seen, Cecily clearly maintained regular warm communication with at least two of her sons and her daughter Elizabeth duchess of Suffolk. In October 1476 Elizabeth Stonor described a family gathering at Greenwich between Cecily, Duchess Elizabeth, the king and the queen: 'and ther I sawe the metyng betwyne the Kynge and my ladye his Modyr. And trewly me thowght it was a very good syght'.[85] The evidence we have suggests that in her sixties Cecily was still close to her powerful children. When she wrote to her son Richard in March 1475 she mentioned that Edward had recently visited her at Berkhamsted but, in lines that echo centuries of mothers' complaints, she continued, 'Son we trusted ye shulde have been at Berkhampstede [too] … ye shulde have been right hertely welcome and so ye shalbe whan soevyr ye wol do the same, as god knoweth'.[86] Now that all of her children were married she also had an increasingly large family of grandchildren. In the 1470s the grandchild whose fortunes probably concerned her most closely was the king's second son, Richard, who was born at Shrewsbury in August 1473 and created duke of York less than a year later.[87] The will that Edward IV drew up in 1475 indicates, as mentioned above, that Edward intended to establish this new Richard duke of York with lands previously held by his namesake, many of which were currently in Cecily's possession.[88] The young duke would not come into his lands until he was sixteen and there was no suggestion that Cecily would be expected to part with her properties if she was still alive at this point.[89] Nonetheless, from now on she must have been conscious that she was holding lands that should one day be his. In the event, young Richard was presumed dead by the time of Cecily's own death and it was her great grandson, Henry duke of York (the future Henry VIII), who acquired those of her lands that were not granted to his mother, the queen.[90] The fact that Cecily made a more generous bequest to Henry in 1495 than that to his older brother, Arthur, suggests that she still consciously identified herself more closely with the boys who shared her husband's title.

Surprisingly there is no mention of her in the extensive records for her husband's sumptuous reburial at Fotheringhay in July 1476. Most likely this was a matter of protocol rather than ill health since no late medieval queen seems to have attended her husband's funeral in public. Richard duke of York's reburial was 'the most lavish of all Yorkist ceremonies' and a celebration of the dynasty's achievements.[91] But Cecily's tempestuous family was on the brink of irrevocable and brutal fracture.

The fall of Clarence

Michael Hicks has traced the origins of the breakdown between George duke of Clarence and Edward IV in George's increasing frustration with his older brother's understandable attempts to control him in the aftermath of the 1469–71 rebellions. Edward resumed some of George's lands and took away his responsibilities and authority as lieutenant of Ireland.[92] In December 1476 George's twenty-five-year-old wife Isabel died shortly after giving birth to their fourth child. His sister Margaret was quick to suggest that George should now marry her stepdaughter Mary, heiress to the duchy of Burgundy.[93] James III of Scotland also suggested a prestigious marriage. He offered the hand of his own sister Margaret.[94] Edward refused to allow either match. It was in this context that the relationship between the brothers broke down completely.

The first sign of George's increasingly reckless mood seems to have been in April 1477 when he had three of his servants tried on charges of poisoning his wife and child.[95] The charges were implausible and did not fit with Isabel's known whereabouts but the jurors were men who did not dare to oppose the duke. The two defendants who had been brought to the court were tried, convicted and executed within one day. One of those executed was John Twyneho's widowed sister-in-law, Ankaret, which may have given Cecily even greater concern about the affair.[96] Michael Hicks has suggested that George's real motive could have been revenge on the three for perceived disloyalty, betraying the secrets of his household by gossiping with those close to the king.[97] Certainly the trial was later reassessed and annulled on the grounds that the jurors had been intimidated.[98]

In the meantime, a yet more dramatic case was unfolding. Master John Stacy, a fellow of Merton College Oxford, had made a startling confession while under torture for alleged necromancy against Richard lord Beauchamp. He claimed that one of the duke of Clarence's close associates, Thomas Burdet, had asked him and the chaplain at Merton, Thomas Blake, to draw up horoscopes for the deaths of Edward IV and his eldest son. All three men were then tried for plotting to undermine the king with their discoveries and for planning to use 'seditious and treasonable' songs and bills to cause an uprising 'to the final destruction of the King and Prince'.[99] Burdet and Stacy were executed at Tyburn on 20 May 1477. The following day Duke George attended a meeting of the king's council, the king himself being absent, and there instructed a friar to read out declarations of innocence that Burdet and Stacy had made before their deaths. Whether George had been trying to disassociate himself from possible implications of treason or arrogantly questioning the king's justice is unclear. Edward summoned Clarence to a meeting at Westminster in the presence of the London mayor and aldermen. Here he spoke of Clarence's support for Burdet 'as if it were in contempt of the law of the land and a great threat to the judges and jurors of the kingdom'.[100] The king then ordered Clarence's arrest and imprisonment in the Tower.

At this point other members of the royal family may not have guessed how far the king's anger went. On 15 January 1478, they gathered together in St Stephen's chapel, Westminster, to celebrate the new Richard duke of York's wedding.[101] His bride was Anne Mowbray, great granddaughter of Cecily's sister Katherine, and sole heiress to the last duke of Norfolk, who had died in 1476. The groom was only four years old and his bride was six, but the match came with a guarantee that young Richard would hold the duchy of Norfolk for his life, even if Anne died as a child. Like the reburial of his namesake, Richard duke of York's marriage was a sumptuous celebration of the Yorkist dynasty, carefully recorded so that the details could be shared across the land. Since George's arrest it also provided an opportunity to emphasize the family's strength. Only Cecily stood in pride of place beneath the canopy with the king and queen and their children, but Richard duke of Gloucester, Henry duke of Buckingham and senior members of the queen's family were all present in the chapel. On the following Sunday twenty-four new knights were created, including Anne duchess of Exeter's second husband and two of the king's Bourchier kinsmen.[102] In choosing to attend this ceremony, despite her absence from many earlier family rituals, Cecily signified that she had not fallen out with the king and that she accepted George's arrest.

Even before the wedding jousts were over, Edward had opened the parliament which would try his brother. Many of the political community seem to have been shocked by the proceedings that followed. 'The mind recoils from describing what happened', wrote the Crowland Continuator, 'so sad was the dispute between two brothers of such noble character'.[103] Edward himself presented the case against his brother, claiming among other charges that 'it is comen nowe of late to his knowlage' that George had 'conspired, compassed and purposed a moch higher, moch more malicious, more unnaturall and lothely Treason than atte eny tyme hertoforn'.[104] This involved accusing the king of crimes including necromancy against his subjects, and 'uppon oon the falsest and moost unnaturall coloured pretense that man myght imagine, [he had] falsely and untruely noysed, published and saide, that the Kyng oure Sovereigne Lorde was a Bastard, and not begottone to reigne uppon us'.[105] This is the earliest surviving instance of that aspersion on Cecily's virtue in an English source. It might possibly be that it was only now that Edward felt sufficiently confident in his own position to risk allowing it public mention, in spite of his mother's feelings. However, it seems more probable that the 'seditious and treasonable' words attributed to Burdet and Stacy were the first instances of Clarence himself recklessly disseminating this story.

The Crowland Continuator expressed disquiet that some of those called to give evidence seemed to be accusers rather than witnesses. Nonetheless, he concluded, '[t]hose in Parliament, believing the information they had heard to be well-founded, formally condemned him; the sentence was pronounced by the mouth of Henry, duke of Buckingham'.[106] What form Clarence's death was supposed to take was not recorded and the king delayed ordering the execution, apparently unwilling to conclude what he had started. The only hint of information about Cecily's response comes from the *Journal* or *Chronique Scandaleuse* attributed to Jean de Roye.[107] This chronicle was composed only a few years later but is a very unreliable source for English history. It asserted that Clarence had originally been sentenced to be hanged, drawn and quartered but this sentence was 'changée et muée' (changed and commuted) to drowning in a barrel of Malmsey wine.[108] The original text attributes this change to 'la grant priere et requeste desdiz Edouard et de Clarence' but a later hand has inserted 'de la mere' so that it reads 'at the great prayer and request of the mother of the said Edward and of Clarence'.[109] Whether this alteration reflects the author's original meaning or is only an assumption made by a later reader is impossible to know. Cecily's involvement is entirely plausible but so too was intervention from a sister or even their brother Richard.

The Crowland Continuator believed that George's death marked a watershed in Edward IV's kingship.[110] Without any possible challenge from his charismatic brother or his cousin Warwick, Edward became more autocratic and arrogant. Unsurprisingly, Cecily too seems to have been changed by her son's trial and death. As will be seen in the next chapter, it was from this point that her religious concerns became far more varied and indeed more visible. She spent more time staying in religious houses or promoting their interests. Yet none of those actions for which evidence survives suggests any particular concern with George's spiritual welfare. Nor did she display concern for George's children. His daughter Margaret, like Anne of Exeter's daughter, received nothing in Cecily's will, even though there can have been no political reason to ignore them. If Cecily was convinced by Edward's arguments in 1478, and the accusation that he had called her an adulteress, then this final betrayal by George may have been too much for even his mother to forgive. It was perhaps grief at her family's brokenness, rather than George's death, that inspired some of her piety, as well as an attempt to refute his now very public slander on her reputation. Within half a decade more slander and far greater tragedy would follow.

10

The End of the House of York: 1478–1485

*In the yere of our lorde M^l iiij^c iiij^{xx} And the xxth yere of the Reigne of King Edwarde
the iiijth on Sainte Martyns even, was Borne the lady Brigette, And Cristened on the
morne on Sainte Martyns daye In the Chappell of Eltham … My lady the Kinges
Mother, and my lady Elizabethe, were godmothers at the Fonte.*

The Christening of Princess Bridget[1]

The last major family celebration of Edward IV's reign was the christening of his
daughter Bridget in November 1480. It is testament to the king's enduringly close
relationship with his mother that he again asked Cecily to be his daughter's godmother.
In the years after George duke of Clarence's death Cecily remained an important
influence at the centre of politics. Her good ladyship was sought by individuals and
local authorities alike. She seems now to have begun to take a more personal interest
in religious life, although her piety remained conventional for a noble widow. Then in
1483 the house of York faced a sudden destabilizing challenge that turned swiftly to
bloodshed and tragedy. Edward IV died shortly before his forty-first birthday, leaving
his twelve-year-old son as his heir. The circumstances in which Cecily's son Richard
seized his nephew's throne are among the most contentious in English history. Cecily's
own role in the events of Richard's reign, and the actions of her servants, are similarly
intriguing.

Dealings with the duke of Suffolk

The year 1480, the year of Bridget's birth, is one of the best recorded years of Cecily's
life. It provides an excellent picture of the variety of roles that the king's mother was
expected to undertake. It also reveals that at sixty-five Cecily was still a figure of
considerable influence and authority. In May she extended her influence beyond her
own landholdings by taking out a lease on the manor of Grovebury in Leighton Buzzard
which had just come into the possession of the dean and canons of St George's Chapel,
Windsor by a grant from her daughter Elizabeth and son-in-law John de le Pole, duke
of Suffolk.[2] It is the only instance among surviving records of Cecily leasing land.
Given the property's proximity to Berkhamsted she may have been acting to provide

extra resources for her household although the involvement of other family members suggests that it was something more complex. Her grandson, Edmund de la Pole, was later to claim that Edward IV had forced his parents into making the grant.[3] It may well be that Cecily's promise to lease the land was part of that original arrangement so that she would now oversee the interests of her daughter and son-in-law's former servants there. Her right to farm these lands and pastures cost her £24 annually, although by the end of her life she was six months in arrears.[4] Later in 1480 she was to have further dealings with the duke of Suffolk in a rather different context.

Cecily spent much of the early summer near Suffolk's lands in East Anglia, principally at the abbey of St Benet at Hulme where she had similarly spent several months in 1475.[5] She travelled with an extensive household and conducted business there as she would at home.[6] During her 1480 stay both the outgoing and newly elected mayors of Norwich seized the opportunity to petition Cecily 'to obtain a remedy for injuries committed against the city'.[7] Although the surviving records do not detail these 'injuries' it appears from later events that they were perpetrated by the duke of Suffolk, or at least men in his affinity.[8] Suffolk had become accustomed to getting his own way in the region through acts of violence to which Edward IV habitually chose to turn a blind eye. In 1465 Suffolk had actually secured support from the mayor of Norwich in his aggressive dispute with the Paston family, but in the early 1470s city officials were expressing their concern about his agents.[9] On 24 May 1480 the mayors visiting Cecily rode with a company of aldermen, sheriffs and wealthier citizens and brought with them a gift of a hogshead of wine for the duchess.[10]

In the following month, she received a similar visit from the bailiffs and jurymen of Great Yarmouth who brought appropriate gifts from a seaside town including a porpoise and twenty lampreys. 'And they had very many thanks and great pleasure, with abundant wine of various kinds, dining with this excellent lady'.[11] The town authorities also cultivated the goodwill of her councillors, various of whom were staying nearby with local gentlemen or in religious houses. The Norwich city council sent gifts of wine to their residences and the bailiffs of Yarmouth entertained her chief councillors and servants with 'a rich feast of the best wines and foods'.[12]

That August, after Cecily had returned to London, the Norwich mayor John Aubry despatched one of his city's chamberlains to Baynard's Castle in company with a servant of the abbot of St Benet's. It appears that whatever resolution Cecily may have brokered on their behalf in May had proved short-lived. Their letters were respectfully directed to 'Master Lessy to inform the said Lady the Kings Mother of the Riots perpetrated a new by the servants & tenants of the said Lord Duke [of Suffolk] at Haveringham etc'.[13] Cecily wrote immediately to the king's chief secretary, Oliver King, and charged the Norwich chamberlain, Robert Hoo, with delivering her letter to Windsor where the king was then in residence. It seems that Cecily felt that the king was now in a position to bring his thuggish brother-in-law to heel and he ought to do so. Cecily's intervention to control Suffolk perhaps marked a turning point in the duke's violent career because when he resorted to force again the following summer his victim successfully reclaimed the manor from which he had personally ejected her.[14]

John duke of Suffolk was not the only significant political figure whom Cecily took to task in 1480. That Easter she had taken Sir Walter Devereux, Lord Ferrers, to court over an unpaid bond of £20.[15] The case was postponed until the summer and seems likely to have been settled in the meantime. This was one of several cases pursued by Cecily's attorney, Peter Benet, that year. Another involved a charge of breach of contract against her receiver in Devon, Thomas Calwodelegh.[16]

Family reunions

Cecily was also engaged in closer family matters through 1480. She had timed her departure from East Anglia to coincide with her daughter Margaret's arrival in London. This was Margaret's only visit home since her marriage in 1468. Margaret's husband, Charles the Bold, had died in 1477 so she was now dowager duchess. She enjoyed a good relationship with the new duchess, her stepdaughter, Mary who now ruled Burgundy with her husband, Maximilian Archduke of Austria. Margaret was seeking military aid against France. This alliance was to be cemented by a marriage between Mary's two-year-old son and heir, Philip, and Edward IV's four and half-year-old daughter, Anne.[17] The crucial negotiations occurred in mid-July at Greenwich. Cecily was present for a banquet that Edward held specifically in honour of his mother and sister on 20 July.[18] She may well have been there for the negotiations with her daughter, too.

In late October Cecily is likely to have taken up residence at Eltham where the queen was preparing for the birth of her last child.[19] The queen's sister Margaret, Lady Mautravers, and Cecily's kinswoman, Lady Margaret Beaufort, would both have prominent roles at the christening and so were likely to have been with the queen at Eltham as well. The baby was born on 10 November and was christened the following day by the bishop of Chichester, Edward Story.[20] The baby's name reflects the interest in St Bridget of Sweden shared by many of the royal family, including both Cecily and Lady Margaret.

Piety

It was also in 1480 that Cecily undertook the unusual devotional act that prompted some early historians to imagine that she had actually become a Benedictine nun. That June Cecily and her sister, Anne duchess of Buckingham, were accepted together into confraternity with the general chapter of the English Benedictines who were meeting at Northampton.[21] It was of course very common to join fraternities associated with particular religious houses, but evidence of those joining the general chapter is surprisingly scarce. This arrangement would have meant that all the abbots present at the meeting would be expected to arrange for their houses to pray for her on a regular basis.[22] Considering the number of Benedictine houses in England this must have led to an extraordinarily large number of prayers for her soul.

The earliest recorded instance of anyone in confraternity with the general chapter of the Benedictines was one of Cecily's predecessors as lord of Brimpsfield, John Lord Giffard, who joined in 1298, before the northern and southern provinces combined in 1338.[23] Another, perhaps more significant predecessor, was Cecily and Anne's own grandfather, John of Gaunt, who had entered into confraternity with these monks in 1366.[24] Cecily's affection for St Benet at Hulme and the house of St Margaret, Ashridge near Berkhamsted may both have played a part in her decision to connect herself to the Benedictines in this way.[25] As Joel Rosenthal observed, her membership 'probably indicates the receipt [by the Benedictines] of various forms of tangible aid' as well as gratitude for her 'moral support' in the past.[26] Anne duchess of Buckingham, like John Lord Giffard, only had a few more months to live when she joined the fraternity, yet she left nothing to the order in her will, so the choice of order was most likely Cecily's. It was the first of a number of indications that Cecily's piety was becoming more central to her life and her identity. In most cases this piety was still closely connected with the religious interests of other family members.

Duchess Anne's interests seem to have been focussed on the newer and more fashionable Carthusians, an order which Edward IV also particularly patronized.[27] The first concrete evidence of Cecily's interest in the Carthusians comes from two years after Anne's death. In 1482 Cecily petitioned Pope Sixtus on behalf of the London Charterhouse whose buildings were then 'in need of great repair'.[28] Pope Sixtus mentioned Cecily's 'singular devotion' to the Charterhouse in his letter encouraging visitors and almsgiving to the house.[29] Cecily was able to share this devotion to the Carthusians with members of her household. Henry Heydon requested in his will that 'devout and virtuous' priests of the Charterhouse should sing mass and pray for him after his death, and Richard Lessy asked to be buried in the Charterhouse cloister.[30] Detailed financial records for the London Charterhouse survive only for the period after 1492 but these mention a gift of £13 6s. 8d. from 'the most serene lady Duchess of York', as well as gifts from her granddaughter, the queen, and from the king's mother, Lady Margaret Beaufort.[31] Lady Margaret was of course daughter-in-law to Cecily's sister Anne and I have already alluded to the likely friendship between these three women. Like Cecily, Margaret also valued the work of Walter Hilton, a writer who was cherished by the Carthusians.[32] Cecily owned a copy of Hilton's *Mixed Life* and in the year before Cecily's death, Lady Margaret arranged for Wynkyn de Worde to print Hilton's *Scala Perfectionis*.[33]

Several of Cecily's other books were similarly associated with 'an elite of Carthusian monks, Bridgettine nuns and devout laywomen'.[34] These books included the works of Catherine of Siena and Bridget of Sweden. Syon Abbey, where Cecily had stayed with Richard to discuss the Prince affair, was the only Bridgettine house in England. Like the Sheen Charterhouse, it was a Lancastrian royal foundation that the house of York had been happy to patronize too. By the time of her death Cecily owned a copy of St Bridget's *Revelations* but it is hard to judge just when her affection for this saint had first developed. A late fifteenth-century manuscript of Syon Abbey's requiem offices included prayers for its benefactors, 'specially for the duce Richard and Cecilye his spowse parenters unto kyng Edward the iiiith'.[35] This might mean that Cecily had been a patron before 1461, although the duke of York's name could easily have been added as a courtesy to the king and his mother in hindsight. The house of York had developed a particular political interest in St Bridget because one of her prophecies, about the importance of the rightful heir, could be read as justification for Edward IV's accession.[36] This had consequently been used in several pieces of Yorkist propaganda.[37]

Cecily's own affection for St Bridget may have developed over the years of her widowhood in response to parallels between her own life and Bridget's. Bridget was a Swedish noblewoman who was widowed when she was forty-one but she engaged in national and international politics, offering advice to kings and popes on the authority of visions she received. Carole Hill argues that Bridget's book of *Revelations* provided particular encouragement to widows who chose to emulate St Bridget's commitment to chastity. Hill also suggests that it gave solace to women trying to manage difficult sons: St Bridget's visions included one in which the Virgin helped her to drag the soul of her dead son Karl to salvation in spite of his degenerate lifestyle.[38] This last may have been especially pertinent to Cecily after George duke of Clarence's death, although there is no evidence in her patronage after 1478 that she was particularly concerned for his soul. It may be that Cecily's interest in St Bridget was initially politically motivated and became spiritually deeper over time. It is a measure of the house of York's shared interest in the Bridgettines that Cecily's granddaughter, Anne de la Pole, eventually became prioress of Syon.[39]

Cecily's daughter-in-law, Anne Neville, duchess of Gloucester, similarly seems to have shared Cecily's interest in the mystical writings propagated by Carthusians and Bridgettines. Both Cecily and Anne owned Mechtild of Hackeborn's *Booke of Gostlye Grace*. Anne's copy still survives in the British Library, signed by herself and her husband Richard.[40] The book's principal owner could have been Richard but, as Ros Voaden has argued, the majority of laypersons associated with manuscripts of Mechtild's visions were women.[41] It was a work that commonly circulated with the works by Bridget of Sweden and indeed Catherine of Siena.[42] When the duchess of Gloucester was in London she would presumably have been able to talk of shared religious interests with her namesake, the duchess of Buckingham, and with Cecily too.

Naturally Cecily still supported the religious interests of those on her estates. In 1480 she persuaded the king to allow six of her tenants at Thaxted to found a fraternity at their parish church, St John the Baptist.[43] Two years later she granted a licence allowing several Suffolk men to alienate the manor of Swifts, near Long Melford, in order to endow a guild of the Holy Name of Jesus in Bury St Edmunds.[44] Her licence mentioned her particular devotion to the Virgin Mary, the Holy Trinity and to the 'Most Sweet Name of Jesus'. This last may have been no more than a polite reference to the name of the guild, but evidence of her devotion to Mary and the Trinity has already been mentioned in the previous chapter so her affection for the Holy Name may well have been genuine too. Indeed, I have already speculated that her prayer beads included some used in this devotion. Ann Hutchison has noted that English manuscripts of Bridget's *Revelations* frequently reveal evidence of this cult which 'emphasized the sweetness, gentleness and accessibility of the human saviour'.[45] The mystics Richard Rolle and Walter Hilton had both written about the name of Jesus as an aid to contemplation. Beyond the small communities with an interest in mysticism, the name of Jesus also had a wide appeal in popular piety because it could be used as something of a talisman on walls, seals and books, often in the form of the monogram 'ihc' or 'ihs'.[46]

The breadth of Cecily's own devotional interests at this period are evident in her connections with the English hospice in Rome. It appears that she commissioned at least one of her chaplains to undertake a pilgrimage to Rome on her behalf. This was William Grave, rector of Sanderton, who stayed at the English hospice in Rome through July and August 1482.[47] It was probably he who delivered to the hospice her gift of a silver and gilt chalice and silver candlesticks.[48] Like her decision to join the Benedictine confraternity, this pilgrimage and the gift to the hospice were less obviously dynastically significant than most of her previous religious acts. It seems that her religion was now genuinely becoming more important to her, perhaps both as a result of increasing age and of the personal losses she had suffered recently. Her daughter Anne duchess of Exeter had died of complications following childbirth in 1476, just two years before George duke of Clarence's death.[49]

Nonetheless, her actual patronage was negligible in comparison with her sons' ambitious religious foundations. On 21 February 1478 Richard duke of Gloucester had acquired a licence to found two new colleges at his northern homes, Barnard Castle and Middleham. Strikingly those who would be prayed for at Middleham included Edward IV, Elizabeth Woodville, Richard's wife, his dead brothers and sisters and his father, but not Cecily.[50] This rather suggests that Richard's own piety was not consciously influenced by hers. By contrast, in 1481, when Cecily's son-in-law, Thomas St Leger, applied for a licence to found a chantry in his wife's memory at St George's, Windsor, he promised to include prayers for Cecily's good estate.[51] Edward also continued to involve his mother in acts of religious patronage with other members of the royal family. For instance, in April 1478 he gave her the right to present the next candidate for a prebend at St Stephen's chapel in Westminster Palace, a role she was to share with her son Richard, her granddaughter Elizabeth of York, and the king's closest friend, William lord Hastings.[52]

The end of Edward's reign

There is further evidence of Cecily's continuing closeness to the king in the fact that Edward IV had by now decided to grant her an annuity of £107 17s. 4d. in addition to all her landed income.[53] Cecily was similarly still managing her own affairs in ways that would benefit the king. In February 1483 she again granted the post of constable of Bridgwater Castle to a man high in the king's favour. On this occasion she appointed Giles Daubeney, a knight of the king's body who was becoming a significant power in the south-west, rather like Sir Humphrey Stafford before him.[54] However, the balance of Cecily's world was about to be overturned once more.

Christmas 1482 had been celebrated with special magnificence, but London gossip held that the king had arranged 'many performances of actors amidst royal splendour' to disguise his melancholy at recent failures in foreign policy.[55] On 23 December 1482 France and Burgundy concluded the Treaty of Arras.[56] This meant that the French dauphin, previously promised to Edward's eldest daughter Elizabeth, was now to marry Mary of Burgundy's daughter Margaret.[57] England was now disappointingly politically isolated once more. The Crowland Continuator dwelt on the new fashions Edward introduced to England that winter and wrote: 'in those days you might have seen a royal Court such as befitted a mighty kingdom, filled with riches and men from almost every nation and (surpassing all else) with the handsome and most delightful children born of the marriage … to Queen Elizabeth'.[58] Yet the Continuator knew he was describing a fool's paradise.

The following Easter Edward suddenly fell mortally ill. As early as 6 April rumours reached York that the king was dead, although it was actually on 9 April that he breathed his last.[59] Cecily had had plenty of opportunity to come to her son's deathbed at Westminster but there is no certain evidence of her whereabouts either then or in the crises that followed.[60] Nonetheless, it is worth examining the immediate aftermath of Edward's death in detail in order to understand the political and family situation in which Cecily found herself.

The crisis of 1483

Cecily must have been devastated at losing Edward. Combined with Cecily's grief there was surely also anxiety about what would happen to the realm under a child king and to her only surviving son, Richard duke of Gloucester. Cecily had grown up in the shadow of infant kings and the dangerous consequences for their uncles, in particular the two previous dukes of Gloucester. Richard himself must similarly have been very aware that his forerunners were both widely believed to have been murdered by men following orders from their royal nephews.

The men closest to Edward V were his Woodville kinsmen. Edward had had his own household since he was two and his time had been divided between his father's court and Ludlow Castle. In both locations his governor and teacher was his uncle Anthony Woodville, Earl Rivers.[61] Before 1483, Richard duke of Gloucester's relations with the Woodvilles seem to have been entirely cordial. Shortly after Clarence's first rebellion, when Richard was just seventeen, Queen Elizabeth had appointed Gloucester to the office of steward of her lands and granted him an annual fee of £100.[62] In subsequent years he was associated with various of the queen's kin, including Richard Haute (whom he knighted) and Katherine Haute (who was possibly his mistress).[63] As Rosemary Horrox has argued, if there had been simmering tensions between the Woodvilles and the duke of Gloucester we would expect to find some evidence of this in those regions where both were important landowners, but there is none.[64]

London gossip in 1483 told that Richard blamed the Woodvilles for the death of his beloved brother George.[65] Yet it is hard to find evidence of this notion before Richard made his bid for the throne. Indeed, Richard had had every reason to resent George in the aftermath of the readeption and their bitter quarrel over the Beauchamp/Neville inheritance. Contrary to Mancini's account, Richard had not withdrawn from the royal court in the aftermath of George's death.[66] Consequently, in April 1483 the queen and her brother, Anthony earl Rivers, clearly expected to be able to work with Richard in governing the realm on Edward V's behalf.

However, the Woodvilles certainly did have powerful enemies elsewhere in the political community. Mancini implied that Henry duke of Buckingham's antagonism was due to loathing for his childhood wife, the queen's sister Katherine, although a sense that he had been excluded from power in Wales by Woodville dominance there may have been equally significant.[67] There was also rivalry between the Woodvilles and William Lord Hastings, who had been Edward IV's closest friend and his chamberlain.[68] According to Mancini, Hastings sent letters to duke Richard claiming that the queen and her kin were trying to exclude Richard from his rightful position of greatest power in the new regime.[69] In practice the council in London were modelling their decisions on those made for the minorities of Henry VI and, particularly, Richard II. Henry VI had acceded as a baby and not been crowned until he was almost eight. Richard II, at the age of ten, was also younger than Edward V when he became king and his lords decided that he should be crowned only twenty-five days after the old king's death.[70] Edward V's council decided to adopt exactly the same time-period and appointed his coronation for 4 May.[71] This decision was made in the absence of Edward V, who had been at Ludlow when his father died, and of Duke Richard.

Richard duke of Gloucester's father had been driven to rebellion and death by his belief that he was being excluded from his birthright as the king's closest kinsman, and by fear of those whom the king loved. Perhaps it was his awareness of this that made Gloucester suspicious of those whom Edward V most trusted. Later writers asserted that Gloucester and Buckingham's initial meeting with Rivers was entirely cordial although it may be that Rivers's confidence in his own position heightened the anxiety already aroused in the dukes by Hastings's letters.[72] On Wednesday 30 April the dukes' retainers arrested Rivers as well as the queen's son, Richard Grey and others in the young king's entourage, 'and ordered them to be taken to the North in captivity'.[73] At this point it is unlikely that either duke had any firm plan of what they would do with the queen's kin except that they wanted them out of the way while the new regime was established.[74]

When rumour of the arrests reached London on 1 May the queen fled once more into sanctuary at Westminster Abbey with all her daughters, and those of her sons not in the duke of Gloucester's keeping: Thomas Grey, marquis of Dorset, and Richard duke of York. This was to prove a tragic miscalculation, perhaps even one that provoked the duke of Gloucester into usurpation. Richard's own childhood experience with Cecily had led him to expect a royal mother to prioritize the needs of whichever of her children was closest to the throne. He must have assumed that Elizabeth Woodville would want to be as close as possible to Edward V and would therefore work with him despite Richard Grey's imprisonment. Elizabeth Woodville chose instead to protect her more obviously vulnerable eldest son, the marquis of Dorset. The fact that Dorset was in his late twenties did not lessen his mother's determination to do all that she could to protect him. It was obvious that he would be the duke's next target and Elizabeth was well aware that Yorkist lords did not always respect the church's right to give sanctuary. She knew that it would be far more controversial for the duke of Gloucester to break sanctuary if the king's own mother and full siblings were there than if he were merely seizing Thomas Grey. Elizabeth may have hoped to bargain from here for the release of her other son, Richard Grey, confident that the duke of Gloucester could not expect to govern without her. If so she must soon have realized her error. The duke of Gloucester was not to be persuaded to backtrack. From now on he saw the queen as his enemy.

It must swiftly have become apparent that Richard duke of Gloucester was now in a very dangerous situation. Mancini is probably broadly right in his depiction of Gloucester's confrontation with the young king: Gloucester naively expecting his nephew to believe that he was acting in his best interests, caught out by the self-confidence of the mature twelve-year-old boy who had 'seen no evil' in his Woodville uncle and had 'complete trust' in the queen.[75] If Richard released Rivers and Grey now he could not hope to build good relations with them, but if he kept them prisoner or killed them then he must live in fear of retribution when the king reached maturity.

On 7 May the dukes of Gloucester and Buckingham, together with nine bishops and some of Edward IV's executors met at Baynard's Castle to consider Edward IV's will.[76] Despite Richard's regular use of the property that summer, it was still understood to be 'the customary residence of the splendid and most illustrious lady, Lady Cecily duchess of York'.[77] She may well have been present at the meeting but in the absence of the king's principal executor, the queen, the others declined to administer the will.[78] Richard's regular residence at Baynard's Castle seems to imply that Cecily was not opposing his policy that summer. No doubt she was very conscious of the political tightrope he was walking. She was only too aware of the turmoil that could surround a child king and may well have brought herself to believe that Richard's accession was God's will. Yet it is highly unlikely that Cecily was actually driving Richard's policy. Had this been the case it is scarcely likely that Henry VII would have given her such a privileged and protected role in his own regime two years later when he would surely have relished an excuse to take control of her extensive properties.

Richard's actions throughout early May 1483 seem to have alarmed few but the Woodvilles. By 8 May he had adopted his father's former title as protector and over the next few weeks he systematically confiscated the lands and offices of almost all the Woodvilles and many of their closest associates.[79] However, rather than promoting his own men in their place, Richard usually demonstrated his continuing commitment to his dead brother by choosing servants of the previous king.[80] One exception to Richard's general preference for the *status quo* was his decision to remove Thomas Rotherham, archbishop of York from his post as chancellor of England.[81] It may be that Gloucester felt Rotherham was too close to the Woodvilles. A more dramatic exception was Gloucester's generosity to Henry duke of Buckingham who was granted what Rosemary Horrox called 'an independent satrapy consisting of Wales, the March and three southern English counties'.[82] All these manoeuvres appeared designed to set up a strong position for the two dukes in Edward V's reign.

Edward V's coronation was rescheduled for 22 June and letters were sent out to the men chosen to receive their knighthoods as part of the ceremony. Those invited included Alexander Cressener who was one of Cecily's officers in Suffolk and the only one of her nephews who would be remembered in her will.[83] Another prospective knight was Henry Heydon, the steward of Cecily's household.[84] They may both have been proposed by Cecily. The letters were despatched on 5 June, the same day that the duke of Gloucester's wife, Anne Neville, arrived in London for the celebration.[85] At about the same time Thomas Grey, marquis of Dorset fled his sanctuary at Westminster, eluding a manhunt with troops and dogs.[86] The queen and her younger children stayed at the abbey, demonstrating her continued protest at the duke of Gloucester's policies while her son Edward V remained in the Tower of London.

The following week there was a dramatic turn of events. On the morning of Friday 13 June William Lord Hastings arrived at the Tower of London for a council meeting and there he was charged with treason and immediately executed. The former chancellor, Thomas Rotherham, archbishop of York and John Morton, bishop of Ely, were both arrested at the same time but, as clergymen, were spared execution. Instead they were imprisoned. 'Thus fell Hastings', Mancini wrote, 'killed not by those enemies he had always feared, but by a friend he had never doubted'.[87] Mancini, like many others later in the year, was convinced that Richard had invented a charge of treason in order to dispose of the men most likely to remain loyal to Edward V when Richard moved to seize his throne. Historians since have been divided on the plausibility of such a plot. A third clergyman arrested at this time, perhaps for the same reason, was Edward IV's secretary Oliver King.[88] King was not only a man with whom Cecily had been accustomed to do business but was also a man she trusted. In 1495 it was his name that headed her list of executors.

On 21 June, which should have been the eve of Edward V's coronation, Simon Stallworth, a servant of Bishop John Russell, the new chancellor, wrote of the fear and confusion among the political elite in London that followed Hastings's death: 'with us is much trouble and every man doubts other'.[89] On the Monday after Hastings's execution, 16 June, Stallworth explained, there 'was at Westminster great plenty of harnessed men'. They were attending a visit by Cardinal Bourchier, Chancellor Russell and other lords who demanded that the queen hand over her youngest son, Richard duke of York.[90] In the face of so many men of authority, accompanied by men at arms, the queen acquiesced. Stallworth reported that the duke of Gloucester welcomed his nephew at the palace of Westminster 'with many loving words'. Thereafter the cardinal took him to join Edward V at the Tower of London where York was, 'blessed be Jesus, merry'. Intriguingly Stallworth added a postscript to the effect that all of Hastings's affinity had become the duke of Buckingham's men. Thus the stage was set for Richard duke of Gloucester to take the throne of England.

Allegations of adultery

Dominic Mancini, writing late in 1483, recalled that Richard first openly showed his ambition when he

> so corrupted preachers of the divine word that in their sermons to the people they did not blush to say, contrary to heaven's law and all religion, that Edward's offspring should be immediately rooted out (*extirpandam*), because he had not been a legitimate king nor could his descendants be so. For Edward having been conceived in adultery was wholly unlike the deceased duke of York, whose son he was falsely said to be. But Richard, duke of Gloucester, who most resembled his father, was being called the legitimate successor to the kingdom.[91]

Mancini was one of many writers to allege that Cecily was accused of adultery by her youngest son. Yet their stories are somewhat different.

The Great Chronicle of London, which was written in about 1512 by a London draper, also recorded that Richard had impugned his mother's virtue. In this later account there was only a single preacher and sermon. The speaker was Ralph Shaw, a Cambridge doctor of theology and brother to the mayor of London. Shaw was specifically preaching in front of the duke of Gloucester and the duke of Buckingham at St Paul's Cross on the Sunday after Hastings's death, 15 June.[92] That of course would have been before Richard duke of York had been removed from sanctuary, allegedly to attend his brother's coronation, so it is generally assumed that the real date of Shaw's sermon must have been a week later, 22 June.[93] The author of the *Great Chronicle* was writing almost thirty years after the events he described. If he had not actually attended the sermon in 1483 that was plenty of time for rumours of scandal to develop into a more attractively coherent but less accurate story.

Polydore Vergil and Sir Thomas More, both also writing early in Henry VIII's reign, similarly recorded a single sermon. Like Mancini, they knew that the justification for calling Edward IV a bastard was his physical dissimilarity to his father. Vergil made this argument sound ridiculous and observed that the audience wondered at the 'foolhardiness and doltishness of the preacher'.[94] Thomas More took the comic possibilities even further, presenting a farce of missed cues and incompetent preaching.[95] Despite the humour in these accounts, there can be little doubt that at least one London preacher did accuse Cecily duchess of York of adultery at some point. Thomas More explained that Shaw began his sermon with a text from the book of Wisdom, '*Spuria vitulamina non agent radices altas*. That is to say bastard slippes shal neuer take depe roote.'[96] Mancini's reference to 'rooting out' Edward's heirs was almost certainly drawn from the same text. It is also very similar to the rhetoric about 'fals heyres fostred' that had accompanied the Yorkists' attacks on the house of Lancaster two decades earlier.[97]

Whether writing of multiple sermons or just one, all four writers considered the topic utterly shameful.[98] Mancini was presumably echoing initial reactions to events when he said he felt that the preachers should have blushed and were immoral (*contra fas*).[99] All of which begs the question, why would the duke of Gloucester have slandered his own mother when it would obviously appal those he needed to impress? This is even harder to fathom when we read Mancini's account of the official explanation for Edward V's deposition. He related that the duke of Buckingham told the other lords that Edward V himself was illegitimate. This was because a certain duke (probably meaning the earl of Warwick) had contracted a proxy marriage with 'another wife … on the continent' on Edward IV's behalf, so that the king had not been free to marry Elizabeth Woodville.[100] It was certainly not unprecedented for fifteenth-century political propaganda to encompass multiple accusations of unsuitability for kingship. However, on 18 July 1483 Richard's signet register referred to Edward IV as 'our derrest Brothere late king' but to Edward V as 'Edward Bastard late called king Edward the Vth'.[101] At this early stage Richard was not supporting his claim to the throne with slanders on his mother's virtue. J. A. F. Thomson speculated that the 'allegations of Edward IV's illegitimacy may originally have emanated from Buckingham rather than Gloucester'.[102]

Alternatively, the story of Cecily's adultery may have begun as a matter of popular gossip. It was only five years since the duke of Clarence had been executed for crimes that allegedly included saying that Edward IV was illegitimate. It is scarcely surprising that the story should have been revived in London amid the uncertainties and fears of June 1483. Some Londoners, anxiously contemplating the rule of yet another child king which had already begun inauspiciously, might well have linked that gossip with memories of adultery allegations at the time that previous child kings had been deposed.[103] In 1483 Mancini recalled scattered preachers to whom he could give no name or audience. With hindsight, after the princes' disappearance, he and others assumed that in that summer the story of Edward IV's illegitimacy had originated with Richard even though such unchivalrous behaviour would have been very obviously politically misjudged. As Michael Hicks has argued, 'it was perverse to trace one's claim from Richard duke of York, who was never a king, rather than from his son, who reigned for over twenty years'.[104]

Perhaps it was because he was aware of these stories that Richard used Cecily's home, rather than his own, to receive the lords of the realm who formally asked him to become king on 26 June 1483.[105] According to Mancini, 'all the lords forgathered at the house of Richard's mother … There the whole business was transacted, the oaths of allegiance given, and other indispensable acts duly performed. On the two following days the people of London and the higher clergy did likewise'.[106] It is not unreasonable to assume that Cecily herself was present alongside Richard's wife at these events, although neither woman is mentioned by the men who recorded it.

Despite Richard's apparent attempt to distance himself from the slanders against his mother, there is further reason to think that his relationship with Cecily may have been complicated at this point. As he prepared for the coronation he drew up a new list of men who would be created knights of the Bath. It is unsurprising that this was significantly different from the list drawn up for Edward V since it should reflect his own connections and affinity. However, both Cecily's nephew, Alexander Cressener, and her steward, Henry Heydon, had been dropped.[107] We can only guess at the reason for this. Perhaps Richard felt that including them among his knights of the Bath might have suggested that he was as much under his mother's influence as Edward IV had been at his accession.

The evidence of Cecily's relationship with Richard throughout his reign, discussed below, is confusingly contradictory. Taken together it seems to suggest that Cecily was not as close to Richard as she had been to Edward, perhaps even that she was not happy about the way that Richard had deposed her grandson. Nonetheless, she was the ultimate political survivor of the Wars of the Roses. Just as she had bided her time in 1470, so in 1483 she was not about to jeopardize the privilege that her motherhood brought by resisting the *status quo*. Sources discussed in the following chapter intimate that she remained proud of her role as Richard's mother, even after his death.

'Buckingham's rebellion'

Richard seems to have spent the night after being acclaimed king at Baynard's Castle. The earliest known document of his reign was issued on 27 June 'in a certain high chamber next to the chapel in the lodging of the lady Cecily duchess of York'.[108]

Cecily may still have been in London but she was certainly absent from Richard and Anne's sumptuous coronation on 6 July. Like her absence from Elizabeth Woodville's coronation, this was probably a matter of protocol rather than a political statement. Cecily's only remaining sibling, the redoubtable Katherine, duchess of Norfolk, did attend.[109] It is the last record we have of Katherine's life. Very likely by the autumn she too had died, leaving Cecily the only Neville of her generation still alive.[110]

It is impossible to know whether Cecily chose to support any of the men who were in Richard's service as she did Edward's because no letters patent from her survive from this period. What we do know is that some men in her service became embroiled in the rebellions against Richard that broke out across England in the autumn of 1483. Most, like Giles Daubeney, were men who had also served Edward IV so their behaviour cannot be used to interpret Cecily's own opinions, especially since local politics tended to play as much of a role as dynastic loyalties in their motivation.[111] That said, just after the rebellion a general pardon was issued to one of the most important members of Cecily's household, the dean of her chapel, Richard Lessy, as well as to three men of Berkhamsted and to one of Cecily's receivers, Richard Manory.[112] The timing may have been mere coincidence but there is every likelihood that these men close to Cecily also had some peripheral connection with the uprising against Richard III.

In its earliest stages, the autumn 1483 rebellion had been aimed at liberating Cecily's grandsons, Edward V and Richard duke of York, from the Tower of London.[113] Lady Margaret Beaufort and the old queen became key players, along with John Morton, bishop of Ely.[114] Much of the impetus seems to have come from gentry families who had long been loyal to Edward IV and were dissatisfied with the legality of Richard III's accession or his changes in administration.[115] Although it is now known as Buckingham's rebellion the duke's true role, motives and intentions remain a matter for considerable debate. Some contemporaries assumed he had come to regret his role in helping Richard to take the throne.[116] There were others who suspected him of masterminding the murder of Edward V and his brother which might imply that he now had designs on the throne himself.[117] The Crowland Continuator, who seems to have been a well-informed civil servant, stated that it had been Buckingham who initially persuaded the council to house Edward V in the Tower rather than at Westminster, even though some 'did not wish it'.[118] This chronicler also explained that it was immediately after Buckingham joined the rebellion that 'a rumour arose that King Edward's sons, by some unknown manner of violent destruction, had met their fate'.[119]

At news of the princes' death, the focus of the rebellion shifted from reinstating Edward V to a potential Lancastrian claimant who could marry the boy's elder sister, Elizabeth. Elizabeth was still in sanctuary at Westminster with her mother. This new focus for the rebellion was Lady Margaret Beaufort's exiled son, Henry Tudor. Tudor could draw on the support of long-standing Lancastrian exiles to join the disaffected Yorkists as well as commanding some foreign aid. This made him far more dangerous to Richard than a child king in the Tower, despite his dubious lineage. Richard took no steps to refute or confirm the rumours of Edward V's death. Tales that the boys had been poisoned, starved, suffocated or even drowned in malmsey wine like their uncle George all eventually circulated, provoking horror and outrage against the man who had imprisoned them.[120] Cecily was surely in a position to demand to know exactly what had befallen her grandsons. For the sake of the security of her dynasty she remained silent about what she knew.

If it had been Buckingham who orchestrated the princes' deaths, then both Richard III and Henry Tudor were significantly tainted by association. This would explain why neither king made a public declaration about the boys' fate. It was only after Henry VII's death that a story surfaced blaming Cecily's former ward, James Tyrrell, for murdering the princes on Richard's orders either in July or August of 1483.[121] Allegedly Tyrell confessed to the murders in 1501, just before being executed for treasonous involvement with Cecily's grandson, Edmund de la Pole, earl of Suffolk. Yet there is no evidence of any attempt to publicize such a confession before 1512.[122] Tyrell had certainly been a loyal servant to Richard III, but Henry VII allowed him to remain in post as lieutenant of Guînes and within three years of Bosworth Tyrell was a knight of the body, as he had been for Richard.[123] Why he should have risked all this to support the disaffected earl of Suffolk remains one of the many mysteries of this period. Thomas More's colourful story of Tyrell smothering the sleeping princes ensured that his name would long be remembered with revulsion despite the demonstrable inaccuracies and contradictions in More's tale.[124]

In the autumn of 1483 contrary winds delayed Henry Tudor from making his planned landing at Plymouth and floodwaters prevented Buckingham from crossing the Severn to join other rebels. The rebellion was swiftly crushed and Tudor retreated to Brittany. Here he was joined by many Yorkist rebels, the queen's only remaining son, Thomas Grey, among them. Buckingham was captured and executed as was Cecily's son-in-law, Thomas St Leger, the widower of her daughter Anne.

The new regime

When parliament was at last able to meet in January 1484 the case for Richard's right to the throne was presented, apparently comprising 'the tenour ... [and] all the continue' of the petition presented to him at Baynard's Castle the previous summer.[125] Here there was no mention of Cecily's adultery. However, there was a slight reference to Edward's possible ineligibility to rule: 'Ye be born withyn this lande' the composer of the *Titulus Regius* told Richard III, 'by reason wherof, ... all the thre estatis of the lande have, and may have, more certayn knowlage of youre byrth and filiacion'.[126] In this there was perhaps an allusion to another popular trope in political propaganda – babies being switched at birth if the true heir died. Just such a story had circulated about the foreign-born John of Gaunt.[127] This added to the broader picture of Edward IV's inappropriate rule, but made no specific allegation against Cecily. It was a minor detail that for most hearers was probably swiftly forgotten in the face of the more serious charges. Richard III's claim to the throne rested first, like all previous such justifications, upon the dissolute rule of his predecessor in which 'the lawe of God and man' had been 'confounded'.[128] Since the child Edward V could scarcely be excluded on the basis of his father's misdemeanours, the explanation then turned to the boy's illegitimacy. His parents' marriage had been made without the knowyng and assent of the lordes of this lond, and also by sorcerie and wichecrafte committed by the said Elizabeth and hir moder Jaquet duchesse of Bedford, as the comon opinion of the people and the publique voice and fame is thorough all this land, and herafter, if and as the caas shall require, shalbee proved sufficiently in tyme and place convenient.[129]

A royal marriage had already been dissolved upon just these grounds forty years before, that of Humphrey duke of Gloucester, and Edward IV's own marriage had been threatened by the story in 1469. This made it a far stronger justification for disinheriting Edward V than any aspersion on Cecily's chastity. Richard probably had no intention of making good this threat to bring Elizabeth Woodville to trial, not least because of the popular sympathy that Eleanor Cobham's experience had aroused. Nonetheless, the threat may have helped force Elizabeth into agreeing to terms for leaving the Westminster sanctuary the following March when she placed her family under Richard's protection.

It was only, as Charles Ross observed, 'as a kind of afterthought' that the idea of a precontract was again introduced at the very end of the *Titulus Regius*.[130] Yet the Crowland Continuator recalled this as the principal justification for Richard III's coup.[131] In contrast to the tale Mancini had heard the previous summer, the supposed prior bride was a woman much like the queen herself, Eleanor Butler (née Talbot), whose parents Cecily had known well in Normandy. Indeed, Eleanor's father, John earl of Shrewsbury, had stood godfather to Cecily's daughter Elizabeth beside the queen's own mother Jacquetta.[132] Eleanor Butler had died more than a decade earlier and was in no position to defend or corroborate the tale. As Anne Crawford noted, if this story were true, it would have been relatively easy for Edward IV to obtain a papal dispensation legalizing his marriage to Elizabeth Woodville before Edward V was even born.[133] The Crowland Continuator described the story as 'sedition and infamy' that no one in London dared admit to having composed.[134] By early 1484 the precise legality or credibility of the justifications Richard put forward were not all that important. Very similar caveats could be made about the claims of Henry IV and Edward IV, as well as Henry VII later. What really mattered was that Richard had full control of the kingdom, he had been crowned by the archbishop of Canterbury, and that parliament acknowledged him as king.

Richard must still have been anxious about further resistance. There is some indication of his sense of vulnerability in a letter he wrote to Cecily from Pontefract on 3 June 1484: 'Madam I recommmaunde me to you as hertely as is to me possible Beseching you in my most humble and effectuouse wise of youre daly blissing to my Synguler comfort & defence in my nede'.[135] The immediate context of this letter was the death of his only legitimate child, Edward of Middleham, two months earlier. This had been a crushing blow which implied to contemporaries that the king was not in God's favour. In an echo of Cecily's earlier requests to see more of her son, Richard continued, 'Madam, I hertely beseche you that I may often here from you to my Comfort'. In the past year Richard's circle of those he trusted had shrunk dramatically. He was now a king without an obvious heir whose wife seemed incapable of producing more children. He was perhaps already considering whether he might eventually have to divorce his wife in order to hold onto his throne. Cecily was almost the only family he had left.

The main purpose of Richard's letter to Cecily related to another potential threat to his security: Cecily's former steward in Wiltshire, William Colyngbourne. Colyngbourne had been a loyal servant to Edward IV throughout his reign, but he had recently been dismissed from Cecily's service.[136] Perhaps there was some suspicion about his loyalty during Buckingham's rebellion or subsequently, but this can only be conjecture. Richard may well have asked Cecily to dismiss Colyngbourne since the king now felt it necessary to provide an alternative officer for her. In the letter he offered the services of his own lord chamberlain, Sir Francis Lovell, who himself owned property in Wiltshire. This arrangement may in part have provoked Colyngbourne to pen his famous doggerel, 'The Catte, the Ratte and Lovell our dogge rulyth all England under a hogge', which he pinned to the door of St Paul's Cathedral the following month. By then Colyngbourne was also involved in more serious treasonable activities, trying to encourage Henry Tudor to make another invasion attempt. Colyngbourne was finally brought to trial that December, along with John Turburvyle of Friar Mayne in Dorset, after which he was hanged, drawn and quartered.[137]

Less than a year after Edward of Middleham's death, the king's family shrunk further still. Shortly after New Year 1485 Queen Anne suddenly fell ill. She died on 16 March 1485, the day of a 'great eclipse of the sun'.[138] Despite his plans to found three colleges in the north of England, Richard decided to bury his queen at Westminster Abbey. Even the critical Crowland Continuator conceded that she was interred 'with honours no less than befitted the burial of a queen'.[139] Queens' funerals were typically occasions for dynastic celebration in which many of the citizens of London were expected to be involved in communal mourning.[140] Usually kings planned to be buried with their queens even if, like Anne of Bohemia or Joan of Navarre, they were not the mother of the king's heir. Richard III's position was somewhat different since he was probably hoping that his second queen would be more prestigious as well as more fertile and may well have been contemplating burial in York, but in 1485 contemporaries would have been aware of the usual precedent associating kings with their queens' burial sites. Henry IV and Edward IV had both chosen to break with the traditions of the line they had usurped and selected new royal burial sites at Canterbury and Windsor. By contrast Richard III seems to have been trying to imply his continuity with earlier kings by burying his queen at Westminster Abbey.

Anne Neville's death caused a sudden change in her mother-in-law's status. As of 17 March, Cecily was once again the most politically senior woman in the kingdom. This is probably why, on 9 May, Cecily's name appeared among those to be prayed for on a licence to found a chantry in the church of St John the Baptist at Marldon in Devon.[141] The founder was Otho Gilbert of Compton who was the local sheriff but seems to have had no obvious connection with Cecily herself. Apparently he felt that, in the absence of a queen, it was appropriate to pair Cecily's name with that of the king, just as many petitioners for such licences had done before September 1464.

The king himself found time in his busy schedules to visit his mother. On Tuesday, 17 May 1485 he arrived at Berkhamsted and stayed with Cecily until the end of the week.[142] He may well have taken the opportunity to ask Cecily's advice or blessing on his plans to marry a Portuguese princess. Cecily's higher status, however, was not to last for long and it is unlikely that she ever saw her son Richard again.

On 7 August 1485 Henry Tudor landed at Milford Haven with a relatively small band of Lancastrian exiles and hired French soldiers. News of the invasion reached Richard four days later. Neither man seems to have attracted as many supporters as they might have hoped as they marched to face each other. On 22 August 1485 the last of Cecily's sons died in battle at Bosworth. As was so often the case, regional conflicts were being fought upon the battlefield as well as the contest for the throne. For once Cecily's Westmorland kinsmen were fighting alongside her York family. The earls of Westmorland had benefited from Richard's lordship in the north. Unfortunately, this had been at the expense of families like the Stanleys who consequently stood aloof at Bosworth, initially refusing to commit to either side. Despite his superior numbers, the king's side seems to have been doing less well. Then Richard made the surprising decision to lead a cavalry charge directly at Tudor. Perhaps it reflected his confidence that God was on his side. Perhaps it was to test just that. It might ultimately have succeeded had William Lord Stanley not then chosen to commit his troops in favour of Henry Tudor, who was his brother's stepson.[143] Like Richard duke of York twenty-five years earlier, Richard III was killed in the heart of battle and his body abused by his victors. Cecily must soon have heard how his corpse was slung naked over a horse to be carried back to Leicester for public viewing and ultimately burial by the Franciscans.[144] It was time for Cecily to reinvent herself once more for the final chapter of her life.

The Queen's Grandmother: 1485–1495

*I Cecill wif unto the right noble prince Richard late Duke of yorke Fader unto the
most christen prince my Lord and son king Edward the iiijth … bequieth and surrender my soule in to the mercifull handes of allmyghty god my maker.*[1]

The most detailed surviving sources for Cecily's everyday life belong to the very last
decade of her life, when she was in her seventies. Her household regulations, her
will and the description of her daily routine are supplemented by a variety of estate
records. As C. A. J. Armstrong argued, the former suggest that in her last years Cecily
possessed a 'tranquillity of spirit' and 'rigid concentration on the Christian life' that
provide a surprising contrast with the political turbulence through which she had
lived.[2] Yet even after the tragic deaths of all her sons and many of her grandsons,
Cecily remained politically active. She drew men who were powerful in the new
regime into her own service and ensured that Henry VII protected her financial
rights. When one of her servants was found guilty of misprision of treason she rallied
her resources to ensure that his fine was paid with speed. This last decade of her life
was dominated by her care for her household members with whom she shared much
of her religious experience. Nonetheless her primary identity was still that of a royal
matriarch. Cecily accepted Henry VII's kingship and celebrated her own status as the
queen's grandmother.

After Bosworth

Naturally a number of Cecily's servants had fought with Richard III at Bosworth. John
Howard, duke of Norfolk was slain on the field.[3] Sir Francis Lovell took sanctuary in
Colchester, presumably at St John's Abbey where Howard himself had taken sanctuary
during the readeption.[4] Intriguingly, at her death Cecily owed £21 to this sanctuary.
Perhaps she had promised to repay extra hospitality provided for her former servant
and other Yorkists. If so she was tardy about repaying her debt, but that was common
among the late medieval nobility. No evidence of this would have survived had it not
been for the fact that the dean of her chapel, Richard Lessy, had failed to carry out her
orders on this matter before he himself died in 1498. Lessy's will included instructions

to purchase five chalices 'clerely worth' £21 to be given to the abbey at Colchester in payment of the debt owed to its sanctuary.[5] The chance survival of this record increases the likelihood that discreet help had occasionally passed from Cecily's household to those in sanctuary on other occasions but, unsurprisingly, no other evidence seems to remain.

By 3 September 1485 Henry VII had arrived in London where he proceeded to St Paul's, as Cecily's sons had done, and then took up residence at the bishop of London's palace.[6] Henry had already despatched Robert Willoughby to Sheriff Hutton to bring Cecily's most important grandchildren back to London: Edward earl of Warwick and Elizabeth of York. Initially both were taken into the household of the new king's mother, Lady Margaret Beaufort, at Coldharbour.[7] A year later Warwick was discreetly moved into lodgings in the Tower of London where he remained until his death in 1499.[8] Henry VII was crowned on 30 October 1485 and his first parliament gathered on 7 November. Over the next few days many of the attainders passed under Richard III and Edward IV were reversed and the act bastardizing Edward IV's children was nullified.[9] However, after months of preparation, it was not until 16 January 1486 that a papal legate issued a satisfactory dispensation for the new king to marry Elizabeth of York.[10] The wedding took place two days later.[11]

Responding to the Tudor victory

Polydore Vergil maintained that early in Henry VII's reign Cecily complained 'to many noble men ... of that great injury which her son Richard had done her' in accusing her of adultery.[12] It seems unlikely that the seventy-year-old duchess voluntarily reminded men of her family's scandal although it is not impossible that she attempted to ingratiate herself with the new regime by distancing herself from her most controversial son. In formal documents intended for the eyes of royal servants Cecily avoided describing herself as Richard III's mother. Her will mentions Edward twice, but Richard not at all. Nonetheless, the actions of her servants indicate that in private Cecily had not disowned Richard and was still proud to have been his mother. Her servant Robert Incent died of the sweating sickness in the first year of Henry VII's reign and his brass memorial plaque in Berkhamsted Church commemorates his service to 'the noble pryncesse lady Cecyle duchesse of Yorke and mother unto the worthy kyng Edward iiij and Richard the thyrde'. Although the surviving brass was probably commissioned as late as Henry VIII's reign, it is unlikely that his family would have used such wording if Richard's name had been a source of embarrassment in the old duchess's household (albeit the inscription suggests that Richard was not 'worthy'). More significantly, in 1489 Richard Lessy described her as 'the most illustrious princess Cecily, duchess of York, mother of Kings Edward IV and Richard III recently kings of England'. He was then arranging for prayers to be said for her welfare at Hurley Priory, near Marlow.[13]

It may be no coincidence that the men whom Henry VII eventually charged with commissioning Richard III's tomb were men whom Cecily also trusted. Both were members of Henry VII's council, Sir Reginald Bray and Sir Thomas Lovell, and she appointed them as executors of her will.[14] Lovell was a Norfolk lawyer closely connected with her household steward, Henry Heydon, and with her constable at Bridgwater, Giles Daubeney.[15] In 1495 Lovell was steward of her estates at Ansty in Hertfordshire although it may be that this appointment had been made after her death.[16] Reginald Bray also had connections with Daubeney, whom he had persuaded to join Buckingham's rebellion against Richard III.[17] More importantly, Bray had long been a servant to Margaret Beaufort and must first have come to Cecily's attention in this capacity.[18]

Cecily seems to have made a very deliberate policy of cultivating men who were in favour with the new regime, many of whom, like Lovell and Bray, had been involved in Buckingham's rebellion. Less than a month after Henry VII's triumphant first entry into London she had appointed Sir Robert Willoughby as her steward in Wiltshire, the post previously held by William Colyngbourne and then Francis Viscount Lovell. She also made Willoughby keeper of her park at Fasterne on a wage of 6d. a day.[19] Willoughby had served in various posts in Edward IV's administration and was a key figure in Buckingham's rebellion for which he had been attainted in January 1484.[20] After Bosworth Cecily reappointed Giles Daubeney as her constable of Bridgwater Castle and she made him her chief steward in Somerset and Dorset.[21] In exile Daubeney had become one of Henry Tudor's closest confidants and he would eventually replace William Stanley as lord chamberlain. Another key rebel in the autumn of 1483 had been Richard Guildford whom Henry VII swiftly appointed master of the ordnance and armoury in the Tower of London, and a chamberlain of the exchequer.[22] Shortly before her death Cecily appointed him steward of her lands in Kent, Surrey and Sussex.[23]

For these men, their service to Cecily was only of minor importance to their careers. For others Cecily's support seems to have helped them to flourish under Henry VII. For instance, in November 1485 the king appointed Ralph Verney, second son of the Yorkist mayor of the same name, to some minor offices in royal service, thereby indicating that he considered Verney a man he was prepared to trust.[24] Shortly afterwards Cecily made him keeper of her parks at Berkhamsted and Kings Langley and steward of these lordships.[25] Cecily's decision to appoint a man with Yorkist credentials but in the king's favour was strategic. The king had previously promised that on Cecily's death those offices would go to James Parker, one of the gentlemen ushers of his chamber. Henry now revised that decision in Verney's favour, presumably with Cecily's encouragement.[26] Verney's career prospered still further when he married Lady Margaret Beaufort's niece, Eleanor Pole. Such interconnections helped to keep Cecily at the heart of the political community. Eleanor Pole was one of the queen's ladies-in-waiting and Ralph eventually became chamberlain to the household of Cecily's great-granddaughter, Princess Margaret.[27] However, Ralph Verney can have had little time to spend on his service to Cecily and it was perhaps for this reason that she eventually limited his responsibilities to Kings Langley and gave his older brother John the more lucrative stewardship at neighbouring Berkhamsted.[28] This was despite the king's earlier promise that Ralph should hold both offices for life.

Henry VII in turn brought Cecily's existing servants into his own administration. Most notably, Henry Heydon finally achieved his knighthood at Henry VII's coronation and carried dishes into the coronation banquet alongside Reginald Bray.[29]

John Gregory gave up some of his service to Cecily when he was made a yeoman of the king's crown, although he remained her bailiff at Hitchin.[30] It is not always clear where original loyalties lay among the men who worked for both Cecily and the king: Sir Roger Cotton and Sir Thomas Gray were both knights of the king's body but the former was her steward at properties in Kent and Hertfordshire whereas the latter was keeper of her parks at Thaxted.[31]

There is no reason to think that Cecily was being forced to take on board the king's choices. Henry made many grants promising positions on her estates after her death to men who clearly did have to wait until 1495 to take up their posts.[32] An extraordinary court case in November 1494 suggests that some of her tenants had a quite extreme confidence in her authority. A certain John Gardyner of Erith, when arrested by the undersheriff of Kent, allegedly argued that the king's officers had 'nothyng to doo here in this fraunches ... for my lady is bothe Kinge and lorde here in this fraunches'.[33] Gardyner then assembled some sixty men who dragged the undersheriff, William Rose, and his servants from their horses, one declaring 'We all be my lady of Yorkis tenants and by goddis bonys we will kepe her franchises heer'.[34] That said, the accusations against Gardyner and his supporters that followed are so bizarre that at some point either the defendants or the plaintiff must have been concocting stories from their imagination so that this is unlikely to represent many people's perception of Cecily's authority.[35]

Throughout the reign Henry consistently safeguarded Cecily's sources of income. In November 1485, during his first parliament, Cecily was among a number of Yorkists who were exempted from the resumptions that were designed to help Henry rebuild the royal finances after Edward IV's expensive last years.[36] She was here styled 'our welbelovid cosyn Cecilie duchesse of York'.[37] The following February Henry reissued her licence to export 250½ sacks of wool duty free each year, a privilege that was expected to provide the equivalent of an annuity of nearly £700.[38] Having confirmed all of Edward IV's gifts of lands and annuities to her in June 1486, the following November the king reminded the bailiffs and receivers at various towns of their obligation to pay these annuities.[39] Much the largest of these sums was £100 due from York. Cecily had been in dispute with successive high sheriffs of Yorkshire over their failure to pay some or all of this annuity since the early 1470s. During her sons' reigns she had taken seven former sheriffs to court over these debts.[40] In the spring of 1486 she began a case against Sir Thomas Markenfield, one of Richard III's affinity, who had been sheriff at the close of his reign, for £50 unpaid.[41] Henry VII subsequently ordered the then sheriff, Sir John Neville, to collect goods to this value (plus expenses) to ensure that Cecily received her dues, yet in 1488 she brought a case against Neville himself for failure to pay any of the £100 during his term of office.[42] Cecily's lack of any other interests in the region, despite her title, probably meant that her annuity was resented as a drain on the county's resources.[43]

Because Cecily was such a significant landowner and shared many servants with the king, they inevitably occasionally transacted business with one another directly. In December 1485 one of the king's sergeants-at-arms was paid 24s. for the six days he spent travelling to and from Berkhamsted with a letter for Cecily regarding the wardship of the five-year-old Thomas Pygot.[44] Pygot's father and grandfather had been

Cecily's tenants in Cambridgeshire and had died on consecutive days in mid-October, very probably from the sweating sickness that ravaged England in the weeks after Bosworth.[45] In August 1487 Henry paid 6s. 8d. to the 'keeper' of 'my lady of York's place', presumably meaning Baynard's Castle, perhaps for providing hospitality for someone there.[46]

Cecily's personal relationship with Henry VII has naturally left little trace. The wording in Cecily's will suggests a genuinely positive relationship. She left Henry a relatively impersonal, if generous, gift: all the money owed to her from customs and two gold cups. Intriguingly she allowed for the possibility that the king might decide that she should be buried somewhere other than Fotheringhay. She also left it to him to name a supervisor to see that her testament was 'perfittely executed'. In making this request she emphasized her 'singuler trust' in 'the kinges habundant grace'.[47]

Of course Cecily and those who helped her to draw up her will had a very strong motive to flatter the king. Her trusted dean of her chapel, Richard Lessy, had only recently been released from the Tower of London. Lessy had been found guilty of misprision of treason in connection with the long-running Perkin Warbeck conspiracy: a plot to replace Henry VII with a boy who claimed to be Edward V's younger brother, Cecily's grandson, Richard duke of York.[48] Cecily wanted Lessy to play a leading role in administering her final wishes and so needed to avoid giving the king any cause to interfere in her bequests, especially those in Lessy's favour. Yet this does not mean that the sentiments expressed in Cecily's will were necessarily insincere. Had there truly been simmering tensions between their households Henry VII would scarcely be fooled by this flattery, nor could Cecily expect him to be. In light of Cecily's many connections with Henry VII's mother, his marriage to her granddaughter and her own experience of the consequences of blood feuds, it seems likely that Cecily had chosen to make her peace with Henry Tudor in spite of Richard III's death.

Cecily's relationship with the queen was clearly very important to her. This is most evident in one of the titles she used after 1485: 'Cecily, grandmother of the queen of England, duchess of York'.[49] As the wording quoted at the head of this chapter indicates, Cecily still sometimes defined herself according to the most important men in her life, Richard duke of York and Edward IV. However, both of them were now dead and Margaret Beaufort had recently taken to emulating Cecily's innovation in using 'the king's mother' as an official title. In some legal documents, such as the lease on her inn at Grantham, when presenting clergy to benefices in her gift, and in grants to her servants she used variants of this new title of 'queen's grandmother'.[50] Her servants occasionally used the same title for her even after her death.[51] It was highly unusual for a woman to define herself according to her relationship to another woman. Cecily may well have felt that Elizabeth of York was no ordinary queen and that, to quote the Crowland Continuator, in her 'there could be found whatever appeared to be missing in the king's title elsewhere'.[52] For Cecily, loyalty to the house of York now meant loyalty to Henry VII's queen.

Just as she shared servants with the king, it seems that some of Cecily's men also worked for the queen. The Sir Roger Cotton mentioned above was probably the same Sir Roger who was Elizabeth's master of the horse.[53] Cecily's yeoman of the chamber, John Gilmyn, was very likely one of Elizabeth of York's footmen by 1497.[54] Cecily's testamentary gifts to the queen were appropriately personal and expensive. One was a 'Crosse croslette' of diamonds that looks to have been her single most valuable bequest and another was an exquisite psalter, bound in green cloth of gold with enamelled clasps of silver and gilt. She also gave Elizabeth her most significant ancient relic, 'the fleshe of Saint Christofer'. Moreover, Cecily used her will to emphasize the dynastic legitimacy of Elizabeth's family as well as her own proximity to that royalty: not once but twice Cecily stated that Richard duke of York was 'Fader unto the most christen prince my Lord and son king Edward the iiij[th]'.

Other than the immediate royal family, Cecily's will mentioned only a small number of her kin. It would be easy to imagine that her daughter Margaret or her grandson Edward earl of Warwick were omitted as a gesture of loyalty to Henry VII. However, it would be impossible to find a convincing diplomatic reason for all the family members not mentioned. We cannot know whether it was protocol, affection or mere practicality that dictated who received bequests. Chief among those who did were the daughters of Edward IV. Strikingly, the youngest, Bridget, was named before Cecily and Anne, perhaps because of her religious status.

The only other close family members mentioned in Cecily's will were the de la Poles. Cecily's daughter Elizabeth duchess of Suffolk received her chariot and the horses used to pull it as well as all of Cecily's palfreys. Elizabeth had been widowed four years earlier and her son Edmund was now earl (not duke) of Suffolk. The demotion was due to the family's reduced income after his elder brother John was attainted for his role in the Lambert Simnel rising in 1487. Cecily clearly chose not to let this taint of political conspiracy affect her bequests to this family since she made gifts to Edmund and two of his younger brothers, William and Humphrey, as well as their sister Anne. Further indications of close relations between Cecily and this family are suggested in the will of her servant, Nicholas Talbot.[55] Talbot seems to have remained living in Berkhamsted even after Cecily's death but in 1501 he made bequests to several servants in the household of William de la Pole who lived at Wingfield. William's brother, Earl Edmund, was by then in exile. Talbot also bequeathed a diamond ring to William's wife, Katherine, and a reliquary pendant which he habitually wore around his own neck to one of Katherine's gentlewomen.[56] Cecily's affection for her daughter's children, or connections between her household and theirs are unsurprising. They do not mean that she felt any sympathy for pretenders to the Tudor throne, despite the dean of her chapel's involvement with Perkin Warbeck.

The Perkin Warbeck conspiracy

Recent historians have suggested that Richard Lessy was part of a 'Berkhamsted network' which was a distinct subset of the Warbeck conspiracy.[57] Evidence for this is extremely thin. It is true that some significant conspirators came from Hertfordshire, but the only rebels other than Lessy who can actually be connected to Cecily even tenuously were Thomas Cressener and the prior of the Domincans at Kings Langley, Thomas Poynes.[58] Cressener's father was Cecily's nephew and servant Alexander, but there is no reason to imagine that his involvement in Perkin Warbeck's rebellion was connected with his father. On the contrary a far more obvious explanation is provided by London chronicles that explained that Thomas Cressener was steward to John Ratcliffe, Lord Fitzwalter, who was himself a key member of the English side of the conspiracy.[59] It should be noted that Alexander Cressener's service to Cecily seems to have been restricted to offices on her lands in Essex, not, as is often assumed, within her household at Berkhamsted.[60]

Thomas Poynes's only connection was that he resided in the manor of Kings Langley which was in Cecily's possession.[61] She may well have given alms to the priory as a matter of course although no record of any such patronage survives. Richard Lessy did have a strong affection for the priory. His donation to Hurley priory, mentioned above, included some provision for Kings Langley too and in his will Lessy bequeathed £6 13s. 4d., all his bedsteads with their furnishings and linen as well as fine table cloths and the green say curtains from his own bedroom to the friars at Kings Langley.[62] Most likely it was Prior Poynes who had told Lessy of the conspiracy. Poynes himself was probably drawn in by his prior provincial, William Richford, who was another of the most senior figures supporting Warbeck.[63]

Polydore Vergil thought that Lessy was one of the 'principal members' of the rebellion, but Vergil was clearly confused about Lessy's identity and did not realize that he was a priest. More contemporary chroniclers indicate that of those arrested Lessy was actually one of the least important, that he was questioned after the others and was found guilty only of misprision of treason – failure to reveal what he knew of the planned treachery.[64] Many of the conspirators truly believed that the boy being fêted at Margaret of Burgundy's court was Cecily's grandson, Richard duke of York. It is easy to see why the prior of Kings Langley would have risked sharing his knowledge with Lessy and why Lessy would have felt reluctant to betray a man he respected. This does not amount to a reason for imagining Cecily at the heart of a network of Yorkist malcontents who sought to depose her granddaughter Elizabeth. The 'Berkhamsted network' of Warbeck's rebellion appears to be yet another myth that needs to be laid to rest.

Daily life at Berkhamsted

Once she had turned seventy it seems that Cecily rarely travelled far from Berkhamsted. There is no mention of her at royal family celebrations such as prince Arthur's christening at Winchester, where the queen's mother took a prominent role, or the celebrations when three-year-old prince Henry was created duke of York at Westminster in 1494.[65] Nonetheless, Cecily still kept a barge as well as a coach and horses which would have enabled her to travel to London on occasion. It was commonplace to move household goods between houses as required, yet there were sufficient goods stored in her kitchen at Baynard's Castle when she died to merit assigning them to one of her gentleman servants in her will. This suggests that the place was in regular use by her council at least, if not by Cecily herself. In May 1489 a messenger from the mayor of Grantham planning to discuss tolls in the town 'with my lady of Yorkes council' was despatched to London rather than Berkhamsted.[66]

I have argued in previous chapters that Cecily's lifestyle in widowhood was not demonstrably more pious than those of many other noblewomen and her household routine closely emulated that which Christine de Pisan had advised for any 'wise princess'. Nonetheless, it appears that during Henry VII's reign her daily routine was held by some to be a worthy model of noble behaviour that would be appropriate to record for posterity and this now survives as the 'order' at the beginning of the 'Compendious recytation' of Cecily's household regulations.[67] The 'order' seems to present a formula that the author meant to be emulated so we must be cautious of accepting it as more than a general guide to her ideal day, but that in itself is a rare insight. It relates that Cecily would wake at seven by which time her chaplain would be ready to say matins of the day and matins of our lady with her, probably in her 'privy closet', which would be a small private chapel near her rooms. The chaplain in question was most likely William Grave who seems to have been her personal chaplain among a number of clerics who served the household.[68] Then 'when she is fully ready', a low mass was said in her chamber before breakfast. According to her household regulations, breakfast was eaten by all the ladies and gentlewomen of the household together as well as all those employed in her chapel, her almoner, gentleman ushers, cofferer, clerk of her kitchen and the marshal. If any of her 'head officers', such as Henry Heydon, happened to be present at her home they would join this meal. The account of her routine implies that immediately after breakfast she went to the chapel to hear divine service and two further low masses and 'from thence to dinner'. Yet there would clearly have been time for other activities in her morning. On most days dinner was served at 11 whereas on Fridays and Saturdays it was at 12 because these were 'fastyng dayes'.[69] It was commonplace in noble households to restrict protein on Saturdays as well as the statutory Fridays to fish (fresh or salted), butter and eggs. Cecily did not go as far as Elizabeth de Burgh or indeed her own sister Anne duchess of Buckingham, who both included Wednesday as a fast day too.[70]

During dinner someone read aloud to the diners from 'holy matter'. Afterwards an hour was spent giving audience to visitors who must have included tenants with disputes and petitioners as in previous decades. A rare surviving example from this period concerns another traditional exemplar of medieval piety, Anne Harling, widow of Sir Robert Wingfield. In 1491 Anne, or her representatives, persuaded Cecily to allow her to alienate 100 acres of land in the honour of Clare so that she could grant them to the College of St John the Evangelist at Rushworth.[71] Cecily's after dinner business hour was also an opportunity to meet with her estate officers or to host the occasional royal messenger.

She then allowed herself a fifteen-minute nap and afterwards 'contynueth in prayer unto the first peale of evensong'.[72] It is this long period spent in unguided prayer which is the most surprising feature of Cecily's day and the only element not suggested by Christine de Pisan in her proposed ideal routine. Cecily presumably used books and prayer rolls to aid her in this as well as her jewelled beads. She could spend time meditating on her relics and devotional images: her will mentioned a sarcenet cloth painted with John the Baptist and a 'crose cloth' which may have been painted with the instruments of Christ's passion.[73] Afterwards she would drink 'wyne or ale at her pleasure' and her chaplain would say two short evensongs with her while the bell continued to chime for the sung evensong service in the chapel. The last peal of the bell marked the moment at which she would leave her rooms to join her household there. Supper was at four or five and was a less formal meal where talking was allowed. Apparently Cecily would take this opportunity to 'recyte' the reading she had heard at dinner for the benefit of those who had not been present then. Presumably the various clerics in attendance could guide any consequent discussion about the subject of the readings. After supper Cecily enjoyed genuine leisure time in 'honest myrth' with her gentlewomen until seven when she took another cup of wine and retired to her chamber. In her privy closet she took 'her leave of God for all night, making end of her prayers for that day' and was in bed by eight.[74]

The very existence of this 'order' reinforces Kate Mertes's observation that household religious observance was manipulated for political purposes.[75] 'I trust to our lords mercy that this noble princesse thus devydeth the howres to his high pleasur', the author concluded with a hint of smugness.[76] Those who read it were meant to be impressed by the Yorkist matriarch's piety, her self-control and indeed the erudition suggested by her recitations of holy matter over supper. It provided a striking contrast to the narratives of scandal and bloodshed being penned about the last years of Yorkist kingship. Its intended readers may well have included Cecily's own granddaughter and namesake, the queen's sister. This younger Cecily acquired a dispensation to maintain a regular pattern of worship in her household in 1499 during her brief widowhood.[77] The 'order' might also have inspired Lady Margaret Beaufort who was particularly close to the younger Cecily. After Lady Margaret's death John Fisher extolled Margaret's pious daily routine in a sermon which made Cecily duchess of York's day look distinctly uninspiring. Fisher claimed that Margaret rose shortly after five and yet did not suggest any time for business in a list of devotions and services that included four or five masses heard on her knees.[78]

The quantity and quality of Cecily's chapel furnishings and vestments similarly suggest that she meant her religious observance to impress. This would be reinforced by the large number of men who seem to have been attached to Cecily's chapel.[79] After Richard Lessy, eight priests were named in her will. Some of these had certainly been connected with parishes in the past, but may have been retired or were perhaps absentee rectors based in her household. For instance, Master Richard Henmershe may still have been rector of Blythburgh in Suffolk but a certain Henry Hymnorth was parson there.[80] As recently as 1489 Cecily had appointed William Grave to the wealthy benefice of Kingsland in Herefordshire, close to Mortimer's Cross.[81] Yet he had clearly been in her service as a chaplain since at least 1482 so he was presumably simply drawing his income from Kingsland as Thomas Banns had done at Folkestone.[82]

The priests' names were immediately followed in her will by those of seven men who were not distinguished by any title but similarly received altar cloths or vestments as well as bedding in some cases. This may mean that they too were connected to her chapel. Laymen could be employed in the role of sacristan or specifically just for singing or for reading the epistles.[83] There were also children attached to the chapel, one of whom received a bequest in Richard Lessy's will three years after Cecily's death.[84] Lessy's exceptional musical education presumably contributed to the high quality of services there. In his own will he mentioned an expensive 'great' organ which he presumably played in Cecily's household. So even in her last years Cecily's chapel must have resembled those of the wealthiest lords in the land or indeed the Chapel Royal.

'The house of the right excellent Princesse Cecill'[85]

There is ample evidence that Cecily's wider household also functioned as a close community with ties that lasted even after her death. Blood and marital kinship between various members naturally strengthened this. It seems likely that Gervase Cressy and Master Richard Cressy, both mentioned in Cecily's will, were related to one another and to Matthew Cressy who received a commission of gaol delivery for Berkhamsted Castle in 1490 along with Sir John Verney, who was by then Cecily's steward at Berkhamsted.[86] Sir John and his wife, Margaret, were both included in Cecily's will. Margaret was probably one of Cecily's principal gentlewomen along with Jane Talbot, Gresild Boyvile, Jane Brocas and Alice Metcalfe all of whose husbands also served Cecily. Jane Talbot's husband Nicholas was Richard Lessy's cousin whereas Jane Brocas's husband, another Richard, would be one of Lessy's executors.[87] Lessy's niece, Jane, received several of Cecily's jewelled girdles and her white amber beads so she may also have been one of Cecily's gentlewomen.

Richard Lessy was godfather to John and Margaret Verney's younger sons and to Richard and Jane Brocas's only daughter. He also left money to pay for the marriage of Richard and Gresild Boyvile's daughter.[88] Cecily herself is likely to have been godmother to many of her servants' children. It was perhaps no coincidence that John and Margaret Verney's eldest daughter, John Clay's daughter and one of Richard Lessy's nieces were called Cecily.[89] There is further evidence of the continuing connections of her household members in Nicholas Talbot's will which was drawn up six years after Cecily's death. This included bequests to four men who were identified as 'persones dwellyng with my lady Cecile duches of Yorke' and five other Berkhamsted men, among them Owen William who had been Cecily's receiver there and was retained in the same role after her death.[90] Among the many priests who received gifts in Talbot's will were Master Richard Henmershe and John More, former rector of Berkhamsted, who had both received gifts in Cecily's will too.[91] Cecily had bequeathed to Nicholas Talbot and his wife Jane a gold spoon set with a diamond, and three highly decorated jewelled girdles.[92] Talbot in turn arranged for a priest to 'syng for my Lady Cecyle, late Duches of Yorke, the space of a hole yeer'.[93]

The sense of community in Cecily's household was tested to the limit in the spring of 1495 when Richard Lessy was arrested. He was imprisoned at the Tower for just over a month but was pardoned once he had been issued with a heavy fine of £400 to be paid in instalments over the next three years.[94] The nine men who stood surety for him were all men of Berkhamsted. They included four men who were to receive gifts in Cecily's will: Lessy's cousin, Nicholas Talbot; Richard Brocas, the clerk of Cecily's kitchen; Thomas Manory, her receiver in Kent, Surrey and Sussex; and Edward Delahay.[95] At least one of the other men was certainly also in Cecily's service, this was Owen William who was at that time her receiver in Berkhamsted and six local counties.[96]

Cecily herself tried to pay off most of Lessy's heavy fine, perhaps as much for the sake of his guarantors as for Lessy himself. She initially drew up her will on 1 April 1495, a month after the fine was agreed. The first instalment, of £200, was due that Pentecost, 29 May. In her will Cecily promised Lessy 'all suche money as is owing unto me by obligacions what soever they be. And all such money as is owing unto me by the Shirfe of yorkeshir to helpe to bere his charges which he has to pay to the kinges grace'. She added the hopeful suggestion that he might achieve the payments 'by the help & socour' of the king himself. The deadline passed before Cecily's death or indeed the successful collection of the debts. Consequently, the final line of her will, perhaps added just before she signed it on 31 May, stated that if necessary Lessy should be 'recompensed of the Revenues of my Landes to the sum of v C marcs at the leest'. Since these lands were all about to pass into the king's hands she was effectively forcing Henry to cancel almost all of Lessy's debt. In the year after her death over £240 from the receipts from her lands were passed to Lessy so perhaps this was all that was needed to pay his bond after the other debts had been pursued.[97]

Some instances of this community's shared religious interests have been mentioned in earlier chapters. Now, as many of them came towards the end of their lives, there were further opportunities to act in concert in their patronage. Sometimes this included arranging prayers for deceased former colleagues as Richard Lessy did in 1489 when he gave £60 to Hurley Priory in Berkshire.[98] The priory was in significant debt and struggling with regular flooding. Almost certainly Cecily's household had been approached for help at the instigation of her former servant, Agatha Flegge, who lived at nearby Marlow.[99] In return for Lessy's gift, the prior and convent committed to praying for Lessy and for Cecily and for the souls of Lessy's parents, and also of Agatha's husband, John Flegge.[100] The following year Lessy also became involved in supporting a small house much closer to Berkhamsted, St Margaret's convent near Ashridge. He joined Richard Woodville earl Rivers and others in holding lands for the prioress and convent's use.[101] Lessy later bequeathed five torches to the convent. Cecily herself gave them two altar cloths, a crucifix and a 'vestment of great velvet'.[102]

Within Ashridge there was a more prestigious and fashionable foundation that also attracted Cecily's attention. This was the college of Bonhommes founded by Edmund earl of Cornwall in 1283. It held a rare phial of the Precious Blood and was consequently a popular site of pilgrimage. It had been a particular favourite of Edward of Woodstock and broadly followed the Augustinian rule, like the friars at Clare Priory.[103] Cecily's patronage was most likely drawn there by Margaret Verney whose family had been patrons of the college for several generations. Margaret and her husband both arranged to be buried there.[104] Cecily gave vestments of embroidered crimson damask to this house. Similarly, at least one of Cecily's servants became involved in supporting a foundation that mattered to her. Lessy bequeathed eight of his books on church law to the college at Stoke by Clare. He also left money to the curate at St Benet's beside Baynard's Castle.[105]

None of the foregoing is particularly surprising. It demonstrates how Cecily's piety very much remained a community activity, interacting with her immediate companions and her wider dynastic connections. All of the religious houses that received bequests in her will can be linked either to her wider family or to her household members. Most were close to London or Berkhamsted. Although she may have spent an hour or so each day in personal prayer, even in the last years of her life she was not the reclusive figure that is often inferred. On the contrary, she operated at the heart of a web of supportive servants and retainers.

The importance of this community is evident in her will which is remarkable for the fact that it is dominated by bequests to those in her service, with only one brief reference to prayers for her soul. This makes it very different from most wills as detailed as hers. Her mother had left gifts to poor tenants and her sister Anne had paid for a London anchorite to say masses and dirges for her own soul and those of her first husband and children. No similar charity appears in Cecily's will. She seems to have been happy to trust in the extensive arrangements for prayers that she had made during her lifetime and was confident that she could expect prayers from the beneficiaries of her will without having to ask.

It was not only her senior officers, ladies and clerics who received bequests in her will. Every gentleman, yeoman, groom and page was promised a monetary gift ranging from £4 to 14s. 4d., depending on their status. The gentlemen who had served her on her estates generally received sumptuous gowns and money although Alexander Cressener was given her 'best bedde of downe and a bolstor to the same'. Her steward Henry Heydon was given 'a tablett and a Cristall garnesshed with ix stones and xxvij perles lacking a ston and iij perles'. With the exception of her bequest to the queen, Cecily granted all the rest of her jewellery, reliquaries and prayer beads to the women who had served her (for married women these bequests were always to their husbands too). Most of her liturgical books she passed to religious houses, principally Fotheringhay and Stoke by Clare, but, like her vestments and chapel furnishings, some went to men who were probably linked to her chapel. Intriguingly, none of the books that she had listened to each day over mealtimes went to her household members. Their dispersal pointed to Cecily's position in a somewhat different community.

Cecily's books

Considerable attention has been devoted to the books that were read to Cecily and her household at dinner. Susan Groag Bell argued that 'because women's public participation in spiritual life was not welcomed by the hierarchical male establishment, a close involvement with religious devotional literature, inoffensive because of its privacy, took on a greater importance for women'.[106] In support of this she cited Cecily's habit of sharing at supper the readings she had heard at dinner. Felicity Riddy emphasized the oral nature of this sharing and located Cecily in a feminine subculture of 'women talking about the things of God'.[107] There were of course men present at Cecily's discussions too and she must have been well aware that men in her household owned copies of some of the same texts. She particularly referred to her copy of the *Golden Legend* as a volume 'in velem' which would distinguish it from Richard Lessy's printed copy.[108] However, like many of the women in Riddy's study, Cecily chose to bequeath her principal devotional books to other women. Strikingly, she did not give them to her servants, the women in whose company she had previously shared them.

Instead they went to her granddaughters. So, while it appears that on some level Cecily may have understood her reading habits to be part of a feminine culture, her bequests were not designed to continue that culture as she had experienced it.

The granddaughters who received Cecily's devotional books were both in holy orders. Edward IV's daughter Bridget, a nun at Dartford, received the *Golden Legend*, the *Life* of St Catherine of Siena and Mechtild of Hackeborn's *Book of Gostlye Grace*. Anne de la Pole, prioress of Syon, received a volume containing works of the pseudo-Bonaventure and Walter Hilton bound together, and a book of the *Revelations* of St Bridget of Sweden. Cecily might have hoped that their holy communities would have the opportunity to share these books as her own household had done. Yet it seems unlikely that the nuns at Syon could have been in need of another copy of Bridget's *Revelations*. Similarly, as Rowena Archer has observed, there seems to be little point in giving Walter Hilton's book on *Mixed Life* to a woman already devoted to the contemplative life. Cecily must have valued these books for something more than their literary content. In passing them to her most devout granddaughters she perhaps attempted to leave a physical connection with herself in their presence. In giving the prioress of Syon another copy of Bridget's *Revelations* she emphasized to her granddaughter that they were bound by their shared spiritual interests.

Her books of hours Cecily gave to lay kinswomen: one to Lady Margaret Beaufort and two to Edward IV's daughter Cecily who was by then married to Lady Margaret's half-brother, John Viscount Welles. It seems likely that the elder Cecily was aware that her younger namesake already had a greater interest in religious observance than Edward IV's other daughters, Katherine and Anne, who received furnishings and a barge. As mentioned above, Duchess Cecily gave a psalter to her granddaughter, the queen, although it was perhaps as much the richness of this book as its content that made it an appropriate bequest for Elizabeth.

The only volume that was mentioned among those read at mealtimes but not bequeathed in Cecily's will was the *Infantia Salvatoris*. Mary Dzon has suggested that this might at first appear to be the 'black sheep' among Cecily's otherwise very orthodox, if sophisticated, collection of books.[109] There were various different Latin and Middle English versions of the *Infantia Salvatoris*. Most included not merely Christ's nativity but also a narrative of his childhood that included some controversial miracles. Nonetheless Dzon argues that the library at Syon included a Latin volume of infancy miracles and she points out that the Carthusian author of the *Speculum devotorum* used a Middle English *Infantia Salvatoris* in his composition. Consequently, it may have been that the *Infantia Salvatoris* was understood to belong with Cecily's more orthodox devotional texts associated with Bridgettines and Carthusians.[110] Its absence from Cecily's will is an important reminder that she may well have owned many more books than those that have been recorded.

It is reasonable to assume that the period of 'honest mirth' that she spent with her ladies each evening included listening to other stories, as well as playing board games or ninepins as the queen and her ladies did.[111] Yet the tranquil picture of her life painted by that record of her daily routine masks the reality of her household's involvement in national politics or the anxieties about her servants that seem to have haunted Cecily's last weeks. The hasty addition to her will which she made in Richard Lessy's favour could only provide for his exceptional immediate needs. She would have been well aware that on her death many of her other servants would lose much of the income she had provided for them. Not only would her household wages cease, but, as mentioned earlier, Henry VII had promised that a number of the offices on her lands would go to men in his own service once she died. She must also have been very conscious that the granddaughter in whom she took such pride, Elizabeth, was still vulnerable to the pretender, Perkin Warbeck, and his foreign allies.

Cecily's choice of executors for her will illustrates her sense of her own identity at this time, confident in her royal status and proud of her Yorkist connections. She was sufficiently sure of her own importance to name no less than three of the king's councillors. These were Oliver King, bishop of Bath and Wells, once secretary to Edward IV, along with two of Henry VII's new men Sir Reginald Bray and Sir Thomas Lovell. She also chose the heads of the two religious houses most closely connected with the house of York: William Pikenham, dean of the college of Stoke by Clare and William Field, master of Fotheringhay. The latter would of course be closely involved with her funeral. Finally there was her most personal choice, Richard Lessy, despite his recent brush with treason. She also expected her grandson-in-law, the king, to involve himself in choosing a supervisor. It is worth contrasting these self-assured choices with those of her daughter-in-law, Elizabeth Woodville, who appointed the prior of the Sheen Charterhouse and two relatively minor churchmen as her executors but asked her daughter, the queen, and her son, the marquis of Dorset, to 'putte there good willes and help for the performans' of her testament.[112] Cecily's mother had similarly looked to a daughter in this capacity. She had named Katherine duchess of Norfolk as her principal executor along with three of her sons and six other men.[113] Cecily's decision not to name her own daughter or any of the other important female beneficiaries of her will among her executors echoes that of her sister Anne who had appointed John Morton, bishop of Ely and William Lord Hastings along with five other laymen.[114] Both women had been part of female networks and communities during their lives and the dispersal of books in their wills suggests the continued importance of these connections for them. However, as powerful widows both were accustomed to operating effectively in a men's world. In 1495 Cecily's position at the heart of the legitimate Yorkist royal family seems to have shaped her sense of who she was far more profoundly than her gender could.

Death

Cecily was well enough to sign her will as well as sealing it on 31 May 1495. Her witnesses were her confessor, Richard Grant, as well as three men of her household: Richard Lessy, Richard Brocas and Gervase Cressy. Hours later she was dead.[115] Unlike her sister Anne or her daughter-in-law Elizabeth Woodville, who had asked for simple funerals, Cecily chose to depart this life with the splendour in which she had lived it.[116] She had arranged that if necessary all the plate belonging to her chapel, pantry, cellar, ewery and scullery should be sold to pay for her body to be taken for burial in the choir at Fotheringhay. Here she asked to be buried 'beside the body of my most entierly best beloved Lord and housbond ... and in his tumbe'. Just over a decade earlier Edward IV had at last arranged for a tomb over his father's body at the considerable cost of £100.[117] John Leland recorded that Richard duke of York was buried 'on the north side of the highe altar where also is buried King Edward the 4. mother in a vault over which is a pratie chapelle'.[118] It has been suggested that Edward IV had installed a tomb similar to that which he had planned for himself including a cage chapel raised over the vault in which a priest could say mass for the couple.[119] Yet less than forty years after Leland's visit all trace of a memorial to Richard duke of York and his son Edmund had disappeared. Like so many other foundations, Fotheringhay College and Church were 'profanely subverted' by reformers in Edward VI's reign.[120]

On a visit to Fotheringhay in 1566 Elizabeth I was made aware of the ruinous state of her ancestors' memorials and six years later she appointed four commissioners to assess the damage there.[121] Their records mentioned only the memorials to Cecily and to Edward duke of York (her husband's uncle who had died at Agincourt). It seems that it was only when the commissioners began to dig up her tomb that they also found Richard duke of York's and consequently reburied them together in a rather plain and comparatively inexpensive limestone and chalk tomb within the surviving body of the church.[122] Surprisingly their son Edmund earl of Rutland was not mentioned by the commissioners at all. Nor were the infants who had been buried there in the 1440s and 50s. The clue to Cecily's more visible memorial is perhaps to be found in Richard Lessy's will. Lessy asked that 'if therbe spared of my detts C marcs then I will that the saide C marcs be bistowed and spente upon my ladies tombe at Fodringhay by the discretion of the master there and of my executores'.[123] Only after this expense had been met should any further spare money be spent upon 'goodely werkis' for the benefit of his own soul. It was an extraordinarily large sum for a servant to spend upon his mistress's tomb. The likelihood is that Cecily had actually made arrangements with Lessy and another of her executors, the dean of Fotheringhay, that they should embellish her tomb to this sum if it could be done so out of the money that she had bequeathed to Lessy in the uncertain days before her death. If so, the 'pratie chapel' that Leland noted may well have been more explicitly linked with Cecily than with her husband. Cecily's willingness to forego this more splendid tomb for her servant's sake is further testimony to her commitment and even devotion to those in her service.

When her body was exhumed in 1573 a silk ribbon was found tied around Cecily's neck from which hung 'a Pardon from Rome, which penn'd in a fine Roman Hand, was as fair and fresh to be read, as if it had been written but the Day before'.[124] Even though her will had lacked the conventional provision for prayers, she was apparently still concerned to employ every means possible to speed her soul through purgatory. The indulgence had of course come to light in an age when such talismans had been abandoned. Yet there is a hint of the reverence for hallowed relics that Cecily's contemporaries would have recognized in the way that observers were impressed by the indulgence's state of preservation.

Since the eighteenth century it has frequently been reported that Elizabeth I herself arranged for new tombs for her Yorkist ancestors at Fotheringhay.[125] Sofija Matich and Jennifer Alexander have recently shown that the queen's involvement was significantly less than had been imagined. They have drawn attention to similarities between the new tombs erected at Fotheringhay and contemporary building work at nearby Deene Park, home of Sir Edmund Brudenell who had been appointed to join the commission on Fotheringhay after the original report had been made. They argue that it was actually Sir Edmund who organized and paid for one tomb for Edward duke of York and another for Cecily and Richard. The original wording on these tombs was inked but never carved and has consequently been lost. According to an eighteenth-century work on Fotheringhay, Cecily had been remembered on her tomb as wife to Richard duke of York and daughter of Ralph earl of Westmorland.[126] Already her power and influence as the mother and grandmother of English monarchs was being written out of the story of her life.

Conclusion

In this verie ceason departed to God Cicile Duches of Yorke, mother to kyng Edward ye fourth and kyng Richard at her castel of Barkamstede, a woman of small stature, but of much honour and high parentage.

Hall's Chronicle, 1548[1]

In a chronicle dedicated to Cecily's great grandson, Edward VI, it is perhaps unsurprising that Edmund Hall summed Cecily up as a woman of 'much honour and high parentage'. What is more striking is that Cecily had retained that honour, consistently avoiding censure throughout her life, unlike so many of her contemporaries. This was despite the fact that Cecily was trusted to act for her rebellious husband in the 1450s, was deemed to 'rule the king as she pleases' in 1461 and came to accommodations with the new regimes in 1470, 1483 and 1485. Her brief appearances in fifteenth- and sixteenth-century chronicles suggest that, despite all the turbulence and tragedies of her life, she appeared to be a model of contemporary education for medieval noblewomen, observing 'quietness of tongue, ... keeping to a relatively limited space' and displaying a 'religious sensibility guiding all actions', just as medieval courtesy books advised.[2] Only in her alleged anger at her eldest son's controversial marriage was Cecily imagined to have overstepped the boundary of ideal feminine behaviour and with this the writers had considerable sympathy. The allegations regarding her eldest son's legitimacy were never intended as a criticism of Cecily herself whereas confidence in her virtue was used in refuting them.[3] Cecily's skill in manipulating her public image is one reason that she has become such a shadowy figure in modern histories despite her political significance.

One consequence of the present study has been to contribute to the already substantial web of scholarship revealing that noblewomen played an integral role in the networks of authority and influence, patronage and piety that shaped medieval Europe. For those who work in women's studies, there is no a longer a question over whether medieval women regularly enjoyed positions of significant power in spite of the deeply patriarchal culture in which they lived. The issue is how that influence was exercised in different contexts. This work has attempted to add to that discussion.

Centuries of chauvinism have skewed society's perception of power so that influence exercised through motherhood, 'pillowtalk' and domestic management has been rated secondary and inferior to influence exerted through presence in a lord's council chamber or on the battlefield. This meant that Cecily was not seen to be challenging male superiority in her letter to Margaret of Anjou when she confidently dared to celebrate the unique potential of a woman's body to create 'the most precious, most ioyfull, and most confortable erthely tresor that myght come unto this land'.[4] This was a form of female power that fifteenth-century men and women were happy to celebrate. In 1475 the painting of Cecily in the Luton Guild Book, which appears on the front cover of this book, set Cecily herself in that same role by dressing her in a cloak of the royal arms of England, the emblem of the 'earthly treasure' that she had borne and nurtured. The author of the Clare Roll apparently saw no incongruity in praising Richard duke of York by means of a lineage of influential holy women and a celebration of the fertility he shared with Cecily. Cecily's novel decisions to identify herself in her business letters as 'the king's mother' and later 'the queen's grandmother' indicate both her sense of her position at the heart of the English power structure and her confidence in the legitimate authority that such a relationship conferred.

Noblewomen fortunate enough to bear children commonly drew influence and power through their responsibility for educating national leaders, through their role in marriage politics or through opportunities for patronage. Richard duke of York's exile and death inevitably increased Cecily's significance as an influence on and decision-maker for her children. The various references to the young children with her at Ludlow may suggest that her motherhood also enhanced her capacity for intercession or negotiation outside her family, a trope often noted in studies of queenship.[5]

In the fifteenth century, stereotypes about weakness, chaos, temptation and untrustworthiness were habitually applied to women in general and occasionally used in particular to shape propaganda about prominent women in controversial roles. Yet specific relationships consistently ignored these negative tropes, hence Cecily could negotiate for the sale of Caister Castle, acquire pardons for Yorkists after Ludford, run Edward IV's household at Baynard's Castle in the spring of 1461 and direct Richard duke of Gloucester's management of the John Prince affair in 1474. She could also administer estates stretching across twenty-one counties and command a household that operated like that of any major lord throughout the thirty-four years of her widowhood. Her surviving letters and her will particularly reveal Cecily's strong commitment to, and success in, defending the interests of those in her service. This commitment was rewarded, for example, by John Prince's dedication and by loyalty expressed in Nicholas Talbot's and Richard Lessy's wills. Such personal relationships were key to successful ladyship as much as they were to lordship. When Cecily felt that those in her service were failing her, she was confident that it would be effective to threaten the 'perill' of her 'hevy ladyship'.[6]

The vast majority of Cecily's ladyship was exercised through relationships with men. The power she exerted through influence and negotiation was also usually with men. Letters she received asking for her intercession looked to her to use her powers of persuasion on the men of her family. Unlike many noblewomen, she chose not to include any women among her executors. It may be that in identifying herself primarily as a mother and in developing an increasingly visible piety she sought to soften the challenge that her position and wealth could pose although there is no direct evidence that this was her intent. Clearly she operated with confidence and respect in primarily male circles.

Cecily's relationships with other women impinged upon both her political activities and her more domestic pursuits. The circle of acquaintances that she developed in France included many women who shared her patronage of Osbern Bokenham and who maintained connections with Cecily throughout their lives. Her first recorded acts of political intercession were with Margaret of Anjou and her later attempts to build bridges with Lancastrian families centred on women invited into her household. The liminal position that Cecily occupied between Beaufort/Neville origins and York marriage as well as contemporary preconceptions about women's political engagement and her own networking skills allowed her, like many women, to transcend political divisions. Her capacity to survive repeated crises and regime changes unscathed was nonetheless remarkable.

Another result of this study has been to provide an examination of politics and noble society in the fifteenth century from a different perspective, so that in asking new questions of familiar sources, and introducing sources not usually used, fresh interpretations could evolve. I have argued that Cecily's religious expression was better recorded and, late in her life, more splendid and visible than that of many of her contemporaries but that this should not be read as evidence of exceptional piety. Rather, they indicate that routines and expressions of faith were an integral part of daily life that should not be ignored in seeking to understand the functioning of good ladyship/lordship. Cecily's piety became more visible in the years after her chastity was questioned in political propaganda and her family began to fracture. It seems likely that, on one level, her ostentatious religion was intended to impress her contemporaries in order to defend both Edward IV's legitimacy and her own righteousness (with implications for her wider capacity for authority and good ladyship). At another level this piety was presumably also intended to impress God so that He would look favourably upon her dynasty. While achieving these aims, it may also have been an increasingly important strength and solace to her amid continuing losses.

In examining political history from Cecily's perspective, the close kinship of the majority of senior protagonists in the Wars of the Roses is especially evident. The notion of a conflict between Lancaster and York is very obviously an inadequate explanation of the complex and shifting loyalties and motives behind each of the military clashes and regime changes of the fifteenth century. The actions of women involved in these politics have rarely received sufficient attention. Alice Chaucer's willingness to marry her only son and heir into the duke of York's family indicates a genuine confidence in the possibility of reconciliation as late as 1457, a reconciliation which may yet have been possible without the earl of Warwick's intervention. I have suggested that by examining Elizabeth Woodville's motives for taking sanctuary in 1483, and the consequences of her decision, a richer understanding of Richard III's coup emerges. Evidence of the relationship between Cecily and Richard at that point, and thereafter, similarly indicates that the 'usurpation' was a result of fear and chaos rather than long-standing conspiracy so that Cecily and others felt moral confusion over Richard's accession and the princes' imprisonment.

However, the principal purpose of this book has been to tell Cecily duchess of York's story for her own sake, to strip away the myths and misconceptions shaped by writers more interested in the lives of her husband and sons, and to draw together what can be known of her eighty years. Cecily emerges as an extraordinary survivor, an astute politician, a conscientious 'good lady', a respected wife and a mother who was most fiercely loyal to her eldest surviving son. Her power to influence Edward IV and other major political figures was clearly recognized by both foreign visitors and town councils as well as those in her service. Along with her role as a major landholder, this influence set Cecily duchess of York at the heart of the fifteenth-century political community, a woman of far more power and significance than many crowned queens of England.

Notes

Introduction

1 '1415: Hoc anno rex Henricus V. crastino Sancti Laurencii, cum xvii. c. iiii. xx. vj. navibus intravit mare apud Southehamptone ... et xxv. die Octobris sequente fuit bellum de Agincourt, quo die devicti sunt Franci, et multi domini capti et occisi. Hoc anno nata est Cæcilia, uxor Ricardi, ducis Eboraci, filia comitis Westmerlandiæ, iij. die Maii.' Joseph Stevenson, ed., *Letters and Papers Illustrative of the Wars of the English in France during the Reign of Henry the Sixth, King of England*, Rolls Series 22, 2 vols (London: Longman, 1864), II, ii: 759.

2 J. T. Rosenthal, 'Aristocratic Widows in Fifteenth-Century England', in *Women and the Structure of Society: Selected Research from the Fifth Berkshire Conference on the History of Women*, ed. Barbara J. Harris and JoAnn K. McNamara (Durham, NC: Duke University Press, 1984), 40.

3 See bibliography of primary sources for what follows.

4 Polydore Vergil, *Three Books of Polydore Vergil's History of England*, ed. H. Ellis, Camden Society, o.s. 29 (London, 1844), 184.

5 Thomas More, *The Complete Works of St Thomas More, Vol. 2: The History of King Richard III*, ed. R. S. Sylvester (New Haven: Yale University Press, 1963), 64.

6 William Shakespeare, *Richard III*, ed. James R. Siemon (London: Bloomsbury, 2014), Act IV, Scene i, ll. 54–5.

7 George Buck, *The History of King Richard the Third (1619)*, ed. A. N. Kincaid (Gloucester: Alan Sutton, 1982), 182.

8 Ibid.

9 J. Nichols, *The History and Antiquities of the Town, College, and Castle of Fotheringhay in the County of Northampton* (London, 1787), 13 n.

10 Horace Walpole, *Historic Doubts on the Life and Reign of Richard III*, ed. P. W. Hammond (Stroud: Sutton Publishing, 1987), 41.

11 Walpole, *Historic Doubts*, 42 n.

12 Mrs Crawford, 'Autobiographical Sketches', *The Metropolitan* 18 (1837), 301.

13 Mark Noble, 'Some Observations upon the Life of Cecily Duchess of York', *Archaeologia* XIII (1800): 7–19. His paper was read to the society in April 1796.

14 Ibid., 16.

15 Ibid., 13.

16 Agnes Strickland, *Lives of the Queens of England from the Norman Conquest*, 12 vols (London, 1840), III:377.

17 Ibid.

18 Caroline A. Halsted, *Richard III as Duke of Gloucester and King of England,* 2 vols (London, 1844), I:61, 153–4.

19 Ibid.

20 C. A. J. Armstrong, 'The Piety of Cicely, Duchess of York: A Study in Late Medieval Culture', in *England, France and Burgundy in the Fifteenth-Century*, ed. Armstrong (London: Hambledon, 1983), 135–56.

21 T. B. Pugh, 'Richard Plantagenet (1411–60), Duke of York, as the King's Lieutenant in France and Ireland', in *Aspects of Late Medieval Government and Society*, ed. J. G. Rowe (Toronto: University of Toronto Press, 1986), 112.

22 T. B. Pugh, 'The Estates, Finances and Regal Aspirations of Richard Plantagenet (1411–1460) Duke of York', in *Revolution and Consumption in Late Medieval England*, ed. M. A. Hicks (Woodbridge: Boydell Press, 2001), 78.

23 J. T. Rosenthal, *Patriarchy and Families of Privilege in Fifteenth-Century England* (Philadelphia: Penn Press, 1991), 243.

24 Ibid., 242.

25 Ibid., 245.

26 Joanna Chamberlayne, 'Cecily Neville, Duchess of York, King's Mother: The Rôles of an English Medieval Noblewoman, 1415–1495', MA diss. University of York, 1994.

27 Michael K. Jones, *Bosworth 1485: Psychology of a Battle* (Stroud: Tempus, 2002), 91, 93.

28 Shakespeare, *Richard III*, IV.iv. 133–4.

29 Rowena Archer, 'Piety in Question: Noblewomen and Religion in the Later Middle Ages', in *Women and Religion in Medieval England*, ed. Diana Wood (Oxford: Oxbow, 2003), 124.

30 Simon Horobin, 'Politics, Patronage, and Piety in the Work of Osbern Bokenham', *Speculum* 82 (2007): 932–49; Horobin, 'A Manuscript Found in the Library of Abbotsford House and the Lost Legendary of Osbern Bokenham', *English Manuscript Studies 1100-1700* 14 (2007): 132–64; Mary Dzon, 'Cecily Neville and the Apocryphal "Infantia Salvatoris" in the Middle Ages', *Mediaeval Studies* 71 (2009): 235–300; Alison J. Spedding, '"At the King's Pleasure": The Testament of Cecily Neville', *Midland History* 35 (2010): 256–72; Sofija Matich and Jennifer Alexander, 'Creating and Recreating the Yorkist Tombs in Fotheringhay Church', *Church Monuments* 26 (2011): 82–103.

31 For example, C. J. Sansom, *Sovereign* (London: Macmillan, 2006).

32 Christopher Harper-Bill, 'Cecily, duchess of York', *Oxford DNB*, *sub nomine*.

33 Anne Crawford, *The Yorkists: The History of a Dynasty* (London: Hambledon Continuum, 2007); Sarah Gristwood, *Blood Sisters: The Women behind the Wars of the Roses* (London: Harper Press, 2012).

34 Amy Licence, *Cecily Neville: Mother of Kings* (Stroud: Amberley, 2014).

35 Kimberley LoPrete, 'Gendering Viragos: Medieval Perceptions of Powerful Women', in *Victims or Viragos?* ed. Christine Meek and Catherine Lawless (Dublin: Four Courts Press, 2005), 18.

36 Ibid., 38.

37 Miri Rubin, 'Small Groups: Identity and Solidarity in the Late Middle Ages', in *Enterprise and Individuals in Fifteenth-Century England*, ed. Jennifer Kermode (Stroud: Alan Sutton, 1991), 141.

1 Daughter of Lancaster: 1415–1425

1 Clare Roll.

2 Joseph Stevenson, ed., *Letters and Papers Illustrative of the Wars of the English in France during the Reign of Henry the Sixth, King of England*, Rolls Series 22, 2 vols (London, 1864), II:759.

3 Ibid.

4 *Testamenta Eboracensia III*, Surtees Society 45 (1865), 321. Cecily's nephew George Lord Bergavenny was baptized at Staindrop according to his entry in the *Complete Peerage*, *GEC*, I:30.

5 B. A. Windeatt, ed., *The Book of Margery Kempe* (Harmondsworth: Penguin, 1985), 94–6; Diane Watt, 'Political Prophecy in *The Book of Margery Kempe*', in *A Companion to Margery Kempe*, ed. John H. Arnold and Katherine J. Lewis (Cambridge: D. S. Brewer, 2004), 149–50; *Testamenta Eboracensia III*, 332.

6 *VCH Durham*, II:129.

7 E. Ann Matter, 'Church', in *Women and Gender in Medieval Europe: An Encyclopedia*, ed. Margaret Schaus (London: Routledge, 2006), 136–9.

8 Katherine L. French, *The Good Women of the Parish: Gender and Religion after the Black Death* (Philadelphia: University of Pennsylvania Press: 2008), 4.

9 *Manuale et Processionale ad Usum Insignis Ecclesiae Eboracensis*, Surtees Society 63 (1874), 5–22.

10 Ibid., 5.

11 Ibid.

12 Ibid., 6.

13 Ibid., 8–9.

14 Ibid., 8.

15 Rosalynn Voaden, *God's Words, Women's Voices: The Discernment of Spirits in the Writing of Late Medieval Women Visionaries* (York: York Medieval Press, 1999), 12–15.

16 Kay Staniland, 'Royal Entry into the World', in *England in the Fifteenth Century: Proceedings of the 1986 Harlaxton Symposium*, ed. Daniel Williams (Woodbridge: Boydell, 1987), 305.

17 Shulamith Shahar, *Childhood in the Middle Ages* (London: Routledge, 1990), 43–7.

18 R. B. Dobson, *Durham Priory 1400–1450* (Cambridge: CUP, 1973), 187.

19 Nicholas Orme, *Medieval Children* (New Haven: Yale University Press, 2001), 37.

20 St Cuthbert was buried at Durham and St William at York.

21 Sherry Reames, 'The Second Nun's Prologue and Tale', in *Sources and Analogues of the Canterbury Tales, Vol. I*, ed. Robert M. Correale and Mary Hamel (Woodbridge: D. S. Brewer, 2002), 491–9.

22 Karen A. Winstead, ed., *Chaste Passions, Medieval English Virgin Martyr Legends* (Ithaca: Cornell University Press, 2000), 50; L. A. Donovan, *Women Saints' Lives in Old English Prose* (Cambridge: D. S. Brewer, 1999), 57.

23 Geoffrey Chaucer, *The Riverside Chaucer*, ed. Larry D. Benson, 3rd edn (London: OUP, 1987), 268.

24 Anthony Emery, *Greater Medieval Houses of England and Wales, 1300–1500*, 3 vols (Cambridge: CUP, 1996–2006), I:17.

25 J. H. Round, *Family Origins and Other Studies* (London: Constable, 1930), 56–8.

26 *GEC*, IX:494–7.

27 Jeanette Lucraft, *Katherine Swynford: The History of a Medieval Mistress* (Stroud: Sutton Publishing, 2006), 1–2; G. H. Martin, ed., *Knighton's Chronicle 1337–1396* (Oxford: Clarendon Press, 1995), 237.

28 Lucraft, *Katherine Swynford*, 57, 73.

29 For plausible dates of birth see G. L. Harriss, *Cardinal Beaufort: A Study of Lancastrian Ascendancy and Decline* (Oxford: Clarendon Press, 1988), 1.

30 Anthony Tuck, 'Beaufort [*married names*, Ferrers, Neville], Joan, countess of Westmorland', *Oxford DNB*, *sub nomine*.

31 Lucraft, *Katherine Swynford*, 14.

32 Ibid., 26.

33 Tuck, 'Beaufort, Joan'.

34 Alastair Dunn, *The Politics of Magnate Power: England and Wales 1389–1413* (Oxford: Clarendon Press, 2003), 11–12.

35 Anthony Tuck, *Richard II and the English Nobility* (London: Edward Arnold, 1973), 215.

36 Thomas Hearne, ed., *Liber Niber Scaccarii, nec non Wilhelmi Worcestrii Annales Rerum Anglicarum*, 2 vols (London, 1761–2), II:525.

37 Tuck, 'Beaufort, Joan'.

38 Anthony Tuck, 'Neville, Ralph, first earl of Westmorland', *Oxford DNB*, *sub nomine*.

39 Reginald H. C. Fitz Herbert, 'Original Pedigree of Tailbois and Neville', *The Genealogist*, n.s. III (1886): 31–5, 107–11. cf. *Visitations of the North III*, Surtees Society 144 (1930), 27–30. The latter appears to be a later genealogy and places Anne as the youngest which contradicts the Clare Roll. However, the Coverham Roll gives her brother Thomas a title for which there seems to be no supporting evidence elsewhere. The Coverham Roll appears to predate 1444 when Humphrey Stafford became duke of Buckingham.

40 Fitz Herbert, 'Original Pedigree', 110.

41 Tuck, 'Neville, Ralph'.

42 J. R. Lander, 'Marriage and Politics in the Fifteenth Century: The Nevilles and the Woodvilles', *BIHR* 63:4 (1963): 119–52, 121.

43 This table is based on Fitz Herbert, 'Original Pedigree', 110. No birth dates are given in the pedigree. I have, like Lander, assumed the earliest possible birth dates in order not to suggest that the children were any younger at the time of marriage than they really were. I have assumed that Richard was born before Bolingbroke became king because it seems unlikely that his family would have given their eldest son the name of a deposed king. I have assumed that George was not born until 1414 when Henry V was significantly promoting the feast of St George. The *Visitations* genealogy does not include Joan.

44 *CPL*, VI:247, 462.

45 Prior John Wessington of Durham stood godfather to a child of Earl Ralph in 1417 which must presumably have been Edward. Dobson, *Durham Priory*, 185.

46 Marina Warner, *Alone of All Her Sex: The Myth and Cult of the Virgin Mary* (London: Picador, 1985), 201–2; J. Backhouse, *The Bedford Hours* (London: British Library, 1990), 15.

47 Nicholas Orme, *From Childhood to Chivalry: The Education of the English Kings and Aristocracy, 1066–1530* (London: Methuen, 1984), 12.

48 Margaret Scott, *Medieval Dress & Fashion* (London: British Library, 2007), 101.

49 1 Tim 2:9–10.

50 Alcuin Blamires et al., ed., *Woman Defamed and Woman Defended: An Anthology of Medieval Texts* (Oxford: Clarendon Press: 1992), 155–6.

51 Christopher Dyer, *Standards of Living in the Later Middle Ages. Social Change in England c. 1200–1520*, rev. edn (Cambridge: CUP, 1998), 88.

52 *PROME*, II:278.

53 Ibid., II:279.

54 Dyer, *Standards of Living*, 89.

55 Christine de Pisan, *The Treasure of the City of Ladies, or, The Book of the Three Virtues*, trans. Sarah Lawson (Harmondsworth: Penguin, 1985), 16–18.

56 Ibid., 19.

57 Ibid., 76.
58 Orme, *Childhood to Chivalry*, 13.
59 Lucraft, *Katherine Swynford*, 10.
60 James Wylie, *History of England under Henry the Fourth*, 4 vols (London: Longmans, Green, 1884–98), IV:242.
61 Susan Groag Bell, 'Medieval Women Book Owners: Arbiters of Lay Piety and Ambassadors of Culture', in *Women and Power in the Middle Ages*, ed. Mary Erler and Maryanne Kowaleski (Athens: University of Georgia Press, 1988), 158–64.
62 Pisan, *Treasure*, 67.
63 Orme, *Childhood to Chivalry*, 116–17.
64 Orme, *Medieval Children*, 264.
65 John Hardyng, *Chronicle*, ed. H. Ellis (London, 1812), 23.
66 Kim M. Phillips, *Medieval Maidens: Young Women and Gender in England, 1270–1540* (Manchester: Manchester University Press, 2003), 64.
67 J. Raine, ed., *Historiae Dunelmensis Scriptores Tres*, Surtees Society, 9 (Edinburgh, 1839), cclviii.
68 Nicholas Orme, *English Schools in the Middle Ages* (London: Methuen, 1973), 25. Carol Meale, '"... alle the bokes that I haue of latyn, englisch, and frensch": Laywomen and Their Books in Late Medieval England', in *Women and Literature in Britain 1150–1500*, ed. Carol Meale, 2nd edn (Cambridge: CUP, 1996), 140. *Testamenta Eboracensia II*, Surtees Society 30 (1855), 13–15.
69 Durham University Library, Cosin MS v.iii.9 f. 95, reproduced in F. J. Furnivall and I. Gollancz, eds, *Hoccleve's Works: The Minor Poems* EETS 61, 73 (1892, 1925), 242.
70 Pisan, *Treasure*, 51.
71 Phillips, *Maidens*, 97.
72 Ibid., 94.
73 Ibid., 95.
74 Pisan, *Treasure*, 75.
75 Ibid., 95–105.
76 Windeatt, ed., *Margery Kempe*, 10–11.
77 Ibid., 172–3.
78 Ibid., 172.
79 *CPL*, VII:220.
80 H. T. Riley, ed., *Annales Monasterii S. Albani a Johanne Amundesham*, 2 vols, Rolls Series 28 (1870–1), I:24.
81 Rowena Archer, 'Piety in Question: Noblewomen and Religion in the Later Middle Ages', in *Women and Religion in Medieval England*, ed. Diana Wood (Oxford: Oxbow, 2003), 128.
82 Will.
83 Ibid.
84 Dobson, *Durham Priory*, 187.
85 Lucraft, *Katherine Swynford*, 150–3.
86 Chris Given-Wilson, ed., *Chronicles of the Revolution, 1397–1400: The Reign of Richard II* (Manchester: Manchester University Press), 239.
87 Dunn, *Magnate Power*, 93.
88 Although her brother Edward was implicated in earlier plotting this cannot be proven and appears unlikely. Dunn, *Magnate Power*, 80–1, 88.
89 E. F. Jacob, *The Fifteenth Century* (Oxford: OUP, 1961), 36–58; J. M. W. Bean, 'Henry Percy, first earl of Northumberland', *Oxford DNB*, *sub nomine*; Simon Walker, 'Sir

Henry Percy', *Oxford DNB, sub nomine*; T. F. Tout rev. R. R. Davies, 'Sir Edmund Mortimer', *Oxford DNB, sub nomine*.

90 T. Walsingham, *The St Albans Chronicle*, ed. J. Taylor, W. R. Childs and L. Watkiss, 2 vols (Oxford: Clarendon Press, 2003–11), II:430–1; K. B. McFarlane, *Lancastrian Kings and Lollard Knights* (Oxford: Clarendon Press, 1972), 67; T. B. Pugh, *Henry V and the Southampton Plot of 1415*, Southampton Record Series 30 (Southampton: Southampton University Press, 1988), 79; Dunn, *Magnate Power*, 111.

91 Rosemary Horrox, 'Edward, second duke of York', *Oxford DNB, sub nomine*.

92 *CPL*, VI:128.

93 Lander 'Marriage and Politics', 121.

94 Tuck, *Richard II and the English Nobility*, 207–9, 219.

95 Dunn, *Magnate Power*, 118.

96 *Testamenta Eboracensia III*, Surtees Society 45 (1864), 321.

97 Phillips, *Maidens*, 37.

98 Ibid., 36.

99 Colin Richmond, 'Mowbray, John (VI), third duke of Norfolk', *Oxford DNB, sub nomine*.

100 R. A. Griffiths, 'Percy, Henry, second earl of Northumberland', *Oxford DNB, sub nomine*.

101 Francis Grose, Thomas Astle et al., eds, *The Antiquarian Repertory*, 4 vols (London: Jeffery, 1807–9), II:112.

102 Arthur Collins, *The Peerage of England*, 8 vols (London, 1779), II:351–8.

103 P. A. Johnson, *Duke Richard of York, 1411–1460* (Oxford: Clarendon Press, 1988), 1.

104 *CPL*, VI:132.

105 The couple seem to have had a son called Henry who died in infancy as well as a daughter Isabel. *A Visitation of the North of England c. 1480 to 1500*, Surtees Society 144 (1930), 4.

106 G. L. Harris, 'Richard, earl of Cambridge', *Oxford DNB, sub nomine*.

107 Pugh, *Southampton Plot*, 128–31.

108 Ibid., 122.

109 Ibid., 134. Cambridge was sentenced only to execution and forfeiture. *PROME*, IV:66.

110 Rymer, *Foedera*, X:290, www.british-history.ac.uk/rymer-foedera/vol10/.

111 *CFR 1422–30*: 64.

112 *GEC*, II:388–9.

113 J. Raine, ed., *Wills and Inventories*, Surtees Society, 2 (1835), 72.

114 Jennifer C. Ward, *English Noblewomen in the Later Middle Ages* (London: Longman, 1992), 12.

115 In 1443–4 revenues from lands in Wales and the Marches came to £3,497 whereas the income from the honour of Clare alone could be £462. T. B. Pugh, 'Richard Plantagenet (1411–60, Duke of York, as the King's Lieutenant in France and Ireland' in *Aspects of Late Medieval Government and Society*, ed. J. G. Rowe (Toronto: University of Toronto Press, 1986),111; J. T. Rosenthal, 'Fifteenth-Century Baronial Incomes and Richard, Duke of York', *BIHR* 37 (1964), 233–9, 235 (quoting WAM 12158).

2 Becoming a Duchess: 1425–1438

1 *CPL*, VIII:124.

2 *CPL*, VIII:132.

3 *PPC*, III:170, 292–3.

4 P. A. Johnson, *Duke Richard of York, 1411–1460* (Oxford: Clarendon Press, 1988), 1; *CPR 1422–29*: 343.

5 Charles Ross quoted in A. Tuck, 'Neville, Ralph, first earl of Westmorland', *Oxford DNB, sub nomine*.

6 A. J. Pollard, 'Neville, Ralph, second earl of Westmorland', *Oxford DNB, sub nomine*; Pollard, 'Neville, Sir Humphrey', *Oxford DNB, sub nomine*.

7 *PPC*, III:170.

8 Rymer, *Foedera*, X:356.

9 Johnson, *York*, 2.

10 Joseph Stevenson, ed., *Letters and Papers Illustrative of the English in France during the Reign of Henry the Sixth*, Rolls Series 22, 2 vols (London, 1861), II:760.

11 C. L. Kingsford, ed., *Chronicles of London* (Oxford: Clarendon Press, 1905), 95; 130.

12 James Gairdner, ed., *The Historical Collections of a Citizen of London in the Fifteenth Century*, Camden Society, n.s. 17 (1876), 159.

13 *PPC*, III:94.

14 *CPR 1422–29*: 343.

15 *CPR 1422–29*: 492.

16 *PPC*, III:292–3.

17 Johnson, *York*, 10.

18 Christine de Pisan, *The Treasure of the City of Ladies, or, The Book of the Three Virtues*, trans. Sarah Lawson (Harmondsworth: Penguin, 1985), 86.

19 D. A. L. Morgan, 'The House of Policy: The Political Role of the Late Plantagenet Household, 1422–1485', in *The English Court: From the Wars of the Roses to the Civil War*, ed. David Starkey et al. (London: Longman, 1987), 45; G. L. Harriss, 'The Court of the Lancastrian Kings', in *The Lancastrian Court*, ed. Jenny Stratford (Donington: Shaun Tyas, 2003), 1–18.

20 Graham E. St John, 'War, the Church, and English Men-at-Arms', in *Fourteenth-Century England VI*, ed. Chris Given-Wilson (Woodbridge: Boydell, 2010), 74–83.

21 *CPL*, VI:357; IV:76.

22 James Robinson, 'From Altar to Amulet: Relics, Portability and Devotion', in *Treasures of Heaven: Saints, Relics and Devotion in Medieval Europe*, ed. Martina Bagnoli et al. (London: British Museum Press, 2010), 112.

23 Dorothy Jones, ed. *Minor Works of Walter Hilton* (London: Burns Oates and Washbourn, 1929), 86.

24 Peter D. Clarke, 'New Evidence of Noble and Gentry Piety in Fifteenth-Century England and Wales', *JMH* 34 (2008): 23–35.

25 B. Zimmerman, ed., *Monumenta Historica Carmelitana*, vol. 1 (Lérins, 1907, no more published), 455. Their next indult for a confessor was granted a couple of weeks before Keninghale's death. *CPL*, X:92.

26 A. B. Emden, *A Biographical Register of the University of Oxford to A.D. 1500*, 3 vols (Oxford: Clarendon Press, 1957–9), II:1035–6.

27 Anne F. Sutton and Livia Visser-Fuchs, *Richard III's Books* (Stroud: Sutton Publishing, 1997), 22. St George was depicted in one of her tapestries, she owned a relic of St Christopher's flesh and St Barbara was depicted on an agnus she owned. She did also mention St Anthony since he was the dedicatee of a college to whom she bequeathed an antiphoner but this was probably mere coincidence. Will.

28 Kingsford, ed., *Chronicles*, 132.

29 Bertram Wolffe, *Henry VI* (London: Methuen, 1983), 54.

30 TNA E 101/408/10 m7.

31 Anne Curry, 'The "Coronation Expedition" and Henry VI's Court in France, 1430–1432', in *Lancastrian Court*, ed. Stratford, 48. When they entertained York, Cecily does not seem to have been present too.

32 *La Chronique d'Enguerran de Monstrelet*, Société de l'Histoire de France, 6 vols (Paris, 1857–72), V:2.

33 Stevenson, *Letters and Papers*, II 2:760; Ralph Griffiths, *The Reign of Henry the Sixth: The Exercise of Royal Authority 1422–1461* (London: Benn, 1981), 191.

34 BnF Lat. MS 1158 f. 34. Catherine Reynolds, 'English Patrons and French Artists in Fifteenth-Century Normandy', in *England and Normandy in the Middle Ages*, ed. David Bates and Anne Curry (London: Hambledon, 1994), 300–3. The Bedford Hours had been a wedding present commissioned by John duke of Bedford for his wife Anne who then gave it to Henry VI at Rouen as a Christmas gift in 1430. Janet Backhouse, *The Bedford Hours* (London: The British Library, 1990), 59.

35 BnF Lat. MS 1158 f. 34.

36 Only two of the ten shields for men bear a distinguishing mark of difference: one of these is that of the earl of Salisbury. The other seems most likely to be Ralph Neville's eldest son by his first marriage, Sir John Neville (d. 1420). The second earl of Westmorland (Sir John's son) would have been using the undifferenced saltire by this time so both he and his uncle Ralph could have been with Joan Beaufort's sons in the picture.

37 Backhouse, *Bedford Hours,* 32. I am grateful to Laurent Ungeheuer for answering various questions of mine on this and confirming, via email, his opinion that the artist was the master himself, rather than a member of his workshop.

38 Pauline E. Sheppard Routh and Richard Knowles, 'The Markenfield Collar', *Yorkshire Archaeological Journal* 62 (1990): 133–40.

39 Ibid., 302–3.

40 I discuss this at greater length in a forthcoming article: ' "To please … dame Cecely that in Latyn hath lityll intellect": Books and the Duchess of York', in *The Fifteenth Century XV*, ed. L. Clark (Woodbridge: Boydell and Brewer, forthcoming).

41 Ibid.

42 Wolffe, *Henry VI*, 30.

43 Janet Shirley, trans. *A Parisian Journal 1405–1449* (Oxford: Clarendon Press, 1968), 263, 268–7.

44 Ibid.

45 Gairdner, ed., *Historical Collections*, 173; Kingsford, ed., *Chronicles*, 97.

46 Kingsford, ed., *Chronicles*, 97–115.

47 *CPR 1429–36*: 207–8.

48 T. B. Pugh, 'The Estates, Finances and Regal Aspirations of Richard Plantagenet (1411–1460), Duke of York', in *Revolution and Consumption in Late Medieval England*, ed. M. A. Hicks (Woodbridge: Boydell, 2001), 71.

49 *CCR 1435–1441*: 305–8.

50 Johnson, *York*, 11–12.

51 Ibid., 229.

52 Ibid., 11. Although York was initially charged a livery fine of 1,000 marks for this inheritance, it was cancelled the following August.

53 H. L. Gray, 'Incomes from Land in England in 1436', *EHR* 49 (1934), 607–39, 614.

54 Pugh, 'Estates, Finances', 74.

55 Gray, 'Incomes', 614–15.

56 Ibid., 619.

57 Kate Mertes, *The English Noble Household 1250–1600* (Oxford: Blackwell, 1988), 43; Carole Rawcliffe, *The Staffords, Earls of Stafford and Dukes of Buckingham 1394–1521* (Cambridge: CUP, 1978), 87.

58 Mertes, *Noble Household*, 57.

59 Ibid., 58.

60 Ibid., 58, 61, 180.

61 Johnson, *York*, 17; *CPR 1422–29*: 395.

62 Barbara J. Harris, *English Aristocratic Women 1450–1550* (Oxford: OUP, 2002), 7.

63 Ibid., 5, 7.

64 Ibid., 5.

65 Pisan, *Treasure*, 52, 60.

66 Ibid., 61.

67 Ibid., 71–4.

68 Ibid., 130–3.

69 *VCH Northamptonshire*, II:573.

70 John Hutchins, *The History and Antiquities of the County of Dorset*, 4 vols, 3rd edn, rev. William Shipp and James Whitworth Hodson (London, 1861), II:378.

71 *CPR 1461–71*: 131–2.

72 York was recorded there in 1439 and 1453. Johnson, *York*, 15.

73 Clare Noble, ed., *Calendar of Inquisitions Post Mortem XXIII: 6 to 10 Henry VI (1472–1432)* (Woodbridge: Boydell Press, 2004), 370.

74 Philip Schwyzer, *Shakespeare and the Remains of Richard III* (Oxford: OUP, 2013), 78.

75 *VCH Shropshire*, II:136.

76 WAM 12165; 12166; 12167 f. 2

77 *VCH Suffolk*, II:145, 127.

78 *VCH Northamptonshire*, II:569.

79 Clive Burgess, 'Fotheringhay Church: Conceiving a College and Its Community', in *The Yorkist Age*, ed. Hannes Kleineke and Christian Steer (Donington: Shaun Tyas, 2013), 350.

80 Burgess, 'Fotheringhay Church', 353–4.

81 John Stow, *A Survey of London*, ed. C. L. Kingsford, 2 vols (Oxford: Clarendon Press, 1971), I:279–80.

82 Ibid.

83 Ibid.

84 *PPC*, IV:210–12.

85 Shirley, *Parisian Journal*, 282.

86 Ibid.

87 Lucia Diaz Pascual, 'Jacquetta of Luxembourg, Duchess of Bedford and Lady Rivers (c. 1416–72)', *The Ricardian* 21 (2011): 67–91, 70.

88 J. G. Dickinson, *The Congress of Arrass 1435* (New York: Biblo & Tannen, 1972), 169.

89 Jenny Stratford, 'John Duke of Burgundy', *Oxford DNB, sub nomine*.

90 Monique Sommé, ed., *La correspondance d'Isabelle de Portugal, duchesse de Bourgogne (1430–1471)* (Ostfildern: Thorbecke, 2009), 169.

91 Johnson, *York*, 28.

92 A. J. Pollard, *John Talbot and the War in France, 1427–1453* (London: Royal Historical Society, 1983), 33, 38, 71.

93 Amy Licence, *Cecily Neville: Mother of Kings* (Stroud: Amberley, 2014), 60.

94 Johnson, *York*, 30.

95 Griffiths, *Henry the Sixth*, 455.

96 Friedrich W. D. Brie, ed. *The Brut, or, The Chronicles of England*, EETS, o.s. 131, 136 (1906), 472; G. L. Harrriss and M. A. Harriss, eds., 'John Benet's Chronicle for the Years 1400 to 1462', in *Camden Miscellany vol. XXIV*, Camden Society, 4th series, 9 (1972), 185.

97 Berkshire RO D/Q1/Z2.

3 Motherhood Begins: 1439–1449

1 Thomas Hearne, ed., *Liber Niger Scaccarii, nec non Wilhelmi Worcestrii Annales Rerum Anglicarum*, 2 vols (London, 1761–2), II:525. Reproduced in English in J. A. Giles, ed., *Chronicles of the White Rose of York* (London: James Bohn, 1845), 213.

2 Bodl. MS Rawlinson A 146 f. 37. Pseudo-Worcester's *Annales* give the date as 10th but give the day as Tuesday whereas the 10th was a Monday. J. Stevenson, ed., *Letters and Papers Illustrative of the Wars of the English in France*, Rolls Series 22, 2 vols (London, 1864), II:762. The lower margin of Anne's own book of hours gives her birthplace as Fotheringhay but unfortunately the bottom of the page has been cut away so that it is impossible to read the date beyond 'post meridiem decimo die augusti'. If the entry were like her brother Edward's (14 hours after midday) then it might still have meant 11th. Rennes, Bibliothèque Municipale MS 22 f. 29. Viewed at http://bvmm.irht.cnrs.fr/sommaire/sommaire.php?reproductionId=815 31/10/ 2016.

3 Clare Roll.

4 Clare Roll.

5 John Carmi Parsons, *Eleanor of Castile: Queen and Society in Thirteenth-Century England* (Basingstoke: Macmillan, 1994), 17, 24–31, 38–42; Michael Prestwich, *Edward I* (London: Methuen, 1988), 573.

6 C. L. Kingsford, ed., *Chronicles of London* (Oxford: Clarendon Press, 1905), 154; Ralph Griffiths, 'The Trial of Eleanor Cobham', *BJRL* 51 (1968–9): 381–99; F. W. D. Brie, ed. *The Brut, or, The Chronicles of England*, EETS, o.s. 131, 136 (1906), 480.

7 Anne had been a ward of Sir John Fastolf. Her first husband was a loyal Yorkist, William Chamberlayne, and her second, Sir Robert Wingfield, became controller of Edward IV's household. However, the earliest surviving evidence of Cecily and Anne's interactions comes from the 1490s. Rev. Dr Bennet, 'The College of S. John Evangelist of Rushworth, Co. Norfolk', *Norfolk Archaeology* X (1888): 277–382; 296–7, 372.

8 Bennet, 'College of S. John', 298 (Bennet's paraphrase of her words).

9 Anne Dutton, 'Women's Use of Religious Literature in Late Medieval England', (DPhil thesis, University of York, 1995), 205.

10 Ibid., 204–5.

11 Joan Cadden, *Meanings of Sex Difference in the Middle Ages* (Cambridge: CUP, 1993), 228–9, 231, 249.

12 Richard Kieckhefer, *Magic in the Middle Ages* (Cambridge: CUP, 1989), 85.

13 Catherine Rider, *Magic and Impotence in the Middle Ages* (Oxford: OUP, 2006), 110, 163.

14 Kristen L. Geaman, 'Anne of Bohemia and Her Struggle to Conceive', *Social History of Medicine* 29 (2015); see also Anne Jeavons, 'Queenship and Power in the Reign of Richard II: The Authority and Influence of Joan of Kent, Anne of Bohemia, and Isabella of Valois' MA dissertation, University of Reading, 2015, 33–5.

15 Osbern Bokenham, *Legendys of Hooly Wummen*, ed. Mary Sergeantson, EETS, o.s. 206 (London, 1938), 57.

16 Janelle Day Jenstand, "'Lying in Like a Countess": The Lisle Letters, the Cecil Family, and a *Chaste Maid in Cheapside*', *Journal of Medieval and Early Modern Studies* 34 (2004): 373–403, *passim*.

17 Susan Broomhall, 'Gendering the Culture of Honour at the Fifteenth-Century Burgundian Court', in *Women, Identities and Communities in Early Modern Europe*, ed. Stephanie Tarbin and Susan Broomhall (Aldershot: Ashgate, 2008), 181–94, 185.

18 Broomhall, 'Gendering the Culture of Honour', 184.

19 BL Add MS 38174; F. Grose and T. Astle, eds., *The Antiquarian Repertory*, 4 vols (London, 1808), I:296–338.

20 This book includes references to the king's brothers and his youngest, unmarried sister, so could not possibly have been composed originally for Henry VII's court. However, it was updated in later decades and the earliest surviving manuscript was produced in the early 1490s. It was Thomas Hearne who first imagined Margaret Beaufort as the compiler and although there is no mention of her name in the manuscript from which it was taken some modern writers have persisted in repeating Hearne's attribution. Staniland, 'Royal Entry into the World', in *England in the Fifteenth Century*, ed. D. Williams (Woodbridge: Boydell, 1987), 299 nn. 8–9; David Starkey, 'Henry VI's Old Blue Gown: The English Court under the Lancastrians and Yorkists', *The Court Historian* 4 (1999): 1–28, 6–12.

21 Grose and Astle, *Antiquarian Repertory*, I:304; Peter Biller, 'Childbirth in the Middle Ages', *History Today* 36 (1986): 42–9, 45.

22 John Leland, *De Rebus Brittanicis Collectanea*, ed. T. Hearne, 4 vols (London, 1774), IV: 249.

23 L. Howarth, 'The Practice of Midwifery in Late Medieval England', MA dissertation, University of York, 1995, 15–18.

24 Peter Biller, 'Childbirth in the Middle Ages', *History Today* 36 (1986): 42–9.

25 Becky R. Lee, "'A Company of Women *and* Men", Men's Recollections of Childbirth in Medieval England', *Journal of Family History* 27 (2002): 92–100, 93–4.

26 J. L. Laynesmith, *The Last Medieval Queens* (Oxford: OUP, 2004), 116.

27 D. Cressy, 'Purification, Thanksgiving and the Churching of Women', *Past and Present* 141 (1993): 112–14.

28 Ibid., 112–14.

29 Brie, ed., *Brut*, 507.

30 P. A. Johnson, *Duke Richard of York, 1411–1460* (Oxford: Clarendon Press, 1988), 28.

31 *PPC*, V:136–8.

32 TNA CP 25/1/22/123 no. 8, CP 25/1/293/71 nos. 343, 344, 346, 347, CP 25/1/191/28 no. 31, CP 25/1/179/95 no. 122, CP 25/1/116/322 no. 715, CP 25/1/192/9 no. 14.

33 John Hutchins, *The History and Antiquities of the County of Dorset*, 4 vols, 3rd edn rev. William Shipp and James Whitworth Hodson (London, 1861), 390.

34 *GEC*, XII:ii, 547.

35 Stevenson, ed., *Letters and Papers*, II:763.

36 Michael K. Jones, *Bosworth,1485: Psychology of a Battle* (Stroud: Tempus, 2002), 68.

37 Giles, ed., *Chronicles of the White Rose*, 213.

38 TNA E 404/57 f. 172.

39 A. J. Pollard, *John Talbot and the War in France, 1427–1453* (London: Royal Historical Society, 1983), 29.

40 TNA E 404/57 f. 172.

41 These jewels have been represented as a gift to Richard duke of York as a consequence of the king's pleasure on learning that the child shared his name. However, the boy's name is not actually mentioned in our only record of the jewels and this states clearly that they were 'sent ... unto the sone of our right dere cousin Richard duc of York ye day of his Baptisme', TNA E 404/57 f. 172. Henry VI had been godfather by proxy to Henry Holland, son of the earl of Huntingdon, who was born in June 1430 while the king was in France (T. B. Pugh, 'Richard, Duke of York, and the Rebellion of Henry Holand, Duke of Exeter, in May 1454', *Historical Research* 63 (1990): 248–62, 249).

42 His death is first mentioned in the Clare Roll in 1456. The Latin version says that he passed 'swiftly' (*cito*) into heaven although the English version seems to imply that he lived longer than some of his younger siblings.

43 *A Visitation of the North of England circa 1480 to 1500*, Surtees Society 144 (London, 1930), 4.

44 Brie, ed., *Brut*, 477.

45 *The Chronicles of Enguerrand de Monstrelet*, trans. Thomas Johnes, 2 vols (London: William Smith, 1840), II:46.

46 *Monstrelet*, trans. Johnes, II:346.

47 The fine of £1,000 that the couple had to pay was a standard charge for a widow of Jacquetta's status 'intermarrying without the king's consent', *CPR 1436–41*: 53.

48 C. L. Kingsford, ed., *Chronicles of London* (Oxford: Clarendon Press, 1905), 95; James Gairdner, ed., *Historical Collections of a Citizen of London*, Camden Society, n.s. 17 (1876), 183.

49 There is no convincing evidence to indicate which of their children was born first or when that was.

50 *GEC*, X:238–9.

51 Ralph Griffiths, *The Reign of Henry the Sixth: The Exercise of Royal Authority 1422–1461* (London: Benn, 1981), 460–1.

52 Pollard, *John Talbot*, 1.

53 BL Egerton Ch. 8782.

54 *Monstrelet*, trans. Johnes, II:114–15.

55 BL Egerton Chs. 7361, 7364, 8786.

56 *CPL*, IX:486; *CPL*, IX:489; *CPR 1476–85*: 411.

57 *Monstrelet*, trans. Johnes, II:115–116.

58 Rouen, Archives départmentales de la Seine-Maritime, G. 43. f. 21. I am grateful to Livia Visser-Fuchs for showing me a copy of this document.

59 *Monstrelet*, trans. Johnes, II:116.

60 *Monstrelet*, trans. Johnes, II:116.

61 Pollard, *John Talbot*, 56; Jones, *Bosworth*, 49–51.

62 Pollard, *John Talbot*, 57.

63 Janet Shirley, trans., *A Parisian Journal 1405–1449* (Oxford: Clarendon Press, 1968), 345–6.

64 Johnson, *York*, 44.

65 L. Stratford, *Edward the Fourth* (London: Pitman, 1910), 11.

66 BL Egerton Ch. 8782.

67 James Gairdner, ed. *The Paston Letters AD 1422–1509*, 6 vols new complete library edition (London: Chatto & Windus, 1904), II:280–1. (This indenture does not appear in the more recent edition of the *Paston Letters* edited by Davies et al. It is dated 1452 and is BL Add Ch. 17,242.)

68 *Paston Letters*, II:574–5.

69 T. B. Pugh, 'Richard Plantagenet (1411–60), Duke of York, as the King's Lieutenant in France and Ireland' in *Aspects of Late Medieval Government and Society* ed. J. G. Rowe (Toronto: University of Toronto Press, 1986), 112; Pugh, 'The Estates, Finances and Regal Aspirations of Richard Plantagenet (1411–1460), Duke of York', in *Revolution and Consumption in Late Medieval England,* ed. M. Hicks (Woodbridge: Boydell, 2001), 73.

70 Pugh, 'Estates, Finances', 73; BL Egerton Ch. 8782.

71 Pugh, 'Richard Plantagenet', 112.

72 I am grateful to Hannes Kleineke for the suggestion that the Yorks' finery should be considered in the light of Valois consumption.

73 Pugh, 'Estates, Finances', 73.

74 Ibid., 74.

75 BL MS Royal 16 G II; Marianne Ailes, 'Deux manuscrits de la chanson de geste de l'automne de Moyen Âge: un renouvellement du genre?', in *Mélanges Roussel*, ed. Françoise Laurent (Presses universitaires Blaise Pascal de Clermont: forthcoming 2017. I am grateful to Marianne for drawing this book to my attention. See also J. L. Laynesmith, '"To please ... dame Cecely that in Latyn hath lityll intellect": Books and the Duchess of York', in *The Fifteenth Century XV*, ed. L. Clark (Woodbridge: Boydell and Brewer, forthcoming).

76 BL MS Royal 19 A xix.

77 Christine de Pisan, *The Book of the City of Ladies,* ed. Rosalind Brown-Grant (Harmondsworth: Penguin, 1999), 6.

78 Ralph Griffiths, 'The Trial of Eleanor Cobham', in *King and Country: England and Wales in the Fifteenth Century,* ed. Griffiths (London: Hambledon Press, 1991), 238–9.

79 Griffiths, 'Trial', 241; Brie, ed., *Brut*, 481.

80 Griffiths, 'Trial', 245–7.

81 Stevenson, ed., *Letters and Papers*, II:762.

82 Jones, *Bosworth*, 49–51.

83 Ibid., 66–7.

84 David Hipshon, *Richard III* (London: Routledge, 2011), 102; *Monstrelet*, trans. Johnes, II:114.

85 http://www.bbc.co.uk/news/health-23594668 consulted 8/1/16.

86 Stevenson, ed., *Letters and Papers*, I:79.

87 Michael Hicks cites this heraldic document, BL Add MS 6113 f. 49 v in Hicks, *Edward V: The Prince in the Tower* (Stroud: Tempus, 2003), 206. In a Channel 4 documentary broadcast on 3 January 2004, 'Britain's Real Monarch', it was stated that material in the Rouen archives revealed that Edward was christened in a mere side chapel while the whole cathedral was opened up for his brother Edmund's christening. However, this seems to have been a mistake by the presenter: all that the chapter book reveals is that there is no mention of Edward's christening whereas Edmund was christened in the cathedral. Michael Jones and Joanna Laynesmith, 'The Debate: Was Edward IV Illegitimate?', *Ricardian Bulletin*, Summer 2004, 18–24.

88 Stratford, *Edward the Fourth*, 12.

89 C. Scofield, *The Life and Reign of Edward the Fourth*, 2 vols (London: Longmans, Green, 1923), I:1.

90 Jones, *Bosworth*, 70.

91 Stevenson, ed. *Letters and Papers*, II:773. Stratford names Richard Neville earl of Salisbury as a second godfather but gives no source. Stratford, *Edward the Fourth*, 12.

92 *PROME*, V:471.

93 Giles, ed., *Chronicles of the White Rose*, 213.

94 Griffiths, *Henry the Sixth*, 469.

95 M. K. Jones and M. G. Underwood, *The King's Mother: Lady Margaret Beaufort, Countess of Richmond and Derby* (Cambridge: CUP, 1992), 30.

96 Griffiths, *Henry the Sixth*, 485.

97 Stevenson, ed., *Letters and Papers*, II:372. Johnson dated this journey to the previous year but seems not to have noticed that Zano was using a system that dated the year AD from Easter rather than Lady Day. This same dating is used in the Caen receipt which Johnson accepts as 1444, leading him to imagine York making two visits to the city (and implausibly being absent from Rouen for Edmund's birth).

98 V. Hunger, *Le Siège et la Prise de Caen par Charles VII en 1450* (Paris: Champon et Pailhé, 1912), lxii.

99 Jones, *Bosworth*, 59.

100 Hunger, *Le Siége*, lxi.

101 BL Egerton Ch. 8782. I have not been able to ascertain why T. B. Pugh interpreted repeated references to Spryng's 'advice' in this account as evidence that Cecily's expenditure was so reckless that York had had to put one of his own servants in charge of her expenditure. Pugh, 'Richard Plantagenet', 112.

102 Griffiths, *Henry the Sixth*, 486.

103 Stevenson, ed., *Letters and Papers*, II:373.

104 Griffiths, *Henry the Sixth*, 358.

105 Peter Spufford, 'Trade in Fourteenth-Century Europe', in *The New Cambridge Medieval History, volume 6, 1300–1415*, ed. Michael Jones (Cambridge: CUP, 2016), 166–7.

106 John Stow, *A Survey of London*, ed. C. L. Kingsford, 2 vols (Oxford: Clarendon Press, 1971), 174–5.

107 Caroline Barron, *London in the Later Middle Ages: Government and People 1200–1500* (Oxford: OUP, 2004), 147.

108 BL Egerton Ch. 8782.

109 Stevenson, ed., *Letters and Papers*, II:468–9.

110 Ibid., II:763.

111 Charles de Beaurepaire, 'Fondations pieuses du duc de Bedford à Rouen', *Bibliothèque de l'école des chartes* 34 (1873), 343–86, 348n. 4.

112 Griffiths, *Henry the Sixth*, 358.

113 *Chronique de Mathieu d'Escouchy*, ed. G. du Fresne de Beaucourt, Société de l'Histoire de France, 3 vols (Paris, 1863–64), I:86.

114 *Escouchy*, ed. Du Fresne de Beaucourt, I:89.

115 Brie, ed., *Brut*, 488.

116 Stevenson, ed., *Letters and Papers*, I:452.

117 A. R. Myers, *Crown, Household and Parliament in the Fifteenth Century*, ed. C. H. Clough (London: Hambledon, 1985), 225.

118 TNA DL 41/145. In 1434 Cecily's brother, Richard earl of Salisbury, had paid 4,700 marks to wed her namesake, his daughter Cecily, to Henry Beauchamp, the short-lived heir of Richard Beauchamp, earl of Warwick. William Dugdale, *The Baronage of England*, 2 vols (London, 1675–76), I:248. The origin of the idea that Anne's dowry was unprecedented occurs in T. B. Pugh, 'The Magnates, Knights and Gentry', in *Fifteenth-Century England 1399–1509: Studies in Politics and Society*, ed. S. B. Chrimes et al. (Manchester: Manchester University Press, 1972), 118. Here Anne's

dower is erroneously given as 6,500 marks. That figure is corrected in the second edition (Stroud: Alan Sutton, 1995), 118.

119 Quoted in Johnson, *York*, 52.

120 Griffiths, *Henry the Sixth*, 674.

121 Pugh, 'Richard Plantagenet', 123.

122 M. H. Keen, *England in the Later Middle Ages* (London: Routledge, 1973), 401.

123 John Watts, *Henry VI and the Politics of Kingship* (Cambridge: CUP, 1996), 237–9; Christine Carpenter, *The Wars of the Roses: Politics and the Constitution in England c. 1437–1509* (Cambridge: CUP, 1997), 99–103.

124 Griffiths, *Henry the Sixth*, 674.

125 Johnson, *York*, 53.

126 Watts, *Henry VI*, 237.

127 Johnson, *York*, 72.

128 Helen Maurer, *Margaret of Anjou: Queenship and Power in Late Medieval England* (Woodbridge: Boydell, 2003), 83–90.

129 Bodl. Rawlinson MS A 146 f. 37.

130 Ibid.

131 David H. Farmer, *The Oxford Dictionary of Saints*, 3rd edn (Oxford: OUP, 1992), 41–2.

132 A. B. Cobban, *The King's Hall within the University of Cambridge in the Later Middle Ages* (Cambridge: CUP, 1969), 75–6.

133 *CPR 1446–52*: 86.

134 Stevenson, *Letters and Papers*, II:764.

135 Ibid.; Hearne, *Liber Niger*, II:525. For debate on this see Christine Weightman, *Margaret of York, Duchess of Burgundy 1446–1503* (Gloucester: Alan Sutton, 1989), 9.

136 Rennes, Bibliothèque Municipale MS 22 f. 28. There may be some connection between this manuscript and the *Generacio* since both mention George's baptism at St Saviour's and both describe Edward IV's birth as the fourteenth hour after noon on 27 April. Curiously the Rennes manuscript, like the *Generacio*, is missing any reference to Richard duke of Gloucester. Yet there are also significant differences, for example, the Rennes manuscript identifies Anne's birthplace as Fotheringhay.

137 Ibid.; *VCH Hertfordshire*, III: 327.

138 Anthony Emery, *Greater Medieval Houses of England and Wales, 1300–1500* (Cambridge: CUP, 1996–2006), II:261; Weightman, *Margaret of York*, 9.

139 Johnson, *York*, 65.

140 Katherine J. Lewis, *Kingship and Masculinity in Late Medieval England* (London: Routledge, 2013), 156–66.

141 Kingsford, ed., *Chronicles of London*, 157.

142 G. L. Harriss and M. A. Harriss, eds, 'John Benet's Chronicle of the Years 1400 to 1462', *Camden Miscellany XXIV*, Camden Society 4th series, 9 (1972), 192.

143 Gairdner, ed., *Historical Collections*, 188.

144 Kingsford, ed., *Chronicles*, 157.

145 Watts, *Henry VI*, 231.

146 Johnson, *York*, 66.

147 Watts, *Henry VI*, 232; *CPR 1446–52*: 78

148 Stevenson, ed., *Letters and Papers*, II:765. There were of course other important men of that name, including Cecily's own brother. However, William Neville was not as politically important as the namesakes of their older children.

149 *Visitation of the North, c. 1480 to1500*, 4.

150 Giles, ed., *Chronicles of the White Rose*, 214; F. H. W. Sheppard, ed., *Survey of London 39* (London: Athlone Press, 1977), 1.

151 Giles, ed., *Chronicles of the White Rose*, 214.

152 Maurer, *Margaret of Anjou*, 31–8.

153 Ibid., 60–2.

154 Ibid., 87–8.

155 Walter F. Schirmer and Ann E. Keep, *John Lydgate: A Study in the Culture of the XVth Century* (Berkeley: University of California, 1961), 130.

156 Christopher Harper-Bill, *The Cartulary of the Augustinian Friars of Clare*, Suffolk Charters XI (Woodbridge: Boydell, 1991), 105.

157 Osbern Bokenham, *Legendys of Hooly Wummen*, ed. Mary Serjeantson, EETS, o.s. 206 (1938), 136; Edward Flügel, 'Eine Mittelenglische Claudian-übersetzung (1445)', *Anglia* 28 (1905): 255–99, 297.

158 Simon Horobin, 'A Manuscript Found in the Library of Abbotsford House and the Lost Legendary of Osbern Bokenham', *English Manuscript Studies 1100–1700*, 14 (2007): 132–64, 151–2. The manuscript can be viewed online at http://lib1.advocates. org.uk/legenda/.

159 Quoted in Simon Horobin, 'Politics, Patronage and Piety in the Work of Osbern Bokenham', *Speculum* 82 (2007), 932–49, 932.

160 Horobin, 'A Manuscript Found', 138; Simon Horobin, 'The Angle of Oblivioun: A Lost Medieval Manuscript Discovered in Walter Scott's Collection', *Times Literary Supplement*, 11 November 2005, 12–13. I am grateful to Geoffrey Wheeler for drawing this to my attention.

161 Narasingha P. Sil, 'Jobson, Sir Francis', *Oxford DNB*, *sub nomine*; *VCH Essex*, X:190.

162 Horobin, 'A Manuscript Found', 151.

163 Bokenham, *Hooly Wummen*, 137, 139, 227, 259.

164 Ibid.; Sheila Delany, *Impolitic Bodies: Poetry, Saints and Society in Fifteenth-Century England: The Work of Osbern Bokenham* (Oxford: OUP, 1998), 19; Bod. Rawlinson MS A 146, ff. 35–6.

165 A number of works on Bokenham have referred to Katherine Howard as Elizabeth de Vere's mother. Elizabeth's maiden name was indeed Howard but her mother was actually Joan Walton. Anne Crawford, *Yorkist Lord: John Howard, Duke of Norfolk, c. 1425–1485* (London: Continuum, 2010), xiii.

166 Ibid., 49.

167 Delany, *Impolitic Bodies*, 16–17.

168 Johnson, *York*, 159; TNA E 28/86 f. 17.

169 John Watts, '*De Consulatu Stilichonis*: Texts and Politics in the Reign of Henry VI', *JMH* 16 (1990): 251–66, 264n. 34. See also Laynesmith, '"To please … dame Cecely"'.

170 An early catalogue asserted that the text was invoking Richard, duke of York, 'in the person of Stilico … to take upon him the kingly state of Sovereign of England', BL Add MS 11,814 f. 2. This interpretation was followed by its editor in 1905, Flügel, 'Eine Mittelenglische Claudian-übersetzung'. Watts, '*De Consulatu*', 257–61 suggests that the work was written in 1455 to encourage York during his second protectorate. Since the manuscript is dated in Arabic rather than Roman numerals such an error seems unlikely to the present author. Other scholars have accepted the 1445 date but argue for a less treasonous interpretation than Flügel, see Delany, *Impolitic Bodies*, 133–42; Livia Visser-Fuchs, '"Honour is the reward of virtue": The Claudian Translation Made for Richard, Duke of York, in 1445', *The Ricardian* 18 (2003): 66–82, 80–1.

171 Despite appearances in published sources, there is no error in this date on the Clare Roll. The mistake was Dugdale's which was copied by Horstman: *Osbern Bokenham's Legenden*, ed. C. Horstman (Heilbronn: Gebr. Henninger, 1883), 269 and n.

172 Clare Hilles, 'Gender and Politics in Osbern Bokenham's Legendary', in *New Medieval Literatures IV*, ed. Wendy Scase, Rita Copeland and David Lawton (Oxford: OUP, 2001), 200.

173 Clare Roll.

4 The Wheel of Fortune: 1449–1459

1 Will.

2 P. A. Johnson, *Duke Richard of York 1411–1460* (Oxford: Clarendon Press, 1988), 68.

3 Stephen G. Ellis, *Ireland in the Age of the Tudors* (London: Longman, 1998), 52.

4 Michael Hicks, 'From Megaphone to Microscope: The Correspondence of Richard Duke of York with Henry VI in 1450 Revisited', *JMH* 25 (1999): 243–56, 253; M. L. Kekewich et al., eds, *The Politics of Fifteenth Century England: John Vale's Book* (Stroud: Alan Sutton, 1995), 185.

5 Johnson, *York*, 13; TNA CP 25/1/22/123, no. 8; CP 25/1/191/28, no. 31; CP 25/1/192/9, no. 14; CP 25/1/293/71, nos. 343, 344, 346, 347.

6 *CPR 1461–67*: 131.

7 TNA CP 25/1/179/95, no. 122.

8 Ellis, *Ireland in the Age of the Tudors*, 52. Benet says 9 July, G. L. Harriss and M. A. Harriss, eds, 'John Benet's Chronicle of the Years 1400 to 1462', *Camden Miscellany XXIV*, Camden Society, 4th series, 9 (1972), 195.

9 John O'Donovan, ed., *Annals of the Kingdom of Ireland by the Four Masters*, 7 vols (Dublin: Hodges, Smith , 1854), IV:965.

10 BL Egerton Ch 8785.

11 Edmund Curtis, 'Richard, Duke of York, as Viceroy of Ireland: 1447–1460', *The Journal of the Royal Society of Antiquaries of Ireland*, 7th series, 2 (1932): 158–86, 165–7; Andrew Ayton, *Knights and Warhorses* (Woodbridge: Boydell, 1994), 63–4.

12 J. A. Giles, ed., *Chronicles of the White Rose of York* (London: James Bohn, 1845), 214.

13 Anne F. Sutton and Livia Visser-Fuchs, *Richard III's Books* (Stroud: Alan Sutton, 1997), 22; Will.

14 Howard B. Clarke, 'Street Life in Medieval Dublin', in *Ireland, England and the Continent in the Middle Ages and Beyond*, ed. Howard B. Clarke and J. R. S. Phillips (Dublin: University College Dublin Press, 2006), 153.

15 Thomas Hearne, ed., *Liber Niger Scaccarii, nec non Wilhelmi Worcestrii Annales Rerum Anglicarum*, 2 vols (London, 1772), II:525.

16 Curtis, 'Richard, Duke of York as Viceroy', 172.

17 T. B. Pugh, 'The Estates, Finances and Regal Aspirations of Richard Plantagenet (1411–1460), Duke of York', in *Revolution and Consumption in Late Medieval England*, ed. M. Hicks (Woodbridge: Boydell, 2001), 75, 77.

18 Quoted in Curtis, 'Richard, Duke of York, as Viceroy', 174.

19 Ralph Griffiths, *The Reign of Henry the Sixth: The Exercise of Royal Authority 1422–1461* (London: Benn, 1981), 545.

20 O'Donovan, ed., *Annals of the Kingdom of Ireland*, 971.

21 Griffiths, *Henry the Sixth*, 518–19; Johnson, *York*, 78.

22 Harriss and Harriss, ed., 'Benet's Chronicle', 198.

23 I. M. W. Harvey, *Jack Cade's Rebellion of 1450* (Oxford: OUP, 1991), 78.

24 Harvey, *Cade's Rebellion*, 191.

25 Griffiths, *Henry the Sixth*, 611.

26 Harvey, *Cade's Rebellion*, 187.

27 Griffiths, *Henry the Sixth*, 616.

28 James Gairdner, ed., *The Historical Collections of a Citizen of London in the Fifteenth Century*, Camden Society, n.s. 17 (1876), 194.

29 O' Donovan, *Annals of the Kingdom of Ireland*, 971.

30 Curtis, 'Richard, Duke of York, as Viceroy', 174.

31 Johnson, *York*, 77.

32 Hicks, 'Megaphone to Microscope', 252.

33 Kekewich et al., eds., *John Vale's Book*, 185.

34 Johnson, *York*, 78, 84.

35 Harriss and Harriss, ed., 'Benet's Chronicle', 202.

36 Griffiths, *Henry the Sixth*, 688; Kekewich et al., eds., *John Vale's Book*, 185; *Paston Letters*, II:47–50; Hicks, 'Megaphone to Microscope', 251–5.

37 Johnson, *York*, 87, 91.

38 Harriss and Harriss, ed., 'Benet's Chronicle', 203.

39 Ibid.

40 Johnson, *York*, 98n.

41 Ibid.

42 N. W. and V. A. James, eds, *The Bede Roll of the Fraternity of St Nicholas*, London Record Society, 39 (2004), I:56–7; *A Visitation of the North of England c. 1480 to 1500*, Surtees Society 144 (London, 1930), 4.

43 Ibid.

44 WAM 12167.

45 Michael Hicks, *Warwick the Kingmaker* (Oxford: Blackwell, 1998), 49.

46 Bodl. Dugdale MS 15 f. 75.

47 Griffiths, *Henry the Sixth*, 692.

48 Johnson, *York*, 102–3.

49 Ibid., 108.

50 Griffiths, *Henry the Sixth*, 696.

51 *PROME*, V: 346–7.

52 C. L. Kingsford, ed., *Chronicles of London* (Oxford: Clarendon Press, 1905), 163.

53 J. L. Laynesmith, *The Last Medieval Queens* (Oxford: OUP, 2004), 167.

54 T. B. Pugh, 'Richard, Duke of York, and the Rebellion of Henry Holland, Duke of Exeter, in May 1454', *Historical Research* 63 (1990): 248–62, 258.

55 Harriss and Harriss, ed., 'Benet's Chronicle', 207.

56 Anne F. Sutton and Livia Visser-Fuchs, *The Hours of Richard III* (Stroud: Sutton, 1990), 44–6.

57 Rowena Archer, 'Piety, Chivalry and Family: The Cartulary and Psalter of Sir Edmund Rede of Boarstall (d. 1489)', in *Soldiers, Nobles and Gentlemen*, ed. Peter Coss and Christopher Tyerman (Woodbridge: Boydell, 2005), 136.

58 *CPR 1476–85*: 374.

59 Thomas More, *The Complete Works of St Thomas More, Vol. 2: The History of King Richard III*, ed. R. S. Sylvester (New Haven: Yale University Press, 1963), 7. There is no reason to imagine that Richard's scoliosis was a consequence of a difficult birth, http://www.nhs.uk/conditions/Scoliosis/pages/causes.aspx consulted 22/06/2016.

60 Monica H. Green, *The Trotula: A Medieval Compendium of Women's Medicine* (Philadelphia: University of Pennsylvania Press, 2001), 125, 159.

61 Carole Rawcliffe, 'Richard, Duke of York, the King's "obeisant liegeman": A New Source for the Protectorates of 1454–1455', *Historical Research* 60 (1987): 232–9, 233.

62 James Gairdner, ed., *The Paston Letters AD 1422–1509*, 6 vols, new complete library edition (London: Chatto & Windus, 1904), II:280–1.

63 Katherine J. Lewis, *Kingship and Masculinity in Late Medieval England* (London: Routledge, 2013), 214–18.

64 Helen Maurer, *Margaret of Anjou. Queenship and Power in Late Medieval England* (Woodbridge: Boydell, 2003), 90–1.

65 *Paston Letters*, I:249. Margaret may have been with Henry at Norwich on 18 February but this was probably too early to be certain of the pregnancy. Bertram Wolffe, *Henry VI* (London: Methuen, 1983), 370.

66 Huntingdon Library, San Marino, California, Battle Abbey MS 937, printed in Rawcliffe, 'The King's "obeisant liegeman"', 237–8. Unfortunately, this is a copy of the original and bears no date but was presumably written before the king's illness since Cecily was asking Margaret to intercede with the king rather than the lords around him.

67 Johnson, *York*, 121.

68 Rawcliffe, 'The King's "obeisant liegeman"', 237–8.

69 BL Egerton Ch 8365. Johnson assumed that this was the same encounter as that mentioned in the letter. (He incorrectly cites Egerton Ch 8364.) No date for the visit is recorded in the manuscript yet it is accounted for between events in June and July of 1453.

70 Ralph Flenley, ed., *Six Town Chronicles* (Oxford: Clarendon Press, 1911), 140.

71 David Grummitt, *A Short History of the Wars of the Roses* (London: I. B. Taurus, 2013), 15–16.

72 Tracy Adams, 'Christine de Pizan's Isabeau of Bavaria', in *The Rule of Women in Early Modern Europe*, ed. Anne J. Cruz and Mihoko Suzuki (Urbana: University of Illinois Press, 2009), 15–16.

73 *CPR 1446–52*: 430.

74 J. H. Harvey, ed., *William Worcestre : Itineraries* (Oxford: Clarendon Press, 1969), 345; A. J. Pollard, 'Neville, Ralph, second earl of Westmorland', *Oxford DNB, sub nomine*.

75 Joan's disability may have been overstated because she had just been widowed and her sons-in-law were keen to ensure that she was unable to transfer any of her daughters' inheritance into the hands of the lowly squire whom she had married so swiftly after William Neville's death. *CPR 1461–67*: 277.

76 *GEC*, VII:480; Pollard, 'Neville, Ralph, second earl'; Hannes Kleineke, 'Robert Bale's Chronicle of the Second Battle of St. Albans', *Historical Research* 87 (2014): 744–50, 747.

77 *CPR 1461–67*: 277; *GEC*, V:285 and n.

78 Kingsford, ed., *Chronicles*, 163.

79 William Marx, ed., *An English Chronicle 1377–1461: A New Edition* (Woodbridge: Boydell, 2003), 72.

80 Griffiths, *Henry the Sixth*, 720.

81 *PPC*, VI:164.

82 Lincoln's Inn Library, Hale MS 12 Item 75.

83 William Say, *Liber Regie Capelle*, ed. Walter Ullman (London: Henry Bradshaw Society, 92 [1961]), 72.

84 Lincoln's Inn Hale MS 12 Item 75.

85 Ibid.

86 Ibid.

87 Maurer, *Margaret of Anjou*, 45.

88 Say, *Liber Regie Capelle*, 72–3.

89 It is likely that Elizabeth Woodville's churching feast was to some extent modelled on that of Margaret of Anjou. Elizabeth's is described in Malcolm Letts, ed. *The Travels of Leo of Rozmital* (Hakluyt Society, 2nd series, 108 [1955]), 47.

90 Harriss and Harriss, ed., 'Benet's Chronicle', 210.

91 Ibid., 211.

92 Gairdner, ed., *Paston Letters*, II:297. This newsletter is the only source we have for Margaret's proposal. It is not part of the Paston correspondence but was published by Gairdner from BL Egerton MS 914.

93 Jean Chartier, *Chronique de Charles VII, Roi de France*, 3 vols (Paris: Vallet de Viriville, 1858), I:209–10.

94 *PROME*, V:239.

95 R. G. Davies, 'Kemp [Kempe], John (1380/1–1454)', *Oxford DNB, sub nomine*.

96 Griffiths, *Henry the Sixth*, 725; John Watts, *Henry VI and the Politics of Kingship* (Cambridge: CUP, 1996), 309.

97 Griffiths, *Henry the Sixth*, 726–7.

98 R. A. Griffiths, 'Local Rivalries and National Politics: The Percies, the Nevilles and the Duke of Exeter, 1452–1454', in *King and Country: England and Wales in the Fifteenth Century*, ed. Griffiths (London: Hambledon, 1991), 338.

99 Ibid., 343–7.

100 Griffiths, *Henry the Sixth*, 730–8.

101 Griffiths, 'Local Rivalries', 352–3.

102 Griffiths, *Henry the Sixth*, 738–9.

103 Griffiths, 'Local Rivalries', 337 and n.

104 Griffiths, *Henry the Sixth*, 740.

105 A. R. Myers, ed., *English Historical Documents, vol. IV, 1327–1485* (London: Eyre & Spottiswoode, 1969), 277.

106 Griffiths, *Henry the Sixth*, 745.

107 Katherine J. Lewis, *Kingship and Masculinity in Late Medieval England* (London: Routledge, 2013), 181.

108 Ibid., 187.

109 J. Stevenson, ed., *Letters and Papers Illustrative of the Wars of the English in France*, Rolls Series 22, 2 vols (London, 1864), II:771.

110 Although Jacobus de Voraigne's Ursula was a British princess marrying into Anglia, Osbern Bokenham's Ursula was a princess from Brittany who married an English prince. http://lib1.advocates.org.uk/legenda/ (accessed 26/06/2016): Abbotsford Legenda Aurea f. 207. Jacobus de Voraigne, *The Golden Legend*, trans. William Granger Ryan, 2 vols (Princeton: Princeton University Press, 1993), II:256–9.

111 Gordon Kipling, ed., *The Receyt of the Ladie Kateryne*, EETS 296 (1990), 15.

112 *Visitation of the North, c. 1480 to 1500*, 4.

113 Griffiths, *Henry the Sixth*, 748.

114 Ibid., 752.

115 Gerald Harriss, 'Richard Duke of York and the Royal Household', in *Soldiers, Nobles and Gentlemen*, ed. Coss and Tyerman, 332.

116 Harriss and Harriss, ed., 'Benet's Chronicle', 216.

117 Griffiths, *Henry the Sixth*, 757.

118 *Paston Letters*, II:43.

119 BL Lansdowne MS 403 f. 49.

120 Robert Davies, *Extracts from the Municipal Records of the City of York during the reigns of Edward IV, Edward V and Richard III* (London: J. B. Nichols and Son, 1843), 227, 230, 244.

121 BL Lansdowne MS 403 f. 49; *The Register of the Corpus Christi Guild in York*, Surtees Society 1 (1871), 55.

122 Davies, *Extracts from the Municipal Records*, 248.

123 Flenley, ed., *Six Town Chronicles*, 144.

124 *Paston Letters*, II:167.

125 Alastair Hawkyard, 'Sir John Fastolf's "Gret Mansion by me late edified": Caister Castle, Norfolk', *Of Mice and Men: Image, Belief and Regulation in Late Medieval England*, in *The Fifteenth Century V*, ed. Linda Clark (Woodbridge: Boydell, 2005), 58.

126 *Paston Letters*, II:355.

127 Ibid., II:167–8.

128 Ibid., II:167–8, 559–60.

129 Ibid., I:149. Gairdner and Davis both located this letter in 1456, assuming that it preceded Cecily's actual visit. However, Fastolf is unlikely to have been expecting an imminent visit from Cecily when she was in Yorkshire. It is more likely that the letter was written as his health worsened towards his death.

130 J. A. F. Thomson, 'John de la Pole, duke of Suffolk' *Speculum* 54 (1979): 528–42, 529; Michael Hicks, 'Pole, John de la, second duke of Suffolk', *Oxford DNB*, *sub nomine*.

131 Ibid.

132 Maurer, *Margaret of Anjou*, 151–7.

133 Stevenson, ed., *Letters and Papers*, I:361–9.

134 Griffiths, *Henry the Sixth*, 807–8; Maurer, *Margaret of Anjou*, 160–7.

135 Griffiths, *Henry the Sixth*, 817.

136 Thomas Harrington's commitment to York and Salisbury in November 1458 has often been cited as evidence of an earlier breakdown but see Hicks, *Warwick the Kingmaker*, 155–6, on why 1458 cannot be the correct date for this.

137 Griffiths, *Henry the Sixth*, 819–22.

5 A Paper Crown: 1459–1460

1 John Hardyng, *Chronicle*, ed. H. Ellis (London: Rivington et al., 1812), 23.

2 Felicity Riddy, 'John Hardyng's Chronicle and the Wars of the Roses', *Arthurian Literature XII*, ed. J. P. Carley and F. Riddy (Cambridge: D. S. Brewer, 1993), 101. Hardyng had written five and a half thousand lines of the new version before York's death on 30 December 1460. It seems unlikely that the eighty-year-old chronicler could have composed this in the two and a half months between the Act of Accord and York's death. He may even have been commissioned to write it before the rout at Ludford.

3 James Gairdner, ed., *Historical Collections of a Citizen of London*, Camden Society, n.s. 17 (1876), 205.

4 Ralph Flenley, ed., *Six Town Chronicles of England* (Oxford: Clarendon Press, 1911), 148; cf Gairdner, ed., *Historical Collections*, 205.

5   Charles Ross suggested that Cecily was actually at Fotheringhay (hence her failure to escape) but *Hearne's Fragment* explicitly located her at Ludlow. *An English Chronicle 1377–1461* and the *Brut* also seem to imply that she was there. Charles Ross, *Richard III* (London: Methuen, 1981), 4; J. A. Giles, ed., *Chronicles of the White Rose of York* (London: James Bohn,1845), 5–6; William Marx, ed., *An English Chronicle 1377–1461: A New Edition* (Woodbridge: Boydell, 2003), 81; F. W. D. Brie, ed., *The Brut, or, The Chronicles of England*, EETS, o.s. 131, 136 (1906), 528.

6   Giles, ed., *Chronicles of the White Rose*, 5–6.

7   C. L. Kingsford, ed., *Chronicles of London* (Oxford: Clarendon Press, 1905), 169.

8   Gairdner, ed., *Historical Collections*, 205.

9   Ibid.

10 'Hearne's Fragment' in Giles, ed., *Chronicles of the White Rose*, 5–6. Brie, ed., *Brut*, 528. Although some popular histories describe a 'tradition' that Cecily encountered Henry's troops at the steps of the market cross, Paul Murray Kendall acknowledges in an endnote that this was purely his own conjecture. Paul Murray Kendall, *Richard III* (London: Sphere, 1972), 35, 439.

11 Gairdner, ed., *Historical Collections*, 207.

12 Marx, ed., *English Chronicle*, 81. This should not be confused with 'A Short English Chronicle', also written by a Yorkist partisan, which makes no mention of Cecily at Ludlow. James Gairdner, ed., *Three Fifteenth-Century Chronicles*, Camden Society, n.s. 28 (1880), 72.

13 Josephine Wilkinson, *Richard III: The Young King to Be* (Stroud: Amberley, 2008), 67; Philippa Langley and M. K. Jones, *The King's Grave: The Search for Richard III* (London: John Murray, 2013), 73.

14 Gairdner, ed., *Historical Collections*, 207. See also Robert Fabyan, *The New Chronicles of England and France* (London: Rivington, 1811), 635; Giles, ed., *Chronicles of the White Rose*, 5 n.

15 W. M. Ormrod, 'In Bed with Joan of Kent: The King's Mother and the Peasant's Revolt', in *Medieval Women: Texts and Contexts in Late Medieval Britain. Essays for Felicity Riddy*, ed. Jocelyn Wogan-Browne et al. (Turhout: Brepols, 2000), 278–9.

16 Marx, ed., *English Chronicle*, xci. It is not entirely clear when the author imagined the assault happening on Cecily since he refers both to this and to the pillaging of Ludlow with events that happened that winter, after the Coventry parliament.

17 Brie, ed., *Brut*, 528.

18 Carole Rawcliffe, *The Staffords, Earls of Stafford and Dukes of Buckingham 1394–1521* (Cambridge: CUP, 1978), 66–7.

19 *PROME*, 'Henry VI: Introduction'.

20 *Paston Letters*, II:187.

21 Ibid.

22 *Paston Letters*, I:87–91, 98–102, 161–2; Colin Richmond, *The Paston Family in the Fifteenth Century: Fastolf's Will* (Cambridge: CUP, 1996), 56–71, 91, 95–101 and *passim*.

23 Ibid., 91. It is possible that she was interested in the fate of Fastolf's college. One suggested option was to connect it to the abbey of St Benet at which Cecily stayed more than once. The persistent dispute over the will and lack of money meant that Fastolf's college never was properly established, although from 1470 fourteen Magdalen scholars were paid to pray for his soul. Richmond, *Fastolf's Will*, 66.

24 Gairdner ed., *Historical Collections*, 206. This chronicler's chronology for 1459 is frequently confused and he does not say where or when Cecily's meeting with the king took place.

25   Ibid.

26   *PROME*, V:349.

27   R. A. Griffiths, 'Devereux, Walter, first Baron Ferrers of Chartley', *Oxford DNB*, *sub nomine*.

28   *CPR 1452–61*: 532, 534, 550.

29   *CPR 1452–61*: 547.

30   *PROME*, V:350.

31   *CPR 1452–59*: 542.

32   The manors included Finmere, Oxon and North Fambridge, Essex, both of which were among lands which Cecily and Richard had mortgaged together in 1449. TNA CP 25/1/293/71, no. 346. Many of the manors were regranted to Cecily by her son Edward in 1461. *CPR 1461–67*: 131.

33   *CPR 1452–59*: 542.

34   Ibid.

35   *PROME*, V:349.

36   R. A. Griffiths, 'Vaughan, Sir Thomas (d. 1483)', *Oxford DNB*, *sub nomine*.

37   I am grateful to Hannes Kleineke for this interpretation (email correspondence).

38   Kingsford, ed., *Chronicles*, 170.

39   Gairdner, ed., *Historical Collections*, 207; Brie, ed., *Brut*, 528.

40   James Gairdner, ed. *The Paston Letters AD 1422–1509*, 6 vols, new complete library edition (London: Chatto & Windus, 1904), III:203. See, for example, Amy Licence, *Cecily Neville: Mother of Kings* (Stroud: Amberley, 2014), 131.

41   Davis reads it as 'my lady Duchesse ys stille ayen returned yn Kent', *Paston Letters*, II:540. Gairdner's version reads 'my Lady Duchesse ys stille ayen received in Kent', Gairdner, ed., *Paston Letters*, III:203. *Egerton MS 1995* reported that Jacquetta had been captured along with her menfolk which would explain Gairdner's assumption that this duchess could not have been Jacquetta given his reading. Gairdner, ed., *Historical Collections*, 206. Davis's reading suggests that Jacquetta was seized initially but was released before the Calais ships set sail.

42   *Paston Letters*, I:162.

43   Jehan de Waurin, *Recueil des Croniques et Anchiennes Istories de la Grant Bretaigne*, ed. William Hardy, Rolls Series 39, 5 vols (1864–91), V:286.

44   *Paston Letters*, II:216.

45   Marx, ed., *English Chronicle*, 80–1; A. J. Otway-Ruthven, *A History of Medieval Ireland*, 2nd edn (New York: Barnes & Noble, 1980), 387.

46   Griffiths, *Henry the Sixth*, 854.

47   Waurin, *Croniques*, V:286.

48   Ibid., V:287.

49   J. Stevenson, ed., *Letters and Papers Illustrative of the Wars of the English in France*, Rolls Series 22, 2 vols (London, 1864), II:772; Marx, ed., *English Chronicle*, 82.

50   The manifesto is printed in Marx, ed., *English Chronicle*, 82–5.

51   *CSP Milan*, 27.

52   Ibid., 22.

53   Ibid., 23.

54   Michael Hicks, *Warwick the Kingmaker* (Oxford: Blackwell, 1998), 177.

55   Stevenson, *Letters and Papers*, II:773; Marx, ed., *English Chronicle*, 89–90.

56   Ibid., 90.

57   Griffiths, *Henry the Sixth*, 710.

58   Ballad printed in Marx, ed., *English Chronicle*, 86–8.

59 G. L. Harriss and M. A. Harriss, ed., 'John Benet's Chronicle of the Years 1400 to 1462', *Camden Miscellany XXIV*, Camden Society, 4th series 9 (1972), 225; Griffiths, *Henry the Sixth*, 862.

60 Marx, ed., *English Chronicle*, 90–1. This may have been the chronicler's typical Yorkist whitewashing, but the small number of casualties has led historians to accept it as true: Griffiths, *Henry the Sixth*, 862.

61 Ibid. Egremont may have been executed after the battle. R. A. Griffiths, 'Percy, Thomas, first baron Egremont', *Oxford DNB, sub nomine*.

62 Meriel Connor, ed., *John Stone's Chronicle: Christ Church Priory, Canterbury, 1417–1472* (Kalamazoo: Western Michigan University, 2010), 106.

63 Marx, ed., *English Chronicle*, 92; Gairdner, ed., *Historical Collections*, 209. Her itinerary is slightly different in each account. The latter identifies her assailant as one of the prince's gentlemen.

64 Rawcliffe, *The Staffords*, 19–21.

65 *CPR 1452–61*: 576.

66 Waurin, *Croniques*, V:302.

67 Gairdner, ed., *Historical Collections*, 211; Stevenson, ed., *Letters and Papers*, II:773.

68 Marx, ed., *English Chronicle*, 91–2.

69 Harriss and Harriss, ed., 'Benet's Chronicle', 227.

70 Stevenson, ed., *Letters and Papers*, II:773.

71 Ibid., II: 773–4; Gairdner, ed., *Three Fifteenth-Century Chronicles*, 75.

72 Griffiths, *Henry the Sixth*, 864.

73 Connor, ed., *John Stone's Chronicle*, 106.

74 *Paston Letters*, II:216.

75 Johnson, *Duke Richard of York 1411–1460* (Oxford: Clarendon Press, 1988), 230.

76 *Paston Letters*, I:158.

77 Stevenson, ed., *Letters and Papers*, II:771.

78 Hicks, *Warwick the Kingmaker*, 180.

79 *Paston Letters*, II:216.

80 Ibid.

81 Gairdner, ed., *Historical Collections*, 208.

82 Johnson, *York*, 211.

83 Waurin, *Croniques*, V:311.

84 Ibid., V:314.

85 Katherine J. Lewis, *Kingship and Masculinity in Late Medieval England* (London: Routledge, 2013), 199–200.

86 Frederic Madden, 'XXV Political Poems Written in the Reigns of Henry VI and Edward IV', *Archaeologia* 29 (1842): 318–47, 335; J. L. Laynesmith, 'Telling Tales of Adulterous Queens in Medieval England: From Olympias of Macedonia to Elizabeth Woodville', in *Every Inch a King: Comparative Studies on Kings and Kingship in the Ancient and Medieval Worlds*, ed. Lynette Mitchell and Charles Melville (Leiden: Brill, 2013), 206–12.

87 Riddy, 'Hardyng's Chronicle', 101.

88 Hardyng, *Chronicle*, 23.

89 Gairdner, ed., *Historical Collections*, 208.

90 Kingsford, *Chronicles*, 171.

91 Johnson, *York*, 214.

92 Nicholas Pronay and John Cox, eds., *The Crowland Continuations:1459–1486* (London: Sutton, 1986), 110–11.

93 *PROME*, V:379.

94 Ibid., V:380–1. 3,600 marks to be given to Edward and £1,000 to Edmund.

95 Gairdner, ed., *Historical Collections*, 208.

96 Harriss and Harriss, ed., 'Benet's Chronicle', 228.

97 Gairdner, ed., *Historical Collections*, 208.

98 Marx, ed. *English Chronicle*, 97.

99 Johnson, *York*, 215–16.

100 Gairdner, ed., *Historical Collections*, 210.

101 Griffiths, *Henry the Sixth*, 866, 869–70.

102 Flenley, ed., *Six Town Chronicles*, 152.

103 Johnson, *York*, 223; Marx, ed., *English Chronicle*, 97.

104 Henry T. Riley, ed., *Ingulph's Chronicle of the Abbey of Croyland* (London: George Bell, 1893), 421.

105 Stevenson, ed., *Letters and Papers*, II:775. However, Edmund Hall's pathetic picture of Rutland kneeling before Clifford, speechless with terror, while his tutor pleaded for his life is a later maudlin fantasy concocted to emphasize the barbarity of the age (Hall imagined that Edmund was only 12). *Hall's Chronicle*, ed. H. Ellis (New York: AMS, 1965), 250–1.

106 Riley, ed., *Croyland*, 421.

107 Stevenson, *Letters and Papers*, II:775.

108 According to the Crowland Continuator they were buried in a 'lowly burial-place in the house of Mendicant Friars'. Pronay and Cox, eds, *Crowland*, 139. A list of burials at the Dominican house in Pontefract that was written before 1504 recorded that the hearts of the Yorkist lords had remained buried at this house. *VCH Yorkshire*, III:272–3. For the suggestion that they were buried in the Cluniac Priory of St John the Evangelist see Anne F. Sutton and Livia Visser Fuchs with Peter Hammond, ed., *The Reburial of Richard Duke of York, 21–30 July 1476* (London: The Richard III Society, 1996), 2 and n. 9.

109 Christine de Pisan, *The Treasure of the City of Ladies, or, The Book of the Three Virtues*, trans. Sarah Lawson (Harmondsworth: Penguin, 1985), 81.

6 Her First Year of Widowhood: 1461

1 *CSP Milan*, I:67.

2 Hannes Kleineke, *Edward IV* (London: Routledge, 2009), 43. See p. 234n. 40 for proof that it was Shrewsbury and not Gloucester.

3 James Gairdner, ed., *Three Fifteenth-Century Chronicles*, Camden Society, n.s. 28 (1880), 77.

4 James Gairdner, ed., *Historical Collections of a Citizen of London*, Camden Society, n.s. 17 (1876), 211. This chronicler dates the battle 2 February, as does Vitellius A XVI: 'at Candilmasse', C. L. Kingsford, *Chronicles of London* (Oxford: Clarendon Press, 1905), 173; Tanner 2 says 'in principio ffebruarii', Ralph Flenley, *Six Town Chronicles of England* (Oxford: The Clarendon Press, 1911), 167; but William Marx, ed., *An English Chronicle 1377–1461. A New Edition* (Woodbridge: The Boydell Press, 2003), 99 dates the parhelia to Candlemas and the battle to 3 February; Benet's chronicle also dates the battle 3 February, G. L. Harriss and M. A. Harriss, eds, 'John Benet's Chronicle of the Years 1400 to 1462', *Camden Miscellany XXIV*, Camden Society, 4th series, 9 (1972), 229.

5 Gairdner, ed., *Three Fifteenth-Century Chronicles*, 77

6 Ibid.; Gairdner, ed., *Historical Collections*, 211.

7 Hannes Kleineke, 'Alice Martyn, Widow of London: An Episode from Richard's Youth', *The Ricardian* 14 (2004): 32–6, 34.

8 C. L. Scofield, *The Life and Reign of Edward the Fourth*, 2 vols (London: Longmans, 1923), I:140.

9 Hannes Kleineke, 'Robert Bale's chronicle of the second battle of St. Albans', *Historical Research* 87 (2014): 744–50, 747.

10 Scofield, *Edward the Fourth*, I:142.

11 Gairdner, ed., *Historical Collections*, 215.

12 Marx, ed., *English Chronicle*, 99.

13 Henry T. Riley, ed., *Ingulph's Chronicle of the Abbey of Croyland* (London: George Bell, 1893), 422–3.

14 B. M. Cron, 'Margaret of Anjou and the Lancastrian March on London, 1461', *The Ricardian* 11 (1999): 560–615; Helen Maurer, *Margaret of Anjou: Queenship and Power in Late Medieval England* (Woodbridge, Boydell, 2003), 192–3.

15 Kingsford, ed., *Chronicles*, 173 (Vitellius A XVI) names the duchess of Bedford and Lady Scales; Marx, ed., *English Chronicle*, 99 names the duchess of Buckingham; pseudo-Worcester's *Annales* names the two duchesses of Bedford and Buckingham, J. Stevenson, ed., *Letters and Papers Illustrative of the Wars of the English in France*, Rolls Series 22, 2 vols (London, 1864), II:776.

16 Jehan de Waurin, *Recueil des Croniques et Anchiennes Istories de la Grant Bretaigne*, ed. William Hardy, Rolls Series 39, 5 vols (1864–91), 308. Waurin reports that Henry had pardoned Rivers and his son at Greenwich. They had of course been acting on his orders in the first place (or those of his ministers) so that it was rather a reconciliation with Warwick, Salisbury and March than with the king. Waurin's story seems to be supported by Benet's observation that in a parliament held in January 1461, under Warwick's direction, Rivers's son, Anthony, was recognized as Lord Scales in right of his wife, whose father's recent murder is referred to above. Harriss and Harriss, eds, 'Benet's Chronicle', 229.

17 A. R. Myers, *Crown, Household and Parliament in Fifteenth Century England*, ed. C. H. Clough (London: Hambledon, 1985), 182. It is just possible that the petitioner was actually Ismanie's daughter, Elizabeth, who had married Jacquetta's eldest son, Anthony, now Lord Scales.

18 Kingsford, ed.,*Chronicles*, 173.

19 Ibid., 174.

20 Marx, ed., *English Chronicle*, 109.

21 P. A. Johnson, *Duke Richard of York, 1411–1460* (Oxford: Clarendon Press, 1988), 45; Richard Vaughan, *Philip the Good: The Apogee of Burgundy* (London: Longmans, 1970), 342.

22 Christine Weightman, *Margaret of York, Duchess of Burgundy, 1446–1503* (Gloucester: Alan Sutton, 1989), 19.

23 *CSP Milan*, 74.

24 Livia Visser-Fuchs, 'Richard in Holland, 1461', *The Ricardian* 6 (1983): 182–9.

25 See C. A. J. Armstrong, *England, France and Burgundy* (London: Hambledon, 1983), 77n. 2 for discussion of the precise date.

26 Stevenson, *Letters and Papers*, II:777.

27 Gairdner, ed., *Three Fifteenth-Century Chronicles*, 76.

28 Kingsford, ed., *Chronicles*, 173–4.

29 Flenley, ed., *Six Town Chronicles*, 161.

30 C. A. J. Armstrong, 'Inauguration Ceremonies of the Yorkist Kings and Their Title to the Throne', *TRHS* 30 (1948): 51–73, 56–63.

31 Waurin, *Croniques*, V:335.

32 Scofield, *Edward the Fourth*, I:194.

33 TNA E 101/411/11. These were initially provided on credit by optimistic Londoners. Four London brewers had to wait more than two years for payment of the £30 worth of beer they had supplied whereas a certain Philip Nele had to wait longer still for payment for 389 muttons. Scofield, *Edward the Fourth*, I:194n.

34 *Paston Letters*, I:165; *CSP Milan*, 65–6.

35 Gairdner, ed., *Historical Collections*, 216; Waurin, *Croniques*, V:335; Kingsford, *Chronicles of London*, 175.

36 *Paston Letters*, I:165; Brie, ed., *Brut*, 533.

37 *Paston Letters*, I:165.

38 A. H. Thomas and I. D. Thornley, eds., *The Great Chronicle of London* (London, 1938, reprinted Gloucester: Alan Sutton, 1983), 197.

39 Gairdner, ed., *Historical Collections*, 217.

40 A list which may also have been circulated in Cecily's household wrongly included Henry of Buckingham, her sister Anne's son, but correctly added her younger Percy nephew, Eleanor's son, Richard. *Paston Letters*, I:165–6; Anthony Lord Scales and Henry of Buckingham were also mentioned as dead in a newsletter from the bishop of Elphin on 7 April, *CSP Milan*, 66.

41 *Paston Letters*, I:166; *CSP Venice*, I:102 cf. H. T. Riley, ed. *Ingulph's Chronicle of the Abbey of Croyland* (London: Bohn, 1854), 425.

42 *CSP Milan*, 69.

43 *CSP Venice*, I:103.

44 Ibid., I:104; *CSP Milan*, 67.

45 Ibid., 72.

46 Ibid., 67.

47 Ibid., 73–4.

48 Marx, ed., *English Chronicle*, 99.

49 *CPR 1461–67*: 6.

50 Ibid., 15.

51 Ibid., 7, 9.

52 Ibid., 196.

53 WAM 12168.

54 *CPR 1461–67*: 131–2.

55 Penny Lawne, *Joan of Kent. The First Princess of Wales* (Stroud: Amberley, 2015), 207.

56 J. L. Laynesmith, *The Last Medieval Queens* (Oxford: OUP, 2004), 234–5.

57 Joel Rosenthal, *Patriarchy and Families of Privilege in Fifteenth-Century England* (Philadelphia: Penn Press, 1991), 239 cf. John Watts, 'Richard of York, third duke of York', *Oxford DNB*, *sub nomine* (Watts suggests £4,500).

58 M. K. Jones and M. G. Underwood, *The King's Mother: Lady Margaret Beaufort, Countess of Richmond and Derby* (Cambridge: CUP, 1992), 102, 115. Because Margaret had been declared *femme sole* in parliament she was permitted to hold land in her own right during her husband's lifetime.

59 *CCR 1461–68*: 257.

60 T. B. Pugh, 'The Estates, Finances and Regal Aspirations of Richard Plantagenet (1411–1460), Duke of York', in *Revolution and Consumption in Late Medieval England*, ed. Michael Hicks (Woodbridge: Boydell, 2001), 78.

61 A. J. Pollard, *Late Medieval England 1399–1509* (Harlow: Longman, 2001), 268.

62 *CPR 1461–67*: 131–2.

63 TNA SC 6/764/10.

64 Ibid.

65 Ibid.; SC 6/1113/16.

66 Johnson, *York*, 228; BL Egerton Ch 8784; T. B. Dilks, ed. *Bridgwater Borough Archives, iv, 1445–68*, Somerset Record Society 60 (1948), 123–4.

67 Scofield, *Edward the Fourth*, I:191.

68 J. T. Driver, 'Richard Quatremains: A 15th-Century Squire and Knight of the Shire for Oxfordshire', *Oxoniensa* 51 (1986): 87–103, 98; Josiah Wedgwood, *History of Parliament*, 2 vols (London: H.M.S.O, 1936–8), II187; *CPR 1461–67*: 129; TNA E 101/195/410.

69 Harriss and Harriss, eds, 'Benet's Chronicle', 231. See below for Cecily's involvement in patronage of religious houses near Sheen which may have been a consequence of petitions in her presence.

70 Robert Fabyan, *The New Chronicles of England and France* (London: Rivington, 1811), 640.

71 Scofield, *Edward the Fourth*, I:182.

72 *CPR 1461–67*: 97.

73 Scofield, *Edward the Fourth*, I:178.

74 WAM 12168; TNA SC 6/764/10.

75 TNA E361/6 roll 54.

76 W. M. Ormrod, *Edward III* (New Haven: Yale University Press, 2011), 57 n.

77 Kingsford, ed., *London Chronicles*, 176.

78 Chronicle records of Richard's elevation are contradictory but a combination of evidence from the patent rolls, close rolls and chronicles points very strongly to 1 November, All Saints Day. *GEC*, V:278.

79 *CPR 1461–67*: 66.

80 There is an entry in the Great Wardrobe accounts for 1461–2 just before entries for the dukes which refers to a suite in a tower at Greenwich being furnished. If it was furnished for them, which is not clear, this is still not evidence of a permanent household, merely of their residence with the king at his palace. Anne Sutton, 'And to be delivered to the Lord Richard Duke of Gloucester …', *The Ricardian* VIII:100 (1988): 20–5, 24n. 9. Cecily also stayed at Greenwich on occasion, for example, WAM 12168.

81 C. D. Ross, *Richard III* (London: Eyre Methuen, 1981), 6–7.

82 Linda Clark, 'Bourchier, Henry, first earl of Essex', *Oxford DNB, sub nomine*.

83 TNA E 361/6 mm 53–6; Sutton, 'And to be delivered', 24n. 5.

84 Christine de Pisan, *The Treasure of the City of Ladies*, trans. Sarah Lawson (Penguin: Harmondsworth, 1985), 68.

85 Rosenthal, *Patriarchy and Families of Privilege*, 205–6.

86 Walter Blount had acquired his title in June 1465, GEC IX:335–6. Because Anne retained the title of her first marriage the date of the second is difficult to judge but it had occurred before November 1467 *CPR 1467–77*: 69. The date of Katherine's marriage is similarly unclear. The grant to John of reversion of her dower lands in August 1467 made no mention that they were married. *CPR 1467–77*: 19.

87 Ibid.

88 R. A. Griffiths, 'Queen Katherine of Valois and a Missing Statute of the Realm', *Law Quarterly Review* 93 (1977): 248–58.

89 J. Taylor, W. R. Childs and L. Watkiss, *The St Albans Chronicle; The Chronica Maiora of Thomas Walsingham*, 2 vols (Oxford: OUP 2003), I:90, 196–7

90 C. Given-Wilson, ed., *The Chronicle of Adam of Usk, 1377–1421* (Oxford: Clarendon Press, 1997), 10. I am grateful to Anne Jeavons for drawing this to my attention.

91 Laynesmith, *The Last Medieval Queens*, 31–4.

92 See Chapter 8.

93 See below.

94 Barbara J. Harris, *English Aristocratic Women 1450–1550* (Oxford: OUP, 2002) 127–34, 143–52.

95 Jennifer Ward, *English Noblewomen in the Later Middle Ages* (London: Longman, 1992), 99.

96 Pugh, 'Estates, Finances', 78.

97 Pugh specifically cites his daughters' unpaid dowries, 'Estates, Finances', 77–8. Another significant debt was compensation owed to the duchess of Somerset. *CPR 1452–61*: 546.

98 Pugh, 'Estates, Finances', 77–8.

99 N. W. James and V. A. James, eds., *The Bede Roll of the Fraternity of St Nicholas*, London Record Society, 39 (2004), I:56–7. The entry for George refers to him as duke of Clarence so the names must actually have been written into the register some time after they joined. Richard is not given a title so it was clearly before November.

100 James and James, eds., *Bede Roll*, 1.

101 *CPR 1461–67*: 41, 56–7, 67, 73, 74, 97–8, 110, 144–5, 148, 160–1, 163, 216, 322, 441–2, 444, 519; *CPR 1467–77*: 584; *CPR 1476–85*: 584.

102 *CPR 1461–67*: 144–5, 160–1, 163. In 1462 institutions included Eton and King's College Cambridge, *CPR 1461–67*: 73, 74.

103 Kingsford, ed., *Chronicles*, 176.

104 WAM 12168; *CPR 1461–67*: 51.

105 For example, WAM 12168; TNA SC 6/1113/16; SC 6/1115/9.

106 Meriel Connor, ed., *John Stone's Chronicle. Christ Church Priory, Canterbury, 1417–1472* (Kalamazoo: Medieval Institute Publications, 2010), 109; *HMC*, 9th Report, I:115.

107 Ibid.

108 WAM 12168; Sutton, 'And to be delivered to the Lord Richard', 24n. 9.

109 WAM 12168; TNA SC 6/870/5.

110 Flenley, ed., *Six Town Chronicles*, 163; Kingsford, ed., *Chronicles*, 177.

111 Ibid.; *CCR 1461–68*: 18.

112 Wedgwood, *History of Parliament*, II:290.

113 WAM 12168; TNA SC 6/740/10. SC 6/850/31, SC 6/850/33.

114 *PROME*, 'Edward IV: Introduction', V:483–4; TNA C 65/106.

115 Myers, *Crown, Household and Parliament*, 253.

116 *PROME*, '1461: Introduction', V:493.

117 Flenley, ed., *Six Town Chronicles*, 163.

118 F. Grose and T. Astle, *The Antiquarian Repertory* (London, 1807), 300.

119 Unpicking which bits of the *Ryalle Book* were composed when is not always possible because the authors reasonably allowed for various situations in the royal family. However, instructions regarding younger sons and a youngest unmarried daughter could not have applied to any other fifteenth-century king's mother.

120 Flenley, ed., *Six Town Chronicles*, 163.
121 Clive Burgess, 'The Benefactions of Mortality: The Lay Response in the Late Medieval Urban Parish', in *Studies in Clergy and Ministry in Medieval England*, ed. D. M. Smith, Borthwick Studies in History, 1 (York, 1991), 72.
122 F. Devon, ed., *Pell Records 3: Issues of the Exchequer* (London: John Murray, 1837), 487.

7 The King's Mother: 1461–1464

1 T. B. Dilks, ed., *Bridgwater Borough Archives 1445–1468*, Somerset Record Society 60 (1948), 118.
2 James Ross, *The Foremost Man of the Kingdom: John de Vere, Thirteenth Earl of Oxford (1442–1513)* (Woodbridge: Boydell, 2011), 38–46.
3 C. L. Scofield, *The Life and Reign of Edward the Fourth*, 2 vols (London: Longman, 1923), I:232.
4 BL Add Ch 16564.
5 Colin Richmond, 'East Anglian Politics and Society in the Fifteenth Century: Reflections 1956–2005', in *Medieval East Anglia*, ed. Christopher Harper-Bill (Woodbridge: Boydell, 2005), 198; BL Add Ch 16564.
6 C. D. Ross, *Edward IV* (London: Eyre Methuen, 1974), 50–1; A. J. Pollard, *Late Medieval England 1399–1509* (Harlow: Longman, 2000), 269–70.
7 James Gairdner, ed., *Historical Collections of a Citizen of London*, Camden Society, n.s. 17 (1876), 219.
8 TNA E 361/6 m. 53.
9 Michael Hicks, *Warwick the Kingmaker* (Oxford: Blackwell, 1998), 227–8.
10 *A Collection of Ordinances and Regulations for the Government of the Royal Household* (London: Society of Antiquaries, 1790), 132.
11 *CPR 1461–67*: 300.
12 Richard Marks, 'The Glazing of Fotheringhay Church and College', *Journal of the British Archaeological Association* 131 (1978): 79–109, 108.
13 For further discussion of this see J. L. Laynesmith, 'The Piety of Cecily Duchess of York: A Reputation Reconsidered', in *The Yorkist Age*, ed. Hannes Kleineke and Christian Steer (Donington: Shaun Tyas, 2013), 38–9.
14 TNA SC 6/1115/9; *CPR 1461–7*, 293; TNA E 364/104 m. 2.
15 Gairdner, ed., *Historical Collections*, 220.
16 Ibid.
17 Pollard, *Late Medieval England*, 271–2.
18 Scofield, *Edward the Fourth*, I:320 and see n. 2.
19 Gairdner, ed., *Historical Collections*, 224.
20 Ibid., 224–5.
21 Scofield, *Edward the Fourth*, I:334.
22 Gairdner, ed., *Historical Collections*, 227.
23 BL Add MS 29616 ff 8–9.
24 BL MS Arundel 68 f. 3. Meriel Connor, 'Brotherhood and Confraternity at Canterbury Cathedral Priory in the Fifteenth Century: The Evidence of John Stone's Chronicle', *Archaeolgia Cantiana* 128 (2008): 143–64, 153.

25 Barrie Dobson, 'The Monks of Canterbury in the Later Middle Ages, 1220–1540', in *A History of Canterbury Cathedral*, ed. Patrick Collinson, Nigel Ramsay and Margaret Sparks (Oxford: OUP, 1995), 143.

26 BL Arundel MS 68 f. 63.

27 Connor, 'Confraternity at Canterbury', 152–3.

28 *HMC*, 9th Report, 115.

29 CCA-CC-F/A/2, f. 81. Susan Rose, *The Wine Trade in Medieval Europe 1000–1500* (London: Bloomsbury Academic, 2011), 102. Cecily's flagon cost 18d.

30 TNA SC 6/1115/9; NRO MS Kirkpatrick Notes 21 F (9), 58 'Annals of the City', f. 1462.

31 W. G. Benham, ed. *The Red Paper Book of Colchester* (Colchester, 1902), 60.

32 J. W. Clay, ed., *Dugdale's Visitation of Yorkshire, with Additions*, 3 vols (Exeter: William Pollard, 1894–1917), II:3.

33 WAM MS 12179; TNA SC 6 HENVII/1448 m. 8.

34 *Paston Letters*, I:297.

35 Josiah Wedgwood, *History of Parliament*, 2 vols (London: HMSO, 1936–38), I:187.

36 *Paston Letters*, I:342–3. The name of the daughter being considered for the Clay marriage was not mentioned but Margaret's age makes her the most likely.

37 Thomas Gascoigne, *Loci e Libro Veritatum*, ed. J. E. T. Rogers (Oxford, 1881), 203; *HMC* 2nd Report, 111–12; A. B. Emden, *A Biographical Register of the University of Cambridge to 1500* (Cambridge: CUP, 1963), 657; BL Egerton Ch 8784.

38 CCCC MS 108, pp. 91–3. I have assumed an early date for these because Cecily uses the title 'The Kynges Moder duchesse of york' (p. 95 is presumably a little later); will.

39 CCCC MS 108, p. 91.

40 TNA SC 6/1115/4.

41 SC 6/1115/9 f. 2.

42 For example TNA SC 6/1114/4.

43 BL Add Ch 15476.

44 R. W. Dunning and T. D. Tremlett, eds., *Bridgwater Borough Archives V 1468–1485*, Somerset Record Society 70 (1971), 68.

45 Brigitte Bedos-Rezak, 'Women, Seals and Power in Medieval France, 1150–1350', in *Women and Power in the Middle Ages*, ed. Mary Erler and Maryanne Kowaleski (Athens: University of Georgia Press, 1988), 63.

46 Susan M. Johns, *Noblewomen, Aristocracy and Power in the Twelfth-Century Anglo-Norman Realm* (Manchester: Manchester University Press, 2003), 127, 131.

47 BL Add MS 16,564; Leicester RO, DE221/10/2/7. The Leicester seal, from 1469, is less clear than the 1462 seal in the British Library so it is not wholly certain whether the royal arms were still being differenced for York that late.

48 Elizabeth New, *Seals and Sealing Practice* (London: British Records Association, 2010), 12.

49 PRO, *Guide to the Seals in the Public Record Office*, 2nd edn (London: HMSO, 1968), 25.

50 Cecily explicitly referred to it as her 'Grete Seall' in BL Add Ch 15478.

51 W. de G. Birch, *Catalogue of Seals in the Department of Manuscripts in the British Museum*, 6 vols (London, 1894), II:475, 483, III:303, 616.

52 Penny Lawne, *Joan of Kent: The First Princess of Wales* (Stroud: Amberley, 2015), 315.

53 Ibid.

54 Birch, *Catalogue*, I:102.

55 F. Sandford and S. Stebbing, *A Genealogical History of the Kings and Queens of England* (London, 1707), 374, 387. This is probably the same seal as that referred to in L. C. Loyd and D. M. Stenton, eds., *Sir Christopher Hatton's Book of Seals* (Oxford: Clarendon Press, 1950), 266.

56 BL Add Ch 15478.

57 Henry VI's Tudor half-brothers surprisingly also signed without their titles. *Collection of Ordinances*, 24.

58 Anne Crawford, ed., *Letters of the Queens of England 1100–1547* (Stroud: Sutton, 1994), 116, 129, 136.

59 Ibid., 136.

60 M. K. Jones and M. G. Underwood, *The King's Mother: Lady Margaret Beaufort, Countess of Richmond and Derby* (Cambridge: CUP, 1992), 86.

61 Johns, *Noblewomen*, 135; Bedos-Rezak, 'Women, Seals, and Power', 72.

62 Bedos-Rezak, 'Women, Seals, and Power', 75.

63 R. A. Griffiths, 'The Crown and the Royal Family in Later Medieval England', in *King and Country: England and Wales in the Fifteenth Century*, ed. Griffiths (London: Hambledon, 1991), 7.

64 Ibid.

65 Anthony Emery, *Greater Medieval Houses of England and Wales, Vol. III Southern England* (Cambridge: CUP, 2006), 416.

66 Thomas Habington, *A Survey of Worcestershire*, ed. John Amphlett (Oxford, 1899), I:456, II:223–4; Ralph H. Richardson, 'A Yorkist Window at Oddingley, Worcestershire', *The Ricardian* 10 (June 1996): 421–8, 424.

67 Ibid.

68 Sandford and Stebbing, *Genealogical History*, 388.

69 Elizabeth de Burgh, Lady of Clare, as widow, granted livery to 268 people of whom about 100 are known to have been attached to her household, Jennifer Ward, ed., *Elizabeth de Burgh, Lady of Clare (1259–1360): Household and Other Records* (Woodbridge: Boydell, 2014), xix–xx; Edward IV considered 100 servants sufficient for his queen, A. R. Myers, ed., *The Household of Edward IV* (Manchester: Manchester University Press, 1959), 93. George duke of Clarence's ordinances for 1469 anticipated a 'standing household' of 144 servants which his wife would oversee in his absence and a 'riding household', always with him, of 188 persons, *Collection of Ordinances*, 99–101.

70 Inner Temple Library Petyt MS 538 vol. 39 ff. 200–1.

71 Christine de Pisan, *The Treasure of the City of Ladies, or, The Book of the Three Virtues*, trans. Sarah Lawson (Harmondsworth: Penguin, 1985), 52, 60.

72 Inner Temple Library Petyt MS 538 vol. 39 f. 201.

73 Ibid.

74 Ibid.

75 *Collection of Ordinances*, 32–3, 37–9.

76 The heading refers to Cecily as 'the right excellent Princesse Cecill late mother unto the right noble Prince King Edw iiijth' but it is unlikely that it was actually drawn up after her death since the following section is in the present tense. Moreover, she was referred to by the very similar title of 'Cecilia Ducissa Ebor nup[er] mater dni E Regis Angli quarti' during her lifetime (TNA E 13/172 r. 44). The 'rules' include a reference to Berkhamsted so must postdate the readeption.

77 Louise J. Wilkinson, 'The *Rules* of Robert Grosseteste Reconsidered', in *The Medieval Household in Christian Europe, c. 850–1550*, ed. Cordelia Beattie, Anna Maslakovic and Sarah Rees Jones (Turnhout: Brepols, 2003), 293–306.

78 Wilkinson, '*Rules* of Robert Grosseteste', 298 n.

79 Dorothea Oschinsky, *Walter of Henley and Other Treatises on Estate Management and Accounting* (Oxford: Clarendon Press, 1971), 389.

80 *Collection of Ordinances*, 15–86, 89–105.

81 Ibid., 20.

82 BL Arundel MS 68 f. 3.

83 *CPR 1461–67*: 46.

84 *CPR 1467–77*: 563; TNA SC 6/1114/14.

85 Wedgwood, *History of Parliament*, I:420.

86 BL Arundel MS 68 f. 3; Wedgwood, *History of Parliament*, I:118–19.

87 Ibid.

88 E. A. Brown, 'Companion Me with My Mistress: Cleopatra, Elizabeth I and Their Waiting Women', in *Maids and Mistresses, Cousins and Queens: Women's Alliances in Early Modern England*, ed. S. Frye and K. Robertson (Oxford: OUP, 1999), 135.

89 BL MS Arundel 68 f. 3. This cannot have been Cecily's future daughter-in-law of that name since she joined the fraternity as queen many years later.

90 *CPR 1441–46*: 353; A. R. Myers, 'The Household of Queen Margaret of Anjou, 1452–3', in *Crown, Household, and Parliament in Fifteenth Century England*, ed. C. H. Clough (London: Hambledon, 1985), 182.

91 *CSP Venice*, I:106, the author of this letter to Francesco Coppini believed Ralph Grey had died fighting for Henry VI at Towton. Scofield, *Edward the Fourth*, I:157, 249; Wedgwood, *History of Parliament*, I:398.

92 Scofield, *Edward the Fourth*, I:157.

93 Wedgwood, *History of Parliament*, I:398.

94 BL Add MS 48976. The inscription states that Baynard's Castle was 'her palace' so may have been an error but the date certainly fits with other evidence for the duchess's death. *CPR 1467–77*: 100.

95 *CPR 1461–67*: 263, 472.

96 *CPR 1461–67*: 130, 227; *CPR 1467–77*: 14; *CPR 1476–85*: 374; *CCR 1461–68*: 28.

97 *CPR 1461–67*: 46, 335, 479. I have assumed that Katherine was retiring to her Yorkshire home because her income was to come from Hatfield Chase and Hull and because the king was in Yorkshire when he made this grant. It is of course possible that she had actually left Cecily's service somewhat earlier.

98 BL MS Arundel 68 f. 3; W. A. Shaw, *The Knights of England*, 2 vols (London, 1906), I:13.

99 *CPR 1461–67*: 300.

100 TNA C 1/27 ff. 293–4. On the basis of inconsistencies and contradictions in Fenewyke's response it seems most plausible that Cokys was telling the truth.

101 Inner Temple Library, Petyt MS 538 vol. 39, f. 201.

102 TNA C 1/61/397; SC 6/1115/2.

103 TNA C 81/795/1281.

104 Rose, *Wine Trade*, xvi. A tun could be as much as 252 gallons, Miranda Threlfall-Holmes, 'Durham Cathedral Priory's Consumption of Imported Goods: Wines and Spices, 1364–1420', in *Revolution and Consumption in Late Medieval England*, ed. Michael Hicks (Woodbridge: Boydell, 2001), 142.

105 Scofield, *Edward the Fourth*, I:287.

106 K. A. Mertes, 'The Household as a Religious Community', in *People, Politics and Community in the Later Middle Ages*, ed. J. T. Rosenthal and C. Richmond (Gloucester: Alan Sutton, 1987), 123–39.

107 Inner Temple Library, Petyt MS 538, f. 201.

108 Ibid.

109 Oschinsky, *Walter of Henley*, 401.

110 Since there are very few green items, for ordinary time, it seems likely that only the finest furnishings were mentioned in the will.

111 *CSP Milan*, I:67.

112 Margaret H. Harvey, *England, Rome and the Papacy, 1417–1464* (Manchester: Manchester University Press, 1993), 34.

113 *CPL* XIII pt 1, 222; David Rundle, 'The Scribe Thomas Candour and the Making of Poggio Bracciolini's English Reputation', in *Scribes and Transmission in English Manuscripts 1400–1700, English Manuscript Studies 1100–1700 vol. 12*, ed. Peter Beal and A. S. G. Edwards (London: The British Library, 2005), 1–25.

114 *CPL*, X:113–14.

115 Ibid. York had appointed him to Tarant Gunville in 1441 and Pimperne in 1447. Although he resigned from the former in 1454 he drew an income from Pimperne until his death which was after 1480. John Hutchins, *The History and Antiquities of the County of Dorset*, 3rd edn, rev. William Shipp and James Whitworth Hodson, 4 vols (London, 1861), I:296, II:461.

116 *CPL*, XIII pt. II. 511.

117 TNA SC 6/1113/16; SC 6/1114/1.

118 Dilks, ed., *Bridgwater 1445–1468*, 118–19.

119 TNA SC 6/1113/16. A William Brownyng was still named as her receiver after this gentleman's death in 1472 so it appears that his son took over the role from him. TNA SC 6/1114/5–8. See History of Parliament Trust, unpublished articles on 'William Browning I/Melbury Sampford' and 'William Browning II/Melbury Sampford' for the 1422–61 section by Linda Clark. I am grateful to the History of Parliament Trust and to Linda Clark for allowing me to see these articles in draft.

120 Dilks, ed., *Bridgwater 1445–1468*, 67–8.

121 Ibid., 113–14.

122 Ibid., 119.

123 Ibid.

124 Ibid., 123–4.

125 Wedgwood, *History of Parliament*, I:699.

126 CPR 1461–7, 96; cf TNA SC 6/1113/16.

127 TNA SC 6/1114/4.

128 R. W. Dunning and T. D. Tremlett, eds., *Bridgwater Borough Archives V 1468–1485*, Somerset Record Society 70 (1971), 68.

129 Ibid.

130 Alan Rogers, 'Late Medieval Stamford: A Study of the Town Council 1465–1492', in *Perspectives in English Urban History*, ed. Alan Everitt (London: Macmillan, 1973), 18–22.

131 Ibid., 22.

132 Alan Rogers, 'The Parliamentary Representation of Stamford', *Nottingham Medieval Studies* 58 (2014): 184–252, 186; Rogers, 'Late Medieval Stamford', 22.

133 *CCR 1461–68*: 31, 51–2.

134 Ibid., 278; W. Campbell, ed., *Materials for a History of the Reign of Henry VII*, Rolls Series 60, 2 vols (London, 1873), II:48.

135 *CPR 1461–67*: 48.

136 J. T. Driver, 'Richard Quatremains: A 15th-Century Squire and Knight of the Shire for Oxfordshire', *Oxoniensa* 51 (1986): 87–103, 96–8, 101.

137 *CPR 1461–67*: 54.
138 Christine Carpenter, ed., *Kingsford's Stonor Letters and Papers, 1290–1483* (Cambridge: CUP, 1996), 270.
139 Christine Carpenter, *Locality and Polity: A Study of Warwickshire Landed Society 1401–1499* (Cambridge: CUP, 1992), 124, 126, 130.
140 L. C. Loyd and D. M. Stenton, eds, *Sir Christopher Hatton's Book of Seals* (Oxford: Clarendon Press, 1950), 266.
141 Anne Crawford, *Yorkist Lord: John Howard, Duke of Norfolk, c. 1425–1485* (London: Continuum, 2010), 21, 145.
142 Crawford, *Yorkist Lord*, 29.
143 BL Add MS 19398 f. 34.
144 Ibid.; CCCC MS 108, pp. 92–6.
145 BL Add MS 19398 f. 34.
146 *HMC 2nd Report*, 112.
147 Nottinghamshire Archives, DD/SR/209/315.
148 *CPR 1452–61*: 532.
149 A. J. Pollard, *North-Eastern England during the Wars of the Roses* (Oxford: Clarendon, 1990), 328.
150 Thomas Phillipps, ed., *Institutiones Clericorum in Comitatu Wiltoniae*, 2 vols (Salisbury: 1825), I:152.
151 BL Arundel MS 68 f. 1; *CPR 1461–67*: 420.
152 CCCC MS 108, p. 93.
153 CCCC MS 108, pp. 93–5. Richard Heggis was nominated to Bisley and Richard Sherborne to Great Dunmow. Both parishes had belonged to the Mortimer family, hence the gift of the churches to the college. In 1481 there was a dispute with Lady Elizabeth Scrope over the college's right to appoint to Great Dunmow. T. W. Scott, *The Antiquities of an Essex Parish, or Pages from the History of Great Dunmow* (London: H. S. King, 1873), 26. In a list of rectors displayed at Bisley (presumably drawn from bishops' registers), the Dean and Chapter at Clare are credited with presenting the rector there in 1480, but since this was Richard Sherborne the choice was presumably still Cecily's. According to the same list, York had presented a Richard Sherborne, presumably a kinsman, to the living in 1441.
154 Ruth Butler, 'Brimpsfield Church History', *Transactions of the Bristol and Gloucestershire Archaeological Society* 81 (1962): 73–97, 76–8.
155 Ibid.
156 Edward Hailstone, *The History and Antiquities of the Parish of Bottisham and the Priory of Anglesey in Cambridgeshire*, Cambridge Antiquarian Society Publications 14 (1873), 294.
157 Ibid., 172.
158 Marks, 'Glazing of Fotheringhay', 81.
159 *CPR 1461–67*: 216.
160 *HMC, 5th Report* (1876), 590–2.
161 TNA CP 40/799 rot. 480 refers to Banns as prior of Folkestone in 1460.
162 *HMC, 5th Report*, 590.
163 Ibid., 591.
164 Ibid., 592.
165 F. R. H. du Boulay, ed., *Registrum Thome Bourgchier: 1454–86*, Canterbury and York Society, 54 (1957), 275, 285–6.

166 TNA CP 40/872 rot. 409D; CP 40/873 rot. 304.
167 *CPL*, XVI:192–3, 304–5; William Dugdale, *Monasticon Anglicanum*, 6 vols (London, 1846), IV:672.
168 *CPL*, XVI:304–5.
169 C. Harper-Bill, 'The Priory and Parish of Folkestone in the Fifteenth Century', *Archaeologia Cantiana* 93 (1977): 195–200, 200.
170 *CPL* XI:569.
171 TNA CP 40/805 rot. 305.
172 TNA SC 6/1115/4.
173 TNA C 139/18/32 mm. 40–1.

8 Wife of the Rightful Inheritor: 1464–1471

1 Thomas More, *The Complete Works of St Thomas More, Vol. 2: The History of King Richard III*, ed. R. S. Sylvester (New Haven: Yale University Press, 1963), 64.
2 *CSP Venice*, I:114.
3 Joseph Stevenson, ed., *Letters and Papers Illustrative of the English in France during the Reign of Henry the Sixth*, Rolls Series 22, 2 vols (London, 1861), II:783.
4 Livia Visser-Fuchs, 'English Events in Caspar Weinreich's Danzig Chronicle, 1461–1495', *The Ricardian* 7 (1985–7): 310–20, 313.
5 James Gairdner, ed., *The Historical Collections of a Citizen of London in the Fifteenth Century*, Camden Society, n.s. 17 (1876), 226; J. A. Giles, ed., *Chronicles of the White Rose of York* (London: James Bohn, 1845), 16.
6 Michael Hicks, *Edward V: The Prince in the Tower* (Stroud: Tempus, 2003), 43–6. It would have been possible for Edward to marry Elizabeth on 1 May since his known itinerary places him at Stony Stratford, less than five miles from her parents' home, on 30 April and in Northampton on 1 May. Most likely Edward would have passed through Grafton Regis en route to Northampton and indeed those who first spread the story may have remembered this. TNA E 101/411/13 f. 20. His supposed stay at Grafton for several days shortly afterwards is clearly fiction. However, on 10 August 1464 Edward IV granted William Lord Hastings the wardship and marriage of Elizabeth's son, Thomas, as part of the deal she had struck with him for helping secure Thomas's hereditary lands. Even if the king was trying to conceal his marriage from his best friend it makes no sense for him to have been undermining Elizabeth's interests or giving Hastings reason for resentment when the marriage was revealed. At that point the arrangements inevitably lapsed so that the king could provide his stepson with a more suitable marriage. Hicks, *Edward V*, 45. Other than a relatively peaceful fortnight in the vicinity of Fotheringhay in early August, Edward was almost constantly on the move that summer until he reached Reading on 13 September. It may actually have been there that the secret wedding occurred to pre-empt those pressing him to marry Bona of Savoy.
7 Dominic Mancini, *The Usurpation of Richard the Third*, ed. C. A. J. Armstrong (Gloucester: Alan Sutton, 1984), 60–3.
8 Jean Chartier, *Chronique de Charles VII, Roi de France*, 3 vols (Vallet de Viriville Paris: Paris, 1858), I:209–210; '"Désirant tout, envahissant tout, ne connaissant le prix de rien": Materiality in the Queenship of Isabeau of Bavaria', Yen M. Duong, MA dissertation, University of Guelph, 2014, 18.

9   A. F. Pollard, 'The Making of Sir Thomas More's Richard III', in *Essential Articles for the Study of Thomas More*, ed. R. S. Sylvester and G. P. Marc'hadour (Hamden, CT: Archon Books, 1977), 422–4.

10 More, *Richard III*, 61–4.

11 Michael K. Jones, *Bosworth, 1485: Psychology of a Battle* (Stroud: Tempus, 2002), 63–4.

12 K. Mertes, *The English Noble Household 1250–1600* (Oxford: Blackwell, 1988), 54.

13 Penny Lawne, *Joan of Kent: The First Princess of Wales* (Stroud: Amberley, 2015), 252.

14 Charity Cannon Willard, 'The Patronage of Isabel of Portugal', in *The Cultural Patronage of Medieval Women*, ed. June Hall McCash (Athens: University of Georgia, 1996), 316.

15 Monique Sommé, ed., *La correspondance d'Isabelle de Portugal, duchesse de Bourgogne (1430–1471)* (Ostfildern: Thorbecke, 2009), 341–5.

16 J. L. Laynesmith, *The Last Medieval Queens 1445–1503* (Oxford: OUP, 2004), 208.

17 George Smith, ed., *The Coronation of Elizabeth Wydeville* (London, 1935), 10; Malcolm Letts, ed., *The Travels of Leo of Rozmital*, The Haklyut Society, 2nd series, 108 (1957), 47.

18 Ibid.; Smith, ed., *Coronation*, 10.

19 Giles, ed., *Chronicles of the White Rose*, 18.

20 In 1467 Joan Peasemarsh was paid 100s. in wages but seems to have been leaving the queen's service that May, presumably to return to Cecily whom she served until the latter's death. A. R. Myers, 'The Household of Elizabeth Woodville', in *Crown, Household and Parliament*, ed. C. H. Clough (London: Hambledon, 1985), 309.

21 K. Dockray, ed., *Three Chronicles of the Reign of Edward IV* (Gloucester: Alan Sutton, 1988), 163.

22 Visser-Fuchs, 'Caspar Weinreich', 313.

23 Jacquetta owned a collection of the works of Christine de Pisan that had once belonged to Isabeau of Bavaria and a copy of Gower's *Confessio Amantis*. Lucia Diaz Pascual, 'Jacquetta of Luxembourg, Duchess of Bedford and Lady Rivers', *The Ricardian* 21 (2011): 67–91, 87.

24 Lawne, *Joan of Kent*, 4, 146–8, 234; M. M. N. Stansfield, 'Holland, John, first earl of Huntingdon and duke of Exeter', *Oxford DNB, sub nomine*.

25 Michael Hicks, *Warwick the Kingmaker* (Oxford: Blackwell, 1998), 258.

26 TNA C49/56/48.

27 For example. WAM 12168 final entry.

28 J. J. Smith, ed., *Abbreviata Cronica 1377–1469*, Publications of the Cambridge Antiquarian Society, 1 (1840), 9.

29 W. de Gray Birch, *Catalogue of Seals in the Manuscripts Department of the British Museum*, 6 vols (London: British Museum, 1887–1900), III:390–1.

30 Birch, *Catalogue of Seals*, III:300.

31 Cameron Louis, 'A Yorkist Genealogical Chronicle in Middle English Verse', *Anglia* 109 (1991): 1–20, 18.

32 Philadelphia Free Library, MS E 201 can be viewed online at http://www.freelibrary.org/medieval/edward.htm (accessed 8/7/2016).

33 BL Add MS 11814 ff. 17, 18, 9, 10, 5, 6, 13, 14, 26. This same white hind (specified as Joan of Kent's emblem) was used beside the lion of the earl of March on the banners at Edward IV's funeral. Anne F. Sutton and Livia Visser-Fuchs, *The Royal Funerals of the House of York at Windsor* (London: Richard III Society, 2005), 46.

34 'sigillum domine Cecilie uxoris veri heredis Anglie et Francie et domini Hibernie, matris Regis Edwardi quarti, ducisse Ebor', Birch, *Catalogue of Seals*, III:300.

35 TNA E 404/73/3. In May 1468 it was referred to as 'her manor'. *CPR 1467–77*: 538.

36 Graham Dawson, *The Black Prince's Palace at Kennington, Surrey*, British Archaeological Reports, 26 (1976), 4–7, 12–19.

37 R. Allen Brown, H. M. Colvin, A. J. Taylor, *The History of the King's Works, vol. 2: The Middle Ages* (London: HMSO, 1963), 969.

38 *CPR 1467–77*: 538; TNA SC 6 1114/4.

39 BL Harley MS 787 f. 2.

40 CCCC MS 108, 95. The letter is undated but it seems most likely that she was staying there before she herself owned the nearby properties of Berkhamsted and King's Langley.

41 H. Falvey, 'The More: Archbishop George Neville's Palace', *The Ricardian* 9 (1992): 290–302.

42 Anne Crawford, ed., *Household Books of John Howard, Duke of Norfolk* (Stroud: Sutton, 1992), 295.

43 Crawford, *Household Books*, 170–1. Cecily's steward for the honour of Clare, John Howard, was tasked with settling the matter. Howard had a further motive of his own for taking up the cause since one of his own servants also wished to marry the widow. Howard duly wrote to Benet's master asking the two of them to visit and discuss the dispute. Howard does not explicitly state that Cecily had asked him to write, but he explains that the widow is a tenant of 'the hy an myty prynses my lady the Kenges moder to wome I hame steward', implying that Cecily had an interest in the matter.

44 Anne Crawford, *Yorkist Lord: John Howard, Duke of Norfolk, c. 1425–1485* (London: Continuum, 2010), 53.

45 *CPR 1461–67*: 89–90.

46 J. C. Ward, 'The Estates of the Clare Family 1066–1317', PhD thesis, Queen Mary University of London, 1962, 85.

47 *CCR 1461–68*: 278.

48 *CPR 1467–77*: 108.

49 *CPR 1461–67*: 438–9.

50 Ibid., 389.

51 *CCR 1468–76*: 73.

52 *CPR 1467–77*: 184.

53 CPR 1467–77, 151; TNA SC 6/1291/3/4/4.

54 M. K. Jones and M. G. Underwood, *The King's Mother: Lady Margaret Beaufort, Countess of Richmond and Derby* (Cambridge: CUP, 1992), 82–3.

55 There had been a great fire at Kings Langley in 1431 but Joan continued to reside there until her death in 1437. David Neal, 'Excavations at the Palace and Priory at Kings Langley, 1970', in *Hertfordshire Archaeology* 3 (1973): 31–77, 34.

56 Jenny Sherwood, 'Influences on the Growth and Development of Medieval and Early Modern Berkhamsted', in *A County of Small Towns: The Development of Hertfordshire's Urban Landscape to 1800*, ed. Terry Slater and Nigel Goose (Hatfield: Hertfordshire Publications, 2008), 224–48.

57 *VCH Hertfordshire*, II:163–4, 168–9.

58 Richard Barber, 'Joan, *suo jure* countess of Kent, and princess of Wales and of Aquitaine', *Oxford DNB*, *sub nomine*.

59 *CPR 1388–92*: 82.

60 *CPR 1436–41*: 92–6; Jones and Underwood, *The King's Mother*, 36.

61 *CPR 1467–77*: 108. Richard III and Henry VII both made similar grants to her early in their reigns. *CPR 1476–85*: 441; *CPR 1485–1509*: I:62.

62 This was expected to compensate her for annuities of £689 6s. 8d..

63 Eileen Power, 'The Wool Trade in the Fifteenth Century', in *Studies in English Trade in the Fifteenth Century*, ed. E. Power and M. M. Postan (Abingdon: Routledge, 2006), 43.
64 TNA E 122/162/1.
65 H. L. Gray, 'Tables of Enrolled Subsidy and Customs Accounts 1399 to 1482', in *English Trade*, ed. Power and Postan, 358.
66 TNA E 122/128/10.
67 TNA E 122/162/1 f. 1.
68 TNA E 122/128/10; all three appear to have been listed in E 179/144/67 and Lewis appears in E 179/236/111 cited on www.englandsimmigrants.com, consulted 5/7/2016.
69 C. L. Scofield, *The Life and Reign of Edward the Fourth*, 2 vols (London: Longman, 1923), II:408; Eileen Power, 'Wool Trade', 39–50, 45.
70 Ibid., 48.
71 Ibid., 49.
72 Jennifer Ward, *English Noblewomen in the Later Middle Ages* (London: Longman, 1992), 118; Jennifer Ward, ed., *Elizabeth de Burgh, Lady of Clare (1295–1360), Household and other Records*, Suffolk Records Society, 57 (2014), xviii, xxvi, 104.
73 Helen Bradley, 'The Datini Factors in London, 1380–1410', in *Trade, Devotion and Governance*, ed. Dorothy Clayton, Richard Davies and Peter McNiven (Stroud: Alan Sutton, 1994), 59.
74 Christine Weightman, *Margaret of York, Duchess of Burgundy, 1446–1503* (Gloucester: Alan Sutton, 1989), 45–7; Michael Hicks, *Warwick the Kingmaker* (Oxford: Blackwell, 1998), 264.
75 C. D. Ross, *Edward IV* (London: Eyre Methuen, 1974), 136.
76 J. J. Smith, ed., *Abbreviata Cronica 1377–1469*, Publications of the Cambridge Antiquarian Society, 1 (London, 1840), 9.
77 Meriel Connor, ed., *John Stone's Chronicle* (Kalamazoo: Medieval Institute, 2010), 126.
78 Scofield, *Edward the Fourth*, I:491–2.
79 Connor, *John Stone's Chronicle*, 126.
80 BL Add MS 29616, ff. 37, 52. The Dover Corporation Accounts mention a gift of trout for the duchess of Clarence and the countess (or earl) of Warwick, wine for the earl of Warwick and both payment and wine for Cecily's minstrels in two separate places. It may well be that one of these entries is incorrect and that the same account has been copied in twice (they appear in the years Sept. 1468 to Sept. 1469 and Sept. 1469 to Sept. 1470). The fact that the payment to Cecily's minstrels appears immediately below the reference both times may indicate that they were paid at the same time and that the minstrels were in Isabel's company.
81 Dockray, ed., *Three Chronicles*, 68–9.
82 Ibid., 28.
83 Ibid., 29; Hannes Kleineke, 'The Five Wills of Humphrey Stafford, Earl of Devon', *Nottingham Medieval Studies* 54 (2010): 137–64, 156–7.
84 Dockray, ed., *Three Chronicles*, 28; Kleineke, 'The Five Wills of Humphrey Stafford', 138–9, 143–7.
85 J. Calmette and G. Périnelle, eds, *Louis XI et l'Angleterre, 1461–83* (Paris, 1930), 306–7.
86 Laynesmith, *Last Medieval Queens*, 138.
87 Hicks, *Warwick the Kingmaker*, 279.
88 A. H. Thomas and I. D. Thornley, eds, *Great Chronicle of London* (London, 1938), 210.
89 Ibid.

90 Jonathan S. Mackman, 'The Lincolnshire Gentry and the Wars of the Roses', DPhil thesis, University of York, 1999, 149.

91 Dockray, ed., *Three Chronicles*, 13.

92 'The Confession of Sir Robert Welles', in *Excerpta Historica*, ed. S. Bentley (London: Samuel Bentley, 1831), 284.

93 Ibid.

94 David Grummit, *The Wars of the Roses* (London: I. B. Taurus, 2013), 93.

95 Ibid., 106.

96 Dockray, ed., *Three Chronicles*, 32.

97 Ibid., 33.

98 C. D. Ross, *Richard III* (London: Eyre Methuen, 1981), 8.

99 Livia Visser-Fuchs, 'Richard Was Late', *The Ricardian* 11 (1999): 616–19.

100 Dockray, ed., *Three Chronicles*, 33.

101 Michael Hicks, *False, Fleeting, Perjur'd Clarence: George, Duke of Clarence 1449–78* (Gloucester: Sutton, 1980), 96; TNA SC 6/1115/4.

102 Hicks, *Clarence*, 96–7.

103 TNA SC 6/1115/4.

104 TNA C 1/61/397. I have assumed a date during the readeption since Cecily is called 'high princesse and duches of York' but not king's mother and because Walter Breche paid Cecily for Compton Bassett in 1469 but not 1470. TNA SC 6/1115/2; SC 6/1115/3. Moreover, Walter Breche was first manumitted by Robert Baynard's grandfather who had died back in 1437 so a case as late as 1480 (when the chancellor was again an archbishop of York) is less likely than one in 1470 (see also *CCR 1461–8*: 361 which may be related). The court found in Baynard's favour. I am grateful to Hannes Kleineke for his advice on this case.

105 Jones and Underwood, *The King's Mother*, 52.

106 WAM 12183 ff. 14, 15, 24, 32.

107 Jones and Underwood, *The King's Mother*, 70, 255.

108 Ibid., 41.

109 Ibid., 47.

110 Ibid.,143; N. H. Nicolas, ed., *Testamenta Vetusta*, 2 vols (London: Nichols, 1826), I:357.

111 For example, Rebecca Krug, *Reading Families: Women's Literate Practice in Late Medieval England* (Ithaca and London: Cornell University Press), 77.

112 Jones and Underwood, *The King's Mother*, 143.

113 WAM 5472 f. 33.

114 Ibid. f. 24.

115 Ibid. ff. 13, 21, 23, 30, 31, 33, 41, 45. For discussions about Lord Richmond see Ibid. 46–8.

116 WAM 12183 f. 4.

117 Jones and Underwood, *The King's Mother*, 58–65.

118 Hicks, *Clarence*, 99.

119 Dockray, ed., *Three Chronicles*, 156.

120 Ibid.

121 Weightman, *Margaret of York*, 93.

122 Dockray, ed., *Three Chronicles*, 156.

123 Ibid., 155–7; Scofield, *Edward the Fourth*, I:572–3.

124 Dockray, ed., *Three Chronicles*, 163.

125 Ibid.

126 Ibid.
127 Ibid.
128 Sommé, ed., *La Correspondance d'Isabelle de Portugal*, 343.
129 Dockray, ed., *Three Chronicles*, 165–6.
130 Ibid., 166.
131 Scofield, *Edward the Fourth*, I:581.
132 Jones and Underwood, *The King's Mother*, 58.
133 Dockray, ed., *Three Chronicles*, 168.
134 Scofield, *Edward the Fourth*, I:587.
135 Dockray, ed., *Three Chronicles*, 176.
136 Ross, *Edward IV*, 172.
137 Dockray, ed., *Three Chronicles*, 180.
138 Ibid., 181.
139 Ibid., 184.
140 *CSP Venice*, I:128.
141 Scofield, *Edward the Fourth*, II:23.
142 Ibid., II:13–20.

9 Queen of Right: 1471–1478

1 W. H. Black, ed., *Illustrations of Ancient State and Chivalry* (London: Roxburghe Club, 1840), 29.
2 C. D. Ross, *Richard III* (London: Eyre Methuen, 1981), 24–5.
3 Ibid., 26.
4 Ibid., 26–7.
5 M. A. E. Wood, *Letters of Royal and Illustrious Ladies of Great Britain* (London: Henry Colburn, 1846), 102.
6 *HMC Ninth Report*, II:140–1; Meriel Connor, ed. *John Stone's Chronicle* (Kalamazoo: Medieval Institute, 2010), 130.
7 CCA-CC-F/A/5 f. 131; *HMC Ninth Report*, II:142. There is a reference to 12d. spent on bread for Cecily early in the 1471–72 entries. The editor, who has already remarked that some entries 'have strayed considerably from their proper chronological places', comments 'It is difficult to understand how the old Duchess Cicely could have visited the city at so cheap a rate'. Consequently, I would suggest that this is another misplaced entry and that the majority of her expenses were subsumed in the general costs of the king's visit.
8 TNA SC 6/850/32; SC 6/1115/4.
9 W. C. Waller, 'An Old Church Chest, Being Notes of that at Theydon Garnon', *Transactions of the Essex Archaeological Society*, n.s. 5 (1895): 1–33, 18.
10 Carpenter, ed., *Kingsford's Stonor Letters and Papers, 1290–1483* (Cambridge: CUP, 1996), 270. It is possible that this particular visit occurred while Cecily was at Baynard's Castle.
11 *A Collection of Ordinances and Regulations for the Government of the Royal Household* (London: Society of Antiquaries, 1790), 38. Inner Temple Library, Petyt MS 538 vol. 39, f. 201.
12 Christine de Pisan, *The Treasure of the City of Ladies*, trans. Sarah Lawson (Penguin: Harmondsworth, 1985), 131.

13 Only the English brass still survives but some of the Latin is quoted in H. Chauncy, *The Historical Antiquities of Hertfordshire* (London: 1826).

14 Jennifer Sherwood, 'Influences on the Growth and Development of Medieval and Early Modern Berkhamsted', in *A County of Small Towns: The Development of Hertfordshire's Urban Landscape to 1800*, ed. Terry Slater and Nigel Goose (Hatfield: University of Hertfordshire Press, 2008), 233, 242.

15 TNA SC 6/1115/9 f. 2.

16 Roger Bray, 'Music and the Quadrivivium in Early Tudor England', *Music and Letters* 76:1 (1995): 1–18, 6.

17 *CPL*, XIII pt I:309–10.

18 Ibid.,106–7.

19 Will.

20 *HMC* Eighth Report, I:268.

21 Ibid. There seems to be no record of a scholar with the surname Stephen at this period. Since men did not always use their father's surname it is impossible to be sure whether Cecily's request was successful but it looks as if Waynflete felt that God had not given Stephen junior sufficient ability and 'conyng'.

22 TNA CP 25/1/293/71 nos. 343, 344.

23 *CCR 1461–68*: 257.

24 *CPR 1476–85*: 278.

25 *CCR 1476–85*: 256; *CPR 1476–85*: 278; *CPR 1467–77*: 439; *CPR 1476–85*: 218.

26 *CPR 1467–77*: 563.

27 Ibid., 447.

28 Ibid., 599. This could have been the alderman John Felde who died in 1477 or his son of the same name.

29 John Whetamstede, *Registra Quorundam Abbatum Monasterii S. Albani*, ed. H. T. Riley, Rolls Series 28, 2 vols (1872), II:167–8.

30 ERO D/Dce L56; Waller, 'Church Chest', 18.

31 Waller, 'Church Chest', 18; W. C. Waller, 'Some Essex Manuscripts', *Transactions of the Essex Archaeological Society*, n.s. 5 (1895): 200–25, 215. Brocas may not yet have held such a senior position in the household. He was named as her clerk of the kitchen in 1495 (Will).

32 This dispute is significantly more complicated than my summary suggests. It is explored in more depth in Waller's articles but the scores of documents now in the Essex Record Office would repay a new and more extensive study.

33 ERO D/DQ 14/124/3/15.

34 Ibid.

35 Ibid.

36 Anne Crawford, *Yorkist Lord: John Howard, Duke of Norfolk, c. 1425–1485* (London: Continuum, 2010), 73.

37 ERO D/DQ 14/124/3/41.

38 ERO D/DQ/14/124/3/42; D/DQ 14/124/3/41.

39 ERO D/DQ/14/124/3/41.

40 Ibid.

41 Colin Richmond, 'East Anglian Politics and Society in the Fifteenth Century: Reflections 1956-2003', in *Medieval East Anglia*, ed. Christopher Harper-Bill (Woodbridge, 2005), 183–208, 198.

42 BL Add MS 19398 f. 34.

43 ERO D/DQ/14/124/3/43.

44 ERO D/Dce/L70.
45 I am here following Rosemary Horrox's interpretation of ERO D/DCe/L57 although the date and context of the letter to John Prince are unclear. Rosemary Horrox, *Richard III: A Study of Service* (Cambridge: CUP, 1989), 4.
46 ERO D/DCe/L83.
47 Crawford, *Yorkist Lord*, 12.
48 WAM 12179.
49 TNA SC 8/337/15918.
50 Ibid.
51 Philippe de Commynes, *Mémoires*, présentation Philippe Contamine (Paris: Imprimerie nationale Éditions, 1994), 258.
52 J. L. Laynesmith, *The Last Medieval Queens: English Queenship 1445–1503* (Oxford: OUP, 2004), 137–8.
53 Commynes, *Mémoires*, 257.
54 Samuel Tymms, ed., *Wills and Inventories from the Commissary of Bury St Edmunds*, Camden Society o.s. 49 (1850), 86.
55 John Hutchins, *The History and Antiquities of the County of Dorset*, 3rd edn rev. William Shipp and James Whitworth Hodson, 4 vols (London, 1861), II:776–7.
56 Despite an oft-quoted tradition that the church was not dedicated to St Lawrence until its patron was Katherine of Aragon, there are references to the church of St Lawrence in Lechlade in wills of 1404 and 1495. TNA PROB 11/2A/143; PROB 11/10/547.
57 Samuel Bentley, ed., *Excerpta Historica* (London, 1831), 371.
58 SC 6/850/31.
59 P. Fleming, *Time, Space and Power in Later Medieval Bristol* (Bristol: University of the West of England, 2013), 218; History of Parliament Trust, unpublished article on 'John Twyneho I/Cirencester' for the 1461–1504 section by Linda Clark. I am grateful to the History of Parliament Trust and to Linda Clark for allowing me to see this article in draft.
60 SC 6/850/33.
61 *CPR 1467–77*: 361.
62 Anne Sutton, 'Edward IV and Bury St Edmunds' Search for Self Government', in *The Fifteenth Century XIV*, ed. Linda Clark (Woodbrige: Boydell, 2015), 146. Ipswich Record Office HD 474/1 f. 164.
63 *CPR 1467–77*: 361.
64 What is left of these windows has been reassembled in a south aisle window.
65 *CPR 1467–77*: 361.
66 John Rhodes, ed. *A Calendar of the Registers of the Priory of Llanthony by Gloucester 1457–1466, 1501–1525*, Bristol and Gloucestershire Archaeological Society 15 (2002), 51. The reference to an obit to be celebrated in January presumably relates to prayers for Richard duke of York who had died on New Year's Eve.
67 *CPR 1467–77*: 446–7.
68 The Luton Guild Book, f. 1.
69 Richard Marks, 'Two Illuminated Guild Registers from Bedfordshire', in *Illuminating the Book: Makers and Interpreters*, ed. M. P. Brown and S. McKendrick (London: British Library, 1998), 122, 130.
70 Martina Bagnoli et al., eds, *Treasures of Heaven: Saints, Relics and Devotion in Medieval Europe* (London: British Museum, 2010), 114–15.
71 John Cherry, *The Middleham Jewel and Ring* (York: The Yorkshire Museum, 1994), 30.
72 Sutton, 'Edward IV and Bury St Edmunds', 146.

73 James Raine, ed., *Historiae Dunelmensis Scriptores tres*, Surtees Society 9 (1839), cclviii.

74 Cherry, *Middleham Jewel*, 34. R.W. Lightbown, *Medieval European Jewellery* (London: Victoria & Albert Museum, 1992), 216.

75 R. Marks and P. Williamson, eds. *Gothic: Art for England 1400–1547* (V&A Publications, 2003), 343.

76 Marks and Williamson, eds, *Gothic*, 343.

77 Ann M. Hutchison, 'Reflections on Aspects of the Spiritual Impact of St Birgitta, the Revelations and the Bridgettine Order in Late Medieval England', in *The Medieval Mystical Tradition. Exeter Symposium VII*, ed. E. A. Jones (D. S. Brewer: Cambridge, 2004), 77; Susan Wabuda, *Preaching During the English Reformation* (Cambridge: Cambridge University Press, 2002), 162.

78 John Ashdown Hill, 'The Suffolk Connections of the House of York', *Proceedings of the Suffolk Institute for Archaeology and History* 41 (2006): 199–207, 201–2.

79 Rev J. C. Coleman, 'Gold Reliquary Cross found at Clare, Suffolk', *The East Anglian*, III (1869), 45. When it was first discovered some writers argued that it was of fourteenth-century work and it was suggested that it was a reliquary cross recorded among Edward III's jewels. However, Augustus Franks considered a date of 1450–80 to be more accurate and this is now generally accepted. Albert Way, 'Gold Pectoral Cross Found at Clare Castle, Suffolk', *The Archaeological Journal* 25 (1868), 62; Marks and Williamson, eds, *Gothic*, 332 and pl. 7.

80 Bagnoli et al., eds, *Treasures of Heaven*, 44.

81 Michael Hicks, 'Anne of York', *Oxford DNB*, *sub nomine*.

82 Ibid.

83 Bodleian Library MS Rawlinson A 146.

84 Bodleian Library MS Rawlinson A 146 ff 2, 4, 35–7, 48, 50.

85 Carpenter, ed. Stonor Letters, 270.

86 Essex Record Office D/DQ 14/124/3/41.

87 C. L. Scofield, *The Life and Reign of Edward the Fourth*, 2 vols (London: Longman, 1923), II:60, 94. Scofield points out that BL Add MS 6113 dates Richard's birth to 17 August 1472 but this must be wrong since his sister Margaret was born in April 1472 whereas Edward IV is known to have been in Shrewsbury in the summer of 1473.

88 Bentley, ed., *Excerpta Historica*, 371.

89 Ibid.

90 WAM 12174.

91 Anne F. Sutton and Livia Visser Fuchs with Peter Hammond, ed., *The Reburial of Richard Duke of York, 21–30 July 1476* (London: The Richard III Society, 1996), 1.

92 Michael Hicks, *False, Fleeting, Perjur'd Clarence: George, Duke of Clarence 1449–78* (Gloucester: Sutton, 1980), 122–7.

93 Ibid.,132.

94 Ibid., 133.

95 Ibid., 167–8.

96 Clark, 'John Twyneho I/Cirencester'; *PROME*, VI:174.

97 Hicks, *False, Fleeting*, 167–8.

98 *PROME*, VI:173–4.

99 Ibid., 135.

100 Nicholas Pronay and John Cox, eds, *The Crowland Continuations:1459–1486* (London: Sutton, 1986), 145.

101 Black, *Illustrations of Ancient State*, 29.

102 Ibid., 31.

103 Pronay and Cox, eds, *Crowland*, 145.

104 *Rotuli Parliamentorum*, VI:193–5. The attainder appears in modern English in the appendix to this parliament in PROME.

105 Ibid., 194.

106 Pronay and Cox, eds, *Crowland*, 147.

107 Bernard de Mandrot, ed., *Journal de Jean de Roye connu sous le nom de Chronique Scandaleuse* (Paris, 1896), II:64.

108 Ibid.

109 Ibid.

110 Prony and Cox, ed., *Crowland*, 147.

10 The End of the House of York: 1478–1485

1 BL Add MS 6113 f. 73 printed in *The Gentleman's Magazine* (Jan. 1831), 25.

2 SGC XV.25.63; *CPR 1476–85*: 172, 178.

3 James Gairdner, ed., *Letters and Papers Illustrative of the Reigns of Richard III and Henry VII*, Rolls Series 24, 2 vols (1861), I:281–1.

4 SGC XV.48.58.

5 *William Worcestre:Itineraries*, ed. John Harvey (Oxford: Clarendon Press, 1969), 347. Worcester refers to the mayors of Norwich visiting her there on 'Wednesday in Whit week, viz __ June', although that date in 1480 fell on 24 May. This must be Worcester's mistake because the city's accounts confirm just such a visit in 1480. NRO Case 18a/3 10; NRO Kirkpatrick Notes, 'Annals of the City 1459–1505', f. 20b. *Paston Letters*, I:377.

6 *CPR 1476–85*: 218.

7 Harvey, ed., *Worcestre: Itineraries*, 347.

8 See below.

9 J. A. F. Thomson, 'John de la Pole, Duke of Suffolk', *Speculum* 54 (1979): 528–42, 538–9; NRO LEST/P 20n. 8.

10 Harvey, ed., *Worcestre: Itineraries*, 347; NRO Kirkpatrick Notes, 'Annals', f. 20b. The city records refer to payment for five officials and 'other citizens and their servants to the number of twenty-four persons' to make the journey, but William Worcester claimed that 'about 100 citizens on horseback' arrived.

11 Harvey, ed., *Worcestre: Itineraries*, 347.

12 Ibid.; NRO Kirkpatrick Notes, 'Annals', f. 20b.

13 Ibid. The location of the riots was possibly Hevingham, just north of Norwich.

14 Thomson, 'John de la Pole', 540.

15 http://www.british-history.ac.uk/no-series/common-pleas/1399–1500/easter-term-1480; http://aalt.law.uh.edu/AALT3/E4/CP40no871/bCP40no871dorses/IMG_1827.htm, consulted 8/7/2016. The same case also charged Thomas Monyngton of Sarnesfeld.

16 http://www.british-history.ac.uk/no-series/common-pleas/1399–1500/hilary-term-1480; http://aalt.law.uh.edu/AALT3/E4/CP40no871/bCP40no871dorses/IMG_1144.htm (consulted 8/7/2016).

17 Christine Weightman, *Margaret of York, Duchess of Burgundy, 1446–1503* (Gloucester: Alan Sutton, 1989), 134.

18 C. L. Scofield, *The Life and Reign of Edward the Fourth*, 2 vols (London: Longman, 1923), II:288.

19 H. E. Malden, ed., *The Cely Papers*, Camden Society, 3rd Series, 1 (1900), 46.

20 *The Gentleman's Magazine* (Jan. 1831), 25.

21 W. A. Pantin, *Documents Illustrating the Activities of the General and Provincial Chapters of the English Black Monks 1215–1540*, 3 vols, Camden Society, 3rd series, 45, 47, 54 (London 1931–37), III:116, 216–17.

22 I am grateful to Brian Kemp for explaining this process to me.

23 Pantin, *Black Monks*, I:137.

24 Ibid., II:57.

25 Will.

26 J. T. Rosenthal, *Patriarchy and Families of Privilege in Fifteenth-Century England* (Philadelphia: Penn Press, 1991), 243.

27 Nicholas Harris Nicolas, ed., *Testamenta Vetusta*, 2 vols (London, 1826), I:356; William St John Hope, *The History of the London Charterhouse* (London: SPCK, 1925), 58–9; *CPR 1461–67*: 120, 161; *CPR 1467–77*: 304; Charles Farris, 'The New Edwardians? Royal Piety in the Yorkist Age', in *The Yorkist Age*, ed. Hannes Kleineke and Christian Steer (Donington: Shaun Tyas, 2013), 58–9.

28 *CPL*, XIII pt I:260.

29 Ibid.

30 TNA PROB 11/14/336; PROB 11/11/458.

31 E. Margaret Thompson, *The Carthusian Order in England* (London: SPCK, 1930), 196.

32 M. K. Jones and M. G. Underwood, *The King's Mother: Lady Margaret Beaufort, Countess of Richmond and Derby* (Cambridge: CUP, 1992), 167, 181–2.

33 *A Collection of Ordinances and Regulations for the Government of the Royal Household* (London: Society of Antiquaries, 1790), 37; Inner Temple Library, Petyt MS 538, vol. 39 f. 200; Jones and Underwood, *King's Mother*, 174.

34 Anne Sutton and Livia Visser-Fuchs, *Richard III's Books* (Stroud: Sutton, 1997), 47.

35 *Catalogue of the Bute Collection of Forty-two Manuscripts and Miniatures*, (London: Sotheby's, 13 June 1983), 62.

36 Sutton and Visser-Fuchs, *Richard III's Books*, 202.

37 Ibid., J. O. Halliwell, 'Observations upon the History of Certain Events in England during the Reign of King Edward the Fourth', *Archaeologia* 29 (1841), 129.

38 Carole Hill, 'St Bridget and the Household Culture of Norfolk Women', in *East Anglia and Its North Sea World in the Middle Ages*, ed. David Bates and Robert Liddiard (Woodbridge: Boydell, 2013), 301–14.

39 Will.

40 BL MS Egerton 2006.

41 Rosalyn Voaden, 'The Company She Keeps: Mechtild of Hackeborn in Late Medieval Devotional Compilations', in *Prophets Abroad: The Reception of Continental Holy Women in Late-Medieval England*, ed. Voaden (Cambridge: D. S. Brewer, 1996), 51–69, 68.

42 Ibid.

43 *CPR 1476–85*: 227.

44 Anne Sutton, 'Edward IV and Bury St Edmunds' Search for Self Government', in *The Fifteenth Century XIV*, ed. Linda Clark (Woodbrige: Boydell, 2015), 146. Ipswich RO, HD 474/1 f. 164; Margaret Statham and Sally Badham, 'Jankyn Smith of Bury St Edmunds and his Brass', *Transactions of the Monumental Brass Society* 18 (2011): 227–50, 235–6.

45 Ann M. Hutchison, 'Reflections on Aspects of the Spiritual Impact of St Birgitta, the Revelations and the Bridgettine Order in Late Medieval England', in *The Medieval Mystical Tradition: Exeter Symposium VII*, ed. E. A. Jones (Cambridge: D. S. Brewer, 2004), 76–81.

46 Hutchison, 'Reflections', 77–8.

47 John Allen, ed., *The English Hospice in Rome* (Exeter: Catholic Records Press, 1962), 119, 189.

48 Ibid., 108, 148.

49 Michael Hicks, 'Holland, Henry, second duke of Exeter', *Oxford DNB*, *sub nomine*.

50 W. Atthill, *Documents Relating to the Collegiate Church of Middleham*, Camden Society, o.s. 38 (1847), 61.

51 *CPR 1476–85*: 269.

52 Ibid., 143.

53 C. D. Ross, *Edward IV* (London: Eyre Methuen, 1974), 329.

54 *CPR 1476–85*: 337.

55 Dominic Mancini, *The Usurpation of Richard the Third*, ed. C. A. J. Armstrong (Gloucester: Alan Sutton, 1984), 59.

56 Ibid., 106.

57 Ibid.

58 Nicholas Pronay and John Cox, eds, *The Crowland Continuations:1459–1486* (London: Sutton, 1986), 149.

59 Ross, *Edward IV*, 415–16.

60 Neither Cecily nor the queen attended Edward IV's funeral (BL MS Stowe 1047 f. 219).

61 Michael Hicks, *Edward V: The Prince in the Tower* (Stroud: Tempus, 2003), 65–6, 75.

62 Rosemary Horrox, *Richard III: A Study of Service* (Cambridge: CUP, 1989), 33.

63 Ibid., 81.

64 Ibid., 121.

65 Mancini, *Usurpation*, 63.

66 A. J. Pollard, 'Dominic Mancini's Narrative of the Events of 1483', *Nottingham Medieval Studies* 38 (1994): 152–63, 158.

67 David Hipshon, *Richard III* (London and New York: Routledge, 2011), 122.

68 Mancini, *Usurpation*, 69; Pronay and Cox, eds, *Crowland*, 155.

69 Mancini, *Usurpation*, 71–3.

70 Nigel Saul, *Richard II* (New Haven and London: Yale University Press, 1997), 22, 24.

71 Charles Ross, *Richard III* (London: Eyre Methuen, 1981), 68.

72 Pronay and Cox, eds, *Crowland*,155.

73 Ibid., 157.

74 Richard later tried to argue that they should be executed for treason but was initially unsuccessful. Ross, *Richard III*, 74–5. Had he planned to kill them from the first then a staged brawl would have been more effective.

75 Mancini, *Usurpation*, 76.

76 F. R. H. du Boulay, ed. *Registrum Thome Bourchier* (Canterbury and York Society 54. 1957), 52–3.

77 Ibid.

78 The king's final will does not survive, but the version we do have gives Elizabeth significant authority over the rest of the executors. Samuel Bentley, ed. *Excerpta Historica* (London, 1831), 378.

79 Horrox, *Richard III*, 99.

80 Ibid., 104–6.
81 Ross, *Richard III*, 76. The only writer to suggest a reason for Gloucester to mistrust Rotherham is Thomas More who claimed that Rotherham had surrendered the great seal to Elizabeth Woodville in sanctuary, but then reclaimed it. John A. F. Thomson, 'Russell, John (c. 1430–1494)', *Oxford DNB*, *sub nomine*.
82 Horrox, *Richard III*, 107.
83 J. G. Nichols, *Grants etc from the Crown during the Reign of Edward V* (London, 1854), 70; SC 6/HENVII/1448 m. 8; will.
84 Nichols, *Grants of Edward V*, 70.
85 Ibid.; Christine Carpenter, *Kingsford's Stonor Letters and Papers 1290–1483* (Cambridge: CUP, 1996), 416 (160).
86 Mancini, *Usurpation*, 91.
87 Ibid.
88 Carpenter, ed., *Kingsford's Stonor Letters*, 417 (161).
89 Ibid.
90 Ibid.
91 Mancini, *Usurpation*, 94, author's translation adapting Armstrong's.
92 A. H. Thomas and I. D. Thornley, eds, *The Great Chronicle of London* (London, 1938, reprinted Gloucester: Alan Sutton, 1983), 232–3.
93 Thomas More, *The Complete Works of St Thomas More, Vol. 2: The History of King Richard III*, ed. R. S. Sylvester (New Haven: Yale University Press, 1963), 235.
94 Polydore Vergil, *Three Books of Polydore Vergil's History of England*, ed. H. Ellis, Camden Society, o.s. 29 (London, 1844), 184.
95 More, *Richard III*, 67–8.
96 Ibid., 66.
97 William Marx, ed., *An English Chronicle 1377–1461: A New Edition* (Woodbridge: Boydell, 2003), 86.
98 See in particular Vergil, *History*, 183.
99 Mancini, *Usurpation*, 94.
100 Ibid., 96. Armstrong translates *dux Berbiciensium* as the earl of Warwick who would certainly have been the most plausible nobleman for such a task.
101 J. A. F. Thomson, 'The Death of Edward V: Dr Richmond's Dating Reconsidered', *Northern History* 26:1 (1990): 201–11, 210.
102 Ibid., 208. Note also the assertion in the Rous Roll that Richard was king 'by true matrimony without discontinuance or any defiling in the law'. This emphasis on legal marriage was probably meant to remind readers that Edward V's parents' marriage had not been legal. John Rous, *The Rous Roll*, ed. Charles Ross (Gloucester, 1980), 63.
103 J. L. Laynesmith. 'Telling Tales of Adulterous Queens in Medieval England: From Olympias of Macedonia to Elizabeth Woodville', in *Every Inch a King*, ed. Lynette Mitchell and Charles Melville (Leiden: Brill, 2013), 206–12.
104 Hicks, *Edward V*, 164. Of the fourteen kings between William the Conqueror and Edward IV, only half were their immediate predecessor's direct male heir.
105 Ross, *Richard III*, 93.
106 Mancini, *Usurpation*, 97.
107 Anne F. Sutton and P. W. Hammond, ed., *The Coronation of Richard III: The Extant Documents* (Gloucester: Alan Sutton, 1983), 273–4.
108 Thomas Rymer, ed., *Foedera* vol. 12 http://www.british-history.ac.uk/rymer-foedera/vol12/pp172-192 *sub* 27 June 1483.
109 Sutton and Hammond, ed., *Coronation of Richard III*, 167, 169, 377.

110 Rowena Archer, 'Neville, Katherine, duchess of Norfolk', *Oxford DNB, sub nomine.*

111 Horrox, *Richard III*, 174.

112 *CPR 1476–85*: 369.

113 John Stow, *The Annales, or Generall Chronicle of England* (London, 1615), 459.

114 Jones and Underwood, *King's Mother*, 62–5.

115 Ross, *Richard III*, 112.

116 Pronay and Cox, eds, *Crowland*, 163.

117 For discussion of this see Louise Gill, *Richard III & Buckingham's Rebellion* (Stroud: Sutton, 1999), 67.

118 Pronay and Cox, eds, *Crowland*, 157.

119 Ibid., 163.

120 A. J. Pollard, *Richard III and the Princes in the Tower* (Stroud: Alan Sutton, 1991), 120.

121 C. S. L. Davies, 'Information, Disinformation and Political Knowledge under Henry VII and Early Henry VIII', *Historical Research* 85 (2012): 228–53, 249–50.

122 S. B. Chrimes, *Henry VII* (London: Eyre Methuen, 1972), 93.

123 Rosemary Horrox, 'Tyrell, Sir James (c.1455–1502)', *Oxford DNB, sub nomine.*

124 Paul Murray Kendall, *Richard III* (London: Sphere, 1973), 398–404.

125 *PROME*, VI:240.

126 Ibid., VI:241.

127 Mancini, *Usurpation*, 109n. 12.

128 *PROME*, VI:240.

129 Ibid., VI:241.

130 Ross, *Richard III*, 90.

131 Pronay and Cox, eds, *Crowland*, 159. Crowland dates the revelation of the Eleanor Butler story to June 1483.

132 Charles de Beaurepaire, 'Fondations pieuses du duc de Bedford à Rouen', *Bibliothèque de l'école des chartes* 34 (1873): 343–86, 348n. 4.

133 Anne Crawford, *The Yorkists: The History of a Dynasty* (London: Hambledon Continuum, 2007), 179–80.

134 Pronay and Cox, ed., *Crowland*, 161. By contrast Philippe de Commynes identified the source as the bishop of Bath and Wells, Robert Stillington, whom he believed helped Richard 'a great deal in the execution of his evil plan' in 1483. However, there are quite a few errors in his brief account and other writers do not mention a central role for Stillington. Philippe de Commynes, *Memoirs*, ed. Michael Jones (Harmondsworth: Penguin, 1972), 354. It seems unlikely that Henry VII would have pardoned the bishop so soon after Bosworth if he had indeed masterminded Richard III's accession, although Stillington was probably involved in drawing up the *Titulus Regius*. Michael Hicks, 'Stillington, Robert (d. 1491)', Oxford DNB, sub nomine.

135 R. Horrox and P. Hammond, *British Library Harleian Manuscript 433*, 4 vols (Gloucester: Richard III Society, 1979), IV:3.

136 Gairdner, ed., *Letters and Papers*, I:8.

137 Kenneth Hillier, 'William Colyngbourne', *The Ricardian* 3 (1975): 5–9.

138 Pronay and Cox, eds, *Crowland*, 175.

139 Ibid.

140 J. L. Laynesmith, *The Last Medieval Queens* (Oxford: OUP, 2004), 119–29.

141 *CPR 1476–85*: 522.

142 Rhoda Edwards, *The Itinerary of King Richard III, 1483–85* (London: Richard III Society, 1983), 36 citing TNA C81/907/1071.

143 Ross, *Richard III*, 224–5.
144 Pronay and Cox, eds, *Crowland*, 183.

11 The Queen's Grandmother: 1485–1495

1 Will.
2 C. A. J. Armstrong, 'The Piety of Cicely, Duchess of York: A Study in Late Medieval Culture', in *England, France and Burgundy in the Fifteenth Century*, ed. C. A. J. Armstrong (London: Hambledon, 1983), 135–56.
3 Anne Crawford, *Yorkist Lord: John Howard, Duke of Norfolk, c. 1425–1485* (London: Continuum, 2010), 62, 132–3.
4 James Gairdner, ed., *Letters and Papers Illustrative of the Reigns of Richard III and Henry VII*, Rolls Series 24, 2 vols (1861), I:234.
5 Although Lessy mentioned that the money was 'for my lady's debts whom god pardon', he included a request that the monks should pray not only for Cecily but also 'for me as procurator of this benefit'. TNA PROB 11/11/458.
6 S. B. Chrimes, *Henry VII* (London: Eyre Methuen, 1972), 52. All his privy seal orders for September are dated 'from our city of London'. TNA PSO2/1. I have been unable to find any source to verify the suggestion that Henry used Baynard's Castle at this point. Michael K. Jones and Malcolm G. Underwood, *The King's Mother: Lady Margaret Beaufort, Countess of Richmond and Derby* (Cambridge: CUP, 1992), 66.
7 Jones and Underwood, *King's Mother*, 67.
8 Ibid., 75.
9 Chrimes, *Henry VII*, 65–6.
10 *CPL XIV*, 14, 19. They were both fourth generation descendants of John of Gaunt.
11 Chrimes, *Henry VII*, 66.
12 Polydore Vergil, *Three Books of Polydore Vergil's History of England*, ed. H. Ellis, Camden Society, o.s. 29 (London, 1844), 185.
13 WAM 2225.
14 TNA C1/206/69.
15 Steven Gunn, 'Sir Thomas Lovell (c. 1449–1524)', in *The End of the Middle Ages? England in the Fifteenth and Sixteenth Centuries*, ed. John Watts (Stroud: Sutton, 1998), 117–53, 122, 133; TNA PROB 11/14/336.
16 WAM 12179.
17 Vergil, *Three Books*, 196.
18 Ibid.; M. M. Condon, 'Bray, Sir Reynold [Reginald] (c.1440–1503)', *Oxford DNB*, *sub nomine*.
19 William Campbell, ed., *Materials for a History of the Reign of Henry VII*, Rolls Series 60, 2 vols (1873), I:468; WAM 12179.
20 Dominic Luckett, 'Willoughby, Robert, first Baron Willoughby de Broke', *Oxford DNB*, *sub nomine*.
21 WAM 12179, 12169.
22 Sean Cunningham, 'Guildford, Sir Richard (c.1450–1506)', *Oxford DNB*, *sub nomine*.
23 *CPR 1494–1509*: 56–7. He was regranted this role in April 1496 but those letters patent specified that he had originally been appointed to this office by the duchess. However, in 1496 Henry Heydon was still being paid 100s. for that service so it is possible that Guildford had not yet taken up the post before she died. WAM 12179.

24 John Bruce, ed., *Letters and Papers of the Verney Family*, Camden Society, o.s. 56 (London, 1853), 29.

25 *CPR 1485–94*: 189, 254.

26 Campbell, ed., *Materials*, I:204; II:198.

27 Bruce, ed., *Verney Family*, 29–33.

28 WAM 12179. Ralph's services to Cecily were then worth only 60s. 8d. a year compared with 100s. for John's. Given John's prominent position in Cecily's will, he may well have been in her service for some time before 1485. It appears that at Cecily's death the king granted the stewardship at Berkhamsted to Giles Daubeney whereas Ralph Verney remained in post at Kings Langley.

29 Mother Mary Gregory, 'Wickham Court and the Heydons', *Archaeologia Cantiana*, 78 (1963); 1–24, 12; TNA SP 9/8 p. 109.

30 Campbell, ed., *Materials*, II:553. However, by 1496 the bailiff at Hitchin was Richard Copcot, despite Henry VII's promise that the office would remain in Gregory's possession beyond Cecily's death. It is possible that Cecily had decided to replace him before her death: WAM 12179.

31 Campbell, ed., *Materials*, II:282, 364. In both cases Cecily's appointments are recorded because Henry VII subsequently confirmed them as appointments for life in the knowledge that the estates in question would eventually pass to the crown. It may be that she eventually appointed John de Vere, earl of Oxford, as constable of Clare Castle and steward of the honour of Clare, anticipating the accession to this role which Henry VII had promised him on her death (*CPR 1485–94*: 142) because his name appears in WAM 12179. Some of the appointments in this document appear to have been made after Cecily's death since they mention successive holders of a certain post but there is no mention of an earlier postholder at Clare.

32 E.g. *CPR 1485–94*: 189; WAM 12179.

33 TNA KB 9/401 no. 9. I am grateful to Hannes Kleineke for drawing this case to my attention.

34 Ibid.

35 Allegedly the men took Rose and his servants to 'John Wethers house' where they proposed to make him eat all his writs, put him in the stocks or bind his legs under his horse and take him to the duchess. Then one speaker asserted that they had done exactly that to a previous royal bailiff at which the duchess had said 'wherefore brynge ye me the persone y had lever ye had brought me a legge or an arme of hym', so they proposed doing that or cutting him into pieces and eating him. Ultimately, however, the terrified official was allowed to flee 'unbetyn and unhurt' having promised not to return.

36 *PROME*, VI:273.

37 Ibid.

38 Campbell, ed., *Materials*, I:288.

39 Ibid., II:48.

40 TNA E 13/161 r. 3 d.; E 13/162 rr. 37, 39; E 13/163 rr. 11 d., 40 d.; E 13/169 rr. 24 d., 57 d. I am grateful to Hannes Kleineke for drawing my attention to these cases.

41 TNA E 13/171 rr. 36–7, 42 d.

42 TNA E 13/172 rr. 44, 44 d.

43 She was still in dispute with Neville's successor, Marmaduke Constable, when she died. TNA E 13/177 r. 33. See also her Will.

44 Campbell, ed., *Materials*, I:226.

45 *Calendar of Inquisitions Post Mortem: Henry VII*, 3 vols (London: HMSO, 1898–1955), I:32, 112.
46 Campbell, ed., *Materials*, II:171.
47 Will.
48 A. H. Thomas and I. D. Thornley, eds, *The Great Chronicle of London* (London, 1938, reprinted Gloucester: Alan Sutton, 1983), 257; *CPR 1494–1509*: 16.
49 BL Egerton MS 2034 (*Cecilia, Regina Anglia Avia Ducissa Ebor*); TNA SC 2/185/38 calls her 'Cecill the qwenys grand moder duchesse of Yorke'. I am grateful to Steven Gunn for drawing my attention to this reference.
50 TNA SC 2/185/38; BL Egerton MS 2034 p. 105; TNA SC6/HENVII/1448 m. 8.
51 WAM 12169.
52 Nicholas Pronay and John Cox, eds, *The Crowland Continuations:1459–1486* (London: Sutton, 1986), 195.
53 Nicholas Harris Nicolas, *Privy Purse Expenses of Elizabeth of York* (London: William Pickering, 1830), 265.
54 *CPR 1494–1509*: 178.
55 Samuel Tymms, ed., *Wills and Inventories from the Register of the Commissary of Bury St Edmunds*, Camden Society, o.s. 49 (1850), 87–8.
56 Ibid.
57 Anne Wroe, *Perkin: A Story of Deception* (London: Jonathan Cape, 2003), 160–1, 497; Ian Arthurson, *The Perkin Warbeck Conspiracy 1491–99* (Stroud: Sutton, 1994), 87.
58 Contrary to Wroe and Arthurson's assertions, Cecily's servant Richard Boyvile was not among those who stood surety for Lessy. They both combine this story with Boyvile's earlier connection to Margaret of Burgundy in order to argue that he was likely to have been involved in the conspiracy too. Wroe, *Perkin*, 161; Arthurson, *Perkin Warbeck*, 87–8; *CCR 1485–1500*: 232, 243–4.
59 C. L. Kingsford, ed., *Chronicles of London* (Oxford: Clarendon Press, 1905), 203; Thomas and Thornley, eds, *Great Chronicle*, 257.
60 WAM 12179. He appears in her will after a list of gifts to churches and just before a gift to Henry Heydon. Heydon seems to be at the head of a list of household men but this does not mean that Cressener also held office in her house. His will of the following year was given at his family home in Essex, Alphamstone near Sudbury, and did not mention any of Cecily's household members. TNA PROB 11/10/605.
61 Thomas and Thornley, eds, *Great Chronicle*, 257; *Hall's Chronicle*, ed. H. Ellis (New York: AMS, 1965), 467; *VCH Hertford*, IV:446–51.
62 WAM 2225; TNA PROB 11/11/458.
63 Kingsford, ed., *Chronicles*, 203.
64 Thomas and Thornley, eds, *Great Chronicle*, 257; Kingsford, ed., *Chronicles*, 203–4.
65 BL Add MS 6113, ff. 76–8; Gairdner, ed., *Letters and Papers*, I:388–404.
66 Mary Bateson, ed., *Records of the Borough of Leicester*, 2 vols (London: C. J. Clay, 1901), II:323–4.
67 Inner Temple Library, Petyt MS 538 vol. 39 f. 200.
68 Grave was the only cleric given books 'that servith for the closett' in her will.
69 *A Collection of Ordinances and Regulations for the Government of the Royal Household* (London: Society of Antiquaries, 1790), 38.
70 Jennifer Ward, ed., *Elizabeth de Burgh, Lady of Clare (1295–1360): Household and Other Records*, Suffolk Records Society 57 (Woodbridge: Boydell, 2014) 81; K. Mertes, 'The Household as a Religious Community', in *People, Politics and Community in the Later Middle Ages*, ed. J. T. Rosenthal and C. F. Richmond (Gloucester: Sutton, 1987), 131. On both Mondays and Wednesdays there was less beef and mutton provided

in Cecily's household than on other 'eatynge dayes'. Whether rabbits, fowl and other smaller meats were restricted too is not mentioned. Friday was a fast day because of the Crucifixion. The Saturday fast was probably originally an extension of this Friday fast and only later did the day become particularly associated with the Virgin Mary. The reason for Wednesday as a fast day is not certain but may have been because that was the day that Judas agreed to betray Jesus. F. L. Cross and E. A. Livingstone, eds, *The Oxford Dictionary of the Christian Church* (Oxford: OUP, 1997), 1456, 1724.

71 Rev. Dr. Bennet, 'The College of S. John Evangelist of Rushworth, Co. Norfolk', *Norfolk Archaeology* 10 (1888): 277–382, 372.

72 Inner Temple Library, Petyt MS 538 vol. 39 f. 200.

73 Armstrong, 'Piety of Cicely', 155. Both cloths were given to John Walter.

74 Inner Temple Library, Petyt MS 538 vol. 39 f. 200.

75 Mertes, 'Household as Religious Community', 129.

76 Inner Temple Library, Petyt MS 538 vol. 39 f. 200.

77 Jones and Underwood, *King's Mother*, 162.

78 J. Fisher, *The English Works of John Fisher*, ed. J. Major, EETS, e.s. 27 (1876), 294–5.

79 Thomas duke of Clarence had twenty-one clerks in his household and this included four choristers whereas the 'Second Northumberland Household Book' required seventeen priests and gentlemen. C. M. Woolgar, *The Senses in Late Medieval England* (New Haven: Yale University Press, 2006), 258.

80 Tymms, ed., *Wills and Inventories*, 88. Nicolas Talbot's will says he was parson of 'Bliburght' but earlier the same document makes several references to the church at 'Blythburght' and subsequently to Talbot's own possessions at 'Blyburght'. It seems unlikely that he would have had an interest in two distinct places with such similar names so they are probably all Blythburgh in Suffolk. The phrasing in Talbot's will suggests that this may have been part of the dower of Cecily's daughter, Elizabeth duchess of Suffolk. Talbot's will does mention that John More (also in Cecily's will) was late parson of Berkhamsted and late parson of Northchurch, implying that he had retired.

81 Arthur Thomas Bannister, ed., *Registrum Thomas Myllyng Episcopi Herefordensis 1474–1492* (London: Canterbury and York Society, 1920), 197.

82 John Allen, ed., *The English Hospice in Rome* (Exeter: Catholic Records Press, 1962), 119.

83 The First Northumberland Household Book required eight adult choristers and a 'gospeller' at matins and evensong. *The Regulations and Establishment of the Household of Henry Algernon Percy: The Fifth Earl of Northumberland* (London: William Pickering, 1827), 367.

84 PROB 11/11/458.

85 Inner Temple Library, Petyt MS 538 vol. 39 f. 200.

86 *CPR 1485–94*: 347. Matthew Cressy was on all the commissions for the peace for Hertfordshire between 1485 and 1494, p. 488.

87 TNA PROB 11/11/458.

88 Ibid., C 1/436/26; Bruce, ed., *Verney Family*, 10–11, 39–40.

89 Ibid., 41; PROB 11/5/96.

90 WAM 12179.

91 Tymms, ed., *Wills and Inventories*, 85–91.

92 Will.

93 Tymms, ed., *Wills and Inventories*, 86.

94 *CCR 1485–1500*: 243–4.

95 Ibid., WAM 12179; Will.

96 Ibid.

97 WAM 1271.

98 WAM 2225.

99 Bodl. Rawlinson MS A 146 f. 35.

100 WAM 2225.

101 London Metropolitan Archives ACC/0312/221.

102 TNA PROB 11/11/458.

103 *VCH Buckinghamshire*, I:386–390.

104 Bruce, ed., *Verney Family*, 37, 39.

105 TNA PROB 11/11/458.

106 Susan Groag Bell, 'Medieval Women Book Owners: Arbiters of Lay Piety and
Ambassadors of Culture', in *Women and Power in the Middle Ages*, ed. Mary Erler and
Maryanne Kowaleski (Athens: University of Georgia Press, 1988), 149–187, 160.

107 Felicity Riddy, '"Women Talking about the Things of God": A Late Medieval
Subculture', in *Women and Literature in Britain 1150–500*, ed. Carol Meale
(Cambridge: CUP, 1993), 111.

108 TNA PROB 11/11/458.

109 Mary Dzon, "Cecily Neville and the Apocryphal 'Infantia Salvatoris' in the Middle
Ages', *Medieval Studies* 17 (2009): 235–300, 236.

110 Ibid., 291–7.

111 C. L. Kingsford, *English Historical Literature in the Fifteenth Century*
(Oxford: Clarendon Press, 1913), 386.

112 J. Nichols, *Wills of the Kings and Queens of England* (London, 1780), 350.

113 TNA C 142/23/155.

114 N. H. Nicolas, ed., *Testamenta Vetusta* (London: Nichols, 1826), I:357.

115 TNA C 142/23/155.

116 Nicolas, *Testamenta Vetusta*, I:357; Nichols, *Wills of the Kings and Queens of
England*, 124.

117 Matich and Alexander, 90–91.

118 Quoted in Sofija Matich and Jennifer Alexander, 'Creating and Recreating the Yorkist
Tombs in Fotheringhay Church', *Church Monuments* 26 (2011): 82–103, 91.

119 Ibid.

120 http://www.philological.bham.ac.uk/cambrit/huntseng.html#norts1 consulted 14/12/
2015.

121 Matich and Alexander, 'Yorkist Tombs', 82.

122 Ibid.

123 TNA PROB 11/11/458.

124 Francis Sandford, *A Genealogical History of the Kings and Queens of England*, cont. by
Samuel Stebbings (London, 1707), 392.

125 Ibid.; Matich and Alexander, 'Yorkist Tombs', 82.

126 J. Nichols, *The History and Antiquities of the Town, College and Castle of Fotheringhay*,
Biblioteca Topographica Britannica, 40 (London, 1789), 33.

Conclusion

1 Edmund Hall, *Chronicle*, ed. H. Ellis (London, 1809), 472.

2 Kim M. Phillips, *Medieval Maidens: Young Women and Gender in England, 1270–1540*
(Manchester: Manchester University Press, 2003), 94, 97. See Chapter 1.

3 Polydore Vergil, *Three Books of Polydore Vergil's History of England*, ed. H. Ellis, Camden Society, o.s. 29 (London, 1844), 185.
4 Carole Rawcliffe, 'Richard Duke of York, the King's "Obeisant Liegeman": A New Source for the Protectorates of 1454–1455', *Historical Research* 60 (1987): 232–6, 237–8.
5 P. Strohm, 'Queens as Intercessors', in *Hochon's Arrow: The Social Imagination of Fourteenth-Century Texts*, ed. Hochon (Princeton: Princeton University Press, 1992), 95–119; J. C. Parsons, 'The Pregnant Queen as Counsellor and the Medieval Construction of Motherhood', in *Medieval Mothering*, ed. J. C. Parsons and B. Wheeler (New York: Garland, 1996), 39–61.
6 BL Add MS 19398 f. 34.

Select Bibliography

Unpublished Primary Sources

Berkshire Record Office, Reading: D/Q1/Z2
Bodleian Library, Oxford: Dugdale MS 15; Rawlinson MS A 146
British Library:
   Additional Charters 15478, 16564, 23855
   Additional MSS 6113, 48976, 11814, 16564, 19398, 24512, 29616, 38174
   Arundel MS 68
   Cotton Julius MS F II
   Cotton Titus MS X XI
   Egerton Chs 7361, 7364, 8364, 8365, 8781–87
   Egerton MSS 2006, 2034, 2895
   Harley MSS 433, 787, 1628
   Lansdowne MS 403
   Royal MSS 16 G II, 19 A XIX
   Stowe MS 1047
Canterbury Cathedral Archives: CCA-CC-F/A/2; F/A/5
College of Arms: MS Num/Sch 3/16
Corpus Christi College, Cambridge: CCCC Parker MS 108
Essex Record Office, Colchester: D/Dce L1, L2, L28, L47 – L93; D/DQ/14/124/2/1 - D/DQ/14/124/3/43
Inner Temple Library, London: Petyt MS 538 vol. 39
Leicester Record Office: DE221/10/2/7
Lincoln's Inn Library, London: Hale MS 12 Item 75
London Metropolitan Archives: COL/CC/01/01/005; COL/CC/01/01/006; ACC/0312/221
The National Archives:
   C 1 (Chancery, Early Proceedings); C 49/56 (Proviso Clauses); C 81/795 (Writs of Privy Seal, 3 Edward IV); C 142 (Inquisitions Post Mortem); C 143/454/22; CP 25/1 (Court of Common Pleas: Feet of Fines); CP 40 (Court of Common Pleas: Plea Rolls); DL 41/145; E 13 (Exchequer of Pleas: Plea Rolls); E 101 (King's Remembrancer: Accounts Various); E 122 (Customs Accounts); E 404 (Warrants for Issues); E 361 (Enrolled Wardrobe and Household Accounts); E 364/104; KB 9/401; PROB 11 (Will registers); PSO 1 and 2 (Privy Seal Office, series 1 and 2); SC 2 (Special Collections: Court Rolls); SC 6 (Special Collections, Ministers' and Receivers' Accounts); SC 8/337/15918; SP 9/8
Norfolk Record Office, Norwich: Kirkpatrick Notes 21 F (9), 58 'Annals of the City'; NRO Case 18a/3 10; NRO LEST/P 20 n. 8
Nottinghamshire Archives, Nottingham: DD/SR/209/315
St George's Chapel, Windsor: SGC XV.25.63; SGC XV.48.58

Suffolk Record Office, Ipswich: Ipswich RO, HD 474/1
Westminster Abbey Muniments: 12165; 12166; 12169; 12167; 12168; 12179; 2225

Published Primary Sources

A Collection of Ordinances and Regulations for the Government of the Royal Household.
   London: Society of Antiquaries, 1790.

Atthill, W., ed. *Documents Relating to the Collegiate Church of Middleham*. Camden
   Society, o.s. 38. 1847.

Bannister, Arthur Thomas, ed. *Registrum Thomas Myllyng Episcopi Herefordensis 1474–*
   1492. London: Canterbury and York Society, 1920.

Bateson, Mary, ed. *Records of the Borough of Leicester*. 2 vols. London: C. J. Clay, 1901.

Bentley, S., ed. *Excerpta Historica*. London: Samuel Bentley, 1831.

Birch, W. de G. *Catalogue of Seals in the Department of Manuscripts in the British Museum*.
   6 vols. London, 1894.

Black, W. H., ed. *Illustrations of Ancient State and Chivalry*. London: Roxburghe
   Club, 1840.

Bokenham, Osbern. *Legendys of Hooly Wummen*, edited by Mary Sergeantson. EETS, o.s.
   206. 1938.

Brie, Friedrich W. D., ed. *The Brut, or, The Chronicles of England*. EETS, o.s. 131,
   136. 1906.

Bruce, John, ed., *Letters and Papers of the Verney Family*. Camden Society, o.s. 56. 1853.

Calendar of Inquisitions Post Mortem: Henry VII. 3 vols. London: HMSO, 1898–1955.

Campbell, W., ed. *Materials for a History of the Reign of Henry VII*. Rolls Series 60, 2 vols.
   London, 1873.

Carpenter, Christine, ed. *Kingsford's Stonor Letters and Papers, 1290–1483*.
   Cambridge: CUP, 1996.

Chaucer, Geoffrey. *The Riverside Chaucer*, edited by Larry D. Benson. 3rd edn.
   London: OUP, 1987.

Chronique de Mathieu d'Escouchy, edited by G. du Fresne de Beaucourt. Société de
   l'Histoire de France. 3 vols. Paris: Société de l'Histoire de France, 1863–64.

Commynes, Philippe de. *Mémoires*. Présentation par Philippe Contamine.
   Paris: Imprimerie nationale Éditions, 1994.

Connor, Meriel, ed. *John Stone's Chronicle: Christ Church Priory, Canterbury, 1417–1472*.
   Kalamazoo: Western Michigan University, 2010.

Crawford, Anne, ed. *Household Books of John Howard, Duke of Norfolk*.
   Stroud: Sutton, 1992.

Crawford, Anne, ed. *Letters of the Queens of England 1100–1547*. Stroud: Sutton, 1994.

Davies, Robert, ed. *Extracts from the Municipal Records of the City of York during the*
   Reigns of Edward IV, Edward V and Richard III. London: J. B. Nichols and Son, 1843.

Davis, Norman et al., ed. *Paston Letters and Papers of the Fifteenth Century*. EETS, s.s. 20–
   22. 2004–5.

De Gray Birch, W. *Catalogue of Seals in the Manuscripts Department of the British*
   Museum. 6 vols. London: British Museum. 1887–1900.

De Mandrot, Bernard, ed. *Journal de Jean de Roye connu sous le nom de Chronique*
   Scandaleuse. Paris, 1896.

De Pisan, Christine. *The Book of the City of Ladies*, edited by Rosalind Brown-Grant.
   Harmondsworth: Penguin, 1999.

De Pisan, Christine. *The Treasure of the City of Ladies, or, The Book of the Three Virtues*, translated by Sarah Lawson. Harmondsworth: Penguin, 1985.

Dilks, T. B., ed. *Bridgwater Borough Archives, IV, 1445–68*. Somerset Record Society 60. 1948.

Du Boulay, F. R. H., ed. *Registrum Thome Bourgchier: 1454–86*. Canterbury and York Society 54. 1957.

Dunning, R. W. and Tremlett, T. D., ed. *Bridgwater Borough Archives V 1468–1485*. Somerset Record Society 70. 1971.

Fabyan, Robert. *The New Chronicles of England and France*. London: Rivington, 1811.

Fisher, J. *The English Works of John Fisher*, edited by J. Major. EETS, e.s. 27. 1876.

Fitz Herbert, Reginald H. C. 'Original Pedigree of Tailbois and Neville'. *The Genealogist*, n.s. III (1886): 31–5, 107–11.

Flenley, Ralph, ed. *Six Town Chronicles*. Oxford: Clarendon Press, 1911.

Flügel, Edward. 'Eine Mittelenglische Claudian-übersetzung (1445)'. *Anglia* 28 (1905): 255–99.

Gairdner, James, ed. *The Historical Collections of a Citizen of London in the Fifteenth Century*. Camden Society, n.s. 17. 1876.

Gairdner, James, ed. *The Paston Letters AD 1422–1509*. 6 vols. New complete library edition. London: Chatto & Windus, 1904.

Gairdner, James, ed. *Three Fifteenth-Century Chronicles*. Camden Society, n.s. 28. 1880.

Giles, J. A., ed. *Chronicles of the White Rose of York*. London: James Bohn, 1845.

Given-Wilson, Chris et al., ed. *The Parliament Rolls of Medieval England*. Leicester: Scholarly Digital Editions, 2005.

Grose, Francis and Astle, Thomas et al., eds. *The Antiquarian Repertory*. 4 vols. London: Jeffery, 1807–9.

Hardyng, John. *Chronicle*, edited by H. Ellis. London, 1812.

Harriss, G. L. and Harriss, M. A., eds. 'John Benet's Chronicle for the Years 1400 to 1462'. In *Camden Miscellany vol. XXIV*. Camden Society, 4th series, 9. 1972.

Harvey, J. H., ed. *William Worcestre: Itineraries*. Oxford: Clarendon Press, 1969.

Hearne, Thomas, ed. *Liber Niger Scaccarii, nec non Wilhelmi Worcestrii Annales Rerum Anglicarum*. 2 vols. London, 1761–62.

Horstman, C., ed. *Osbern Bokenham's Legenden*. Heilbronn: Gbr. Henninger, 1883.

James, N. W. and James, V. A., ed. *The Bede Roll of the Fraternity of St Nicholas*. London Record Society 39. 2004.

Kekewich, M. L. et al., eds. *The Politics of Fifteenth Century England: John Vale's Book*. Stroud: Alan Sutton, 1995.

Kingsford, C. L., ed. *Chronicles of London*. Oxford: Clarendon Press, 1905.

Kingsford, C. L., *English Historical Literature in the Fifteenth Century*. Oxford: Clarendon Press, 1913.

La Chronique d'Enguerran de Monstrelet. Société de l'Histoire de France, 6 vols. Paris. 1857–72.

Leland, John. *De Rebus Brittanicis Collectanea*, edited by T. Hearne, 4 vols. London, 1774.

Letts, Malcolm, ed. *The Travels of Leo of Rozmital*. Hakluyt Society, 2nd series, 108. 1955.

Louis, Cameron. 'A Yorkist Genealogical Chronicle in Middle English Verse'. *Anglia* 109 (1991): 1–20.

Loyd, L. C. and Stenton, D. M., ed. *Sir Christopher Hatton's Book of Seals*. Oxford: Clarendon Press, 1950.

Malden, H. E., ed. *The Cely Papers*. Camden Society, 3rd series, 1. 1900.

Mancini, Dominic. *The Usurpation of Richard the Third*, edited by C. A. J. Armstrong. Gloucester: Alan Sutton, 1984.

Manuale et Processionale ad Usum Insignis Ecclesiae Eboracensis. Surtees Society 63. 1874.

Marx, William, ed. *An English Chronicle 1377–1461: A New Edition.*
Woodbridge: Boydell, 2003.

More, Thomas. *The Complete Works of St Thomas More, Vol. 2: The History of King Richard III*, edited by R. S. Sylvester. New Haven: Yale University Press, 1963.

Nichols, J., ed. *Wills of the Kings and Queens of England.* London, 1780.

Nicolas, Nicholas Harris. *Privy Purse Expenses of Elizabeth of York.* London: William Pickering, 1830.

Nicolas, Nicholas Harris, ed. *Testamenta Vetusta*, 2 vols. London: Nichols, 1826.

O'Donovan, John, ed. *Annals of the Kingdom of Ireland by the Four Masters.* 7 vols. Dublin: Hodges and Smith, 1854.

Pantin, W. A. *Documents Illustrating the Activities of the General and Provincial Chapters of the English Black Monks 1215–1540.* 3 vols. Camden Society, 3rd series, 45, 47, 54. 1931–37.

Proceedings of the Privy Council of England, 7 vols. London: Commissioners of the Public Records of the Kingdom, 1834.

Pronay, Nicholas and Cox, John, ed. *The Crowland Continuations: 1459–1486.* London: Sutton, 1986.

Raine, J. *Historiae Dunelmensis Scriptores Tres.* Surtees Society 9. 1839.

Raine, J. ed. *Wills and Inventories.* Surtees Society 2. 1835.

Rhodes, John, ed. *A Calendar of the Registers of the Priory of Llanthony by Gloucester 1457–1466, 1501–1525.* Bristol and Gloucestershire Archaeological Society 15 (2002).

Riley, H. T., ed. *Annales Monasterii S. Albani a Johanne Amundesham.* Rolls Series 28. 2 vols. 1870–1.

Riley, H. T., ed. *Ingulph's Chronicle of the Abbey of Croyland.* London: George Bell, 1893.

Say, William. *Liber Regie Capelle*, edited by Walter Ullman. Henry Bradshaw Society, 92. 1961.

Shirley, Janet, tr. *A Parisian Journal 1405–1449.* Oxford: Clarendon Press, 1968.

Smith, George, ed. *The Coronation of Elizabeth Wydeville.* London, 1935.

Smith, J. J., ed. *Abbreviata Cronica 1377–1469.* Publications of the Cambridge Antiquarian Society 1. 1840.

Stevenson, Joseph, ed. *Letters and Papers Illustrative of the Wars of the English in France during the Reign of Henry the Sixth, King of England.* Rolls Series 22. 2 vols. London: Longman, 1861-4.

Stow, John. *A Survey of London*, edited by C. L. Kingsford, 2 vols. Oxford: Clarendon Press, 1971.

Sutton, Anne F. and Hammond, Peter, ed. *The Coronation of Richard III: The Extant Documents.* Gloucester: Alan Sutton, 1983.

Sutton, Anne F. and Visser-Fuchs, Livia with Hammond, Peter, eds. *The Reburial of Richard Duke of York, 21–30 July 1476.* London: The Richard III Society, 1996.

Testamenta Eboracensia III, Surtees Society 45. 1865.

The Chronicles of Enguerrand de Monstrelet, translated by Thomas Johnes. 2 vols. London: William Smith, 1840.

Thomas, A. H. and Thornley, I. D., ed. *The Great Chronicle of London.* London, 1938, reprinted Gloucester: Alan Sutton, 1983.

Tymms, Samuel, ed. *Wills and Inventories from the Commissary of Bury St Edmunds.* Camden Society, o.s. 49. 1850.

Vergil, Polydore. *Three Books of Polydore Vergil's History of England*, edited by H. Ellis, Camden Society, o.s. 29. London, 1844.

Visser-Fuchs, Livia. 'English Events in Caspar Weinreich's Danzig Chronicle, 1461–1495'. *The Ricardian* 7 (1986): 310–20.

Walsingham, Thomas. *The St Albans Chronicle*, edited by J. Taylor, W. R. Childs and L. Watkiss. 2 vols. Oxford: Clarendon Press, 2003–11.

Ward, Jennifer C., ed. *Elizabeth de Burgh, Lady of Clare (1259–1360): Household and Other Records*. Woodbridge: Boydell, 2014.

Waurin, Jehan de. *Recueil des Croniques et Anchiennes Istories de la Grant Bretaigne*, edited by William Hardy. Rolls Series 39, 5 vols. 1864–91.

Whetamstede, John. *Registra Quorundam Abbatum Monasterii S. Albani,* edited by H. T. Riley. Rolls Series 28. 2 vols. 1872.

Windeatt, B. A., ed. *The Book of Margery Kempe*. Harmondsworth: Penguin, 1985.

Wood, M. A. E., ed. *Letters of Royal and Illustrious Ladies of Great Britain*. London: Henry Colburn, 1846.

Worcester, William. *Itineraries,* edited by John Harvey. Oxford: Clarendon Press, 1969.

Secondary Sources

Allen, John, ed. *The English Hospice in Rome*. Exeter: Catholic Records Press, 1962.

Archer, Rowena. '"How Ladies … Who Live on Their Manors Ought to Manage Their Households and Estates": Women as Landholders and Administrators in the Later Middle Ages'. In *Woman Is a Worthy Wight: Women in English Society c. 1200-1500,* edited by P. J. P. Goldberg. Stroud: Alan Sutton, 1992.

Archer, Rowena. 'Piety in Question: Noblewomen and Religion in the Later Middle Ages'. In *Women and Religion in Medieval England*, edited by Diana Wood. Oxford: Oxbow, 2003.

Archer, Rowena. 'Piety, Chivalry and Family: The Cartulary and Psalter of Sir Edmund Rede of Boarstall (d. 1489)'. In *Soldiers, Nobles and Gentlemen*, edited by Peter Coss and Christopher Tyerman, 126–49. Woodbridge: Boydell, 2005.

Armstrong, C. A. J. 'The Piety of Cicely, Duchess of York: A Study in Late Medieval Culture'. In *England, France and Burgundy in the Fifteenth-Century*, edited by Armstrong, 135–56. London: Hambledon, 1983.

Ashdown-Hill, John. 'The Suffolk Connections of the House of York'. *Proceedings of the Suffolk Institute for Archaeology and History* 41 (2006): 199–207.

Bagnoli, Martina et al., ed. *Treasures of Heaven. Saints, Relics and Devotion in Medieval Europe*. London: British Museum Press, 2010.

Barnardiston, K. W. *Clare Priory: Seven Centuries of a Suffolk House.* Cambridge: Heffer, 1962.

Barron, Caroline. *London in the Later Middle Ages: Government and People 1200–1500.* Oxford: OUP, 2004.

Bates, David and Curry, Anne, ed. *England and Normandy in the Middle Ages.* London: Hambledon, 1994.

Bates, David and Liddiard, Robert, ed. *East Anglia and Its North Sea World in the Middle Ages.* Woodbridge: Boydell, 2013.

Bennet, Rev. Dr. 'The College of S. John Evangelist of Rushworth, Co. Norfolk'. *Norfolk Archaeology* X (1888): 277–382.

Brown, E. A. 'Companion Me with My Mistress: Cleopatra, Elizabeth I and Their Waiting Women'. In *Maids and Mistresses, Cousins and Queens: Women's Alliances in Early Modern England*, edited by S. Frye and K. Robertson. Oxford: OUP, 1999.

Brown, R. Allen, Colvin, H. M. and Taylor, A. J. *The History of the King's Works, vol. 2: The Middle Ages*. London: HMSO, 1963.

Butler, Ruth. 'Brimpsfield Church History'. *Transactions of the Bristol and Gloucestershire Archaeological Society* 81 (1962): 73–97.

Carpenter, Christine. *The Wars of the Roses: Politics and the Constitution in England c. 1437–1509*. Cambridge: CUP, 1997.

Chamberlayne, Joanna. 'Cecily Neville, Duchess of York, King's Mother: The Rôles of an English Medieval Noblewoman, 1415–1495', MA diss. University of York, 1994.

Cherry, John. *The Middleham Jewel and Ring*. York: The Yorkshire Museum, 1994.

Chrimes, S. B. *Henry VII*. London: Eyre Methuen, 1972.

Connor, Meriel. 'Brotherhood and Confraternity at Canterbury Cathedral Priory in the Fifteenth Century: The Evidence of John Stone's Chronicle'. *Archaeolgia Cantiana* 128 (2008): 143–64.

Crawford, Anne. *The Yorkists: The History of a Dynasty*. London: Hambledon Continuum, 2007.

Crawford, Anne. *Yorkist Lord: John Howard, Duke of Norfolk, c. 1425–1485*. London: Continuum, 2010.

Cunningham, Sean. *Henry VII*. London: Routledge, 2007.

Curtis, Edmund. 'Richard, Duke of York, as Viceroy of Ireland: 1447–1460'. *The Journal of the Royal Society of Antiquaries of Ireland*. 7th series, 2 (1932): 158–86.

Davies, C. S. L. 'Information, Disinformation and Political Knowledge under Henry VII and Early Henry VIII'. *Historical Research* 85 (2012): 228–53.

Delany, Sheila. *Impolitic Bodies: Poetry, Saints and Society in Fifteenth-Century England. The Work of Osbern Bokenham*. Oxford: OUP, 1998.

Diaz Pascual, Lucia. 'Jacquetta of Luxembourg, Duchess of Bedford and Lady Rivers (c. 1416–72)'. *The Ricardian* 21 (2011): 67–91.

Dobson, R. B. *Durham Priory 1400–1450*. Cambridge: CUP, 1973.

Driver, J. T. 'Richard Quatremains: A 15th-Century Squire and Knight of the Shire for Oxfordshire'. *Oxoniensa* 51 (1986): 87–103.

Dunn, Alastair. *The Politics of Magnate Power: England and Wales 1389–1413*. Oxford: Clarendon Press, 2003.

Dyer, Christopher. *Standards of Living in the Later Middle Ages: Social Change in England c. 1200–1520*. Rev. edn. Cambridge: CUP, 1998.

Dzon, Mary. 'Cecily Neville and the Apocryphal "Infantia Salvatoris" in the Middle Ages'. *Mediaeval Studies* 71 (2009): 235–300.

Edwards, Rhoda. *The Itinerary of King Richard III, 1483–85*. London: Richard III Society, 1983.

Emden, A. B. *A Biographical Register of the University of Cambridge to 1500*. Cambridge: CUP, 1963.

Emery, Anthony. *Greater Medieval Houses of England and Wales, 1300–1500*, 3. vols. Cambridge: CUP, 1996–2006.

Erler, Mary and Kowaleski, Maryanne, eds. *Women and Power in the Middle Ages*. Athens: University of Georgia Press, 1988.

Falvey, H. 'The More: Archbishop George Neville's Palace'. *The Ricardian* 9 (1992): 290–302.

Gill, Louise. *Richard III & Buckingham's Rebellion*. Stroud: Sutton, 1999.

Gregory, Mary. 'Wickham Court and the Heydons'. *Archaeologia Cantiana* 78 (1963): 1–24.

Griffiths, Ralph. 'Queen Katherine of Valois and a Missing Statute of the Realm'. *Law Quarterly Review* 93 (1977): 248–58.

Griffiths, Ralph. *The Reign of Henry the Sixth: The Exercise of Royal Authority 1422–1461.* London: Benn, 1981.

Griffiths, Ralph. *King and Country: England and Wales in the Fifteenth Century.* London: Hambledon Press, 1991.

Groag Bell, Susan. 'Medieval Women Book Owners: Arbiters of Lay Piety and Ambassadors of Culture'. In *Women and Power in the Middle Ages*, edited by Mary Erler and Maryanne Kowaleski. Athens: University of Georgia Press, 1988.

Grummitt, David. *A Short History of the Wars of the Roses.* London: I. B. Taurus, 2013.

Hailstone, Edward. *The History and Antiquities of the Parish of Bottisham and the Priory of Anglesey in Cambridgeshire.* Cambridge Antiquarian Society Publications 14. 1873.

Halsted, Caroline A. *Richard III as Duke of Gloucester and King of England.* 2 vols. London, 1844.

Harper-Bill, Christopher. 'The Priory and Parish of Folkestone in the Fifteenth Century'. *Archaeologia Cantiana* 93 (1977): 195–200.

Harris, Barbara J. *English Aristocratic Women 1450–1550.* Oxford: OUP, 2002.

Harvey, I. M. W. *Jack Cade's Rebellion of 1450.* Oxford: OUP, 1991.

Hawkyard, Alastair. 'Sir John Fastolf's "Gret Mansion by Me Late Edified": Caister Castle, Norfolk'. In *Of Mice and Men: Image, Belief and Regulation in Late Medieval England, The Fifteenth Century V*, edited by Linda Clark. Woodbridge: The Boydell Press, 2005.

Hicks, Michael. *Warwick the Kingmaker.* Oxford: Blackwell, 1998.

Hicks, Michael. 'From Megaphone to Microscope: The Correspondence of Richard Duke of York with Henry VI in 1450 Revisited'. *JMH* 25 (1999): 243–56.

Hicks, Michael. *Edward V: The Prince in the Tower.* Stroud: Tempus, 2003.

Hillier, Kenneth. 'William Colyngbourne'. *The Ricardian* 3 (1975): 5–9.

Hipshon, David. *Richard III.* London: Routledge, 2011.

Horobin, Simon. 'Politics, Patronage, and Piety in the Work of Osbern Bokenham'. *Speculum* 82 (2007): 932–49.

Horobin, Simon. 'A Manuscript Found in the Library of Abbotsford House and the Lost Legendary of Osbern Bokenham'. *English Manuscript Studies 1100–1700* 14 (2007): 132–64.

Horrox, Rosemary. *Richard III: A Study of Service.* Cambridge: CUP, 1989.

Hutchins, John. *The History and Antiquities of the County of Dorset.* 4 vols. 3rd edn. Revised by William Shipp and James Whitworth Hodson. London, 1861.

Hutchison, Ann M. 'Reflections on Aspects of the Spiritual Impact of St Birgitta, the Revelations and the Bridgettine Order in Late Medieval England'. In *The Medieval Mystical Tradition: Exeter Symposium VII*, edited by E. A. Jones. Cambridge: D. S. Brewer, 2004.

Jacob, E. F. *The Fifteenth Century.* Oxford: OUP, 1961.

Johns, Susan M. *Noblewomen, Aristocracy and Power in the Twelfth-Century Anglo-Norman Realm.* Manchester: Manchester University Press, 2003.

Johnson, P. A. *Duke Richard of York, 1411–1460.* Oxford: Clarendon Press, 1988.

Jones, Michael. K. and Underwood, Malcolm G. *The King's Mother: Lady Margaret Beaufort, Countess of Richmond and Derby.* Cambridge: CUP, 1992.

Jones, Michael K. *Bosworth, 1485: Psychology of a Battle.* Stroud: Tempus, 2002.

Keen, M. H. *England in the Later Middle Ages.* London: Routledge, 1973.

Kleineke, Hannes. 'Alice Martyn, Widow of London: An Episode from Richard's Youth'. *The Ricardian* 14 (2004): 32–6.

Kleineke, Hannes. *Edward IV*. London: Routledge, 2009.

Kleineke, Hannes. 'The Five Wills of Humphrey Stafford, Earl of Devon'. *Nottingham Medieval Studies* 54 (2010): 137–64.

Kleineke, Hannes. 'Robert Bale's Chronicle of the Second Battle of St. Albans'. *Historical Research* 87 (2014): 744–50.

Kleineke, Hannes and Steer, Christian, ed. *The Yorkist Age*. Donington: Shaun Tyas, 2013.

Lander, J. R. 'Marriage and Politics in the Fifteenth Century: The Nevilles and the Woodvilles'. *BIHR* 63:4 (1963): 119–52.

Lawne, Penny. *Joan of Kent. The First Princess of Wales*. Stroud: Amberley, 2015.

Laynesmith, J. L. *The Last Medieval Queens: English Queenship 1445–1503*. Oxford: OUP, 2004.

Laynesmith, J. L. 'Telling Tales of Adulterous Queens in Medieval England: From Olympias of Macedonia to Elizabeth Woodville'. In *Every Inch a King*, edited by Lynette Mitchell and Charles Melville. Leiden: Brill, 2013.

Lee, Becky R. '"A Company of Women *and* Men", Men's Recollections of Childbirth in Medieval England'. *Journal of Family History* 27 (2002): 92–100.

Lewis, Katherine J. *Kingship and Masculinity in Late Medieval England*. London: Routledge, 2013.

LoPrete, Kimberley. 'Gendering Viragos: Medieval Perceptions of Powerful Women'. In *Victims or Viragos?* edited by Christine Meek and Catherine Lawless. Dublin: Four Courts Press, 2005.

Lucraft, Jeanette. *Katherine Swynford: The History of a Medieval Mistress*. Stroud: Sutton Publishing, 2006.

McFarlane, K. B. *Lancastrian Kings and Lollard Knights*. Oxford: Clarendon Press, 1972.

Marks, R. 'The Glazing of Fotheringhay Church and College'. *Journal of the British Archaeological Association* 131 (1978): 79–109.

Marks, R. and Williamson, P., eds. *Gothic. Art for England 1400–1547*. London: V&A Publications, 2003.

Matich, Sofija and Alexander, Jennifer. 'Creating and Recreating the Yorkist Tombs in Fotheringhay Church'. *Church Monuments* 26 (2011): 82–103.

Maurer, Helen. *Margaret of Anjou: Queenship and Power in Late Medieval England*. Woodbridge: Boydell, 2003.

Meale, Carol, ed. *Women and Literature in Britain 1150–1500*. 2nd edn. Cambridge: CUP, 1996.

Mertes, Kate. *The English Noble Household 1250–1600*. Oxford: Blackwell, 1988.

Mertes, Kate. 'The Household as a Religious Community'. In *People, Politics and Community in the Later Middle Ages*, edited by J. T. Rosenthal and C. Richmond, 123–39. Gloucester: Alan Sutton, 1987.

Myers, A. R. *Crown, Household and Parliament in the Fifteenth Century*, edited by C. H. Clough. London: Hambledon, 1985.

Nichols, J. *The History and Antiquities of the Town, College, and Castle of Fotheringhay in the County of Northampton*. London, 1787.

Noble, Mark. 'Some Observations upon the Life of Cecily Duchess of York'. *Archaeologia* XIII (1800): 7–19.

Orme, Nicholas. *From Childhood to Chivalry: The Education of the English Kings and Aristocracy, 1066–1530*. London: Methuen, 1984.

Ormrod, W. M. *Edward III*. New Haven: Yale University Press, 2011.

Phillips, Kim M. *Medieval Maidens: Young Women and Gender in England, 1270–1540*. Manchester: Manchester University Press, 2003.

Pollard, A. J. *John Talbot and the War in France, 1427–1453*. London: Royal Historical Society, 1983.

Pollard, A. J. *Late Medieval England 1399–1509*. Harlow: Longman, 2001.

Pollard, A. J. *North-Eastern England during the Wars of the Roses*. Oxford: Clarendon Press, 1990.

Pollard, A. J. *Richard III and the Princes in the Tower*. Stroud: Alan Sutton, 1991.

Power, Eileen. 'The Wool Trade in the Fifteenth Century'. In *Studies in English Trade in the Fifteenth Century*, edited by E. Power and M. M. Postan. Abingdon: Routledge, 2006.

Pugh, T. B. 'The Estates, Finances and Regal Aspirations of Richard Plantagenet (1411–1460) Duke of York'. In *Revolution and Consumption in Late Medieval* England, edited by M. A. Hicks. Woodbridge: Boydell Press, 2001.

Pugh, T. B. *Henry V and the Southampton Plot of 1415*. Southampton Record Series 30. Southampton: Southampton University Press, 1988.

Pugh, T. B. 'Richard, Duke of York, and the Rebellion of Henry Holand, Duke of Exeter, in May 1454'. *Historical Research* 63 (1990): 248–62.

Pugh, T. B. 'Richard Plantagenet (1411–60), Duke of York, as the King's Lieutenant in France and Ireland'. In *Aspects of Late Medieval Government and Society*, edited by J. G. Rowe. Toronto: University of Toronto Press, 1986.

Rawcliffe, Carole. 'Richard, Duke of York, the King's "Obeisant Liegeman": A New Source for the Protectorates of 1454–1455'. *Historical Research* 60 (1987): 232–9.

Rawcliffe, Carole. *The Staffords, Earls of Stafford and Dukes of Buckingham 1394–1521*. Cambridge: CUP, 1978.

Reames, Sherry. 'The Second Nun's Prologue and Tale'. In *Sources and Analogues of the Canterbury Tales, Vol. I*, edited by Robert M. Correale and Mary Hamel. Woodbridge: D. S. Brewer, 2002.

Richardson, Ralph H. 'A Yorkist Window at Oddingley, Worcestershire'. *The Ricardian* 10 (1996): 421–8.

Richmond, Colin. 'East Anglian Politics and Society in the Fifteenth Century: Reflections 1956–2005'. In *Medieval East Anglia*, edited by Christopher Harper-Bill. Woodbridge: The Boydell Press, 2005.

Richmond, Colin. *The Paston Family in the Fifteenth Century: Fastolf's Will*. Cambridge: CUP, 1996.

Riddy, Felicity. 'John Hardyng's Chronicle and the Wars of the Roses'. In *Arthurian Literature XII*, edited by J. P. Carley and F. Riddy. Cambridge: D. S. Brewer, 1993.

Riddy, Felicity. '"Women Talking about the Things of God": A Late Medieval Subculture'. In *Women and Literature in Britain 1150–500*, edited by Carol Meale. Cambridge: CUP, 1993.

Rogers, Alan. 'Late Medieval Stamford: A Study of the Town Council 1465–1492'. In *Perspectives in English Urban History*, edited by Alan Everitt. London: Macmillan, 1973.

Rose, Susan. *The Wine Trade in Medieval Europe 1000–1500*. London: Bloomsbury Academic, 2011.

Rosenthal, J. T. 'Aristocratic Widows in Fifteenth-Century England'. In *Women and the Structure of Society: Selected Research from the Fifth Berkshire Conference on the History of Women*, edited by Barbara J. Harris and JoAnn K. McNamara. Durham, NC: Duke University Press, 1984.

Rosenthal, J. T. 'Fifteenth-Century Baronial Incomes and Richard, Duke of York', *BIHR* 37 (1964): 233–40.

Rosenthal, J. T. *Patriarchy and Families of Privilege in Fifteenth-Century England*. Philadelphia: Penn Press, 1991.

Ross, Charles D. *Edward IV*. London: Eyre Methuen, 1974.

Ross, Charles D. *Richard III*. London: Methuen, 1981.

Ross, James. *The Foremost Man of the Kingdom: John de Vere, Thirteenth Earl of Oxford (1442–1513)*. Woodbridge: Boydell, 2011.

Sandford, Francis. *A Genealogical History of the Kings and Queens of England: Continued by Samuel Stebbings*. London, 1707.

Schnitker, Harry. *Margaret of York: Princess of England, Duchess of Burgundy*. Donington: Shaun Tyas, 2016.

Scofield, Cora. *The Life and Reign of Edward the Fourth*. 2 vols. London: Longmans, Green, 1923.

Slater, Terry and Goose, Nigel, eds. *A County of Small Towns: The Development of Hertfordshire's Urban Landscape to 1800*. Hatfield: University of Hertfordshire Press, 2008.

Spedding, Alison J. '"At the King's Pleasure": The Testament of Cecily Neville'. *Midland History* 35 (2010): 256–72.

Staniland, Kay. 'Royal Entry into the World'. In *England in the Fifteenth Century: Proceedings of the 1986 Harlaxton Symposium*, edited by Daniel Williams. Woodbridge: Boydell, 1987.

Starkey, David. 'Henry VI's Old Blue Gown: The English Court under the Lancastrians and Yorkists'. *The Court Historian* 4 (1999): 1–28.

Starkey, David et al., eds. *The English Court: From the Wars of the Roses to the Civil War*. London: Longman, 1987.

Statham, Margaret and Badham, Sally. 'Jankyn Smith of Bury St Edmunds and his Brass'. *Transactions of the Monumental Brass Society* 18 (2011): 227–50.

Stratford, Jenny, ed. *The Lancastrian Court*. Donington: Shaun Tyas, 2003.

Sutton, Anne F. 'And to Be delivered to the Lord Richard Duke of Gloucester ...' *The Ricardian* 8 (1988): 20–5.

Sutton, Anne F. 'Edward IV and Bury St Edmunds' Search for Self Government'. In *The Fifteenth Century XIV*, edited by Linda Clark. Boydell: Woodbridge, 2015.

Sutton, Anne F. and Visser-Fuchs, Livia. *The Hours of Richard III*. Stroud: Sutton, 1990.

Sutton, Anne F. and Visser-Fuchs, Livia. *Richard III's Books*. Stroud: Sutton Publishing, 1997.

Tarbin, Stephanie and Broomhall, Susan. *Women, Identities and Communities in Early Modern Europe*. Aldershot: Ashgate, 2008.

Thompson, E. Margaret. *The Carthusian Order in England*. London: SPCK, 1930.

Thomson, J. A. F. 'The Death of Edward V: Dr Richmond's Dating Reconsidered'. *Northern History* 26 (1990): 201–11.

Thomson, J. A. F. 'John de la Pole, Duke of Suffolk'. *Speculum* 54 (1979): 528–42.

Tuck, Anthony. *Richard II and the English Nobility*. London: Edward Arnold, 1973.

Visser-Fuchs, Livia. '"Honour Is the Reward of Virtue": The Claudian Translation Made for Richard, Duke of York, in 1445', *The Ricardian* 18 (2003): 66–82.

Visser-Fuchs, Livia. 'Richard Was Late'. *The Ricardian* 11 (1999): 616–19.

Voaden, Rosalynn. 'The Company She Keeps: Mechtild of Hackeborn in Late Medieval Devotional Compilations'. In *Prophets Abroad: The Reception of Continental Holy Women in Late-Medieval England*, edited by Rosalynn Voaden. Cambridge: D. S. Brewer, 1996.

Waller, W. C. 'An Old Church Chest, Being Notes of That at Theydon Garnon'. *Transactions of the Essex Archaeological Society* n.s. 5 (1895): 1–33.

Waller, W. C. 'Some Essex Manuscripts'. *Transactions of the Essex Archaeological Society* n.s. 5 (1895): 200–25.

Walpole, Horace. *Historic Doubts on the Life and Reign of Richard III*, edited by P. W. Hammond. Stroud: Sutton Publishing, 1987.

Ward, Jennifer C. *English Noblewomen in the Later Middle Ages*. London: Longman, 1992.

Watt, Diane. 'Political Prophecy in *The Book of Margery Kempe*'. In *A Companion to Margery Kempe*, edited by John H. Arnold and Katherine J. Lewis. Cambridge: D. S. Brewer, 2004.

Watts, John. '*De Consulatu Stilichonis*: Texts and Politics in the Reign of Henry VI'. *JMH* 16 (1990): 251–66.

Watts, John, ed. *The End of the Middle Ages? England in the Fifteenth and Sixteenth Centuries*. Stroud: Sutton, 1998.

Watts, John. *Henry VI and the Politics of Kingship*. Cambridge: CUP, 1996.

Way, Albert. 'Gold Pectoral Cross Found at Clare Castle, Suffolk'. *The Archaeological Journal* 25 (1868): 60–71.

Wedgwood, Josiah. *History of Parliament*, 2 vols. London: HMSO, 1936–38.

Weightman, Christine. *Margaret of York, Duchess of Burgundy 1446–1503*. Gloucester: Alan Sutton, 1989.

Wilkinson, Louise J. 'The *Rules* of Robert Grosseteste Reconsidered'. In *The Medieval Household in Christian Europe, c. 850–1550*, edited by Cordelia Beattie, Anna Maslakovic and Sarah Rees Jones. Turnhout: Brepols, 2003.

Winstead, K. A., ed. *Chaste Passions, Medieval English Virgin Martyr Legends*. Ithaca: Cornell University Press, 2000.

Wolffe, Bertram. *Henry VI*. London: Methuen, 1983.

Woolgar, C. H. *The Senses in Late Medieval England*. New Haven: Yale University Press, 2006.

Wylie, James. *History of England under Henry the Fourth*. 4 vols. London: Longmans, Green, 1884–98.

Websites

aalt.law.uh.edu

bvmm.irht.cnrs.fr/sommaire/sommaire.php?reproductionId=815

gallica.bnf.fr/ark:/12148/btv1b10532608h

lib1.advocates.org.uk/legenda/

www.british-history.ac.uk

www.englandsimmigrants.com

www.freelibrary.org/medieval/edward.htm

www.philological.bham.ac.uk/cambrit/huntseng.html#norts1

Index

Note: Page numbers in bold refer to illustrations.

Lightning Source UK Ltd.
Milton Keynes UK
UKHW021834170821
389016UK00007B/1417